PREJUDICE AND PRIDE
Canadian Intellectuals Confront the United States, 1891–1945

DAMIEN-CLAUDE BÉLANGER

Prejudice and Pride

Canadian Intellectuals Confront the United States, 1891–1945

UNIVERSITY OF TORONTO PRESS
Toronto Buffalo London

© University of Toronto Press Incorporated 2011
Toronto Buffalo London
www.utppublishing.com
Printed in Canada

ISBN 978-1-4426-4045-0

Printed on acid-free, 100% post-consumer recycled paper with
vegetable-based inks.

Library and Archives Canada Cataloguing in Publication

Bélanger, Damien-Claude, 1976–
    Prejudice and pride : Canadian intellectuals confront the United States,
1891–1945 / Damien-Claude Belanger.

    Includes bibliographical references and index.
    ISBN 978-1-4426-4045-0

    1. United States – Foreign public opinion, Canadian.   2. United States –
Civilization.   3. Canada – Relations – United States.   4. United States –
Relations – Canada.   5. Intellectuals – Canada – Attitudes.   6. Canada –
Intellectual life.   7. Public opinion – Canada.   I. Title.

E169.1.B445 2011   973.91   C2010-904478-9

University of Toronto Press acknowledges the financial assistance to its
publishing program of the Canada Council for the Arts and the Ontario
Arts Council.

University of Toronto Press acknowledges the financial support of the
Government of Canada through the Canada Book Fund for its publishing
activities.

This book has been published with the help of a grant from the Canadian
Federation for the Humanities and Social Sciences, through the Aid to
Scholarly Publications Program, using funds provided by the Social Sciences
and Humanities Research Council of Canada.

Contents

Acknowledgments

This study has benefited from the advice and support of numerous friends, family, and colleagues, and I am pleased to record my appreciation to them. I am particularly indebted to Professors Yvan Lamonde and Brian Young, who supervised the doctoral dissertation from which this book originated. Their guidance, encouragement, and patience made this study possible. Professors Pierre Trépanier and Ramsay Cook provided early comments and suggestions on my research. Later comments by Professor Reginald Stuart and the anonymous reviewers of the University of Toronto Press helped guide the extensive revision process, as did the suggestions of my judicious editor, Len Husband. Juliet Sutcliffe provided translations for the French-language quotes. Pauline Grégoire's support, affection, editing skills, and critical eye were indispensable to my work. My parents, Claude and Janice Bélanger, have been a constant source of love and support throughout my life. I also wish to thank Janet Miron, Dimitry Anastakis, Michel Ducharme, and Sophie Coupal, as well as my colleagues from *Mens*. Their advice and camaraderie have been a source of encouragement on more than a few occasions.

I gratefully acknowledge the assistance of the personnel of McGill's McLennan Library, the Bibliothèque nationale du Québec, the Centre de recherche Lionel-Groulx, and Library and Archives Canada. I also wish to express my appreciation to the McGill Institute for the Study of Canada, the Fonds québécois de la recherche sur la société et la culture, the ACA Education Fund, the University of Ottawa, and Trent University for their generous support of my research.

PREJUDICE AND PRIDE
Canadian Intellectuals Confront the United States, 1891–1945

Introduction

'The average Canadian attitude towards the United States and all things American cannot be permanently based upon pride and prejudice, or, to use one word, ignorance,' warned Douglas Bush (1896–1983) in 1929.[1] Bush, who would spend most of his career teaching English at Harvard University, was part of a new and, some believed, irreverent generation of thinkers who came of age during the Great War and dominated English Canadian discourse during the 1920s and 1930s. Rejecting the imperialism that had largely permeated Canadian thought before the First World War, these intellectuals sought to affirm the inherently American nature of Canadian society and to draw the nation out of Britain's orbit. This implied a redefinition of the Canadian experience and a rapprochement between Canada and its neighbour to the south.

There was nothing exceptionally novel in the outlook of this continentalist cohort. Many of its arguments had been plainly stated a generation before by the bête noire of Canadian imperialists, Goldwin Smith (1823–1910). Indeed, when it comes to the United States and the issue of Canadian-American relations, Canadian thought and writing has been characterized by a great deal of continuity: the broad ideas and sensibilities that emerged in the late eighteenth century are still with us today. This is scarcely surprising, since the various questions surrounding the Canadian-American relationship are existential for Canada. From the time of the American Revolution, Canada's writers and intellectuals have pondered the extent to which Canadian and American society differ. They have also argued over just how close Canada's relationship with the United States should be. These issues have generated a torrent of prose. Most Canadian intellectuals have published some material related to the United States and Canadian-American relations and a number of Canada's most significant works, including Goldwin Smith's *Canada and the Canadian Question* (1891), Edmond de Nevers' *L'Avenir du peuple canadien-français* (1896), and George Grant's *Lament for a Nation* (1965), have dealt in some way with the 'American question.'

This prose has, in turn, generated a good deal of scholarly interest. By and large, scholars have focused their attention on anti-American sentiment in Canada.[2] The general consensus surrounding this writing is fairly straightforward: anti-Americanism is viewed as a facet of Canadian nationalism and an expression of the nation's struggle to maintain its sovereignty and distinctiveness.[3] Carl Berger's writing is typical of this perspective. In *The Sense of Power* (1970), he argues that imperialism was a form of Canadian nationalism and that a vigorous critique of the American republic was a key ingredient of that nationalism. Indeed, he writes, 'what lay behind this Canadian critique of the United States was not malevolence but nationalism.'[4]

Most of the scholars who have examined anti-Americanism have regarded it as essentially harmful to both the Canadian mind and the Canadian-American relationship. J.L. Granatstein is fairly representative of this attitude. 'With all its hatred, bias, and deliberately contrived fearmongering, anti-Americanism ... never was and never could become the basis of any rational national identity,' he writes in *Yankee Go Home?* (1996). Granatstein's monograph is the most comprehensive study of Canadian anti-Americanism published to date. It links anti-Americanism to nationalism, but also points out its more instrumental side: 'anti-Americanism was almost always employed as a tool by Canadian political and economic élites bent on preserving or enhancing their power. It was largely the Tory way of keeping pro-British attitudes uppermost in the Canadian psyche.'[5]

By and large, the anti-American tradition has not generated a significant historical debate in English-speaking Canada. In contrast, as a political ideal, the continentalist tradition has led to some debate.[6] The prevalent attitude within English Canada's intellectual and academic community is to dismiss continentalism as an anti-nationalist and indeed menacing doctrine. By the 1960s, writes Reginald C. Stuart, 'continentalism acquired a musty, quaint, anachronistic, even sinister quality to those who now asserted that Canada was rather too much like, and too peaceful toward, the American neighbor.'[7] The handful of the scholars who have seriously studied the continentalist impulse have sought to counter this impression. Continentalist intellectuals, they argue, have traditionally sought to harness American wealth and power to strength-en the Canadian nation. Indeed, in the continentalist perspective, closer Canadian-American relations were viewed, notes Allan Smith, as 'per-fectly compatible with – and would indeed serve – Canadian survival.'[8] Continentalism, therefore, was not an anti-nationalist doctrine.

In Quebec, the scholarship surrounding late nineteenth and early twentieth century intellectual attitudes towards the United States has often sought to understand the dichotomy between elite and popular attitudes regarding America.[9] It is widely assumed that anti-American-ism was rampant among the province's elite, while the rest of the popu-lation held a more positive view of the United States. Like in English Canadian scholarship, anti-American rhetoric in Quebec is assumed to be an expression of nationalism.

More recent work on the intellectual history of Quebec-U.S. rela-tions has been centred on the concept of *américanité*. According to Yvan Lamonde, who initiated the historical profession to the concept in the 1980s, Quebec's history has been marked by a long struggle between those who embraced the province's *américanité* and those who rejected it. *Américanité* refers to Quebec's fundamentally American nature, to its Americanness, and should not, insists Lamonde, be confused with Americanization. From the mid-nineteenth century until after the Sec-ond World War, the bulk of Quebec's intellectuals would reject the prov-ince's *américanité*. 'The faithfulness of these elites to a largely imaginary past,' writes Gérard Bouchard, whose recent work has also explored Quebec's *américanité*, 'served as an action plan for future generations, with the memory of their origins being substituted for the excitement of the North American dream.'[10] As a result, the bulk of Quebec's elite was out of step with both the populace and the continent's wider ethos of rupture and renewal.[11]

The present book differs from previous research in three significant ways. To begin with, it examines and compares the intellectual dis-course of both English and French Canada.[12] Earlier work on the sub-ject has tended to focus on a single language group. Next, this study is more concerned with Canadian intellectuals as thinkers on the left, the right, and the centre than as nationalists or non-nationalists.[13] Most significantly, however, it argues that late-nineteenth- and early-twentieth-century intellectual discourse regarding American life and the Canadian-American relationship was not simply an expression of nationalism or a reaction to United States foreign or commercial policy. Rather, it was primarily the expression of wider attitudes concerning modernity.[14]

Modernity is a complex concept whose multiple dimensions are difficult to circumscribe. Above all, it entails the erosion of traditional values and practices and the rise of mass society. Modernity is expressed on three basic levels. At the technical level, it is tied to industrialization and the technological advances of the industrial era. The emergence of industrial society, the proletariat, and mass production are fundamental to the modern ethos, as are large-scale urbanization, mechanization, and mass communications. These technological advances were undoubtedly the most tangible expressions of modernity. Indeed, during the period under study, the industrial metropolis, the automobile, and the radio were all powerful symbols of a new age. The technological aspects of modernity marginalize traditional modes of production.

At the philosophical and intellectual level, modernity is tied to a strong faith in science and technology and in the illimitable progress of society. Unlike traditionalism, which is a theocentric doctrine, modernity is anthropocentric. It seeks to affirm the central place of man in the universe and does not view material considerations as inevitably subordinate to spiritual ones. Modernity is not necessarily an atheistic sensibility, but it is invariably tied to some form of secularism. 'Hunched over the present while at the same time constantly focusing on what will overtake it, on its own negation,' writes Alexis Nouss, 'modernity has nothing to learn from the past.'[15] The modern ethos is obsessed with change and newness. As a result, it invariably leads to a penchant for rupture and, in some cases, to outright revolutionism. Politically, it can lean towards either democracy or totalitarianism, but in both instances it will invariably corrode the power of traditional elites, particularly that of the clergy.

Lastly, at the cultural level, modernity is tied to mass culture and mass consumption. Its rise signals the erosion of both traditional and elite culture and the rise of urban leisure. Culture becomes a commodity that is sold or broadcast to the masses. Modernity also progressively emancipates art and literature from traditional notions of æsthetics, propriety, and utility. The notion that art can exist for its own sake is an expression of the modern ethos. Modernity is a powerful and revolutionary force. It spawns new social groups and new forms of expression. In doing so, it produces a cultural and status revolution that overwhelms tradition and erodes established social relations and customs.

Along with Great Britain, the United States played a key role in the conceptual universe of the Canadian intellectual. Both nations were generally represented as antithetical archetypes: Britain embodied tradition and conservative values, while the United States came to symbolize modernity and the liberal ethos.[16] America represented both the promise and the dangers of the mass age. 'The United States is dealing with some of those great social and economic problems which, if not altogether peculiar to the great democracy of the West, seem to be more acute there than elsewhere,' wrote James Cappon (1855–1939) in 1912. Born in Scotland, Cappon had immigrated to Canada in 1888 to teach English at Queen's University in Kingston, Ontario. Regarding the United States, he worried, as did most Canadian imperialists, that 'the problems which are theirs to-day may be ours to-morrow.'[17] Indeed, America has long presented a vision of the future, albeit a blurred one, to the intellectuals of the world.[18]

In the Dominion of Canada, as elsewhere in the late nineteenth and early twentieth centuries, democracy, urban and industrial society, mass culture, and secularism – in a word, modernity – became increasingly identified with the United States. Consequently, resistance to modernity was expressed, in part, through anti-American rhetoric, while faith in the mass age was expressed, again in part, through continentalism. The dialectic between these two sensibilities was a struggle involving two different understandings of Canada, one of which was fundamentally antimodern.

The tension between continentalist and anti-American sentiment emerged during the crucible of Canadian discourse – the American Revolution – when rebel and loyalist elements struggled for the very soul of the Province of Quebec. By the late nineteenth and early twentieth centuries, Canadian hostility to the United States and continental integration was expressed in two conservative discourses: English Canadian imperialism and French Canadian nationalism. Despite their fundamental divergence on the national question, both imperialists and *nationalistes* shared an essentially antimodern outlook, and anti-Americanism was their logical point of convergence. Continentalism was expressed in liberal and socialist discourse. Liberals and socialists tended to diverge on issues related to freedom, equality, and property, but they generally agreed on the opportunities that continental integration would bring to Canada.

Anti-Americanism was largely present in the discourse of English and French Canadian intellectuals from the early 1890s to the Great

War. By the 1920s, however, continentalism became increasingly common in the work of English Canadian intellectuals. Clearly, the era of Andrew Macphail (1864–1938), Stephen Leacock (1869–1944), and the conservative *University Magazine* had come to an end, and the era of Frank Underhill (1885–1971), F.R. Scott (1899–1985), and the left-of-centre *Canadian Forum* had begun. Though several English Canadian thinkers continued to denounce the United States, an emerging generation of progressive intellectuals embraced modernity and continentalism. In French Canada, the process was quite different. The anti-Americanism that had dominated the prewar generation of intellectuals was renewed and reinforced in the 1920s and 1930s as a new cohort of conservative thinkers led by abbé Lionel Groulx (1878–1967) stiffened the resistance to modernity and America that had characterized many of their precursors. French Canadian continentalism, by contrast, grew increasingly marginal.

English and French Canadian intellectuals shared common preoccupations with respect to the United States. However, the tone and emphasis of their commentary often differed. In English Canada, where political institutions and the imperial bond were viewed as the mainstays of Canadian distinctiveness, writing on the United States tended to deal primarily with political and diplomatic issues. In Quebec, where political institutions were not generally viewed as vital elements of national distinctiveness, social and cultural affairs dominated writing on the United States. Anti-American rhetoric tended to be more radical in French Canada, but it was also less prevalent in French Canadian discourse than in English Canadian writing.

The period under study begins in 1891 – a significant year in the intellectual history of Canadian-American relations. One of the most momentous federal elections in Canadian history – and Sir John A. Macdonald's last – was held in March of that year. The election pitted an ailing Macdonald and his National Policy against a youthful Wilfrid Laurier and his promises of unrestricted reciprocity with the United States. The old chieftain prevailed. The campaign revolved around anti-Americanism and, in a pattern that would be repeated time and again in Canadian politics, anti-American rhetoric was used by the Conservatives to attack their Liberal opponents.[19] The Tories had successfully portrayed the election not as a contest between free trade and protectionism, but as a mortal struggle pitting the forces of loyalty against those of treason. The campaign galvanized English Canadian imperialists. In effect, the challenge posed by the advocates of unrestricted reciprocity, commercial union, and annexation in the late 1880s and early 1890s had given Canadian imperialism its raison d'être.

The 1891 election also produced one of the most important Canadian works of non-fiction: Goldwin Smith's best-selling *Canada and the Canadian Question*. Its publication stands out as one of the key moments in Canadian intellectual history. In a sense, *Canada and the Canadian Question* was English Canada's Durham Report. The irreverent essay argued that the Dominion of Canada was a geographic, ethnic, economic, and political absurdity whose ultimate destiny lay in political union with the United States. Smith had rejected almost every principle held by nineteenth-century Canadian imperialists, and much in the same way that the indignation generated by Lord Durham's infamous report sparked an intellectual and literary explosion in French Canada, *Canada and the Canadian Question* generated a similar torrent of nation-affirming prose in English Canada. According to Carl Berger, Smith's book 'is supremely important in Canadian nationalist thought because he asked the question which all Canadian nationalists have since tried to answer: what positive values does the country embody and represent that justifies her existence?'[20]

Canada and the Canadian Question had actually been written as a campaign document for the Liberal party – Smith endorsed reciprocity – but failed in this purpose since it was not off the press until April 1891.[21] Rabidly anti-Catholic and francophobic, the book was the product of a deeply pessimistic time. Less than twenty-five years after the British North America Act was passed, Canada was suffering from a profound malaise. The enthusiasm generated by Confederation had been battered by economic depression and washed away by a torrent of ethnic, religious, and sectional strife. To make matters worse, emigration to the United States was undermining Canada's population growth, and annexationism, that unmistakable sign of national despair, reared its ugly head for one final encore. Clearly, some Canadians shared Smith's profound defeatism. As the nation lurched from recession to recession, it became clear that the National Policy had not delivered on its promises of prosperity.

There was, however, some light at the end of the tunnel. A few years after Smith's indictment of Canada, the nation was enjoying rapid economic expansion and a period of unbridled optimism under the stewardship of Sir Wilfrid Laurier and his 'sunny ways.' The next decades would witness the birth of a new independent, urban, and industrial Canada. By the late 1890s, Canada had shaken off a decade of pessimism and discord and had begun to grow as never before. 'The poor relation has come into her fortune,' wrote British observer J.A. Hobson at the turn of the century.[22] Between 1901 and 1945, emigration ebbed, immigration soared, and Canada's population nearly tripled. In addition, rapid, though at times intermittent, industrial growth brought the nation's urbanization rate from 35 to 59 per cent. Industrial expansion also fuelled the rise of consumerism which, in turn, helped to homogenize North American lifestyles.

The Dominion of Canada emerged from the Great War a nation transformed. Canadian independence had been consecrated at Vimy and Versailles and the nation was taking its first steps on the world stage. Continental integration was proceeding apace: American investments in Canada grew rapidly as Britain's decline in the years after the First World War pushed Canada into the arms of the United States, and American mass culture displaced British popular culture in Canada.[23] 'Like all the great empires before it,' writes Stephen Brooks, 'America had begun to export its culture – its values, lifestyles, dreams, and self-image – through what were then the new media of film and mass advertising,' and had proven her mastery of the mass age.[24] By the end of the Second World War, the United States was fully poised to assume its new role as a global superpower. All the pieces were now in place: America had become a military, economic, and cultural powerhouse. America's symbolic significance would shift accordingly. In post–Second World War Canada, anti-American rhetoric would become increasingly identified with the left and would gradually cease to express a distaste for modernity.

This study explores the intellectual history of Canadian-American relations through an extensive corpus of fiction and non-fiction. It does not focus on specific events like, for instance, the Spanish-American War or the New Deal. Instead, the study offers a thematic examination of Canadian viewpoints on a variety of issues ranging from American forms of freedom to cross-border migration. This thematic method avoids some of the pitfalls of more biographical or event-based methods of intellectual history, which often neglect the internal dynamics of discourse and the continuity of ideas over time.[25] Major quotations are included in the text to illustrate the nature and evolution of Canadian commentary. Quotes were generally selected for inclusion based on their representativeness, though many quotations were also included to illustrate atypical discourse. To facilitate comprehension, French-language quotes have been translated into English. The original quotes can be found in the endnotes.

The intellectuals whose work is examined in these pages were essentially cultural figures – most intellectuals in late-nineteenth and early-twentieth-century Canada could be found in the academic community, in journalism, or in the ranks of the clergy – who became involved in sociopolitical debate without directly entering the world of partisan politics.[26] Indeed, as S.E.D. Shortt notes, 'rather than actively participating in politics, they preferred to confine themselves to critical observations in academic journals or membership in quasi-clandestine organizations, a tradition beginning with the Canada Firsters, carried on by the Round Table Groups, and culminating in the League for Social Reconstruction.'[27] Many of the radicals involved in the League, in particular Frank Underhill, F.R. Scott, Edgar McInnis (1899–1973), and King Gordon (1900–1989), are good examples of the *intellectuel engagé* whose action lies somewhere between the cultural and political spheres. This grey zone is the realm of the intellectual.

For the purposes of this study, intellectuals were considered Canadian if they were born in Canada and received the greater part of their education there, or if they immigrated and settled permanently in the Dominion. As a result, work by expatriate intellectuals who showed a sustained interest in Canadian affairs throughout their careers was examined. Indeed, exiled authors like John Bartlet Brebner (1895–1957) or Edmond de Nevers (1862–1906) were full participants in the development of Canadian discourse and played a key role in disseminating American ideas north of the border.

The present study rests on a corpus of over 500 texts written by Canadian intellectuals between 1891 and 1945. Texts were selected for inclusion in the study's corpus if they contained a substantive discussion of American life or Canada's relationship with the United States. Not surprisingly, given that the 'American question' has played a key role in Canadian discourse since the late eighteenth century, several of the most influential Canadian books published between 1891 and 1945 can be found in this study's corpus. Works of fiction account for roughly 5 per cent of the corpus.

The study's corpus was intended to be comprehensive, not exhaustive. It contains work written by most of the era's prominent intellectuals and offers a cross-section of late-nineteenth and early-twentieth century Canadian discourse. In all, work by over 250 authors was analysed. French-language texts represent a little less than a third of the corpus. Women authors account for about 2 per cent of the study's corpus. To a large extent, this underrepresentation is a reflection of women's relative exclusion from the professions most closely associated with intellectual discourse in late nineteenth and early twentieth century Canada.

Articles gleaned from journals make up roughly three-quarters of the corpus. The bulk of these texts was located through an examination of the era's periodical literature. Detailed scrutiny of this literature was confined to a selection of over one hundred of Canada's leading English- and French-language political, religious, literary, business, labour, legal, military, student, university, learned, and scholarly journals published no more than once a month between 1891 and 1945. Efforts were made to include journals that were both regionally and ideologically representative of the diversity of the Canadian mind. However, due to the sheer volume of material, articles in daily, weekly, and bi-monthly publications were excluded from the study. A few American and British periodicals, including the *North American Review* and the *Round Table*, were also scrutinized.

In an effort to grasp the various contexts that surround a given text, biographical information on the various intellectuals whose work is examined in these pages was collected and analysed. That said, this is not a prosopographical study. Rather, the group approach was primarily employed to uncover intellectual generations, their principal characteristics, and the key events that shaped their evolution. Generations are important to the study of intellectual history. Indeed, as historian Jean-François Sirinelli has noted, 'the effects of age in intellectual circles are ... numerous and significant' and can affect discourse as profoundly as the left-right cleavage. Intellectual generations are not homogeneous groups, but the events that shape a generation's consciousness during its formative years will deeply affect its outlook on the world. Every generation, writes Sirinelli, 'brings *genetic baggage* from its gestation and a *common memory*, at the same time both innate and acquired, from the first years of its existence, which mark it for life.'[28] The Great War, for instance, deeply affected the outlook of the generation of English Canadian intellectuals born roughly between 1880 and 1900. As we shall see, their penchant for continentalism was largely an expression of their profound disillusionment with imperialism and Europe.

My work rests on the assumption that ideas have consequences; that they can be powerful and autonomous historical forces, but that they can also serve as pragmatic tools or instruments for socioeconomic and political control.[29] The attitude of Canadian intellectuals towards the United States has affected the relationship between the two nations. Several key observers, most notably O.D. Skelton (1878–1941) and Hugh L. Keenleyside (1898–1992), would eventually help shape Canadian policy towards the United States from inside the Department of External Affairs, while others would influence the course of Canadian-American relations through their essays, lectures, and sermons. For instance, in the 1880s and 1890s, Erastus Wiman's (1834–1904) tireless promotion of a Canadian-American customs union helped convince many North Americans that continental integration was both feasible and desirable. His numerous articles and pamphlets nourished the wider social discourse regarding reciprocity and no doubt encouraged the Liberal party in its late-nineteenth century campaign to liberalize Canadian-American trade. That this campaign was unsuccessful is beside the point. Wiman's ideas – and those of other Canadian intellectuals – are important to the study of Canadian-American relations because they helped shape larger attitudes towards the United States and continental integration.

The present study is divided into three parts. The first chapter, Canadian-American Relations: An Intellectual History, amounts to an *entrée en matière*. It defines and dissects Canadian continentalism and anti-Americanism, and traces their general evolution. The foreign sources of Canadian commentary are also discussed. The next four chapters explore how Canada's intellectuals have viewed the various aspects of American society, from its philosophical bases to its practical workings. American politics and government are discussed, as are religion and culture, race and gender, and various issues related to order and industrial capitalism. Finally, the last four chapters examine how Canadian intellectuals have applied their reading of American history and society to the field of Canadian-American relations and to the politics of Canadian identity. The spectres of annexation and Americanization, as well as American foreign policy and Canadian-American trade, unionism, and migration are also discussed.

1 Canadian-American Relations:
An Intellectual History

Though it has been argued that early Canadian views of America 'were lacking in both understanding and information,'[1] this was certainly not the case by the turn of the twentieth century. Many Canadian intellectuals studied, worked, and travelled in the United States, and American newspapers, magazines, literature, and eventually, radio and film combined to make Canadians keenly aware of events and trends in the United States. Canadian interest in American affairs and in the Canadian-American relationship ebbed and flowed during the period under study, but it never ceased to occupy a prominent place in Canadian discourse. This was largely because, as George Grant (1918–1988) noted, 'to think of the U.S. is to think of ourselves – almost.'[2] This chapter examines the two opposing sensibilities, anti-Americanism and continentalism, that emerge from Canadian writing on the United States and continental integration. Both sensibilities were often inspired by the same writers, but they expressed very different world views. The same could be said of English and French Canadian commentary: while the two shared wider concerns regarding the United States and the modern ethos, the manner in which these ideas were developed and expressed often significantly differed.

Most Canadian intellectuals showed some interest in the 'American question.' Commentary on American affairs and on Canadian-American relations nonetheless remained more prevalent in English Canadian discourse. Generally speaking, English Canadian intellectuals were better informed of American affairs than were their French Canadian counterparts. Indeed, by the late nineteenth century, English Canadian society was awash in American ideas and culture. English Canadians read American books and magazines, studied with American readers, and enjoyed American mass entertainment. Their exposure to American news, writes Allan Smith, 'played a particularly important role in the creation of a continental frame of reference. The fact that they were so fully provided with knowledge of public controversies in the United States transformed those controversies into matters which seemed less newsworthy items from a foreign country and more vital matters which penetrated into the heart of Canada.' The pervasiveness of American ideas and culture in English Canada was not fully reproduced in Quebec. The United States certainly loomed large in Quebec, but the province was partially insulated from American ideas by its distinct language and culture.[3]

Moreover, in spite of Quebec's geographic contiguity with the United States and its large Franco-American diaspora, much of the readily available information on the republic was the work of French authors. Very little American history was taught in the province's classical colleges and universities. Eurocentric and preoccupied with antiquity, the whole structure of classical education did not lend itself to the study of American affairs. This situation troubled A.D. DeCelles (1843–1925): 'Is it not remarkable to see educated Canadians, well informed about the doings of the Greeks and the Egyptians, the causes of the rise and fall of the Romans, the annals of Europe, who are scarcely or not at all informed about the United States? Here, we must admit, is an anomaly that should not exist, since no country in the world has as much influence as the American Confederation on our interests and our economic situation.'[4] An admirer of American institutions, DeCelles sought to remedy this situation by publishing Les États-Unis. Origine, institutions, développement (1896), French Canada's first full-length study of American history and government. His book was widely read and received a prize from the French Académie des sciences morales et politiques. Re-issued in 1913 and 1925, with additional new sections, its success inspired Sylva Clapin (1853–1928) to write a similar but more generally accessible Histoire des États-Unis (1900) for use in French Canadian and Franco-American schools. However, despite the best efforts of DeCelles and Clapin, Quebec's intellectuals remained underinformed when it came to American affairs. And the situation did not improve with time. A generation after DeCelles criticized Quebec's classical colleges for neglecting the United States, American studies remained underdeveloped in Quebec and the province's intellectuals continued to look to France for analysis of American affairs.

During the period considered here, the average Canadian observer of the United States was a middle-class man born sometime between 1860 and 1900. Two intellectual generations dominate this study. The first, born between the late 1850s and the late 1870s, was profoundly affected by the wave of imperialism that washed over the British Empire during the second half of Queen Victoria's reign. It was most active in the early twentieth century. The second generation, born roughly between 1880 and 1900, was deeply scarred by the Great War. It reached its peak of influence during the 1930s and 1940s.

For Canada's intellectuals, interest in American affairs increased in proportion to contact with the United States. Many of Canada's most persistent observers of American life had studied or worked in the United States. A handful of prominent Canadian intellectuals, including Jules-Paul Tardivel (1851–1905) and John Castell Hopkins (1864–1923), were born in the United States. Others, like George M. Wrong (1860–1948), R.G. Trotter (1888–1951), Jean-Charles Harvey (1891–1967), and Harry Bernard (1898–1979), spent part of their childhood there. Not surprisingly, expatriate intellectuals proved to be among the most prolific observers of the United States. Indeed, writers like abbé Henri d'Arles (1870–1930), who was attached to the Roman Catholic diocese of Manchester, New Hampshire, for almost two decades, or John Bartlet Brebner, who spent most of his career teaching history at New York's Columbia University, could offer a unique perspective on American life to Canadians.

Many key observers experienced American society through its universities. Indeed, though higher education grew rapidly in late nineteenth and early twentieth century Canada, graduate studies remained underdeveloped in Canada until well into the 1960s. As a result, a significant number of the intellectuals whose work is examined in these pages completed their studies abroad, often in American universities. Stephen Leacock, O.D. Skelton, and Harold Innis (1894–1952), for instance, all earned doctoral degrees from the University of Chicago, while James T. Shotwell (1874–1965) received his Ph.D. from Columbia University.

Moreover, as Canada's economic and intellectual development perennially lagged behind that of the United States, a number of intellectuals left Canada to find work south of the border. American universities proved to be particularly fertile ground for Canadian scholars in search of employment and good wages. Queen's University graduate William Bennett Munro (1875–1957), for instance, headed Harvard's Bureau of Municipal Research in the 1920s, while P.E. Corbett (1892–1983), who served as McGill University's Dean of Law in the 1930s, left Canada and joined the faculty of Yale University in 1942. The world of American journalism also proved particularly enticing to Canadian intellectuals. Sara Jeannette Duncan (1861–1922), one of the most prominent women authors of her generation, got her start at the Washington *Post*, while John MacCormac (1890–1958) made a name for himself at the *New York Times*.

The 'brain drain' was particularly acute among English Canadian thinkers, whose upward mobility in America was not generally hampered by the 'foreign' label. In his memoirs, Arthur Lower (1889–1988), who studied and taught history at Harvard University, reflected on this reality: 'In that first week [at Harvard], I also went to a reception for foreign students. The gentleman receiving me said, "You do not seem like a foreigner." I replied that I did not know whether I was or not, since I was a Canadian. "Oh, Canadians are not foreigners," he said. No one ever treated me as one.'[5]

The French Canadian experience in America was different. Emigrants from Quebec had long suffered the stigma of the 'Chinese of the Eastern States' epithet that the Chief of the Massachusetts Bureau of Statistics of Labor, Carroll D. Wright, had heaped on them in 1881. Nonetheless, many French Canadian intellectuals followed the hundreds of thousands of their compatriots who emigrated to the United States in the late nineteenth and early twentieth centuries. And though latent nativism and linguistic barriers effectively excluded most of them from mainstream American intellectual life, many found work in the lively world of Franco-American journalism. In fact, the emigrant press served as a training ground for several of French Canada's most prominent journalists, including the enfant terrible of French Canadian journalism, Olivar Asselin (1874–1937), who began his career at the age of eighteen writing articles for the *Protecteur canadien* of Fall River, Massachusetts. Others, like Catholic clergymen Édouard Hamon (1841–1904) and Antonio Huot (1877–1929), served God in various American dioceses.

The Canadian fascination with the United States grew steadily during the period under study. Writing on America responded to a variety of stimuli, both domestic and foreign. Canadian commentary was primarily a reflection of national concerns, but American events and policy affected its intensity. Canadian interest in American affairs and Canadian-American relations increased during the reciprocity elections of 1891 and 1911. Later, the Great Depression, the New Deal, and the King-Roosevelt reciprocity agreement produced a fair amount of discussion in 1929–31 and in 1935–36, while American neutrality and the outbreak of the Second World War, the fall of France, the Ogdensburg and Hyde Park agreements, which significantly increased Canadian-American wartime defence and economic cooperation, and the Japanese attack on Pearl Harbor brought Canadian commentary to a fever pitch in the years 1939–42. The fall of France was indirectly responsible for the burst of interest in American affairs and in Canadian-American relations that occurred in 1940 and 1941. As the British Empire faced the Axis powers alone, Canada's sense of vulnerability reached its highest levels since the 1860s, and Canadians increasingly turned to the United States for protection and leadership. As a result, Canadian intellectuals produced more commentary on American affairs in 1940–41 than at any other point during the period studied here.

Canadian independence and Canada's entry into the League of Nations generated a great deal of writing on international relations in general, and on Canadian-American relations in particular, during the interwar years. International affairs literally fascinated the English Canadian intellectuals born in the 1880s and 1890s. They had come of age with the Dominion and were anxious to see it assume its rightful place in the concert of nations. The Canadian Institute of International Affairs, which was founded in 1928, helped nurture their interest in international relations by sponsoring a number of conferences and studies that explored Canada's place in the world.

English Canadian intellectuals showed greater interest in American affairs and a more pronounced tendency to view American issues as though they were their own than did their French Canadian counterparts. Nevertheless, Quebec's interest in America grew rapidly after the First World War. As in English Canada, French Canadian interest in American affairs peaked in 1941, which André Laurendeau (1912–1968) hailed as the year of Quebec's belated discovery of America.[6]

While French Canadian intellectuals, on the whole, showed less sustained interest in the United States than did their English Canadian counterparts, they did, however, produce several of Canada's full-length examinations of American life. It is indeed Edmond de Nevers, not Goldwin Smith, who stands out as the most sophisticated Canadian observer of his era. Born Edmond Boisvert in Baie-du-Febvre, Canada East, de Nevers was educated at the Séminaire de Nicolet. Called to the bar in 1883, he appears to have taken a job as a provincial inspector of asylums rather than practise law. Shortly thereafter, he adopted the pseudonym Edmond de Nevers. In 1888, he left Canada for Germany.

Brilliant and multilingual, he travelled extensively throughout Europe during the next several years and worked at the Agence Havas in Paris as a translator and writer. In 1895, he returned to North America, going first to Rhode Island, where his family had previously emigrated, then to Quebec City, where he had numerous friends and relatives. The following year he was back in Europe, but he returned to Quebec in 1900, stricken with locomotor ataxia. He spent the next couple of years working as a publicist for the provincial Department of Colonization and Mines. Debilitated by his illness, he returned to Rhode Island sometime in late 1902 or early 1903 to die among his family.[7] In many ways, de Nevers was Canada's answer to Alexis de Tocqueville. Like the author of *De la démocratie en Amérique*, de Nevers was a liberal with marked conservative tendencies who devoted several years of his life to analysing American society, which he admired, though certainly not unquestioningly. He published his monumental *L'âme américaine* in 1900 and translated Matthew Arnold's 1888 essays on *Civilization in the United States* into French. In 1900, French literary critic Ferdinand Brunetière published a forty-page review of *L'âme américaine* in the prestigious *Revue des deux mondes*. He believed that the two-volume essay was 'one of the most interesting that had been published on America for a long time.'[8]

Despite sharing common preoccupations regarding the United States, English and French Canadian commentary differed in several respects. English Canadian discourse on America tended to centre on political and diplomatic affairs. As Louis Balthazar has pointed out, 'Canadian-American relations, even in a political light, have been on the whole the almost exclusive domain of English Canadians.'[9] Writing on Canadian-American diplomatic relations was largely the domain of English-speaking Canadians. Conversely, French Canadian intellectuals were inclined to concentrate on social issues – religion, education, and culture – which English Canadian intellectuals were less likely to examine, and they showed far less interest in American political affairs and in Canadian-American diplomacy. Quebec's intellectuals did, however, devote a great deal of energy to Canadian-American economic, demographic, and cultural relations. To be sure, while it was at best a minor theme in English Canadian writing, emigration loomed large in the French Canadian psyche. Economic affairs were of great interest in both English and French Canada, though issues related to trade were not as important in French Canadian discourse. Indeed, while reciprocity served as the flashpoint for the 'American question' in English Canada,

this issue was far less contentious in Quebec. Interwar American investment, by contrast, does not appear to have generated a debate as intense
in English Canada as it did in Quebec.

A great deal of Canadian commentary on America can be found
in texts on emigration and the Loyalist experience. For many English Canadian intellectuals, the Loyalists acted as a springboard for
discussing the merits of the American Revolution and the foundations of American politics and government. However, interest in the
Loyalist tradition was tied to the vitality of English Canadian imperialism, and both declined after the Great War.[10] For its part, Quebec
frequently viewed the continent through the eyes of its diaspora and, to
a lesser extent, through the experience of various other Roman Catholic groups. Emigration and Franco-America generated a great deal of
commentary in Quebec, which, in turn, often led to an examination of
the merits of American society. Roughly one-fifth of the French Canadian texts selected for inclusion in this study deal directly with emigration, Franco-America, or Louisiana, making diaspora-related issues the
most significant topic discussed in French Canadian commentary on
the United States. Interest in emigration and Franco-American affairs
declined rapidly after 1930, when the United States severely curtailed
immigration from Canada.

Canadian intellectuals, particularly those who were most critical of
the United States, tended to homogonize the American experience. Regional, class, and ethnic differences in the United States were not particularly well assessed in Canadian commentary. In this sense, Canadian
commentary was very similar to European writing on America, which
also tended to represent the United States homogeneously. Unlike European commentary, however, Canadian writing on the United States
rarely took the form of the travel narrative. The European observer usually saw America through a transatlantic haze or from the perspective
of a traveller, while the Canadian observer merely peered over a fence,
glanced at his neighbour, and jotted down his impressions.[11]

The themes and arguments used to debate the 'American question' were more or less constant during the period examined here. As
Ramsay Cook has noted, 'George Grant succeeds Robinson and Principal Grant as the spokesman for "British" Canada, while Professor
Underhill is the successor of Goldwin Smith as the spokesman for
"American" Canada.' Their arguments regarding the United States
and continental integration, however, remained largely unchanged.[12]
Canadian commentary was indeed repetitive and, as we shall see,
somewhat derivative. Some scholars bemoan this fact. They argue that

Canada, as a North American nation, should have produced some of the more perceptive analyses of American civilization; instead, they claim, it generated among the most unoriginal work ever written about the United States.[13] There is some truth to these assertions. But the importance of Canadian interpretations of American life is lost when they are compared with European analyses. Canadian commentary is not significant because it offers any particular insight into the American experience; it is worthy of study because it provides a great deal of insight into the Canadian mind. Besides, the American commentary of Edmond de Nevers, Jules-Paul Tardivel, or Goldwin Smith easily ranks with that of Georges Duhamel or Charles Dickens. Their work has undoubtedly attracted scant attention in the United States and Europe, but this is largely the reflection of a wider ignorance of Canadian thought and writing.

In Canada, resistance to American domination has taken a number of forms since the War of 1812: the National Policy, Defence Scheme No. 1, the Canadian Broadcasting Corporation, Canadian content regulations, the Foreign Investment Review Agency, and the National Energy Program, to name only a few. And from Confederation to the present day, cultural and economic protectionism has generally found its most vocal supporters among Canada's intellectual elite. Indeed, though the nation's intellectual culture has changed fundamentally since the late nineteenth century, anti-American sentiment continues to play a key role in Canadian thought. This apparent continuity masks a fundamental inversion in the underpinnings of anti-American rhetoric in Canada: largely a left-wing idea today, anti-Americanism was primarily a right-wing doctrine until the 1960s.

Anti-Americanism has historically implied a reasonably systematic hostility to American society, not merely a punctual criticism of American policy or life. Moreover, anti-American thinkers were generally opposed to continental integration and they rejected the notion that Canada was above all an 'American' nation. It should be noted, however, that the anti-American ethos was neither uniformly unsympathetic nor wholly uninformed; certainly, it was not entirely the product of bitterness and traditional animosity.[14] Prominent anti-American thinkers could indeed, on occasion, wax sentimental about Anglo-Saxon unity or the Dominion of Canada's critical role as the linchpin of Anglo-American relations. And while anti-American rhetoric frequently involved inaccurate representations and irrational delusions, irrationality was not intrinsic to anti-Americanism. Canadian critics could, at times, prove surprisingly insightful and accurate in their assessment of American society.

Anti-Americanism was fundamentally different from the other major negative faiths, anti-Semitism and anticommunism, because it lacked their unconditional nature.[15] Indeed, as Charles F. Doran and James P. Sewell note, Canadian hostility to the United States tended 'to dissolve when brought directly into contact with the individual American.'[16] Anti-American sentiment rarely prevented Canadian conservatives from befriending Americans, from adopting American practices, from contributing to American periodicals, or from studying, working, lecturing, or vacationing in the United States. Speaking before the Young Men's Liberal Club of Toronto in 1891, Goldwin Smith offered an amusing anecdote to this effect: 'The other day I was myself reviled in the most unmeasured language for my supposed American proclivities. Soon afterwards I heard that my assailant had accepted a call as a minister to the other side of the line.'[17]

Though American actions and policy have historically intensified or lessened Canadian hostility, especially among the masses, they have never proved fundamentally causal to elite anti-Americanism. This was particularly true after Confederation. Certainly, American expansionism did threaten Canada before the Great War, but it had been a mitigated menace since the 1871 Treaty of Washington. Besides, American forcefulness never upset all Canadian thinkers – there has always been a group of continentalist intellectuals willing to forgive America for even its most serious misdeeds. Instead, anti-Americanism expressed a series of ideas – anti-Americanism is not an ideology – that were integral to the conservative ethos.

The premises upon which anti-American discourse rested were indeed those of conservative nationalism. These were relatively straightforward in English Canada. Imperialists insisted that an unbroken bond existed between Canada and Great Britain. They viewed Canadian society as fundamentally different from American society and argued that Canadian nationhood was intrinsically precarious. French Canadian nationalism rested on comparable premises. The continuity between French Canada and pre-revolutionary France was affirmed. So too was the extent to which French Canadian society was fundamentally different from American (and English Canadian) society. French Canadian nationalists also viewed their nation as a vulnerable and fundamentally precarious entity and, like imperialists, they had a tendency to downplay the regional, cultural, and social diversity of their nation.[18]

By and large, American society before the Second World War presented a greater affront to traditionalists than it did to Marxists.[19] This is why Canadian anti-Americanism was expressed most fully in the discourse of the nation's dominant conservative families: imperialism[20] and French Canadian nationalism.[21] Certainly, anti-Americanism has historically made for strange bedfellows, but more to the point, as Sylvie Lacombe has shown, French Canadian nationalism and English Canadian imperialism were not antithetical ideologies.[22] Despite their fundamental divergence on the national question, they both possessed an essentially antimodern outlook, and anti-Americanism was their logical point of convergence.

Imperialists and *nationalistes* shared a number of overarching conservative values. These included a firm belief in communitarianism, elitism, and a transcendent order; an appreciation of organic, evolutionary change; a profound devotion to tradition, continuity, and order; and a deep conviction that freedom, order, and private property were closely linked.[23] It is worth noting, however, that Canadian conservatives were rarely satisfied with the status quo. As a result, they produced some of the most sweeping critiques of modern industrial society to be published in Canada. Conservatism itself would not have existed without the challenge of modernity; only the erosion of traditional values and customs forces reflection on the value of tradition.

That said, the average English Canadian critic of American society was both more fixated and more temperate than his French Canadian counterpart. This apparent paradox was the result of two basic factors: English Canada's more moderate conservative intellectual tradition and the traditional focus of its nationalism. French Canadian nationalism was, on the whole, more conservative than imperialism. English Canadian conservatism was essentially British and Protestant in inspiration; Quebec's right, on the other hand, was fundamentally Catholic and bore the influence of France's far less temperate conservative tradition.[24] These factors combined to ensure that French Canadian intellectuals would offer a stiffer resistance to modernity and the United States. Unlike many Protestant denominations, Catholicism stood fast against modernism as the twentieth century began. The English Canadian critique of America also lacked the fundamental pietism that was the hallmark of conservative French Canadian commentary.

English Canada's ethnocultural proximity to its southern neighbour has historically made the United States the main focus of its nationalism, of its efforts at survival. Quebec's distinctiveness from the United

States has long been more readily apparent than English Canada's and, during the period under study, English Canadian conservatives were more fixated on America than were their French Canadian counterparts. Nevertheless, the intellectual's rapport with modernity was closely tied to the construction of identity and nationalism in both English and French Canada, and imperialists and *nationalistes* both were similarly driven to construct a national identity on traditional (and therefore anti-American) precepts.

Modernity renewed the intellectual's function. The expansion of public and higher education, urbanization, the growth of journalism and the press, the development of a network of public libraries, and most importantly, the expansion of literacy that occurred in the late nineteenth century, all contributed to the emergence of the modern Canadian intellectual.[25] Yet most Canadian thinkers around 1900 were resolutely antimodern, and a moderate traditionalism born of Canada's basically temperate political and intellectual culture formed the core of their thought. In the United States, the antimodern impulse expressed itself, among other things, through orientalism, medievalism, and the exaltation of martial virtues.[26] These values could be found in Canadian thought, but Canadian antimodernism found its principal outlet in anti-American rhetoric.

But why lash out at the United States? Because America, like the former Soviet Union, is more than a nation; historically, it has embodied both a way of life and an ideological system with pretensions to universality.[27] The American Republic is built on specific conceptions of liberty, equality, individualism, and secularism, and has come to epitomize an implicitly liberal version of modernity. Moreover, America was a revolutionary nation built on an ethos of rupture, and it had been quick to embrace the mass age and its social, cultural, and technological transformations. Revealingly, the Canadian critique of the United States centred on a rejection of republicanism, egalitarianism, individualism, secularism, mass culture, materialism, and large-scale industrialization. America was a nation where continuity, order, and deference had vanished; it was, as George Grant asserted in *Lament for a Nation*, 'the heart of modernity.'[28]

The dynamism of American society has often been viewed as a threat by conservative elites intent on the preservation of traditional values, institutions, and social relationships.[29] Accordingly, anti-American rhetoric was tied to a wider denunciation of the status revolution that followed the rise of modernity.[30] Industrialization eroded premodern social relations, and new groups assumed some of the power and prestige that traditional elites, especially the clergy and the liberal professions, had wielded. A new and grandiosely wealthy industrial bourgeoisie had emerged and was stamping out traditional notions of status and deference. The growing power and size of the proletariat was also a source of anxiety for conservative intellectuals. Many worried that capitalist exploitation would push the proletariat to revolution. Like a number of American progressives, Canadian conservatives were nostalgic for an era when society was characterized, writes Richard Hofstadter, by 'a rather broad diffusion of wealth, status, and power,' and where 'the man of moderate means, especially in the many small communities, could command much deference and exert much influence.'[31]

Intellectual concerns about the ill-effects of the status revolution were tied to more general middle-class anxieties that invariably follow rapid social change. These apprehensions were not confined to the Dominion of Canada; they could be found throughout Western Europe and the United States. 'In both Europe and America, the antimodern impulse was rooted in what can aptly be called a crisis of cultural authority,' writes Jackson Lears.[32] The power and prestige of intellectuals has always rested on their role as arbiters of culture. As a result, many Canadian thinkers felt dispossessed by mass, or as they saw it, American culture, which was completely out of their control. That said, antimodernism and its principal Canadian expression, anti-Americanism, were also the result of a sincere effort to impose moral meaning on a rapidly changing society, and it would be a mistake to reduce this impulse to a simple quest for social control.

English Canadian imperialism experienced its golden age during the years that separated the 1891 and 1911 reciprocity elections. Imperialist anti-Americanism reached its zenith during the latter federal election, when inflammatory rhetoric was successfully used by the Conservative party to scuttle a reciprocity agreement that promised to revolutionize Canada's economy. The imperialist movement, which had close ties to the Conservative party, was a loose collection of individuals that gravitated around a number of associations, including the Imperial Federation League and, later, the Round Table groups. A few dozen intellectuals constituted the vanguard of the imperialist movement, which could, in turn, count on hundreds of thousands of sympathizers in Canada at the turn of the twentieth century. Most of these intellectuals were Canadian-born, but the imperialist movement itself found its greatest appeal among Canada's large population of British immigrants. During the 1890s and the early 1900s, two influential journals of intellectual commentary, the *Queen's Quarterly* (founded in 1893) and the *University Magazine* (founded in 1907), were tied to the imperialist movement. During the period examined here, these reviews played a key role in the intellectual culture of English-speaking Canada.

An aging generation of imperialists, among them George Monro Grant (1835–1902), John G. Bourinot (1836–1902), Colonel George T. Denison (1839–1925), and George R. Parkin (1846–1922), faced the continentalist challenge in the 1890s. Born in the 1830s and 1840s, these men came of age around the time of Confederation and were mesmerized by the new nation's potential. They were also appalled by the American Civil War, which seemed to confirm the folly of the American experiment. The American menace loomed large in the 1860s, as the long-standing quarrel between Britain and the United States worsened, and the Fenian raids nourished both anti-Irish and anti-American – the two were often related – sentiment in the young Dominion of Canada.

Principal Grant's generation of imperialists was most active during the Dominion's first twenty-five years, when sectionalism, economic marasmus, sectarianism, and ethnic conflict threatened to tear apart what the Fathers of Confederation had built. Yet their faith in the Dominion remained unshaken and their desire to ensure its survival found its expression in a longing for imperial federation and a forceful anti-Americanism. They were convinced that Canada was seriously threatened by Americanization and Manifest Destiny, and that only British power could guarantee the nation's sovereignty.

Born roughly between the late 1850s and the late 1870s, the generation of imperialists who rose to prominence in the early twentieth century was brought up in the midst of the status revolution. Its leading lights, which included George M. Wrong, Andrew Macphail, Robert Falconer (1867–1943), and Stephen Leacock came of age during the late 1880s and early 1890s. The rancorous debate over unrestricted reciprocity and commercial union helped shape their anti-Americanism. Macphail and his associates followed their imperialist predecessors in arguing that Canadian sovereignty would be best preserved and enhanced through imperial solidarity. Their anti-Americanism deepened in the whirlwind of change that struck Canada in the late nineteenth and early twentieth centuries. It was this generation of imperialist intellectuals that helped bring popular anti-American sentiment to a fever pitch during the 1911 federal election. Stephen Leacock, for instance, actively campaigned in favour of the Conservative party in 1911, and wrote anti-reciprocity articles for various newspapers, for which he was paid, indirectly, by the Canadian Manufacturers' Association.[33]

During the 1920s and 1930s, the imperial federation movement withered away as the Empire gave way to the Commonwealth, the *University Magazine* ceased publication, and the exaltation of Canada's Loyalist heritage, which had been intimately linked to the imperialist movement, waned. But imperialism lived on: its Tory core was preserved by intellectuals like R.G. Trotter who refused to follow the leadings lights of their generation into continentalism. Besides, several of the Dominion's most prominent pre–First World War imperialists, including Stephen Leacock and Andrew Macphail, remained active until the late 1930s. Their time, however, had passed, and their anti-Americanism had considerably mellowed since 1911. That said, though elite anti-American sentiment waned in the 1920s, it nevertheless became more organized with the creation of a number of lobby groups such as the Canadian Authors' Association, the Magazine Publishers' Association of Canada, and the Canadian Radio League, which were set up to defend Canada against Americanization and promote Canadian cultural autonomy.

During the 1930s, many Canadians turned their backs on protectionism once it became apparent that the Depression was going to last longer than a few months, and the nation generally applauded when Prime Minister Mackenzie King negotiated a major trade agreement with the United States in 1935. By the late 1930s, the continental debate in English Canadian intellectual circles had partially shifted from Americanism to pan-Americanism. But the discussion surrounding the possible entry of Canada into the Pan-American Union was in fact a renewal of one of the oldest debates in Canadian intellectual history. Tories like R.G. Trotter refuted pan-Americanism with essentially the same arguments that their predecessors had used to reject reciprocity twenty-five years before. In essence, they feared that pan-Americanism would corrode Canada's British essence.

By the early 1940s, even the staunchest imperialists generally accepted the necessity of wartime continental integration. Few Tories protested the August 1940 Ogdensburg Agreement, which linked Canada and the United States in a permanent defensive alliance. Ogdensburg indeed marked the nadir of English Canadian anti-Americanism. In a world gone mad, the United States appeared increasingly familiar and sane to even the most vigorous proponents of imperial unity. As Canada held its breath after the fall of France, anti-American sentiment seemed totally out of place. German U-boats prowled the Gulf of St

Lawrence, the Japanese mauled the American fleet at Pearl Harbor, and the very survival of Britain and, indeed, of the free world, seemed to rest in the hands of the United States. But anti-American sentiment had not disappeared. It would re-emerge in the writing of a new generation of conservatives born between 1900 and 1920. Led by Donald Creighton (1902–1979) and George Grant, this generation of Tory intellectuals was too young to have fought in the Great War and, in many cases, too old to have fought in the Second World War. It turned up on Canada's cultural radar in the late 1930s and early 1940s, and came to dominate the nation's intellectual discourse in the 1950s and early 1960s. In the context of the Cold War and the atomic age, their anti-Americanism reflected new concerns regarding modernity and American power.

Several scholars maintain that Ontario has historically been the epicentre of anti-American sentiment in Canada.[34] Certainly, fragmentary evidence would suggest that anti-Americanism has generally been stronger in Ontario than in the rest of Canada. The results of the 1911 federal election, for instance, do reveal that support for reciprocity – the litmus test of anti-American sentiment – was weaker in Ontario than in most of the rest of Canada. Things become far less clear, however, when gauging the regional distribution of anti-American sentiment among intellectuals. Undoubtedly, several of Canada's most prominent anti-American thinkers were Ontarians. This is hardly surprising since nineteenth-century Ontario had received large numbers of British immigrants, the province's industrial structure relied heavily on the National Policy, and the province possessed a dynamic United Empire Loyalist movement that was more militantly anti-American than its Maritime counterpart.[35] Nevertheless, Ontario did not have anything approaching a monopoly on anti-Americanism. A number of imperialist intellectuals born in the Maritimes, most notably John G. Bourinot, Andrew Macphail, and George R. Parkin, made major contributions to Canada's anti-American canon. Moreover, during the period under study, Quebec's intellectual culture was notoriously anti-American. In fact, if anything, Quebec was the epicentre of elite anti-Americanism in Canada.

A general hostility to the United States was one of the hallmarks of traditional French Canadian nationalism. Closely tied to the Roman Catholic Church, the nationalist movement was a fairly diverse group of individuals gravitating around a number of associations and publications, which included, at various times, *Le Devoir*, *L'Action française*, the Ligue des droits du français, and the Jeune-Canada. The movement could count on some degree of sympathy from a fairly significant proportion of Canada's French-speaking population. That said, the nationalist movement was not a mass movement. Its members were drawn largely from the clergy and the liberal professions, and many of its campaigns, most notably its crusade against emigration and Americanization, were less than successful. Like the imperialist movement, the nationalist movement contained various divisions and was scarcely a homogeneous bloc. That said, during the period examined here, it rallied a significant proportion of Quebec's intellectual elite.

During the decades that preceded the Great War, French Canadian anti-Americanism never attained the level of intensity that it would reach in the 1920s and 1930s. The combined impact of the imperial federation movement, the South African War, and the Conscription Crisis left nationalist intellectuals like Henri Bourassa and Olivar Asselin thoroughly convinced that imperialism – both British and English Canadian – was the primary external threat to the French Canadian nation. Accordingly, their Ligue nationaliste, though concerned about Quebec's progressive Americanization and deeply troubled by emigration, found its raison d'être in the anti-imperialist struggle. In the wake of the 1911 election, Bourassa went as far as to denounce the manipulation of anti-American rhetoric by imperialists. Though he acknowledged that Americanization threatened French Canada, he skilfully argued that annexation was in fact less of a threat to *la survivance* than was imperial federation. English Canadian opinion was mortified.

After the Great War, the decline of imperialism in English Canada, the concretization of Canadian independence, the decline of British power, and the dramatic rise of America's commercial and cultural influence all combined to make the United States appear increasingly threatening to French Canadian conservatives. Perhaps worse still, emigration, which had been steadily declining since the late 1890s, suddenly kicked back into high gear – almost 150,000 Quebecers left for the United States between 1919 and 1929. Nationalist intellectuals answered this new *saignée* with a torrent of anti-American prose. Moreover, the French intelligentsia was growing increasingly hostile to the United States, and French Canadian conservatives, who took some of their cues from the French right, were inclined to follow suit.

In effect, the United States was in the process of replacing Britain as the leading outside menace to French Canadian traditionalism. The shift was evident. 'The English influence might seem formidable,' André Laurendeau asserted in 1937, 'but it is exerted at a distance and, considered as a civilization, is less hostile to us [than] American civilization.'[36] Shortly after the Great War, as Henri Bourassa's influence began to decline and abbé Lionel Groulx came to dominate Quebec's nationalist movement, interest in imperial affairs waned, and anxiety over French Canada's progressive Americanization grew apace. The abbé had shared Bourassa's concerns in the prewar years, but in the 1920s his attention increasingly shifted from imperialism and constitutional issues to Americanization and economic affairs. Bourassa's unruly collaborator, Olivar Asselin, followed suit. Groulx exerted a great deal of influence on the generation of nationalist intellectuals who, like Anatole Vanier (1887–1985) and Esdras Minville (1896–1975), came of age during the Great War, and he galvanized the Jeune-Canada movement, whose most prominent figures, Dostaler O'Leary (1908–1965), Gérard Filion (1909–2005), André Laurendeau, and Roger Duhamel (1916–1985), would burst onto the scene in the 1930s.

By 1920, the era of the moderately conservative *Revue canadienne* had passed. The French Canadian right would now take its cues from the militant *L'Action française* and its heir apparent, *L'Action nationale*. Many nationalists argued that the Great Depression was the logical consequence of materialism and capitalism. In their eyes, this confirmed the failure of the American experience. In both Quebec and France, the Great Depression would bring intellectual anti-Americanism to a fever pitch. In 1936, the *Revue dominicaine* published a series of exceptionally virulent articles devoted to 'notre américanisation.' The review's staunchly conservative editor, Father M.-A. Lamarche (1876–1950), was particularly harsh in his assessment of the United States: 'this residue of Anglo-Saxon civilization, thrown into an immense test-tube, has produced an extraordinary civilization, dazzling from certain angles. But *there is a massive amount of rubbish, and we collect the rubbish.*'[37] He concluded the 1936 inquiry by calling for a vast anti-American public education campaign. French Canadian anti-Americanism had reached its zenith.

By the 1940s, however, a noticeable shift had occurred in French Canadian commentary: elite anti-Americanism had begun to recede. Wartime anxiety also worked its magic on French Canada, and nationalist intellectuals like Édouard Montpetit (1881–1954), Gustave Lanctot (1883–1975), Léopold Richer (1902–1961), and André Laurendeau began to explore Quebec's relationship with the United States in a new way. The tone remained largely critical, but a new interest in American affairs was emerging. French Canada, it was argued, needed to learn more about its southern neighbour. Laurendeau, who was poised to assume the leadership of Quebec's nationalist movement, played a particularly important role in this wartime development. In a 1941 article published in the normally sedate *L'Enseignement secondaire*, he scathingly criticized the lack of attention paid to American affairs by the province's classical colleges:

> If Edmond de Nevers spent ten years of his life scrutinizing documents, if he turned his original and perspicacious gaze towards our neighbours to the south, it was because in his opinion *the destinies of the United States are of the utmost importance to us French Canadians*. We would not demand such a sustained effort from all educated minds, let alone from students studying for the baccalaureat. But with the future of the United States weighing so heavily on our own national future, is it not legitimate to expect that college students be given some simple, fair, and true ideas about the past and present of the great Republic? ... If we ask around we discover, by and large, the same weaknesses, the same emptiness. Some friends, whose sympathy has been awakened in this respect, have given themselves a personal half-education. Their specialism has forced others to search further. Many have travelled to the other side of the forty-fifth parallel, sealed business relations, etc. But everyone is in agreement: at college they were warned against Americanism, that is to say against a very real sickness of the soul and the mind, against a national, moral, and religious peril, but were told very little about the American reality.[38]

This was hardly an endorsement of American society, but the shift was palpable. Liberal intellectuals like Edmond de Nevers, A.D. DeCelles, and Sylva Clapin had urged Quebecers to show more interest in American affairs at the turn of the twentieth century, but this was the first time that a major intellectual identified with the province's conservative nationalist movement – Laurendeau was the editor of *L'Action nationale* – had called for the same thing. The 1940s indeed witnessed a fundamental shift in French Canadian intellectual history. After dominating French Canadian discourse for the better part of a century, conservatism had begun to recede. Laurendeau and his acolytes were undoubtedly conservative, but their rapport with tradition – and America – was different.

To describe the continentalist ethos as pro-American – sympathetic to the interests of the United States and favourable to American society

– is simplistic. Rather, continentalism was a complex and specifically Canadian version of pro-Americanism. It was a *sensibility* that implied far more than a general sympathy to American society. Continentalists embraced the essentially North American nature of Canadian society and were favourably inclined towards some form of continental integration. They believed that Canada was sufficiently resilient to survive – and would, in fact, benefit from – continental integration. Moreover, they were more likely to view the Canadian-American relationship in terms of similarities and concord, rather than in terms of differences and conflict. Perhaps most of all, notes Allan Smith, continentalists shared the deep conviction 'that nation-building had to involve working with, rather than against, the grain of American strength.'[39]

That said, continentalists did not accept North American integration unquestioningly. And they did not systematically gloss over or ignore America's shortcomings either; they relativized them. Canada, continentalists believed, suffered from many of the ills that affected its neighbour. Above all, Canada and the United States shared a common North Americanism; they were nations of the New World. Continentalists rarely suggested that American society was in any way superior to Canadian society. Their differentialism was usually aimed at Europe, not America. Continentalists believed that Canada, as a North American nation, possessed a social order that was fundamentally different from that of Europe.

Continentalism was endemic to the centre and the left in pre-1945 Canada. Indeed, though liberalism and socialism are antithetical ideologies in the sense that they are respectively founded on individualism and collectivism, they also share a profoundly modern ethos. Liberals and socialists possess a common passion for change. As a result, they are largely contemptuous of tradition, which they reject as a guide to social welfare in favour of reason or materialistic determinism. Moreover, they regard humanity as the central fact of the universe (anthropocentrism), and have a profound faith in its perfectibility and in the illimitable progress of society (meliorism). Privilege is condemned, and democracy, as direct as practicable, is the professed ideal (egalitarianism).[40]

To continentalists, the United States more or less embodied these core modern values. America was a liberal republic that embraced a certain conception of progress, equality, and secularism. Moreover, the United States had detached itself from the Old World; it had made a genuine attempt to build a new society and, by extension, a new man. Unhindered by the burden of tradition, America was a nation on the move. To defend America was to defend the promise of the New World, which continentalists wanted Canada to enter unreservedly. During the interwar years, the rise of continentalism was also tied to a more general shift in Canadian society: as anxieties regarding industrialization and urbanization lessened, the middle class increasingly embraced progress and materialism.[41]

Left-wing discourse and pro-American sentiment may seem irreconcilable today, but they were frequently allied in late nineteenth and early twentieth century Canada. The United States projected a different image before 1945. It had embarked on a number of progressive experiments, including the New Deal, and was often perceived as a nation that eschewed militarism. For the prewar left, European imperialism and militarism were generally viewed as the world's principal obstacles to progressivism, and the United States had not yet come to fully embody the abuses of industrial capitalism. But all this would change with the Cold War. To the left, the United States became a quintessentially reactionary nation whose military-industrial complex conspired to stifle radicalism on an international scale. 'For Canadians who wish to pursue the elusive goal of an egalitarian socialist society,' wrote James Laxer in 1970, 'American imperialism is the major enemy.'[42] And so the die was cast.

Socialism aside, annexationism was continentalism's most radical expression. Articulated by liberal intellectuals who had lost all faith in Confederation, it was an idea born of nineteenth-century despair and depression – its fortunes were invariably tied to some form of economic or political malaise. And though continentalists as a group were frequently accused of favouring the union of Canada and the United States – the stigma attached to annexation stuck to continentalism – most were firmly opposed to the idea of political union. No longer able to rally more than a handful of malcontents, annexationism basically disappeared from Canadian discourse around 1900.

Continentalism and nationalism were not necessarily opposing doctrines and, contrary to what many scholars would argue, Canadian nationalism has never been intrinsically anti-American. Certainly, some continentalists, most notably Goldwin Smith, James T. Shotwell, and Jean-Charles Harvey were antinationalists, but the majority, in fact, were not. Continentalism was a key ingredient in the anti-imperialist Canadian nationalism professed by intellectuals like John S. Ewart (1849–1933), Arthur Lower, and F.R. Scott. Canada, they believed, would only become truly independent from Britain if it fully embraced its North American nature. Moreover, in Quebec, several liberal nationalists at the turn of the twentieth century, including Errol Bouchette (1863–1912) and Edmond de Nevers, were keen proponents of continentalism.

As a doctrine, continentalism was hardly univocal. Unlike the anti-American ethos, which was essentially conservative, the continentalist impulse could be either liberal or socialist in inspiration. But the divisions did not end there: continentalism was also tied to four larger geopolitical sensibilities. All shared the wider continentalist ethos described earlier, but could also diverge on a number of issues.

In its purest form, continentalism could be described as North American isolationism. Indeed, many diehard continentalists believed that the Old and the New World were antithetical entities and that America's vitality was the product of its early separation from Europe. Isolationism was the most intrinsically nationalistic form of continentalism. This radical doctrine was popular during the turbulent 1930s and found its most articulate spokesman in Frank Underhill, a scholar who taught history at the University of Toronto from 1927 to 1955. Deeply scarred by his service in the Great War, Underhill's contempt for Europe was far-reaching.

On the other hand, moderate continentalists such as John Bartlet Brebner saw the United States as a key component in an enduring axis – the 'North Atlantic triangle' – that no revolution could sunder. In essence, their continentalism was tied to a wider Atlanticism. Atlanticists argued that history, geography, and culture made Canada, the United States, and North-Western Europe (usually Britain) members of a wider Atlantic community. As a result, the nations of the North Atlantic, not simply Canada and the United States, needed to draw together for the purposes of trade and defence. Atlanticism reached its height of popularity in the 1940s and found its most concrete expression in the creation of the North Atlantic Treaty Organization (NATO) in 1949.

Pan-Americanism was occasionally tied to the wider continentalist ethos. Though most early continentalists gave little thought to hemispheric integration and the Pan-American Union, some later proponents of continental integration, including John P. Humphrey (1905–1995), also hoped to see Canada draw closer to the wider pan-American community. Pan-Americanism reached its apex in the late 1930s and early 1940s. With wartime Europe essentially closed to Canadian goods, several continentalists argued that the time had come for Canada to seek out new markets in Latin America and join the Pan-American Union.

An internationalist seam also ran through Canadian continentalism. It postulated that all the nations of the world, not merely Canada and the United States, shared a broad community of interests. Internationalism's most prominent Canadian advocate was James T. Shotwell, an idealistic intellectual born in Strathroy, Ontario, who dedicated his life to the promotion of multilateralism and disarmament. Strangely, in Canadian discourse, internationalism was not necessarily an anti-nationalist doctrine. Unlike Americans, who have often viewed international organizations and multilateralism as possible threats to their national sovereignty, Canadians have long tended to view their participation in multilateral bodies as the fulfilment of their sovereignty.

These four sensibilities were not all mutually exclusive. For instance, Canada's keenest advocate of hemispheric integration, John P. Humphrey, was also a proponent of internationalism. In his 1942 essay entitled *The Inter-American System*, he argued that regional organizations, including the Pan-American Union, could form the building blocks for a 'universal World Order.'[43] In practice, Humphrey's pan-Americanism was a facet of his wider internationalism. Born in Hampton, New Brunswick, Humphrey practised law in Montreal before joining McGill's Faculty of Law in 1936. He briefly served as the faculty's dean before being appointed director of the Human Rights Division of the United Nations Secretariat in 1946, where he helped draft the Universal Declaration of Human Rights. Humphrey would remain with the United Nations for the next twenty years. In 1966, he returned to teaching at McGill and lectured well into his eighties. He was awarded the U.N.'s Human Rights Award in 1988.

Continentalism predates Confederation – its earliest proponents were to be found among the Quebecers and Nova Scotians who supported the American Revolution. In the late nineteenth century, most of its intellectual proponents were close to the Liberal party and gravitated around various Liberal organs, including the Toronto *Globe*. The presence of a certain number of outspoken annexationists in Canada's liberal intellectual circles lesssened the appeal of continentalism among the general population, and helped the larger and better organized imperialist movement in its efforts to portray continentalism as a disloyal doctrine.

Goldwin Smith and Erastus Wiman were continentalism's elder statesmen in the late nineteenth century. Their writing was often tinged with despair – Canada, they believed, was on its last leg – and a number of Canadians shared their pessimism. Indeed, when Goldwin Smith published *Canada and the Canadian Question*, the communal confidence of Canadians in their national experiment had just about hit rock bottom.

Born in Reading, England, Smith taught modern history at Oxford University from 1858 to 1866. In 1868, he accepted the professorship of English and constitutional history at the newly formed Cornell University at Ithaca, New York. He left Cornell after a few years and settled in Toronto, eventually marrying William Henry Boulton's widow, Harriet Elizabeth Mann (née Dixon), in 1875. Harriet possessed a sizeable fortune, which gave Smith a degree of financial independence that few intellectuals enjoyed in his era. Shortly after settling in the Dominion, Smith became active in the Canada First movement, but soon lost all faith in the new nation. Ever the prophet of gloom and despair, he saw Canada's only possible salvation in annexation, and played a key role in annexationism's last gasp in the late 1880s and early 1890s. By contrast, the less pessimistic Wiman merely prescribed commercial union as a cure for Canada's ills. Unlike Smith, who had studied at Eton and Oxford, Wiman had little formal education. Nevertheless, Wiman's success as an entrepreneur – he was known as the 'Duke of Staten Island' for his attempts to develop the New York island – lent a great deal of credibility to his ideas regarding a North American customs union. Both Smith and Wiman had a significant following in the late 1880s and early 1890s, but their ideas were repellent to the imperialists who dominated English Canadian discourse in the late nineteenth century.

By 1900, however, the storm clouds that had hung over the Dominion of Canada in the early 1890s had cleared and continentalism began to shed its gloomy aura. Reciprocity was now cheerfully advertised as a tool for economic development and prosperity rather than as a desperate measure to preserve Canada from economic collapse. And though aging continentalists like John S. Ewart remained active well into the new century, it was the younger generation of pro-American thinkers – Sara Jeannette Duncan, John W. Dafoe (1866–1944), James T. Shotwell, William Bennett Munro, and O.D. Skelton – that took centre stage in the crusade for continental integration. Born in the 1860s and 1870s, these intellectuals bucked the trend and supported reciprocity in 1911. Like their predecessors, they had come to realize, writes Allan Smith, that 'American might could in fact be interpreted not as a threat to, but as a source of assistance for, Canada's growth and development.'[44] And though theirs was a rearguard action, they helped lay the framework for the dynamic continentalism of the interwar years.

The interwar continentalists were born roughly between 1880 and

1900 and, as an intellectual generation, they came of age during the Great War. Their wartime experience profoundly shaped their continentalism. Idealistic and naïve, many rushed to answer their nation's call in 1914. A number of those lucky enough to survive the carnage would return profoundly disillusioned with imperialism and, more generally, with Europe.[45] Canada may indeed have been born at Vimy Ridge, but nineteenth-century Canadian imperialism died at the Somme. Traumatized by the horror of gas and trench warfare, the *génération massacrée* no longer saw Europe as a genteel land of universities, libraries, museums, and cafés, but as a seething cauldron of hatred and militarism. Europe's seamy side had been exposed.

In the years that followed the Great War, national self-confidence swelled and anti-Americanism receded as Canada entered the concert of nations. The Dominion could stand on its own, and the United States, many argued, was no longer a threat to Canadian nationhood. Indeed, unlike the imperialists who had previously dominated English Canadian discourse, the interwar continentalists tended to view Britain as the principal obstacle to national sovereignty. European imperialism had claimed over sixty thousand Canadian lives and had torn the Dominion apart, and intellectuals like Frank Underhill vowed that Canada would not be sucked into the swirling vortex of European militarism again. Besides, Europe was incorrigible: a mere fifteen years after the Treaty of Versailles, rearmament was proceeding apace and the rhetoric of war was becoming omnipresent. By comparison, North America was an oasis of peace, and the much vaunted undefended border stood in stark contrast to the endless cycle of European conflict. Accordingly, Canada had to realign itself and embrace its North American destiny. Tradition and imperialism had brought war and devastation; modernity and continental integration promised peace and prosperity.

During the nineteenth century, continentalism was an overwhelmingly liberal doctrine, and it found its political expression in the policies of the Liberal party. However, in the 1930s, the continentalist ethos took a left turn. After the Great War, socialists like Frank Underhill and F.R. Scott were among the nation's leading promoters of continentalism; they condemned British imperialism, criticized economic protectionism, and held the New Deal in high regard. Scott and Underhill also played a key role in the emergence of the socialist Co-operative Commonwealth Federation, a political party that received the support of a number of interwar continentalists. Nevertheless, liberalism and the Liberal party continued to play an important role in continentalist discourse, and a number of the interwar generation's leading lights, including P.E. Corbett and John Bartlet Brebner, were staunch liberals.

Interwar continentalism was born with the left-of-centre *Canadian Forum* in 1920, and reached maturity in the 1930s with the publication of a landmark series of studies on Canadian-American relations sponsored by the Carnegie Endowment for International Peace. Edited by James T. Shotwell, the twenty-five-volume series played a notable role in the development of North American sentiment among Canadian intellectuals. According to Carl Berger, Shotwell 'immediately grasped the significance of Canadian-American history for the lesson it would convey as a model of peaceful international relations.'[46] Shotwell believed that the healthy state of Canadian-American relations confirmed that arbitration and trade could foster international peace and good will. Some of the volumes published in the Carnegie series, in particular Donald Creighton's *Commercial Empire of the St Lawrence* (1937), did not reflect Shotwell's continentalism, but the series nonetheless represented the pinnacle of North American idealism in Canada.

Expatriates like Shotwell and Brebner played a key role in the development of Canadian continentalism. For the most part, notes Graham Carr, they 'approached the border eagerly, and many of those who eventually returned to Canada were candid about their fondness for the United States.'[47] American-educated intellectuals were particularly drawn to continentalism. In most cases, however, expatriation merely heightened pre-existing continentalist tendencies; it confirmed that the United States was not a cultural backwater. American schooling or residency, moreover, hardly guaranteed a continentalist outlook. For instance, the years Stephen Leacock spent studying under Thorstein Veblen at the University of Chicago may have strengthened rather than lessened his anti-Americanism.

Continentalism had a profound impact on the writing of Canadian history. During the interwar years, writes Carl Berger, 'a systematic and determined effort was made to explore in detail the interconnections between Canada and its southern neighbour.'[48] Led by Lower, Underhill, and Brebner, the continentalist school tended to emphasize the North American nature of the Canadian experience. Above all, continentalism was an environmental creed that focused on the ways in which the continent and the frontier had transformed Canada's European settlers into North Americans.

Even at its height, intellectual continentalism was not always favourably viewed by the general population. Indeed, in August 1940, Frank

Underhill came close to being dismissed from his teaching position at the University of Toronto after the following statement caused a public outcry: 'We now have two loyalties – one to Britain and the other to North America. I venture to say it is the second, North America, that is going to be supreme now. The relative significance of Britain is going to sink, no matter what happens.'[49] Popular anti-Americanism may have reached its nadir during the war, but some English Canadians, especially in Ontario, undoubtedly continued to equate continentalism with treason. In the end, the enthusiasm with which the Canadian population greeted the Ogdensburg and Hyde Park agreements was largely the result of fear. With Britain teetering on the edge of collapse and Nazi legions streaking across Europe, most Canadians had more important things than Americanization to worry about. Predictably, public support for continental integration declined after the Second World War. The postwar years would also witness the steady decline of continentalist sentiment among Canadian intellectuals.

Continentalist sentiment appears to have been stronger in Canada's more peripheral regions. The Prairie Provinces, with their important American-born population and wheat economy, were especially receptive to continentalist ideas. Indeed, a number of Canada's leading continentalist intellectuals, in particular John W. Dafoe, were Westerners. Others, like Frank Underhill and John S. Ewart, lived for a time on the Prairies. That said, though the Western experience of several Canadian intellectuals appears to have contributed to their continentalism, its impact on their thought should not be overestimated. Underhill's continentalism, to be sure, was far more a product of his war service than of his years at the University of Saskatchewan, where he taught from 1914 to 1915 and from 1919 to 1927. Besides, during the period under study, many of the West's leading continentalists were born and raised in Ontario. Dafoe, Western Canada's most fervent champion, did not settle permanently in Manitoba until he was thirty-five years old. Above all, he was a product of Ontario's intellectual culture, which also possessed a continentalist tradition.

Among intellectuals, continentalist sentiment was weakest in Quebec. Conservative nationalism dominated the province's intellectual culture from the mid-nineteenth century to the end of the Second World War, and continentalist sentiment, which had been steadily diminishing in Quebec intellectual discourse since the 1840s, reached its low-water mark during the interwar years. The failure of the 1837–38 rebellions seriously disrupted the development of continentalism in Quebec.

Traumatized by military and political defeat, a generation of young *Canadiens* turned their backs on radical republicanism – continentalism's core constituency in nineteenth-century Quebec – and embraced more moderate theses. Pro-American and annexationist sentiment, however, lived on in the Institut canadien and in the writing of prominent *rouges* like Louis-Joseph Papineau's nephew, Louis-Antoine Dessaules (1819–1895), and the anticonfederate poet Louis-Honoré Fréchette (1839–1908). Still, republicanism declined further after Confederation: the Roman Catholic Church condemned the Institut canadien and Laurier repudiated *rougisme* in favour *le libéralisme politique* – British-style (i.e., moderate) liberalism. Denounced by Quebec's civil and religious leaders, radicalism was on the ropes.

Consequently, by 1900, continentalist sentiment was becoming increasingly uncommon in Quebec intellectual discourse. Continentalism's most radical seam was preserved in the writing of aging annexationists like Fréchette and Jean-Baptiste Rouilliard (1842–1908). However, after experiencing a brief period of popularity in the late 1880s and early 1890s, militant annexationism basically disappeared from the province's intellectual culture – prosperity had been as lethal to annexationist sentiment in Quebec as it had been in English Canada. By the turn of the twentieth century, French Canadian continentalism's leading lights – A.D. DeCelles, Sylva Clapin, Edmond de Nevers, and Errol Bouchette – embraced the moderate liberalism of the age of Laurier. They held American civilization in high regard, but were not shy about pointing out its shortcomings. Still, in an era dominated by Jules-Paul Tardivel and Henri Bourassa, their ideas – though appealing to Quebec's population at large – had a relatively limited impact on the evolution of French Canadian discourse.

Expatriates were responsible for a good deal of the pro-American prose published in Quebec. Indeed, a number of the province's prominent continentalist thinkers resided for a time in the United States. Edmond de Nevers, for instance, spent the last years of his all-too-short life in Rhode Island, while Sylva Clapin lived in Massachusetts for nearly a decade and served in the U.S. Navy in the early 1870s and again during the Spanish-American War. Expatriates often acted as vectors of intellectual and cultural transmission. Immersed in a different political culture, they were sometimes drawn to the radical republican theories that were becoming increasingly taboo in late-nineteenth-century Quebec. Annexationism was reasonably popular in the Franco-American communities of New England and the Midwest, and prominent French

Canadian annexationists like Louis-Honoré Fréchette and Jean-Baptiste Rouilliard found a receptive audience for their corrosive ideas in Franco-America. Fréchette lived in Chicago from 1866 to 1871. It was during these formative years that he published *La voix d'un exilé*, a popular poem denouncing Confederation. For his part, Rouilliard spent the last years of his life, from 1893 to 1908, in New England. Shortly after leaving Quebec, he founded *L'Union continentale*, a monthly review advocating annexation. Both men left Quebec under a cloud of suspicion; Fréchette is believed to have disclosed sensitive information to a Fenian spy, while Rouilliard was tarnished by the scandal that toppled the provincial government of Honoré Mercier.[50]

Interwar English Canadian continentalism had little or no influence in Quebec, and even the Carnegie series' volume on Quebec, *Les Canadiens français et leurs voisins du sud* (1941), edited by Gustave Lanctot, was basically anti-American in its conclusions. However, despite reaching its nadir during the interwar years, continentalist discourse did not disappear from Quebec's intellectual culture. Its leading light was the irreverent novelist and journalist Jean-Charles Harvey. The anticlerical Harvey was Quebec's enfant terrible in the 1930s, but he showed less interest in American affairs than many previous continentalists had. The interwar years also witnessed the appearance of a new modernist current in French Canadian literature led by Alfred Desrochers (1901–1978) and Robert Choquette (1905–1991). Like Harvey, Desrochers and Choquette had spent part of their childhood in New England, and though they also showed relatively little interest in American affairs, their work nonetheless explored Quebec's *américanité*.

There was no significant socialist voice among the French Canadian elite during the period under study – even radical republicanism had been whittled down to a mere shadow of its former self by 1900. As a result, by the 1930s, a fundamental divergence existed between English and French Canadian thought. This dichotomy is dramatically reflected in the ideological gulf that separates the two documents that respectively embody the reformist impulse in Depression-era English and French Canada: the socialist *Regina Manifesto* (1933) and the conservative *Programme de restauration sociale* (1934). The ethno-religious nature of French Canadian nationalism did not lend itself to radicalism because it hindered the discussion of political institutions. This, in turn, could have but one consequence: the marginalization of radical social thought in interwar Quebec.[51] This dearth of radicalism prevented the emergence of a vigorous continentalism in the prewar intellectual circles of French Canada. Nevertheless, the United States has traditionally exerted a powerful attraction on Quebec's masses, and there existed an evident disparity between elite and popular attitudes on the question of *américanité*. Put simply, ordinary French Canadians do not appear to have embraced the negative image of America propagated by most of their intellectuals.

In some senses, Canadian commentary was derivative. Indeed, though analysis of Canadian-American relations and the Dominion's *américanité* was overwhelmingly Canadian in inspiration, writing centred on domestic American issues tended to rest on sources from the United States, Great Britain, and France. Moreover, intellectuals with vastly different perspectives on the United States were often drawing on the same sources. Foreign interpretations were not being bought wholesale, however, and Canadian observers were both critical and selective when it came to their foreign sources. André Laurendeau, for instance, was impressed by Georges Duhamel's sweeping indictment of American society in *Scènes de la vie future* (1930), but nevertheless warned the readers of *L'Action nationale* to take the French writer's 'caricatured anti-Americanism' with a grain of salt.[52]

Even the most hostile Canadian intellectuals drew a great deal of inspiration from American sources. Historically, American writers and intellectuals have not shied away from critical introspection, and Canadian criticism has been inspired by this rich tradition since the era of Alexander Hamilton. The American Federalist tradition cast a long shadow across several strains of Canadian thought and Hamiltonian ideas can be found in the work of thinkers as seemingly antithetical as Goldwin Smith and Bishop John Strachan. As John Herd Thompson and Stephen J. Randall note, 'even the Loyalist elite's anti-American critique was copied directly from the writings of American Federalists, who were similarly alarmed with what they saw as the democratic excesses of the Jeffersonian Republicans.'[53]

Likewise, the idealized, anti-American narratives produced by Loyalist historians were also inspired by American sources. Arthur Johnston's (1841–1919) *Myths and Facts of the American Revolution*, published in 1908, was one of these. Dedicated 'to the memory of the Loyalists,' the book was largely based on the work of American historians James Hosmer and Moses Tyler.[54] In a similar vein, George M. Wrong drew heavily on the work of George Louis Beer and, more widely, on the so-called imperial school of American history, to produce his 1935 monograph entitled *Canada and the American Revolution*. Like Beer, Wrong was critical of the American Revolution and mourned the great rift of 1776.

However, it was the American progressive tradition and its scathing critique of political corruption and plutocracy that most inspired English Canadian anti-American commentary in the early years of the twentieth century. Many American progressives shared with Canadian imperialists a fundamentally antimodern sensibility. Andrew Macphail, for instance, was a keen observer of the progressive movement. He considered his critique of the United States to be tied to 'that undertone of doubt, suspicion and fear, which a fresh perception detects in growing volume in the minds of the best Americans who meditate upon their own problems.'[55] Thorstein Veblen, progressive America's most articulate critic of plutocracy and consumption – he coined the phrase 'conspicuous consumption' – was particularly influential in the Dominion. Stephen Leacock helped to popularize his ideas in Canada. Inspired by Veblen's seminal critique of American wealth, *The Theory of the Leisure Class* (1899), Leacock's celebrated cycle of humorous sketches, *Sunshine Sketches of a Little Town* (1912) and *Arcadian Adventures with the Idle Rich* (1914), are a witty commentary on the ill-effects of the status revolution. Woodrow Wilson was also popular among Canadian intellectuals. Before entering the political arena, the twenty-eighth president of the United States published several studies that criticized American politics and government. Moreover, Wilson held certain aspects of the British parliamentary tradition in high regard. As a result, a number of imperialists writing in the early 1900s eagerly drew anti-American arguments from his work.

Because their work addressed American concerns and was partially inspired by progressivism, some English Canadian critics of the republic, most notably Stephen Leacock, enjoyed a wide audience in the United States at this time. Antimodernism was common in American intellectual discourse, and the progressive mind was receptive to critical assessments of American life. As a result, many Americans were more than ready for the critique of American wealth in Leacock's *Arcadian Adventures* or Robert Barr's (1850–1912) tale of political corruption in New York City, *The Victors*, published in 1901, which had the added attraction of an anti-Irish subtext.[56]

American progressivism also had a profound effect on the work of many English Canadian continentalists, in particular James T. Shotwell, O.D. Skelton, and Frank Underhill. However, unlike their conservative rivals, continentalists did not draw a series of anti-American arguments from progressive writing. Underhill's historical materialism was particularly influenced by the work of Charles Beard, whose economic interpretation of American history revolutionized historical thought in the United States.[57]

American writing had a greater impact on English Canadian commentary than it would in Quebec. However, directly or indirectly, French Canadian intellectuals were absorbing a fair amount of American ideas. American authors were read in Quebec. Francis Parkman's work on colonial North America, for instance, was widely read among intellectuals. Besides, French commentary on the United States, which played an important role in nourishing French Canadian thought, was often inspired by American writing. American Catholic sources, moreover, were important in the formulation of French Canadian commentary. The pastoral letters of many American bishops, especially Cardinal James Gibbons, the primate of the American Church, were widely circulated within Quebec's Catholic clergy. And a variety of Catholic periodicals, principally *America*, New York's Catholic weekly, but also the *American Catholic Quarterly Review* and the *Catholic World*, were an important source of information for many French Canadian intellectuals. These periodicals were particularly inspiring for writers seeking to pass judgment on American morality and public education. Taken individually, however, few American Catholic writers appear to have had a significant impact on French Canadian commentary. Jules-Paul Tardivel, who stands out as the French Canadian intellectual who drew most heavily on American Catholic sources, was particularly fond of the writing of outspoken Catholic convert and journalist James A. McMaster. In his influential essay on *La situation religieuse aux États-Unis* (1900), which denounced theological modernism in the American Church, Tardivel referred to McMaster, 'that great Catholic polemicist,' as 'one of the most noble figures of the American Church, and altogether comparable to Louis Veuillot.'[58] This was the ultimate compliment that Tardivel, an ultramontane who consciously modelled himself on Veuillot's example, could pay to a fellow journalist.

Canadian observers drew heavily on British sources for inspiration. The American commentary of Charles Dickens, Walter Bagehot, Frances Trollope, or Matthew Arnold, for instance, was widely read and commented in Canada. However, no British – or indeed foreign – observer could rival the impact of James Bryce on Canadian commentary, especially in English Canada. *The American Commonwealth* (1888), Bryce's essentially positive, though certainly not uncritical assessment of American politics offered a great quantity of arguments to both continentalist and anti-American thinkers. As a result, Bryce's ideas permeated Canadian commentary and helped heighten some of its repetitive tendencies. Intellectuals from across the political spectrum were inspired by his work and used it in a variety of ways: Edmond de Nevers quoted Bryce a number of times in his two-volume essay on *L'âme américaine*; George R. Parkin's critique of American politics and government was influenced by *The American Commonwealth*; and Sara Jeannette Duncan evoked Bryce in one of her novels.[59] As a young man, James T. Shotwell was in absolute awe of Bryce. In his autobiography, he fondly recounted meeting the author of *The American Commonwealth* while on an 1899 visit to the British House of Commons:

> The House was in session, and gathering together all the courage I could muster I sent in my card, inscribed 'as 'a student of history,' to the Right Honorable James Bryce, former ambassador to the United States, whose brilliant essay The Holy Roman Empire had been published ten years before I was born, and whose American Commonwealth, with its penetrating analysis of United States politics, we were using in my class. He came out to see me, and instead of dismissing me with formal courtesy sat down to ask me all about history at Columbia – a half hour worth to me all the cycles of Cathay.[60]

The American Commonwealth was an important source of anti-American arguments for turn-of-the-twentieth-century imperialists. With chapters entitled 'Why Great Men Are not Chosen Presidents,' 'Why the Best Men Do not Go into Politics,' and 'The True Faults of American Democracy,' the two-volume essay was bound to please many imperialists. Bryce was undoubtedly a liberal, but his strong conservative tendencies endeared him to many Tories who were inspired by his forceful critique of American political corruption and his distrust of the separation of powers.

France produced the first truly classic interpretation of American society in Alexis de Tocqueville's *Democracy in America* (1835–40). The two-volume essay was widely read in the Dominion, but as Michel Winock notes regarding French commentary, 'people only took from Tocqueville what they were looking for.'[61] Like Bryce, Tocqueville was read very selectively. His overall assessment of American society was too positive to be accepted by Canadian conservatives. That said, the right did appreciate his rejection of American individualism and materialism and his critique of the republic's supposed cultural anemia. Not surprisingly, Tocqueville also inspired a number of continentalist intellectuals. For instance, the work of Goldwin Smith, Edmond de Nevers, A.D. DeCelles, and Sylva Clapin echoed several of Tocqueville's ideas, including the value of social mobility in the United States and the overall stability of American democracy.

For most English Canadian observers, French commentary began and ended with *Democracy in America*. But Tocqueville's opus was only the beginning of a very rich tradition. Indeed, over the years, French intellectuals have shown a great deal of interest in American society. This was particularly the case during the 1920s and 1930s, when the rise of American power and the steady decline of the French Republic led many thinkers to wonder who would dominate the new world order: Europe or America? As a result, several influential books on the United States were published in France during the interwar years. This sudden increase in French interest in the United States contributed to the rise of American commentary and anti-Americanism in post–First World War Quebec.

French political scientist André Siegfried stands out as the most important foreign source for interwar anti-American rhetoric in Quebec. As a Protestant who had authored a highly controversial study on the French Canadian question, *Le Canada: les deux races* (1906), his work was generally regarded with suspicion. 'André Siegfried tries to be objective, but in spite of himself, his judgements, his assessments, leave it very visible that he is Protestant. His beliefs prevent him from having an overall view of the question,' warned Hermas Bastien (1897–1977), who taught Latin at Montreal's Mont-Saint-Louis, in 1928.[62] Nevertheless, Siegfried's *Les États-Unis d'aujourd'hui* (1927) was very well received in Quebec. His interest in Canadian affairs gave him a degree of prominence that other French authors did not necessarily enjoy. Consequently, his 1927 study of American society appears to have had a greater impact on French Canadian interwar commentary than the works of Georges Duhamel or Lucien Romier, whose studies on America are generally regarded as more significant. Siegfried, like Tocqueville and Bryce, was a liberal with strong conservative tendencies, and many *nationalistes* shared his aversion to American cosmopolitanism and industrialism.

French Canadian intellectuals were influenced by the work of Lucien Romier and Georges Duhamel. In his *Scènes de la vie future*, Duhamel warned that America offered a glimpse of Europe's future degeneracy: 'Our future! All the scars of that devouring civilization – we will find them, within twenty years, on Europe's limbs.'[63] Duhamel's monograph exerted a good deal of influence over the various authors who contributed to the *Revue dominicaine*'s 1936 inquiry into 'Notre américanisation.' Lucien Romier, a conservative republican who would eventually serve as a minister in Marshall Pétain's ill-fated *État français*, went even further than Duhamel in his rejection of the mass age and America. In *Qui sera le maître, Europe ou Amérique?*, Romier warned that 'the current cycle of human evolution is leading, little by little, to a '"depersonalisation" of the individual, who has become a machine himself.'[64] America, as he saw it, was the embodiment of this post-human era. Romier's 1927 monograph was widely read in Quebec's intellectual circles and appears to have exerted a particular influence over the anti-American commentary of Lionel Groulx and Hermas Bastien.

Quebec before the Second World War was certainly not an intellectual province of France.[65] French texts were read selectively and other sources were consulted. English Canadian commentary was no different in that regard. Britain and America loomed large in the English Canadian mind, but never overwhelmed Canadian concerns. These concerns evolved over time, and various events helped shape the evolution of Canadian commentary. The Great War, for instance, was a watershed event in the intellectual history of Canadian-American relations. It announced both the decline of anti-American sentiment in English Canada and its intensification in Quebec.

During the period under study, Canada experienced rapid social change and the erosion of premodern status and deference. American society came to embody these changes to the Canadian intellectual. As a result, Canadian writing on America contained an encrypted commentary on the mass age. Conservatives expressed many of their misgivings regarding modernity through anti-American rhetoric while liberals and socialists often signalled their acceptance of the modern ethos by adopting the continental perspective. In effect, the essential dichotomy between modern and antimodern thought was partially masked by a debate centred on the nation's *américanité*.

The 'American question' loomed large in Canadian discourse. It is hardly surprising, therefore, that most of Canada's intellectuals devoted some energy to analysing the various philosophical, political, cultural, social, racial, and economic elements that were believed to define the American experience. What emerges from this writing is the image of a society that embodied both the hopes and the fears of Canada's intellectual elite.

2 American Politics and Philosophy

Since its founding, the United States of America has embodied a variety of principles to the intellectuals of the world. These principles reflect, to a large extent, the intellectual's era and perspective. In the 1830s, for instance, Tocqueville saw equality as one of the essential features of American society. On the other hand, more than a century later, Simone de Beauvoir, who also spent several months travelling across the nation, saw inequality as one of the hallmarks of the American experience. In the late nineteenth and early twentieth centuries, Canadian intellectuals were inclined to view materialism, freedom, individualism, and equality as the core principles of the American experience. The United States was a revolutionary nation; this was reflected, for better or for worse, in its politics and government.

'It does not seem quite intelligent to denounce the American pursuit of wealth when we calculate our own progress mainly in material terms,' reasoned Douglas Bush in a 1929 diatribe against anti-Americanism.[1] A literary critic and frequent contributor to the *Canadian Forum*, Bush had little patience, writes Brandon Conron, 'for the introspective and moral seriousness of both Canadian literature and the Canadian character.'[2] Arthur Lower, who had taught history at Tufts College, Massachusetts, and at Harvard before accepting a position at United College, Winnipeg, was equally sceptical when it came to Canadian criticism of American materialism. 'We worship [the great god Dollar] just as faithfully but with less success,' he wrote in 1939.[3] Materialism – the tendency to treat material possessions, wealth, and physical comfort as more important or desirable than spiritual values – was no more specific to the United States, English Canadian continentalists argued, than the setting of the sun.

Tories, for their part, saw materialism as central to the American experience. The mass age, which America was believed to have embraced wholeheartedly, corroded religious values and undermined intellectual endeavours. As a result, Americans only attached importance to the tangible, the quantifiable, and the material. Materialism marginalized the intellectual's moral authority and was, many believed, the Trojan horse of a status revolution. Beckles Willson (1869–1942), a staunch Canadian imperialist who worked as a freelance writer in Great Britain, was blunt on the subject of American materialism. 'If a neighbour critic may say so frankly,' he wrote in *The New America: A Study of the Imperial Republic*, published in 1903, 'there is no people which has greater need to hold up to itself constantly high ideals of conduct and morals – because there is no people who struggle passionately for material advantages, and are, therefore, most exposed to temptation in the methods by which they may gain it. They may be said to have, at present, chiefly executive energy without depth of idea or spiritual direction.'[4] Willson, the neighbourly anti-American, hoped that imperialism and Anglo-Saxon unity would give the United States the spiritual and intellectual direction it lacked.

Along with American secularism, materialism was denounced far more frequently by French Canadian conservatives, principally because Catholicism played such a major role in the formulation of French Canadian discourse. 'Materialism takes up the greatest portion of American energy,' warned the Université de Montréal's professor of American literature, Hermas Bastien, in 1936. America, he continued, was a 'civilization based on economics' that embodied 'liberalism in its pure form, indifferent to people and ethnic distinctions.'[5] Others went further still. Drawing on the work of French intellectuals Jacques Maritain and Lucien Romier, Lionel Groulx, who had studied theology and philosophy in Rome and philosophy and literature at the University of Fribourg, in Switzerland, offered a searing indictment of American materialism to a Catholic student association in 1928: 'In brief, it seems that these people are setting their sights lower than God, which, for a Christian civilization, is the beginning of all disorder.'[6]

Most French Canadian continentalists refused to buy in to the Manichean logic that opposed materialism to intellectualism. Quebec's leading turn-of-the-twentieth-century economist, Errol Bouchette, warned his compatriots not to snub material progress under the pretext that it was incompatible with spiritual and intellectual pursuits. Of America, he wrote in 1905 that 'its outstanding quality is its energy, and people accuse it of too much aggression in its pursuit of material riches. But it is as untrue to say that Americans love nothing but the dollar as it is to claim that the English are a nation of shopkeepers.' The United States, Bouchette continued, 'does not lack for intellectual life,' and had produced, among other things, 'a literature that is more dazzling and varied than our own.'[7] Jean-Charles Harvey, whose economic thought drew heavily on Bouchette's liberal nationalism, was also reluctant to denounce American materialism. In fact, Harvey was convinced that the conservative rejection of materialism was entrenching, indeed celebrating, the economic marginalisation of French Canadians. Harvey's first novel, *Marcel Faure* (1922), grappled with these issues. The story's hero, young industrialist Marcel Faure, and monsieur Brégent, an aging Tory, cross swords on the question of American materialism:

> – Ah! The Americans! Let's talk about them, said old man Brégent, his face red with anger. A bunch of boors! A nation of pagans where marriage is a game and divorce is a sport. The Americans! Pleasure seekers, always looking for sensual stimulation, who find no other purpose in life than making suspenders and sowing their wild oats! Not intelligent, not artistic, stuffed with literature about football and stupefied by jazz music. Ah! Ah!
> – Please calm down. I know their flaws. It is a young country, too strong for its age. It has the exuberance of a teenager who has understood, too early, his own power: it is overflowing with life. But let's stay on the subject: material prosperity, I tell you, brings comfort to the household and the state, pride to the citizens, who become enamoured of a land where one can live better than elsewhere. Along with wealth, science, literature and the arts become the privilege of the majority; great institutions multiply; in short, civilization can be bought.[8]

Born in La Malbaie, Quebec, Harvey studied at the Séminaire de Chicoutimi for three years before entering the Society of Jesus in 1908. He left the order in 1913 and briefly studied law at the Montreal campus of Université Laval. In 1914, he began his career as a journalist with *Le Canada*. Four years later, he took a job as a publicist with the Machine agricole nationale of Montmagny, Quebec. The firm went bankrupt in 1922 and Harvey soon returned to journalism, this time at Quebec City's *Le Soleil*. In April 1934, Harvey's second novel, *Les demi-civilisés*, which was harshly critical of Quebec's Roman Catholic clergy, was placed on the Index by Cardinal Villeneuve. Shortly thereafter, he was dismissed as *Le Soleil*'s editor-in-chief. Harvey was appointed the head of Quebec's Bureau of Statistics a few months later by Premier Louis-Alexandre Taschereau, but was dismissed from this position after the 1936 victory of Maurice Duplessis' Union nationale. In September 1937, Harvey founded *Le Jour*, a weekly newspaper devoted to political and cultural commentary. The paper ceased publication in 1946 and Harvey would spend the rest of his career working as a radio journalist and tabloid editor in Montreal.

Whether taken to mean an exemption from arbitrary or despotic control or the capacity to act without hindrance or restraint, freedom remains a largely abstract concept. Yet from its inception, America has been understood to be a land of freedom – a nation built on the very idea of liberty. As a result, the concept of liberty loomed large in Canadian commentary on the United States. And not surprisingly, freedom of speech – the right to freely express one's opinions without fear of sanction – was of particular interest to intellectuals.

Canadian conservatives were generally critical of American liberty. They valued liberty as a traditional right, but saw American freedom as a modern deviation from British tradition. Some argued that the United States suffered from a deficit of liberty, while others contended that the republic was handicapped by an excess of freedom. In either case, it was assumed that freedom and order were out of balance in America. 'It is difficult, often amusingly difficult,' wrote Beckles Willson at the turn of the twentieth century, 'to make the mass of Americans understand that Britain is also a republic and a democracy; that there is far more justice and freedom there than in their own country.'[9] Robert Falconer was more elaborate in his critique of America's dearth of liberty. An astute observer of American life, the Presbyterian minister and president of the University of Toronto saw pervasive conformism in the United States as a powerful obstacle to freedom of expression. Speaking before an English audience in 1925, he noted that 'there is less freedom of speech in America, east or west, than in Britain; in the East this may be due to the innate timidity of the propertied classes, in the West to the fear lest the principles of society are not so strongly rooted as to be able to resist the convulsive shock of new ideas should they gather volume.'[10] Falconer, like many other Burkean conservatives, had an English liberal's tolerance for dissent. As a result, he had a deep aversion for the republican conformism that he believed was stifling freedom in America.

Most conservatives, however, argued instead that the United States suffered from an excess of freedom. Born of the Age of Reason, American liberty was abstract, self-seeking, and unbalanced; it was an irresponsible and licentious form of freedom. The American, remarked George Grant in a 1945 pamphlet on Canada's place in the North Atlantic triangle, emphasized 'the inalienable right to be free to do as he chooses, whatever the effect it might have on society as a whole.' 'We in Canada,' he continued, 'have put the balance far more on the side of order or the good of society. The individual has certain rights, but these rights must be strictly prevented from causing any disruption to society as a whole.' Grant argued that 'the great question of the modern world is going to be to what extent, within the complicated pattern of industrialized civilization, freedom and authority can be truly integrated.' American society, however, had proven itself incapable of reconciling liberty and order.[11] Educated at Upper Canada College, Queen's, and Oxford, where he was a Rhodes Scholar, Grant's conservative pedigree was impeccable; he was the son of Upper Canada College headmaster William Lawson Grant (1872–1935) and the grandson of two of Canada's most influential late nineteenth century imperialists: George Monro Grant and George Parkin. He joined Dalhousie University's Department of Philosophy in 1947. By the late 1950s, Grant had emerged as Canada's leading critic of the mass age.

Quebec's critique of American liberty was more moral and religious in tone. Licentiousness, claimed some French Canadian conservatives, was the major consequence of American freedom. While serving as a chaplain in turn-of-the-twentieth-century Mississippi, Antonio Huot warned the readers of *La Revue canadienne* that 'the greatest moral problem of the American people today, for which a solution is vital, is this: where should the line be drawn between freedom and licentiousness?'[12] American society, he argued, was too permissive, relativistic, and secular. Jules-Paul Tardivel agreed:

In England they have some knowledge of freedom. In the United States, freedom is talked about a lot. The English language even has two words to express it: *liberty* and *freedom*; two great words, to be sure, that nicely round out a sentence and always, as long as they are spoken with a slight emphasis, cause applause to burst out. But the Land of Freedom does not actually have the slightest idea of what true freedom is ... The freedom that exists in the United States is liberal freedom, or Masonic freedom. And this freedom – a false freedom – is harmful to the Church, in the sense that it takes away numerous children from the flock and weakens the faithful spirit in many of those that it does not entirely uproot from the Church.[13]

Like Huot, Tardivel drew a great deal of inspiration from France's counterrevolutionary tradition, and was correspondingly obsessed with the *fléau maçonnique*. In his influential monograph on American Catholicism, published in 1900, Tardivel contended that American-style liberty threatened society's moral order because it inevitably led to secularism and to religious free thought.

Continentalists hardly shared these concerns. Order did not loom as large in their thought, and they considered American freedom to be an offshoot, rather than a perversion, of British liberty. As a result, they saw Canada and the United States as two nations possessing similar conceptions of freedom. And though Canadian socialists wrote precious little on the subject of American freedom, most liberal continentalists argued that the New World had, in fact, revitalized British liberty. Freedom was central to the 'community of dominant ideas' that formed the basis for 'our North American civilization,' contended one of Wilfrid Laurier's most trusted advisers, Reverend James A. Macdonald (1862–1923). 'More than that,' he wrote in the *North American Idea* (1917), 'it is by the ties of their great ideas … that the peoples of the United States and Canada are bound up in the great bundle of life with all the free peoples of the English-speaking fraternity over all the world. The idea of freedom is the badge of their North American brotherhood.'[14] Later, the erosion of civil liberties in wartime North America, though deplored by many continentalists, was cited as proof that American, British, and Canadian forms of freedom were essentially the same – at least in practice. In *Canada Fights* (1941), a collaborative volume edited by John W. Dafoe, several of Canada's leading liberal intellectuals argued that 'in times of crisis, even the written safeguards of the American Constitution have not availed the citizen much, for judges and juries interpreting that Constitution are no more immune from any general inflammation of public opinion than the judges and juries of Canada who today have the task of defining the rights of the subject.'[15]

Criticized by many Canadian intellectuals, individualism – self-centred feeling or conduct as a principle – was seen as one of the foundations of American society. Conservatives viewed American individualism as corrosive and antisocial; it eroded the traditional solidarity of family and community. In 1900, Jules-Paul Tardivel noted that 'American individualism … is called, in correct French, a spirit of insubordination.'

'Indeed,' he continued, 'American individualism has a horror of discipline, of anything that could restrict its movements. It wants to believe
in dogmas, but does not wish to have rules of behaviour imposed on
itself.' And though Tardivel understood that individualism 'is a quality
... when it does not exceed the limits of moderation,' he could not condone a form of individualism which he believed destabilized society.[16]
Similarly, but several decades later, George Grant warned Canadians
not to follow the American model, which placed an undue emphasis on
the individual. Instead, he argued that Canada should continue to chart
a 'middle course between individual liberty and social order.'[17]

Individualism is tied to the liberal ethos, and many nineteenth-
century liberals, including A.D. DeCelles, saw individualism as the
root of American success. 'Founded by individualism, having reached
the highest prosperity by relying on its own strengths, the Republic
will have to repugn the law of the community, which would be a com-
mandeering of the energy of each, to the profit of all,' DeCelles argued
in 1896.[18] However, by the interwar years, a growing number of continentalists began to view American individualism as too extreme.
Invariably described as 'rugged,' American individualism held little
attraction for these intellectuals, particularly for those on the left. Colin
McKay (1876–1939), for instance, applauded the New Deal's 'apparent
dethronement of the time-honoured fetishes of rugged individualism
and *laissez faire*.' However, the radical labour activist warned the readers of the *Canadian Unionist* that this 'apparent revolution in sentiment
and temperament' might prove ephemeral 'since it was effected under
the influence of a fear that troubled the plutocracy.'[19]

Equality is a relatively abstract concept with a number of legal, political, social, and economic implications. The United States was founded
on egalitarian principles, but equality has meant different things at different times in American history. Generally speaking, American egalitarianism has been political and legal in nature and has corresponded to
the liberal concept of equality of opportunity. Canadian conservatives
held a low view of egalitarian doctrines, which they tended to present
as a threat to traditional social relations, but they also had little use for
hereditary privilege. Many conservatives came from relatively modest
backgrounds, and their elitism, though commonly tinged with some
form of racialism or sexism, was largely based on merit and talent, not
on birth. Some imperialists, including James Cappon, correspondingly
praised American notions of equality. 'We in Canada owe much to that
great American democracy,' Cappon wrote in 1904, 'it taught Europe

to respect what is good in our standards and in our ways. It broke the mountain barriers of aristocratic prejudice and arrogance for us.'[20] Other turn-of-the-twentieth-century conservatives, in particular Beckles Willson, held a dimmer view of American egalitarianism. Where Cappon saw equality of opportunity, Willson saw radical utopianism. 'Had the founders of the republic attempted to apply the doctrines of equality which they proclaimed,' he argued in 1903, 'the whole social fabric would very quickly have gone to pieces.' Happily, however, 'they one and all shrank from applying them,' and 'an aristocracy, not as ungenerously charged, merely of money, but of manners and culture, is growing, and class distinctions are widely and properly recognized.'[21]

Sustained contact with right-wing French discourse made Quebec's conservatives even more likely to see American egalitarianism as a radical attempt at class levelling. They believed that French society had been thoroughly dislocated under the republican triptych of *Liberté, Égalité, Fraternité*, and held a correspondingly low view of egalitarian doctrines. Like many Roman Catholic clerics, Antonio Huot saw any attempt at social equality as an aberration. In the United States, he wrote in 1907, 'the egalitarian utopia … is in every orator's speech, but barely exists in society. It is the most stupid nonsense that has ever come out of a man's mouth. And even worse, it is against nature.'[22] Abbé Huot had formulated a classic conservative statement: no society could flaunt human nature and found itself on abstract principles. Jules-Paul Tardivel, whose contempt for liberal doctrines was almost boundless, agreed. Like Huot, Tardivel was usually quick to liken the American Revolution to its more radical French counterpart. This was one of the preferred anti-American strategies of Quebec's right, and it was used with brio by the radically anti-egalitarian Tardivel:

Men are created equal in the sense that they are all made up of a soul and a body, that they are all mortal, that they all come to the same supernatural end that can only be achieved with the same help from on high, by demonstrating the same virtues and distancing themselves from the same sins. But this metaphysical sense is not what the revolutionaries, whether American or French, mean by equality. They talk about social and political equality. Yet such an equality has never existed, will never exist, cannot exist. There are perhaps not two men 'created equal' in that sense; there are not two men who possess exactly the same intellectual qualities, the same aptitudes, the same physical gifts. Not everyone is called to the same role in society. Is the son 'created equal' to his father? The idiot, the moron, is he the equal, socially and politically speaking, of the learned man or the genius? [23]

The continentalist understanding of American equality was quite different. Equality of opportunity and a porous class structure were assumed to be among the principal hallmarks of North American civilization and liberal continentalists consistently praised American egalitarianism. Many socialists were sceptical of American notions of equality, but their generally favourable outlook on the United States limited their capacity to criticize these notions. The value of American equality was a recurring theme in continentalist literature. Sara Jeannette Duncan, who successfully explored the differences between the Old and the New World in several of her novels, was fond of contrasting the egalitarianism of the New World with the rigid social stratification of Europe. In *A Daughter of Today* (1894), her rebellious and Bohemian heroine, Elfrida Bell, depicted American equality thusly: 'you see, our duchesses were greengrocers' wives the day before yesterday, and our greengrocers' wives subscribe to the magazines. It's all mixed up, and there are no high lights anywhere.'[24] Immigrant novelist Frederick Philip Grove (1879–1948) dealt with a similar theme, namely, the New World's caustic effect on aristocratic pretence, in *A Search for America* (1927). Shortly after arriving in North America, ruined patrician Phil Branden realizes that breeding counts for little on an egalitarian continent:

No matter how miserable I might – in Europe – have felt in my innermost heart, the mere deference shown by 'subordinates' to my appearance, my bearing, and my clothes would have kept up the pretence of a certain superiority. In Europe I should have lapsed into the most comfortable of all deceptions, self-commiseration: 'a smile on the lips, and death in my heart.' Here I was simply roused to revolt. Nobody paid the slightest attention to me. If in all this gaiety a girl or a boy had a look for me at all, the girl betrayed no admiration in her eye, the boy felt not subdued by my mere presence. This was truth![25]

Branden, who personifies Grove in this semi-autobiographical novel, eventually accepts and embraces New World egalitarianism.

Edmond de Nevers, who saw deference as 'a hangover from times of servitude,' praised democratic egalitarianism in *L'âme américaine* (1900). De Nevers had been repelled by 'the servility of cafe waiters, workers, labourers' that he had encountered while travelling in Europe. By contrast, he marvelled at American society, where 'every man treats his peer like a *man*.' Indeed, in spite of America's insidious love of titles, 'equality reigns in the United States, as utterly as is compatible with the laws of nature, which always make equality something of a paradox. The movement of wealth, the setting up of great fortunes have not been fatal to it, as one might have believed.'[26] Nevertheless, many Canadian observers saw American egalitarianism as threatened or inoperative. The growth of an irresponsible plutocracy was generally cited as the main reason for the erosion of America's egalitarian ideals. Nevertheless, liberal continentalists viewed American equality, along with freedom and individualism, as fundamental to the American experience.

For the intellectual right, the philosophical underpinnings of American society found their expression in the nation's political system. Born of a violent revolution, this system was democratic, republican, and secular. America's political institutions, like the political philosophy that underpinned them, were essentially modern in their postulates. They derived their legitimacy from the people, rather than from God. Imperialists were the most active detractors of American politics and government, and a vigorous critique of the nation's politics and government lay at the heart of imperialist anti-Americanism. By contrast, *nationaliste* intellectuals centred their critique of the United States on social and cultural issues. These different approaches to a common American threat reflected a profound divergence in the politics of Canadian identity. English Canadian nationalists have traditionally viewed their nation primarily as a political entity. Ethnicity and religion were important to imperialists, but they were less significant to the construction of Canadian distinctiveness than political institutions and the imperial bond. Indeed, many imperialists were willing to acknowledge that Canada and the United States shared a number of ethnic and religious affinities. The main distinction between Canadian and American society lay therefore in its political institutions and its membership in the British Empire. As a result, anti-American rhetoric in English Canada largely centred on political themes. French Canadian nationalists, on the other hand, saw their nation primarily as a spiritual, ethnic, and cultural entity and produced relatively little comment on American politics and government. In the end, the nature of political institutions was less important to intellectuals whose conception of *la race française en Amérique* was essentially ethno-religious and cultural.

Conservative intellectuals believed that America, as a revolutionary nation, had unwisely founded its national experiment on discontinuity. 'A nation must grow from the roots,' argued Andrew Macphail in 1909, 'and in this process of growth a thousand years are as one day.' To Macphail, the American nation was an ill-conceived tabula rasa founded on abstract principles. Indeed, while Canadians 'are following a course which the English have travelled ever since they landed in Britain at least. The people of the United States broke into a new direction, chiefly under the persuasion of certain guides who lived in France, and in accordance with the genius of that race had drawn up as rules for guidance certain theoretical propositions based upon hypothetical considerations. It has come to be a question between experience and theory.'[27] Abstract principles, to be sure, could not serve as a nation's bedrock. Born in Orwell, Prince Edward Island, Macphail was a graduate of McGill University and a licentiate of the Royal College of Physicians. After practising medicine and teaching at Bishop's University from 1893 to 1905, he was appointed McGill's first professor of the history of medicine in 1907, a position he would hold for thirty years. That same year he became the editor of the prestigious and influential *University Magazine*. Deeply disheartened by modernity, Macphail saw the United States as the antithesis of his conservative political, religious, and social values.

In spite of their dread of rupture, many conservative intellectuals were not as dismissive of the American Revolution as might be expected – Edmund Burke, after all, had shown some sympathy for the Patriot cause. They tended to blame Georgian absolutism for the conflict, and even the most radical Tories who, like Colonel George T. Denison, Arthur Johnston, or George Sterling Ryerson (1854–1925), were steeped in the Loyalist tradition, often showed little sympathy for George III. Indeed, though Denison attributed the revolution to 'lawless elements' led by 'impecunious lawyers and unsuccessful merchants, by ship owners who lived by smuggling, and by men on the verge of bankruptcy,' he did not hesitate to write in 1895 that 'misunderstandings, negligence, ignorance, what Lord Beresford describes as the "savage stupidity of the British Government of 1774–1776," led to the loss by the Empire of the thirteen colonies.'[28] Although he was perhaps the pre-eminent Loyalist mythmaker of his time, Denison's loyalty to Britain was not blind: he did not hesitate to criticize Britain if he felt that its actions were endangering the cause of imperial unity.

Like most nineteenth-century Tories, the colonel saw the revolution as a cataclysm that would forever destabilize the American nation. Some later conservative writers were willing to acknowledge, however, that the American Revolution, at heart, had been less a revolution than an unhappy civil war that had pitted the two branches of the English race against each other. This view was shared by many continentalist writers. 'In one sense the American Revolution was not a revolution at all,' argued William Bennett Munro on the first page of his popular 1919 textbook on American government. 'It was not a cataclysm like the French Revolution of the eighteenth century; it did not sweep away the fundamental institutions, or transform political ideals, or shift the weight of political power from one class among the people to another.'[29] A.D. DeCelles agreed. 'Washington, Hamilton, and the main constituents of Philadelphia were absolutely moderate men,' Parliament's head librarian wrote in 1896 in his *Les États-Unis. Origine, institutions, développement*. 'It would be wrong to see them as revolutionaries; they were only such for an instant, and only reluctantly and in self-defence. Deeply imbued with English traditions, they remained, under the republic, prisoners of their past and their traditions.'[30]

DeCelles's work was at odds, however, with the conservative reading of the American Revolution that prevailed among Quebec's *nationaliste* intellectuals. Many French Canadian nationalists were not willing to attach a moderate label to the revolution. 'The spirit of the American Revolution scarcely differs, no matter what people say, from the spirit of the French Revolution,' wrote Jules-Paul Tardivel in 1900.[31] There was nothing temperate about 1776 – it was radical revolution in the French mould. Indeed, noted Father Louis Chaussegros de Léry (b. 1895) several decades later in *Relations*, the organ of Quebec's Jesuits, many of the leading Patriots were heavily influenced by French freemasonry and by Voltairean ideas. Worse still, he wrote, 'several leaders of the American Revolution tended towards deism.'[32]

A deep sense of loss emerges from much of the English Canadian writing on the American Revolution. Had 'tact prevailed in England,' Robert Falconer told a British audience 1925, 'a compromise might have resulted and the radical thinkers would not have been able to go to the extreme.'[33] For imperialists like Falconer, the revolution has forever weakened both the British Empire and the cause of Anglo-Saxon unity. Continentalist writing could be equally sorrowful. 'Looking back,' wrote John W. Dafoe of his Loyalists ancestors, 'one can only ponder on how different the history of the world might have been if their suggestions had been followed. If there had been a little more statesmanship in England and a little more patient application of constitutional methods in the colonies, how different history would have been. But men are not wise enough. The appeal was to the sword, and the English race was tragically divided.'[34]

In spite of some residual nostalgia for Anglo-Saxon unity, English Canadian continentalists nonetheless argued that American independence had been both necessary and inevitable. Many also believed that a singular kinship had fortunately survived the great rift of 1776. For instance, in 1942, John MacCormac argued metaphorically that 'a man may cast his mother off and grow up to hate her, and she may have given him cause for it, but he cannot banish her from the deeps of his mind or legislate her out of his blood.'[35] Similarly, Ray Palmer Baker (1883–1979), whose *History of English-Canadian Literature to the Confederation* (1920) was written, in part, to illustrate the intellectual kinship that united the English-speaking peoples, contended that the North American continent had remained English in both speech and thought after 1776.[36] There was more than a touch of Atlanticism in Baker's work. Like many moderate continentalists, he was eager to show that a wider continuity had survived the American Revolution.

The revolution produced a new nation, a new political system and, some believed, a new man. Yet the Founding Fathers drew on the British political tradition to elaborate their new republic. As a result, there exists a certain continuity between the British and American political traditions. The extent of Anglo-American continuity, however, has preoccupied a number English-speaking writers since the days of the early republic, and Canadian intellectuals frequently addressed this question. In fact, much of the Canadian debate surrounding the value of the American system often revolved around its perceived deviation from British tradition. Most of Canada's intellectuals believed that the British political system, and by extension the Canadian one, were fundamentally sound. Even among the most ardent continentalists, precious few would have agreed with annexationist Samuel R. Clarke (1846–1932) when he wrote in wake of the 1891 federal election in Canada that the American system of government, 'though possessing some defects, is on the whole, so far as I am able to judge, superior to our own.'[37] In fact, even during the early 1890s, only a limited number of radical intellectuals hoped to see Canada become an American-style republic or a series of American states.

Always quick to minimize Canadian-American divergences, continentalists insisted that the American political tradition was, like its

Canadian counterpart, largely British in inspiration, and that both nations had adapted British ideas and institutions to suit the conditions
of a new continent. Canada and the United States 'received the matrix
of their laws and government from England,' wrote John Bartlet Brebner in 1934, 'and both have North-Americanized it.'[38] He believed that
many Canadian-American political divergences were essentially superficial in nature. In the end, both Canada and the United States were
New World democracies. O.D. Skelton, a professor of political and economic science at Queen's University, had a more unusual perspective
on the continuity that existed between the British and American political traditions: 'When the United States took over the task of governing
itself, the Great Britain it knew and imitated in its political institutions
was a Great Britain in which the cabinet system had not yet secured a
definite and recognized place, and where the official exponents of the
constitution declared that the first condition of liberty was to keep the
executive and legislative separate.'[39] Skelton, who would later serve
as Queen's dean of arts, saw America's chief political weakness – the
separation of powers – as the result of an unfortunate reproduction of
Georgian England's inchoate political system.

Anti-American intellectuals generally insisted on the revolutionary
nature of the republic, and aside from a few moderates, notably George
M. Wrong and Robert Falconer,[40] most imperialists argued that only
residual traces of British tradition could be found in the American polity. The United States was not built on the bedrock of tradition, but on
the shifting sands of abstract theory. Indeed, as Andrew Macphail put
it it 1911, 'British institutions work well because they are based upon
fictions which we all understand to be so. American institutions work
with noise and friction because people think that they are founded
upon realities.'[41] The republic possessed a flawed system based on
egalitarian illusions. At heart, American institutions were alien to the
Anglo-Saxon race.

The United States is a democratic republic; Canada is a constitutional monarchy. Therein lies the fundamental political difference between the two nations. In Quebec, where the Westminster system was
not generally viewed as an element of national distinctiveness, most
nationaliste intellectuals were largely indifferent to the whole question
of American republicanism versus British monarchy. Even Jules-Paul
Tardivel, who held democratic republicanism in very low regard, noted
in 1900 that 'the diverse forms of government that people set up, as
long as they do not stray outside legitimate limits, do not interest the
Church.'[42]

Things were quite different in imperialist circles. For imperialists, constitutional monarchy was fundamental to Canadian distinctiveness and tradition. Republicanism was viewed as poisonous to tradition, and the superiority of British constitutional monarchy over American republicanism was held to be self-evident. In a paper read before the Toronto branch of the Imperial Federation League in 1891, A.H.F. Lefroy (1852–1919) dismissed the whole issue in one sentence: 'I do not purpose dwelling this evening upon any of the advantages which may be supposed to accrue to us from having at the apex of our political system the representative of our ancient and historic monarchy, rather than a mere passing politician elected for four years, whose very mediocrity often recommends him as a safe candidate to the party tacticians.'[43] Born into a prominent Toronto family – his father, John Henry Lefroy, had been one of Canada's most renowned scientists and served as the governor of Bermuda, while his grandfather, Sir John Beverley Robinson, had been the chief justice of Upper Canada – Lefroy was educated at Oxford University. He practised law in Toronto during the 1880s and 1890s and was appointed professor of Roman law, jurisprudence, and the history of English law at the University of Toronto in 1900, a position he would hold for the rest of his life. Inspired in part by the work of Sir John George Bourinot, Lefroy's essays frequently emphasized the superiority of British and Canadian forms of government over American ones. An ardent imperialist, he frequently sought to refute English jurist Albert Venn Dicey's assertion that the Canadian Constitution was essentially similar to the American one.[44]

Lefroy's negative assessment of republican government was thoroughly rejected by some radicals. Radical republicanism experienced a brief surge in the late 1880s and early 1890s, and during those years, Jean-Baptiste Rouilliard was at the centre of Quebec's republican movement. He firmly believed that 'the Republican system ... possesses an undeniable, unquestionable superiority, because it could not, unlike heredity, produce ignorant, coarse or even criminal leaders and pontiffs.'[45] For Rouilliard, the superiority of American republicanism was yet another argument in favour of annexation. Goldwin Smith concurred. He believed that monarchy and aristocracy were aberrations in the context of the Americas. 'On the soil of the New World hereditary monarchy and aristocracy can never grow,' he wrote in 1891.[46] The very essence of the New World, Smith believed, required American nations to break with European monarchies and their political systems.

Most continentalists, however, were fairly comfortable with constitutional monarchy. In practice, they argued, Canada was as democratic as the United States. As a result, many continentalists deplored what James T. Shotwell regarded as the 'inveterate tendency in American opinion to regard monarchy as synonymous with reaction because it has been reminiscent of oppression.' 'The answer to this historical barrier to American-Canadian understanding,' he wrote in 1934, 'is surely to be found in the principles upon which the British Commonwealth is founded, which makes the Crown itself the conservator of the ordered processes of freedom.'[47]

During the period under study, the issue of American political secularism did not generate a great deal of commentary in English Canada. Mainstream Protestant culture, indeed, had come to accept the formal separation of church and state, and even imperialists like Andrew Macphail, who were inclined to view 'the utter divorce of government from piety' with alarm, did not view political secularism as much of an issue.[48] French Canadian conservatives viewed things somewhat differently. Catholicism was paramount to the French Canadian identity, and at the turn of the twentieth century, the ultramontane impulse was particularly strong among Quebec's nationalists. Not surprisingly, therefore, an overwhelming proportion of Canadian commentary on American secularism was written in Quebec.

The province's most forceful critic of American secularism was none other than Jules-Paul Tardivel. Born in Covington, Kentucky, Tardivel's parents were recent immigrants to the United States from England and France. He was sent to Canada in 1868 by his maternal uncle, a parish priest in Mount Vernon, Ohio, to study at the Séminaire de Saint-Hyacinthe. After graduating, Tardivel began his career as a journalist at *Le Courrier de Saint-Hyacinthe*. Shortly thereafter, he briefly worked at Montreal's *La Minerve* before settling down in Quebec City and joining the staff of *Le Canadien* in 1874. In 1881, he founded *La Vérité*, French Canada's most influential ultramontane newspaper, which he would continue to edit until his death in April 1905. In the wake of the 1899 papal condemnation of 'Americanism,'[49] Tardivel published an influential three-hundred-page essay on *La situation religieuse aux États-Unis* that denounced the separation of church and state in the United States. American secularism, Tardivel warned, was not a model for church-state relations:

Ever since JESUS CHRIST came to earth, there are only two ideas that motivate both individuals and governments: the Christian spirit and the anti-Christian spirit. The governing spirit of the United States, being manifestly not the Christian spirit, necessarily must be the anti-Christian spirit. If the anti-Christian spirit seems to be less violent there than elsewhere, it is only because it meets less resistance. The river, wide and deep, flows silently towards the sea, whereas the small stream, whose course is obstructed by dykes and rocks, makes a lot of noise. However, the power of the river is far superior to that of the stream.

Ultimately, despite an 'official recognition of the existence of a Supreme Being' by the American republic, Tardivel believed that 'the real GOD of the American people and the American government is humanity, is man.'[50]

Many French Canadian conservatives held a more moderate view of the separation of church and state in America. Henri Bourassa, for instance, argued in 1912 that the First Amendment to the American Constitution was hardly a radically secular clause, and noted that 'the Catholic Church is not "established" in Quebec, at least in the sense meant by the framers of the American constitution.'[51] In the end, most of Quebec's intellectuals recognized that church and state could hardly be linked in a society divided into a number of Christian confessions. Even Jules-Paul Tardivel was willing to acknowledge that 'the heterogeneous population of the United States, the many faiths found there, the very absence of any religious faith among a great number of people, have made [secularism] necessary. In such circumstances, it is incontestably the least bad option.'[52] Indeed, as several of the province's observers were quick to point out, American theocratism had historically led to the persecution of Roman Catholics. Many conservatives were fairly disinclined, therefore, to condemn the wider secularism of American government. Their critique of the separation of church and state centred instead on the practical application of political secularism, particularly in the public school system.

American democracy has long provided the intellectuals of the world with a working model to applaud or criticize. In Canada, 'democracy' was understood to possess two separate yet related meanings. In the writing of some purists it corresponded to the Greek notion of δημοκρατία – rule of the people – and referred to a form of government where sovereign power resided with the people. The term was more generally employed, however, to designate any system of representative government involving free elections. Hence, Canada, though a constitutional monarchy in the strict sense, was often referred to as a democracy.

Democratic notions are tied to the modern ethos, which favours political systems founded on some form of popular sovereignty. That said, most conservative intellectuals did not condemn democracy per se, whether American or otherwise, mainly because they understood the term to refer to representative government which, of course, was seen as a key element of the British political tradition.[53] As a result, only the most immoderate conservatives criticized American democracy, because they alone understood it to be a radical political system.

Until the 1960s, ultramontanism lingered in Quebec's intellectual culture. Imported from continental Europe, this theocratic doctrine rejected the very notion of popular sovereignty as an affront to God. Accordingly, Quebec's nationalists were most likely both to equate democracy with popular sovereignty and to reject it wholesale. By the turn of the century, both France and the United States provided convenient foils for their antidemocratic rhetoric. Among the province's nationalists, Jules-Paul Tardivel emerged as one of American democracy's most persistent critics. Indeed, in 1900, Quebec's most theocratic intellectual saw blasphemy at the very root of American politics and government: 'The Declaration of Independence contains a priniciple that is essentially false and subversive. '*Deriving their just powers from the consent of the governed*.' The creators of the American republic thereby formally attributed a human origin to civil power. The Church, speaking through Leo XIII in the encyclical *Diutumum*, declared 'that we must seek the source of power in the state in GOD.'[54] Henri Bourassa was not far behind Tardivel when it came to criticizing democracy in America. Indeed, though Bourassa's thought possessed a strong liberal component – he sat as a Liberal in the House of Commons for the riding of Labelle, Quebec, from 1896 to 1899 – the enigmatic *castor rouge* viewed democracy with a certain disdain. American democracy was contemptible, he believed, because it entertained a dangerous illusion: egalitarianism.[55] Similarly, Andrew Macphail insisted in 1908 that equality, political or otherwise, was a fallacy that American democracy perpetuated: 'To preserve the fiction that all men continue on the same plane of equality is an essential of democratic government.'[56] Like many imperialists, Macphail believed that egalitarian democracy was an unworkable charade.

More generally, however, Canadian conservatives merely criticized the breadth of suffrage in the United States. Commenting on the wave of nativist legislation that followed America's entry into the First World War and that threatened Franco-American parochial schools, abbé

Henri d'Arles lamented in 1919 that the American republic 'is really the people's affair; it has universal suffrage, which is, for great minds, "the reign of incompetence."'[57] The self-styled Viscount de Fronsac (b. 1856) agreed. Born Frederic Gregory Forsyth in Montreal, the viscount received most of his education in the United States. The American political system, he wrote in 1893, was 'radically wrong.' Democracy, Fronsac argued, 'renders government into the hands of the worthless and ignoble.' Worse still, it shuts out of power 'the silent, unrepresented minority of wise and cultured men, who of right are the natural rulers, but in democracies never have a right.'[58] By granting suffrage to the urban proletariat, many conservatives believed that the United States had destabilized existing social relations and rejected political elitism and deference.

Goldwin Smith, whose liberalism had congealed in the mid-nineteenth century, was not far behind Fronsac when it came to condemning universal suffrage. He noted in 1891 that 'among the American errors of which even Liberals who took part in founding the Canadian Confederation promised themselves to steer clear, was universal suffrage.'[59] Like many of his conservative adversaries, Smith feared the extension of suffrage to the proletariat, women, and non-whites.

By the early twentieth century, however, precious few continentalists shared Smith's aversion to universal suffrage. On the contrary, his intellectual successors saw the expansion of suffrage in the United States as a brilliant experiment in democracy. The democractic ideal was viewed as one of the pillars of North American civilization, and continentalists insisted that American democracy, like its Canadian counterpart, had been inherited from Britain and nurtured in the soil of the New World. For Reverend James A. Macdonald, democracy, in spite of its European origins, found its incarnation in 'the North American idea': 'America, with its United States and Canada, prides itself against Europe, as embodying the world's idea of democracy. Here on this continent has been asserted and made good the right of a free people to govern themselves.'[60] Educated at Knox College, Toronto, and at the University of Edinburgh, Macdonald was ordained a minister of the Presbyterian Church in 1891. In 1896, he founded the *Westminster*, a monthly religious journal published in Toronto. Later, he reorganized and edited the *Presbyterian*, a weekly journal devoted to the interests of the Presbyterian Church. In 1902, he was appointed managing editor of the Toronto *Globe*, where he would remain until his retirement in 1916. Macdonald believed that Canada and the United States possessed a common English-speaking civilization founded on the twin ideals of democracy and liberty. He expressed this idea in two collections of essays, *Democracy and the Nations* (1915) and *The North American Idea* (1917).

There were aspects of American democracy, however, that few Canadian intellectuals, continentalist or anti-American, endorsed. Before the First World War, imperialists like John Castell Hopkins believed that America suffered from 'the cost and turmoil of ... almost continual elections.'[61] On this issue, many continentalists saw eye to eye with their anti-American adversaries. Edgar McInnis, who taught history at the University of Toronto and whose widely used textbooks helped diffuse continentalist ideas in Canada's colleges and universities, held the idea of frequent fixed-term elections in low regard. In a 1929 article published in the *Canadian Forum*, McInnis argued that excessive democracy had the paradoxical effect of alienating the American voter:

> It is not merely the choice of a President that faces the voter, or even of Senators and Congressmen. He has his state elections, his county elections, his municipal elections; and the class of elective officials is far more extensive than under our own system. And he has in addition the burden of the primary, which seeks to assure to the people the right of nomination as well as of election. Small wonder if the average voter finds the task of selection beyond his powers, and frequently abandons all intelligent interest, if not all participation, in politics generally.[62]

Democracy had limits, many continentalists insisted, and its application should not act as an impediment to good government. Indeed, their understanding of democracy certainly did not require the election of all public officials.

No single element of American government was rejected more vigorously in Canada than the separation of powers. In the United States, constitutional checks and balances have historically been viewed as integral to democracy and indispensable to the prevention of tyranny. But most Canadian intellectuals believed that they hindered both democracy and good government. For instance, A.H.F. Lefroy insisted, as did most imperialists, that 'the fundamental defect of the American system ... seems to lie in the separation and diffusion of power and responsibility, and on both points it is obviously less favourable than our system to the speedy and safe carrying into effect of the popular will.'[63] Many continentalists also vigorously criticized the separation of powers in the United States. Socialists tended to view constitutional checks and balances as an obstacle to progressive legislation, while liberals, like their conservative adversaries, often suggested that they hampered the whole working of government. In *The Government of the United States*, a successful textbook which went through five editions and two title changes between 1919 and 1946, William Bennett Munro offered a tactful – and essentially liberal – critique of the separation of powers to American college students:

> The notion that there can be no liberty without a separation of govern-
> mental powers, without a system of checks and balances, is one that might
> easily be expected to find favor a century ago; to-day it is far from com-
> manding general acceptance by students of political science. The federal
> governments of Canada and Australia, for example, with no separation of
> powers, have demonstrated Montesquieu's dread of centralization to have
> been in large measure imaginary. It is impossible to say, of course, whether
> the United States would have fared better or worse under a constitution
> framed by men who knew not Montesquieu; but there are many thought-
> ful Americans who nowadays believe that the theory of checks and bal-
> ances is a delusion and a snare, that it has made for confusion in the actual
> work of government, that it divides responsibility, encourages friction, and
> has balked constructive legislation on numberless occasions.[64]

Only a handful of continentalists fully embraced constitutional checks and balances. Samuel R. Clarke was one such thinker. Like the American republicans he so admired, the Toronto jurist and advocate of continental union saw the separation of powers as an indispensable obstacle to tyranny. By contrast, he argued in early 1891 that the Canadian prime minister was endowed with the powers of a dictator: 'A few sickly theorists with the tinsel of royalty dazzling their mental vision are laboring painfully to disseminate the notion that our system of government is superior to the American. According to these gentlemen the initiative in American legislation belongs to nobody in particular. I quite agree this objection will not lie in respect of our system. Sir John Macdonald is a kind of emperor, king, president and British prime minister all combined.'[65]

The American Constitution is one of the most enduring instruments of government in the world. Yet many Canadian intellectuals refused to acknowledge its resilience. For many imperialists, it was little more than a rigid and overly decentralized piece of legislation that had stifled American life since the late eighteenth century. Moreover, though Tories were willing to acknowledge that the Constitution of 1787 contained fragments of the British political tradition, they also believed that it had failed its ultimate test: the Civil War. Canadian conservatives favoured measured change guided by tradition, and they correspondingly rejected what they saw as the American effort to produce permanence out of nothing. 'A community cannot adopt a constitution any more than a child can adopt a father,' wrote Andrew Macphail, quoting Walter Bagehot, in 1911.[66] Constitutions had to evolve over hundreds of years; they could not simply be drafted by a convention of delegates. The whole issue was summarized by John G. Bourinot in a paper read before the Royal Society of Canada – of which he was a founding member – in 1893: 'The great source of the strength of the institutions of the United States lies in the fact that they have worked out their government in accordance with certain principles, which are essentially English in Origin, and have been naturally developed since their foundation as colonial settlements, and what weaknesses their system shows have chiefly arisen from new methods, and from the rigidity of their constitutional rules of law.'[67] A foremost authority on constitutional law and parliamentary procedure – his *Parliamentary Procedure and Practice in the Dominion of Canada,* published in 1884, was the standard work on the subject for several decades – Bourinot's writings consistently emphasized the superiority of British and Canadian political institutions over American ones.

Continentalists and anti-Americans could agree on a number of America's political shortcomings, but they often held diametrically opposed positions when it came to its Constitution. Like many American intellectuals, continentalists tended to praise the Constitution of 1787 for its stability and flexibility. 'It is not true that the constitution of the United States has shown itself to be far less flexible than the constitution of England,' wrote William Bennett Munro in 1919.[68] Indeed, while he acknowledged that the American Constitution was difficult to amend, Munro also noted that constitutional interpretation had allowed the document to evolve a great deal since 1787. In practice, therefore, the British and American constitutions were quite similar. Born in Almonte, Ontario, Munro was one of Canada's most influential interwar continentalists. The Harvard professor of government showed a sustained interest in Canadian affairs throughout his career, and some of his most significant work was aimed at revealing the common features of North American politics and government.

Continentalists and anti-Americans also diverged on the level of influence that American constitutional thought had exerted on the drafting of the Canadian Constitution, the British North America Act, 1867. English Canadian conservatives were usually not keen on admitting that the Fathers of Confederation had drawn heavily on American political ideas and institutions to craft the British North America Act. To do so would compromise the anti-American nature of the Canadian nation. If anything, America had provided an example of what *not* to do when drafting a constitution. For his part, Donald Creighton vigorously rejected the idea that the BNA Act was an essentially American document. In 1942, he published an article in the *University of Toronto Quarterly* to affirm the anti-American integrity and the centralized nature of the Canadian Constitution:

> The chief sentiments which the Fathers of Confederation entertained with respect to the United States were a lively desire to escape being annexed and a firm determination to avoid what were popularly regarded in British North America as the mistakes of American federalism. Besides the United States was not the only federal system with which the provinces were acquainted: they had, in fact, been long and intimately related to another organization, which, though much less systematic than the American, was definitely federal in character. This was, of course, the British Empire itself, with its central imperial parliament and its subordinate colonial legislatures. And it would not be difficult to prove that the main ideas and a good deal of the political machinery of Canadian federalism were taken over directly from the Old Colonial System of Great Britain.[69]

Creighton was reacting to the ideas contained in William Bennett Munro's *American Influences on Canadian Government* (1929). In this widely read essay, Munro had insisted that, in spite of some superficial institutional differences, the political systems of Canada and the United States were very much alike. In fact, he argued that the Fathers of Confederation had borrowed heavily from American constitutional thought and practices while drafting the British North America Act. Consequently, they had produced an essentially Hamiltonian – and therefore American – document. 'If Macdonald is entitled to be called the "Father of the Canadian Constitution,"' Munro remarked, 'it would appear that Alexander Hamilton has some claim to be designated as its grandfather.'[70]

By the early twentieth century, one of the few elements of the American political system that aroused genuine interest in Quebec was the constitutional division of powers between the federal government and the states. This is hardly surprising given that the struggle for provincial autonomy rallied a significant proportion of the province's intellectuals. In their calls for constitutional decentralization, French Canadian nationalists occasionally cited the American division of powers as a model. Indeed, many believed that the American state possessed a greater degree of sovereignty than the Canadian province. In *Reflets d'Amérique*, a 1941 collection of essays which urged French Canadians to resist Americanization, Édouard Montpetit, who taught political economy at the Université de Montréal for almost three decades, wrote approvingly of the American Constitution: 'the American states receive and exercise the powers that the Constitution does not reserve for the federal government, whereas in Canada, it is the central government that retains the powers that the Constitution does not give to the provinces. In other words, the American state possesses, as regards legislation, a much wider field, a broader authority.'[71]

Canadian imperialists often cited state sovereignty as one of the great weaknesses of the American political system. Centralism, to be sure, was an imperialist mantra, and English Canadian conservatives regularly condemned the fact that American states retained all residual powers not specifically granted to the federal government by the Constitution. This could only have a centrifugal, and therefore negative, effect on American life. Indeed, for many Tories, including Andrew Macphail, the Civil War was the direct result of constitutional decentralization: 'The people of the United States have not yet decided wherein the real sovereignty lies. Calhoun believed that it lay in the individual states. Madison also was of the opinion that the union was an operation of the states and not of the whole people. The Civil War was an argument to the contrary; but nothing is ever settled by force.'[72]

Beyond the theories and institutions lay the actual practice of politics and government in the United States which, perhaps not surprisingly, generated a great deal of commentary Canada. For the most part, Canadian intellectuals held American political culture in low regard. 'There can be no doubt that political corruption in the United States has, in particular instances, surpassed anything the world has seen,' remarked William S. Milner (1861–1931), the University of Toronto's influential professor of classics, in 1903.[73] This belief was widespread in Canada, where many conservatives regarded corruption as the primary characteristic of American political culture, indeed of its politics and government. The issue even crept into Canadian literature. In 1901 alone, two Canadian novels, James Algie's (1857–1928) *Bergen Worth* and Robert Barr's *The Victors*, explored political corruption in American cities. A few years later, Stephen Leacock ridiculed American political culture in his humorous *Arcadian Adventures with the Idle Rich* (1914). In the final instalment of this celebrated cycle of stories, even the Clean Government League becomes an instrument of political corruption and violence:

> There is no need to recount here in detail the glorious triumph of the election day itself. It will always be remembered as the purest, cleanest election ever held in the precincts of the city. The citizen's organization turned out in overwhelming force to guarantee that it should be so. Bands of Dr Boomer's students, armed with baseball bats, surrounded the polls to guarantee fair play. Any man wishing to cast an unclean vote was driven from the booth: all those attempting to introduce any element of brute force or rowdysm into the election were cracked over the head. In the lower part of the town scores of willing workers, recruited often from the humblest classes, kept order with pickaxes. In every part of the city motor cars, supplied by all the leading business men, lawyers, and doctors of the city, acted as patrols to see that no unfair use should be made of other vehicles in carrying voters to the polls.[74]

Canadian conservatives attributed political corruption in the United States to a number of causes, including the nation's revolutionary heritage, the structure of its politics and government, and the impact of immigration and plutocracy on its body politic. Continentalists also acknowledged that political corruption was a problem in the United States. However, they were usually quick to minimize and relativize the phenomenon. American corruption, they insisted, was not as widespread as many believed. Besides, bossism and bribery were hardly confined to the United States. In *American Influences on Canadian Government*, William Bennett Munro pointed out that, in spite of the creation of the Civil Service Commission, cronyism and political corruption were very much alive in Canada. He argued that 'in the government and politics of Canada, most of what is superimposed is British; but most of what works its way in from the bottom is American.'[75]

But corruption was not the only blemish that Canadian intellectuals detected on America's body politic. Like Bryce, many anti-Americans were convinced that the United States consistently produced politicians of inferior quality. A number of continentalists were inclined to agree. William Bennett Munro lamented the fact that America 'has failed to utilize in the presidential office a long line of notable statesmen: Hamilton, Marshall, Gallatin, Webster, Clay, Calhoun, Seward, Sumner, Hay, and others. On the other hand, it has bestowed its highest honor on men like Polk, Fillmore, Pierce, and Arthur, of whom no one now knows much except that they are on the roll of the presidents.'[76] American parties, Munro remarked in 1919, generally picked inoffensive, and often untalented, presidential candidates simply because they could garner votes in pivotal states. This, he believed, was hardly a recipe for great statesmanship.

That said, most continentalists refused to see intermittent presidential mediocrity as a sign of American inferiority. Some claimed that Canadian political culture was scarcely more adept at producing great statesmen. Frank Underhill, whose contempt for Canada's political establishment reached its paroxysm during the Great Depression, argued that socioeconomic factors common to both Canada and the United States produced inferior politicians. 'The real test of a government is in the character of the men who are attracted to public life, and in this respect there is no appreciable difference between Canada and the United States,' he wrote in the *Canadian Forum*. 'We habitually talk as if the British system in Canada habitually produced Balfours and Asquiths whereas we all know in our hearts that it only produces – well, the reader can fill in the names for himself.'[77] Underhill joined the *Forum*'s editorial staff in 1927 and authored its irreverent 'O Canada' column in the 1930s. In 1932, he played an active role in the founding of both the League for Social Reconstruction, which was intended to be a Canadian version of the British Fabian Society, and the Co-operative Commonwealth Federation. He authored the first draft of the CCF's 1933 Regina Manifesto.

In the late nineteenth and early twentieth century, many Canadian intellectuals saw the two-party system of the United States as one of its few political assets. In 1904, Queen's James Cappon argued that the two-party system checked the spread of radicalism and provided the United States with a great measure of unity and stability:

Consider the practical efficiency of an organization which keeps nearly 80 millions [*sic*] of people, so diverse in their interests, so heterogeneous in blood and instincts and spread over so vast a space, within the political unity of the Republican and Democratic parties, with clearly defined and concerted programmes for each, and think of the confusion that would exist, and the danger for the body politic, if that political unity were split up into the confused conflict and uncertain, changing combinations of half a dozen parties as in the German Empire, an Irish party, a German party, a Socialist party, a Labour party, a Western party, and so forth.[78]

A number of liberals were inclined to agree with Cappon. A.D. DeCelles held radicalism in low regard and viewed federalism as the principal barrier to subversion in the United States. 'Does not the federal system constitute a formidable force for order? Indeed, over the vast expanse of the Republic stand forty-five separate governments, like so many citadels in the way they intimidate the enemies of society,' he wrote in 1896.[79]

By the interwar years, however, classical liberals like DeCelles no longer held a monopoly on pro-American sentiment and the America's dearth of radicalism was often criticized by continentalists. In a 1929 article published in the *Canadian Forum*, Edgar McInnis lamented that 'the most arrogantly progressive nation in the world has, of all civilized nations, the most unreasoning terror of any political change whatever.' He insisted, moreover, that the Democratic and Republican parties had virtually become political clones. 'Such differences as originally existed between Republicans and Democrats – and these differences were once very real – have one by one been obliterated.'[80] For Frank Underhill, ideological convergence was a problem common to both Canada and the United States. 'A party in North America is nothing but a bundle of sectional factions held together by a common name and a common desire for the spoils of office,' he wrote in 1930.[81] Aside from a lack of ideological distinctiveness, many continentalists also believed that both the Democratic and Republican parties suffered from an absence of ideas, which Underhill attributed to the two-party system's deleterious effect on politics. Like many left-of-centre intellectuals, he considered third parties to be the primary matrix of political change in North America.

Nevertheless, from the late nineteenth century to the opening of the Cold War, and particularly during Roosevelt's New Deal, Canadian reformers regularly looked south for successful examples of state interventionism. Before the Second World War, the United States was seen as a fairly progressive nation and, in many respects, its social legislation was assumed to be ahead Canada's. The Canadian voter, bemoaned a group of liberal continentalists in 1941, 'has a greater reverence for the past than his neighbor; for precedent, position and old custom; and he is correspondingly slower to accept economic and social experiments. Thus Canada watched the New Deal with scepticism. In social legislation it is relatively a backward nation and one which is extraordinarily loyal to economic orthodoxy.'[82] By the late 1940s, however, Canada had begun to pull ahead of the United States in terms of social legislation and few progressives longed for the Dominion to follow America's lead.

American statism was not universally praised in interwar Canada. Antistatist sentiment was strong in Canada, particularly in Quebec where Catholic doctrine made many intellectuals wary of the state. Like most *nationalistes*, Hermas Bastien was concerned by the effects of 'the deification of the state' on society. In a 1936 article published in the *Revue dominicaine*, he argued that American statism produced 'a rupture in the hierarchy of people and a confusion in their relations with politics and culture. In the last few years, such symptoms have appeared here at home and we believe ourselves authorized to denounce them as an American influence on political morality.'[83] Nationalist intellectuals believed that excessive state intervention destabilized society because it threatened established social relations. Nevertheless, nationalist reactions to the New Deal were mixed, as various intellectuals believed that some of its measures could be likened to corporatism, a system of economic and political organization that elicited a great deal of enthusiasm among clerical and nationalist elites in the 1930s.

During the period under study, few Canadian intellectuals wholeheartedly embraced the American political system. Indeed, on several issues, there was little to distinguish the anti-American and continentalist positions. The conservative critique of American politics and government, however, was deep-seated. For conservative intellectuals, the core principles of the American experience, which included revolutionism, materialism, and individualism, were viewed as the underpinnings of an undesirable social order. These modern ideals were expressed, among other things, through the American polity. The Americans had established their nation on the very unsound idea of popular sovereignty and, as a consequence, suffered from permanent political instability.

Continentalists scarcely embraced the American political tradition. Like their anti-American contemporaries, they often had doubts concerning its effectiveness. Yet their critique of certain aspects of American politics and government did not lapse into anti-Americanism. On the contrary, they generally sought to relativize Canadian-American divergences. Putting aside what they considered to be superficial differences, continentalists argued that Canada was fundamentally an 'American democracy' that possessed many of the strengths and weaknesses of its neighbour. True to form, they constructed an image of the United States that corresponded to their aspirations regarding continental integration and, in a wider sense, to their appreciation of the modern ethos.

An overwhelming proportion of the Canadian commentary on American politics and government was published by English-speaking Canadians. This reflected the importance of political themes in the English Canadian debate surrounding Canadian distinctiveness and identity. Quebec's intellectuals, by contrast, showed relatively little interest in the American polity. During the period examined here, French Canadian nationalists generally portrayed their nation as an ethno-religious and cultural entity. As a result, they rarely felt compelled to denounce American republicanism in order to assert French Canada's distinctiveness. Quebec's intellectual right, moreover, did not exhibit a fervent attachment to a given political system. It did, however, possess a powerful attachment to Catholicism which, as we shall see in the next chapter, generated a strong dislike of the moral and religious laxity that America apparently embodied.

3 Religion and Culture in the United States

The emergence of mass culture is a key element in modernity. In the modern world, culture is a commodity to be purchased and consumed like any other good or service. Moreover, it is standardized and relentlessly advertised and promoted by a cultural industry that seeks to generate vast profits and anticipate or create the next trend. In North America, culture began to experience its first signs of commodification and standardization in the mid-nineteenth century. Later, the spread of mass culture was hastened by the emergence of mass media and advertising, as new technologies like broadcasting became effective instruments of cultural standardization. Mass culture marginalized both folk culture and elite culture. As folk culture receded, the relative cultural autonomy that had characterized most North American communities was slowly ground down. Moreover, the elite's professed role as the arbiter of culture became increasingly tenuous.

From the very start, the United States emerged as the hub of mass culture. The country appeared to embrace technology and the mass age like no other, and, for many observers, mass culture and American culture became indissociable. This was certainly the case for Canadian conservatives, who saw the commodification and standardization of culture as an American poison. Mass culture appealed to the lowest common denominator; it was violent and sensual, and it sought only to entertain, not to educate and elevate. Worse still, conservatives argued that it corroded Canadian culture and Canada's more traditional way of life. American intellectual culture did not usually fare any better. In imperialist and *nationaliste* commentary, Americans were often described as unintelligent rubes. The intellectual sterility of the United States was a popular theme in anti-American discourse. Materialism had corroded every possible aspect of America's cultural life, and the nation suffered from its premature separation from Europe, a continent which conservatives believed was the ultimate source of all proper culture. In 1922, Victor Barbeau (1896–1994), who would spend most of his career teaching French language and literature at the École des Hautes Études commerciales, summed up the whole issue up in this oft-quoted passage from his irreverent *Cahiers de Turc*: 'Let us look to New York when it comes to finance, and to Chicago when it comes to pigs. But when it comes to literature, art, science, culture, we should remember that the Gods have not yet crossed the Atlantic.'[1] Barbeau was an unorthodox nationalist in many ways – he was, for instance, a frequent critic of literary regionalism – but his anti-Americanism was typical of Quebec's interwar right.

American culture, it was argued in conservative circles, married vulgarity with technology. By the 1920s, it had acquired a new means of propagation: the radio. During the interwar years, many Canadian conservatives railed against American radio, especially in Quebec, and demanded that the federal government intervene to sanitize Canada's airwaves. Indeed, not only were many Canadians able to pick up American signals over the air, but Canadian stations were eagerly retransmitting American programs. The *nationalistes* feared that American radio would be an instrument of linguistic assimilation, but all conservatives worried about the moral content of American programs. American stations, for instance, facilitated the spread of jazz, a form of entertainment that Lucien Desbiens (b. 1907) found utterly repugnant. In a 1936 article published in the *Revue dominicaine*, the junior editor of Montreal's *Le Devoir* argued that jazz was more akin to noise than music: 'The jazz most often put out by the American radio stations has not been refined by the art of remarkable composers; it is handled not by musicians but by ordinary noisemakers. What we are offered is therefore *original* jazz, which is, according to Paul Whiteman – one of the reformers of syncopated music – an epileptic noise penetrated by a shapeless, idiotic music.'[2]

In a similar vein, American movies were often cited as a major source of low-brow depravity. Conservative intellectuals argued that Hollywood producers would stop at nothing in their race to appeal to the lowest common denominator. In a 1931 tirade against the raciness of American movies, the assistant editor of the Toronto *Star Weekly*, John Herries McCulloch (b. 1892), lamented that 'of all the monstrosities of the cinemas, the kiss is far and away the worst. It is revolting. Deliberately or unconsciously – it doesn't matter which – Hollywood has made it symbolize sexual contact ... And as we become accustomed to it, our artistic senses are dulled, and we are made ready for the next crudity that will emanate from Hollywood.'[3]

Observations on the immoral nature of American cinema were also a staple of *nationaliste* anti-Americanism, which intensified along with America's cultural influence during the interwar years. In 1924, Harry Bernard warned the readers of *L'Action française* that Hollywood hypnotized moviegoers and made them yearn for material possessions: 'For ordinary people, the cinema is something like a waking dream. Concrete, almost palpable, it is a beautiful illusion that everyone, without perhaps believing in it much, keeps in a little corner of their soul. The spectacle detaches people from lived reality and its sorrows to transport them to an artificial world from which they can only return with difficulty. For many, this journey into the unreal has the effect of making life, and the renouncement it entails, more difficult.'[4] The son of a restless French Canadian businessman, Bernard was born in London, England, and attended school in Soissons, Paris, and St Albans, Vermont. In 1906, his family returned to Canada and settled in Quebec's Eastern Townships before relocating to Saint-Hyacinthe. From 1911 to 1919 Bernard studied at the Séminaire de Saint-Hyacinthe. He entered the world of journalism at Ottawa's *Le Droit*, and became the editor of the *Courrier de Saint-Hyacinthe* in 1923, where he would remain until his retirement in 1970. Bernard was the founding editor of one of Quebec's most influential intellectual journals, *L'Action nationale*, from 1933 to 1934. In the early 1940s, he received a grant from the Rockefeller Foundation to study literary regionalism in the United States, and his attitude towards American culture softened correspondingly. Indeed, though Bernard continued to disapprove of mass culture in the United States, his eyes had been opened to the nation's literary and cultural accomplishments.

The United States had also turned the written word into mass entertainment, and anti-Americans frequently railed against the abject commercialization and the utter degradation of the American press. They believed that American newspapers and magazines had been reduced to mere forms of entertainment. For Jean Bruchési (1901–1979), the American magazine embodied the worst tendencies of yellow journalism. Born in Montreal, Bruchési was admitted to the Quebec bar in 1924, but never practised law. Instead, he pursued graduate studies at the Sorbonne and taught history and political science at the Université de Montréal. A vocal supporter of the Union nationale, Bruchési was appointed to a key position within Quebec's civil service in 1937 by Maurice Duplessis. In 1959, he was named Canadian ambassador to Franco's Spain by Prime Minister John Diefenbaker. Like many nationalists of his generation, Bruchési saw American culture as utterly debased. 'Even if there can still be found, in the United States, several magazines whose tone and literary form recall the first publications of the genre,' he wrote in 1936, 'the great majority of American magazines have become synonymous with one of the most despicable and dangerous forms of advertising for the lowliest expressions of the morals of our neighbours.' These included 'apologies for crime, divorce and free love,' and 'the glorification of cinema stars and baseball aces.'[5] The Canadian critique of American magazines was, of course, tied to a campaign to protect Canada's periodicals from foreign competition. Moral outrage was good business for Canadian intellectuals, and the literary nationalism of the Canadian Authors' Association was, to be sure, the cultural equivalent of the self-serving economic nationalism of the Canadian Manufacturers' Association – both groups intended to protect Canadian producers from their American competitors.

Stephen Leacock, for his part, denounced 'the literary sterility of America.' This was a recurring theme in anti-American thought. Americans, it was argued, simply could not write. Leacock was therefore not alone in believing that 'the quantity of American literature – worthy of the name – produced in the last one hundred years is notoriously small.' Furthermore, he wrote in 1909, 'its quality is disappointingly thin.' It was Britain, not America, that had produced 'the great bulk of our reputable common literature of the past one hundred years.' Above all, Leacock believed that Americans were not a literary people. Their education system was too utilitarian to foster the growth of literary genius. Worse still, the affluence and materialism of American life was scarcely conducive to the development of great literature. In the United States, Leacock remarked, 'all less tangible and proveable [sic] forms of human merit, and less tangible aspirations of the human mind are rudely shouldered aside by business ability and commercial success.' He argued that 'literature and progress-happiness-and-equality are antithetical terms.' As a result, 'American civilization with its public school and the dead level of its elementary instruction, with its simple code of republicanism and its ignorance of the glamour and mystery of monarchy, with its bread and work for all and its universal hope of the betterment of personal fortune, contains in itself an atmosphere in which the flower of literature cannot live.'[6]

The conservative critique of American culture was tied to more general anxieties regarding the status revolution. Conservative thinkers
believed that mass culture threatened the social status of the intellectual and cultural elite. The right was particularly dismayed by the status granted by American society to sports stars and entertainers, those
adulated heroes of mass culture. Indeed, while industrial capitalism
produced a new plutocracy and a growing urban proletariat, mass culture spawned the modern superstar. Like many interwar *nationalistes*,
the dean of the Université de Montréal's Faculty of Philosophy, Father
Ceslas Forest (1885–1970), was horrified by the rise of the superstar and
its implications for the status of the traditional elite. America's scale of
values, he reasoned, was upside down:

> Who do young Americans know, admire, and envy? Men of letters, schol-
> ars, artists? Not at all. They admire stars of the screen for their beauty,
> and sports stars for their strength and skill ... Some of them are verita-
> ble national treasures. They enjoy a level of fame that no public figure,
> no scholar, no artist could ever dare hope for. Their features, which the
> newspapers never grow weary of reproducing, are often more familiar to
> young Americans than those of the President of the United States. During
> the Chicago Eucharistic Congress, a newspaper printed a photo of Babe
> Ruth shaking the Cardinal Legate's hand. There is no doubt that for a large
> number of Americans, the honour belonged to the Legate of the Holy See.[7]

The conservative critique of American culture was not restricted to
arts and entertainment. The quality of American English also spawned
a fair amount of criticism among English Canadian Tories. Countless
Americans, it was argued, did not speak properly. Their pronunciation
was atrocious and their spelling was appalling. In 1942, while still an
unknown quantity in the field of literary theory, Northrop Frye (1912–
1991) lamented that 'untold millions of Americans tawk through their
nowses and hawnk like fahghorrns; some whine like flying shells; some
sputter and gargle like cement mixers. The average American pronunciation of "yes" or "now" is hardly a human sound at all.'[8] The Canadian critique of American English was generally tied to a desire to attach
Canadian English to its British parent. Imperialists were always quick
to point out even the minutest divergences between American and
Canadian English and, unlike many of their continentalist opponents,
they usually made a point of using British spelling in their publications.
The continentalist defence of American culture rarely included a plea

for mass culture. Instead, continentalists usually chose to defend the instruments of mass culture, which they generally portrayed as possible means of intellectual upliftment. For instance, one of the most significant Canadian playwrights of the interwar years, Merrill Denison (1894–1975), defended the promise of American radio in a 1931 collection of essays: 'United States radio programs are claimed to exert a deplorably bad cultural influence. Is this actually a fact? I doubt it. The reverse is true, it seems to me. Consider, for a moment, this much discussed matter of musical taste and appreciation. There can be no question that both are improving, and that thousands of people today can enjoy music that they would neither have tolerated nor understood three years ago.'[9] Born in Detroit of a Canadian mother and an American father, Denison studied architecture at the universities of Toronto and Pennsylvania before turning to writing. He wrote several plays for Toronto's Hart House Theatre and was a leading figure in the Little Theatre movement. His plays often cast a satirical gaze at Canadian life. Denison also made a significant contribution to the development of North American radio drama.

Continentalists often tried to highlight America's intellectual vigour. The United States, with her countless colleges, graduate schools, solvent journals, and vast market for erudite publications seemed like an eldorado to intellectuals reared in a society with a limited cultural capacity. During the interwar years, notes Graham Carr, continentalists believed that 'American writing had overtaken British writing at the cutting-edge of English-language literature.'[10] Unlike their anti-American adversaries, a number of continentalists believed that the republic's intellectual emancipation from Europe was the necessary precondition to its cultural development. In the conclusion to *L'âme américaine* (1900), Edmond de Nevers warned that 'the great obstacle to the advent of the state of absolute liberty to which all sincere patriots should aspire is the intellectual vasselage in which America still finds itself in relation to Europe and above all to England.'[11] Decades later, in 1941, E.G. Faludi, an architect and urban planner whose postwar designs would leave a permanent imprint on Toronto's urban landscape, anticipated that 'the influence of the European culture on the American continent will slowly cease.' American affluence and innovation would then propel the United States to the forefront of the artistic world. 'America will become the centre of art,' he confidently predicted in the *Canadian Forum*. Moreover, the widespread affluence of the United States would contribute to an artistic boom: 'In America, there are no limitations. There are free masses which are in considerably better economic conditions than the Europeans and there are now 140 millions all speaking the same language and having the same understanding for many human feelings, expressions and actions. *These masses will be the greatest consumer market for artists ever known in history.*'[12]

Likewise, some continentalists noted that America's literate masses were an extraordinary market for the written word. In 1896, A.D. De-Celles, who had spent his early career as a journalist in Quebec City, marvelled at the U.S. newspaper's ability to reach and inform the masses: 'In the field of journalism the superiority of the Americans over their rivals establishes itself without contest. Under the pressure of their enterprising genius, the short-lived pages have developed in line with the thirst for knowledge that is devouring their feverish society ... Admittedly, newspapers ought to achieve this phenomenal development in a country where education seeps everywhere.'[13] Goldwin Smith was less impressed by American journalism. He believed, however, that Canadian journalism shared many of the weaknesses of its U.S. counterpart: 'The Canadian Press is, in the main, American not English in character. It aims at the lightness, smartness, and crispness of New York journalism rather than at the solidity of the London *Times*.'[14]

Continentalists usually defended American English with a little more vigour. After all, Canadian English was basically American in its pronunciation and syntax. In the preface to his *New Dictionary of Americanisms* (1902), Sylva Clapin, who worked as a translator at the House of Commons in Ottawa from 1902 to 1921, praised American English. He believed that the English spoken in Canada and the United States was a distinct improvement on its British parent: 'As regards the great bulk of the people of the United States, there can be no question but that they speak purer and more idiomatic English than do the masses in the Old Country. In every State of the Union, the language of the inhabitants can be understood without the slightest difficulty. This is more than can be said of the dialects of the peasantry in various parts of England, these being in many instances perfectly unintelligible to a stranger.'[15] Clapin's argument was a continentalist classic. Indeed, he skilfully turned anti-American rhetoric on its head by arguing that Britain, not America, suffered from poor English. The implication was clear: the New World had improved upon the Old.

Modernity marginalizes religion, and established religion in particular. In its liberal form, it is quite tolerant of religious devotion, but rejects religious absolutes. As a result, the modern ethos refuses to accept that a particular religion or denomination possesses a monopoly on truth. The religious constellation, liberals believe, is marked by some degree of moral equivalency. These ideas were anathema to Canadian conservatives, particularly in Quebec. Indeed, traditionalism is inherently theocentric, and it cannot embrace a fully secular outlook. The United States, conservatives believed, was a modern society where faith was marginal; it was a secular nation in every sense of the word. In their writing, conservative intellectuals often contrasted American worldliness with Canadian spiritualism. Once again, anti-Americanism served to affirm the essentially conservative nature of Canadian society.

By and large, anti-American sentiment was strongest among the followers of the least evangelical forms of Christianity – Roman Catholicism and Anglicanism – whose conservative theology stressed order and hierarchy. More than a few anti-Americans, including Donald Creighton, were also sons of the manse. In contrast, continentalism was most prevalent among intellectuals who were raised in or practised nonconformist Christianity. The Quaker upbringing of James T. Shotwell, for instance, appears to have played an important role in the development of his principled internationalism and pacifism. Religious free thinkers like Goldwin Smith were common in continentalist circles, and continentalism appears to have held a particular appeal for agnostics and spiritual eccentrics – religious syncretism and continentalism went hand in hand for Theosophist literary critic William Arthur Deacon (1890–1977), for example. In Quebec, anticlericalism and continentalism were undoubtedly correlated. Indeed, impious dissidents like Louis-Honoré Fréchette and Jean-Charles Harvey invariably professed a deep admiration for American secularism.

For French Canadian nationalists, the critique of American faith – or lack thereof – and of Protestantism was indissociable. America was a secular nation, but it was also an essentially Protestant nation. And Protestantism, the *nationalistes* believed, was a worldly faith. It encouraged individualism, materialism, and secularism, which in turn spawned religious indifference. In 1930, Georges-Marie Bilodeau (1895–1966), a Roman Catholic missionary in the Canadian West, argued that American spirituality had been thoroughly vitiated by Protestant materialism. The American, he wrote, 'is not always an atheist, but the supernatural side of religion does not preoccupy him. Moreover he is the product of a Protestantism whose founding principle rests on faith alone, without charity. The free interpretation of the Bible, another Protestant principle, pushes him to make his own religion, and this is how the ever-growing naturalism, according to the appeal of tainted nature, essentially makes a heathen of him.'[16] In a similar vein, Lionel Groulx warned in 1928 that 'this population of 120 million men' was ravaged by 'all the microbes of its neo-paganism.' 'Is it not in the process of making its way towards an atheist civilization,' he asked, 'accepting no laws other than the hard law of economic supermen, no goals other than sensual pleasure or producing better breeds of the human animal?'[17] The last segment was a reference to the practice of eugenics in the United States, which Groulx found deeply troubling. By the late 1920s, the abbé's influence over Quebec's nationalist movement was nearing its summit. Appointed professor of Canadian history at the Montreal campus of Université Laval in 1915, his position at the university only became permanent after he resigned as the editor of the combative L'Action française, whose position on a number of issues had upset the Liberal provincial government of Louis-Alexandre Taschereau. Undeterred, Groulx played a key role in the 1933 creation of L'Action nationale, a journal whose nationalism was no less combative.

French Canadian nationalists were not alone in criticizing American worldliness. Imperialists also believed that the United States had lost its moral and spiritual compass. Their critique of religious practice in America, however, was far more moderate, and obviously did not include an anti-Protestant component. Stephen Leacock, for instance, poked a good deal of fun at the religious practices of the American elite in his 1914 Arcadian Adventures with the Idle Rich. In his humorous sketches, the wealthy socialites of Plutoria Avenue practised an utterly superficial form of Christianity. They measured faith in dollars and cents, complained that their pastor's sermons were 'always so frightfully full of religion,' and were enthralled with 'Oriental Occultism.'[18] Born into an Anglican family in Swanmore, England, Leacock was not a particularly devout Christian. Nevertheless, he was critical of the hollow religion of the 'leisure class.'

During the interwar years, the state of American Protestantism worried many imperialists. America's various Protestant denominations, they believed, were drifting further and further apart. Some sects had become horribly worldly, while others were embracing an apocalyptic brand of fundamentalism. In the wake of the 1925 Scopes Trial, Reverend Robert Falconer expressed great concern at the rise of Protestant fundamentalism in the United States: 'The fundamentalist appeals to the authority of post-reformation Confessions and lives theologically in an era of arrested development. Though this attitude of mind is found in all countries, it is relatively much stronger in the United States than elsewhere. Churches are being riven twain and some fear a permanent cleavage in American Protestantism.'[19] Born in Charlottetown, Prince Edward Island, Falconer spent much of his youth in the West Indian island of Trinidad, where his father, a Presbyterian clergyman, had been posted. He was himself ordained a minister of the Presbyterian Church in 1892. Shortly thereafter, he joined the faculty of Pine Hill College, Halifax, where he taught New Testament Greek and New Testament Exegesis. He was appointed the college's principal in 1904. Like many Canadian imperialists, Falconer was a religious moderate and a proponent of church union. The idea of denominational schism and estrangement pained him.

Lionel Groulx was equally concerned by the rise of Protestant fundamentalism in 1920s America, but for different reasons. He warned that 'the largest and most active sect, that of the Calvinists,' was 'split by two opposing tendancies, that of the modernists in the process of emptying religious life of all dogma and rite, and that of the fundamentalists who, as much as a religion, represent a nationalist Anglo-Saxon reaction against foreign races and beliefs.'[20] The persecution of American Catholics was indeed a recurring theme in French Canadian commentary, and many intellectuals insisted on the limits of religious freedom in the United States. 'The Catholic Church is free in America,' wrote Jules-Paul Tardivel in 1900, 'as long as it never ventures out, never leaves its councils, its temples, its schools. But whatever desire it might have to make itself small, to stay in the background, to get lost in the crowd of religions, it must, necessarily, make contact with the authorities. And there begins the real persecution.' Indeed, he continued, 'public opinion and the authorities are hostile to the Church and to Catholics.' Roman Catholics, Tardivel noted, were effectively barred from such highly symbolic offices as the presidency: 'No political party would dream of nominating a Catholic for the highest public office of the Republic. If, by some remote chance, one of the parties did make such a nomination, it would be literally swept away in the elections like a vile dust. One cannot imagine a *Catholic* or a *Negro* as president of the United States. It is a moral impossibility.'[21]

Nevertheless, French Canadian nationalists insisted that Roman Catholicism alone could preserve the United States from complete degeneracy. 'Divorce, secular teaching and socialism: the three social wounds that threaten to completely ruin, in this day and age, the vital strength of the American Republic,' warned abbé Antonio Huot in 1908. Mercifully, however, 'the Catholic Church rises up, in all the majesty of its unchanging doctrine, to bar the way to these three enemies of social order.'[22] Though he acknowledged that persecution and heresy threatened the American Catholic Church, Huot insisted that Catholicism was advancing in the United States. Ordained in 1899, the abbé taught philosophy at the Séminaire de Québec in 1900 and 1901, but resigned due to ill-health. He spent the next decade in Mississippi and became the editor of the *Semaine religieuse de Québec* sometime after his return to Canada.

The continentalist response to the conservative critique of America's religious atmosphere was relatively muted. By and large, continentalists praised American religious freedom, but did not linger on the issue. The continentalist ethos was indeed too ideologically diverse to present a common position on religious affairs. The state of American faith generated some debate in continentalist circles. For instance, A.D. DeCelles believed, like Tocqueville, that religious conviction was strong in the United States. 'Our neighbours have another force militating in favour of order, which is the religious sentiment that still permeates all classes of society and establishes itself in circumstances that are fairly important in national life.'[23] DeCelles' contemporary, Edmond de Nevers, disagreed. He claimed in 1900 that 'in the United States, whatever the optimists might say, religions are in decline; in every denomination ruins have accumulated, and a gust of scepticism and indifference blows over people's consciences.'[24] A conservative liberal, de Nevers was hardly ultramontane. Yet like many traditionalists, he firmly believed that widespread irreligion was a threat to the United States. Unlike Louis-Honoré Fréchette, whose anticlericalism was a source of irritation to Quebec's Roman Catholic clergy, de Nevers and DeCelles showed a great deal of respect for the Church. By and large, their work did not offend the sensibilities of the province's conservative and clerical elite.

For the most part, English Canadian continentalists simply noted that Canada and the United States shared a fair amount when it came to religious affairs. Goldwin Smith, for instance, listed religious affinities among the factors that would facilitate continental union. Later, the president of the Canadian Historical Association, Fred Landon (1880–1969), argued that religion played a key role in the history of Canadian-American convergence. In a 1941 monograph on *Western Ontario and the American Frontier*, he remarked that 'American influences upon the religious life and denominational characteristics of Upper Canada were widespread and their effects were often permanent in character.' In fact, Landon continued, 'the two most distinctively evangelistic sects, the Methodists and the Baptists, first entered the province from the United States, and though each increased its membership at a later date through immigration from the British Isles their American characteristics persisted for a long time.'[25]

Like religion, American education generated a great deal of commentary in Canada. Many Canadian intellectuals were educators, and in their eyes, the schools and colleges of the United States embodied a distinctly new form of learning. American education was often viewed as secular, egalitarian, and utilitarian. This, of course, could only draw the ire of Canadian conservatives, who held these values in low regard. Education, they believed, was primarily a moral and spiritual endeavour whose purpose was to separate the wheat from the chaff and, ultimately, to prepare an elite for the challenges of leadership. Education was not a purely utilitarian undertaking and both imperialists and *nationalistes* agreed that a classical education was the most suitable method to forge moral and intellectual leaders.

Anti-American tendencies were often reinforced by a British education. This is not to say that Oxford, Cambridge, or Edinburgh were necessarily hotbeds of anti-American sentiment. Indeed, a number of continentalists, including F.R. Scott and P.E. Corbett, studied in Britain. Rather, a British education tended to reinforce imperialist sentiment among English Canadian intellectuals which, in turn, almost invariably strengthened pre-existing anti-American sentiment. At any rate, Canadian intellectuals hardly needed to study in Britain in order to cultivate anti-American prejudices. Anti-Americanism thrived in Canada's schools and universities. Upper Canada College, for instance, was a breeding ground for anti-American sentiment, particularly under the headmastership of George R. Parkin, who ran the college at the turn of the twentieth century. Likewise, Quebec's classical colleges all appear to have been disseminating some form of anti-Americanism.

The secularism embodied in American education was most fiercely resisted in Quebec, where the entire school system rested on a confessional base. And secularism's most forceful French Canadian opponent was none other than Jules-Paul Tardivel. In his 1900 essay entitled *La situation religieuse aux États-Unis*, Tardivel lashed out at American common schools: 'There is perhaps one thing that Europe has really borrowed from America: the radically false and supremely harmful principle that makes a child's education a function of the state, a political work, a doctrine which, in the hands of the Freemasons, has led to schooling without GOD.'[26] The state, he believed, had no real role to play in education. The moral and intellectual edification of children was the responsibility of their parents and of the Roman Catholic Church. Education, Tardivel argued, should be founded on a moral and spiritual base. To reject this assumption was to flirt with disaster. Indeed, he firmly believed that modern, American-style secular education produced morally stunted non-believers who were drawn to crime and perversion. These ideas were widely held in pre-1945 Quebec's intellectual circles.

Some nationalists believed that American education was not only secular; it was, at times, blasphemous. Darwinian theory, they noted, was taught in many U.S. schools and colleges. Father M.A. Lamarche, for instance, was absolutely scandalized by the scientific curriculum of many American universities. 'In *biology* the system of evolution without God prevails exclusively, all idea of creation having disappeared,' he wrote in 1936. 'Every vital phenomenon, including thought, is caused by a chemical change in the organism. The right to abortion and suicide naturally stem from this.'[27] Nationalist assumptions about secularism and Darwinism were not generally shared by their imperialist contemporaries. By the early twentieth century, most imperialists had embraced common schools and had more or less accepted Darwinian theory as objective truth. Reverend Robert Falconer, for instance, was a delegate to the 1909 centenary celebration of the birth of Charles Darwin held in Cambridge, England.

When it came to criticizing the egalitarian and utilitarian aspects of American education, however, there was greater consensus among Canadian conservatives. The American system, they believed, was too concerned with elevating the masses and with the schooling of women. American attempts at coeducation were particularly criticized in Quebec, where higher education for Catholic women did not emerge until the École d'enseignement supérieur pour jeunes filles (later renamed the Collège Marguerite-Bourgeoys) was founded in 1908. The whole issue upset a number of conservatives. Coeducation, it was argued, destabilized both the education process and society in general. It was also suggested that women were a disruptive presence on campus because they distracted male students. Besides, higher education was often assumed to be unsuitable for women, and admitting women into colleges and universities was viewed as a step towards gender equality, which most pre-1945 conservatives resisted fiercely. In a 1902 pamphlet on U.S. colleges, abbé Henri d'Arles offered a comprehensive critique of coeducation:

> It does not seem to us that a woman's mental constitution is suited to subjects that are intended mainly for the positive, cool and reasoning minds of men, nor is it fitted to a programme of classical education ... Moreover, whatever the feminists think of it, it is completely misunderstanding a woman's social role as set out by God, her mission, her vocation in the world, to prepare her, by this sort of study, to leave her natural sphere of influence and action, not to help men later in life but to supplant them, not to be an accomplished wife but a companion who is absolutely his equal in the liberal professions, previously considered his exclusive domain. Such work seems to us a distortion of God's plan.[28]

Born Henri Beaudet in Princeville, Quebec, d'Arles was educated at the Séminaire de Québec and entered the Dominican Order in 1889. Over the next several years, he served God in various Quebec and New England dioceses. He adopted the pseudonym Henri d'Arles during a 1906 trip to France. In 1912, he left the Dominican Order and settled in Manchester, New Hampshire, eventually becoming the chaplain of the Association canado-américaine, a Franco-American fraternal organization. He became an American citizen in 1924. A profound conservative, d'Arles' revolt against the mass age was at once moral, philosophical, and æsthetic.

The democratism of U.S. schools and colleges did not end with coeducation. The American system, many conservatives argued, was also excessively focused on educating and elevating the lowest common denominator. This, of course, could only be done at the expense of the elite. Even moderate conservatives like University of Toronto president Robert Falconer lashed out at what they saw as American attempts at class levelling. Falconer, indeed, was not a fervent critic of American education. His imperialism was barely anti-American. Yet he rejected American education as altogether too democratic and utilitarian. 'Democracy as it exists in America is willing to educate the masses but is careless of the few who must be carried to a high degree of proficiency,' he wrote in 1925. Appointed president of the University of Toronto in the wake of a 1906 royal commission recommending the complete reorganization of the university, Falconer thoroughly reformed its structure during his twenty-five year presidency. The fundamental purpose of higher education, he argued, was 'the cultivation of those who are to become the intellectual leaders of the people.' And the 'mass production' of college graduates in the United States endangered his elitist conception of education.[29] Andrew Macphail was of the same opinion. In a 1910 collection of essays, he praised the British education system for its elitism and derided American attempts to elevate the masses. 'The main result of the English method was that boys with minds which were capable of improvement were educated and became leaders of men. The boys without such minds were relegated to their own place without loss of time to their teachers or waste of their own.' However, Macphail continued, 'the aim of the American method is to bring the whole mass up to the same level, with the result that there are few leaders and many ill-educated. This principle finds its ultimate expression in those schools which are designed for the instruction of the imbecile, and the re-education, as it is called, of those who have lost their reason by accident or disease.'[30]

Along with Macphail, Stephen Leacock emerges as one of Canada's most influential critics of American education. A graduate of Upper Canada College and the University of Toronto, Leacock joined UCC's faculty in 1889. He left the college in 1898 to pursue doctoral studies in political economy at the University of Chicago. After receiving his degree, he returned to Canada and was appointed lecturer in economics and political science at McGill University. In 1907, with the active encouragement of Governor-General Lord Grey, Leacock embarked on a triumphant and lucrative lecture tour of the British Empire to promote imperial unity. A year later, he was named professor of political science at McGill and head of the department, a position he would hold until his retirement in 1936. Like Falconer, Leacock rejected American education as too utilitarian and specialized. 'The older view of education,' he wrote in 1909, 'which is rapidly passing away in America, but which is still dominant in the great Universities of England, aimed at a wide and humane culture of the intellect.' This was not the goal of modern North American educators. 'Our American system,' Leacock continued, 'pursues a different path. It breaks up the field of knowledge into many departments, subdivides these into special branches and sections, and calls upon the scholar to devote himself to a microscopic activity in some part of a section of a branch of a department of the general field of learning.' As a result, 'the American student's ignorance of all things except his own part of his own subject has grown colossal ... The unused parts of his intellect have ossified.'[31] As far as Leacock was concerned, only a broad curriculum based on the classical humanities could be used to educate young minds.

In the end, however, the conservative assessment of American education was not entirely negative. Many anti-Americans were impressed by certain aspects of the system of higher education in the United States, particularly its facilities and endowments. Even a persistent critic like Henri d'Arles could find things to marvel at. In fact, the abbé was so impressed by Rhode Island's Brown University that he published a short monograph praising *Le collège sur la colline* in 1908.

In continentalist writing, education in the United States was the object of a fair amount of praise, which extended far beyond the facilities and endowments of the nation's institutions of higher learning. A number of continentalists had received part of their education in the United States, and some even taught in American colleges and universities. Unlike their anti-American adversaries, continentalists regularly paid tribute to the democratic and utilitarian aspects of education in the United States. Indeed, for liberals and socialists, a widely accessible system of education was vital to the development of a democratic society. In Errol Bouchette's only work of fiction, *Robert Lozé*, which he published in 1903, the year he was appointed assistant librarian of the Library of Parliament, the narrator praises the democratic nature of American education: 'In this country, education is within everyone's reach, and the business of educating oneself is not hindered by insurmountable obstacles. Everyone has free access to the source of knowledge, but not everyone draws on it.'[32] American education, however, was not only accessible, it also actively strove to elevate the masses and prepare them for the challenges of citizenship. The American system, continentalists argued, did not leave behind the weaker student; it strove to improve his chances of success. In a 1931 article, John Bartlet Brebner contrasted the three universities he had attended, Oxford, Toronto, and Columbia, in an effort to evaluate the higher education systems of the three nations. Uncharacteristically – Brebner usually preferred not to dwell on Canadian-American differences – he lauded the American system and heaped criticism on higher education in Britain and Canada:

American social democracy, the idea of every individual's right to education and a preoccupation with Americanization which unconsciously makes for confidence in indoctrination, press upon, indeed are part of, Columbia in interesting and intangible ways which make it more experi-

mental and less static than Oxford or Toronto, more continuously conscious of the responsibility of its aristocracy to the surrounding democracy,
and public and self-assured than Toronto in manifesting its conviction that
the gifted and self-reliant student is entitled to the better, more expensive
instruction which the tutorial system provides. Oxford ignores the weaker
brethren, Toronto segregates them and Columbia gives greatly of her ener-
gies to teach them to be strong.[33]

Many continentalists also praised the apparently practical nature
of an American education. They often argued that education should
be better adapted to the challenges of the industrial age, though they
usually did this without rejecting the classical humanities outright. In
Quebec, classicism reigned supreme in higher education, and its detractors were generally restrained in their criticism. In his 1896 outline
of American history, A.D. DeCelles, who had studied at the Séminaire
de Québec and the Université Laval, chose to obliquely criticize the
French Canadian system by praising the American one. Although he lamented the overly secular and practical nature of American education,
DeCelles felt that it nonetheless achieved laudable results. 'Nowhere
in the world more than in the United States do we see the adolescent
better prepared for life's struggles, for envisaging the future with more
confidence,' he wrote. 'The young American leaves school perfectly
equipped to accomplish his mission. His knowledge is the result of a
fully positivist instruction, from which is excluded as useless baggage
the ornamental knowledge that is regarded as indispensable in Europe.
He will acquire this knowledge later, once he has made his fortune. In
sum, a very democratic education, very precise, and leading towards a
clear goal: comfort or wealth.'[34]

Outside of Quebec, most continentalists were usually quick to acknowledge the essentially American nature of Canadian education.
'Incidentally,' remarked William Bennett Munro in his 1929 study of
American Influences on Canadian Government, 'it may be mentioned that
almost every feature of the Canadian public school system (save in the
Province of Quebec) is measurably like that in the United States – not
because it has been borrowed therefrom, perhaps, but because similar educational problems have been encountered in the two countries
and have been dealt with in much the same way.'[35] The Canadian correspondent for the New York Times, John MacCormac, was of the same
opinion. In Canada and the United States, he noted in 1940, 'educational
facilities have been almost interchangeable. Canadians have the same

faith as Americans in the advantage of education for all. They cherish the same belief that there is nothing degrading in a boy's working his way through college, whereas in Britain only in London University has anything of the kind been known.'[36] At heart, Canada and the United States shared an essentially democratic philosophy of education.

Canada was, in the continentalist mind, an American nation. As a result, pro-American writers devoted a great deal of energy to pointing out the cultural and spiritual similarities that existed between the two nations. Though this pattern was less pronounced in Quebec, where ethno-religious differences were more evident, continentalists throughout Canada usually cast a favourable gaze on American culture and religion. They were not generally alarmed by the secularism, mass culture, or utilitarian pedagogy that many intellectuals identified as being integral to the American experience. On the contrary, in many instances, these were interpreted as signs of social progress.

Conservative intellectuals viewed the rise of mass culture, secularism, and progressive education as a threat to traditional Canadian society. These expressions of modernity were often identified with the United States, especially in Quebec, where culture and religion were central to national distinctiveness. The United States came to symbolize the widespread irreligion that French Canadian nationalists believed invariably accompanied Protestantism and secular education. Moreover, as America's cultural influence grew after the Great War, its French Canadian detractors became more vocal. They were following a well-beaten path. A number of leading imperialists had strongly criticized American mass culture at the turn of the twentieth century, and their assessment of the state of religion and education in the republic was basically negative, as was much of their commentary related to race and gender in the United States, which are discussed in the next chapter.

4 Race and Gender in the United States

Ethnic and racial pluralism are not intrinsic to the modern ethos; neither is tolerance, for that matter. In fact, in the nineteenth century, modern science and scientism intensified rather than lessened racial exclusion. The modern ethos can indeed flourish in homogenous societies or within the confines of racial exclusivism. As a result, at the turn of the twentieth century, American segregationism was not inherently antimodern, and the nation's rising multiculturalism was not necessarily a sign of modernization. However, in the United States, ethnic pluralism accompanied the rise of industry and urbanization, and a number of Canadian intellectuals considered the increasingly cosmopolitan nature of America's cities to be an essentially modern phenomenon.

Many Canadian conservatives suffered from an essential dilemma: how could they criticize America's mistreatment of its racial minorities without actually appealing for racial equality? Most resolved this quandary with a healthy dose of paternalism. African Americans and First Nations were viewed as the 'white man's burden': they deserved protection, but not necessarily equality. For many anti-Americans at the turn of the twentieth century, both the republic's treatment of its Black population and African Americans themselves were viewed as blemishes on American society. Indeed, though segregation and racial violence were frequently denounced in conservative writing, Blacks were seldom treated as intellectual and moral equals.[1] For instance, in 1902, abbé Antonio Huot condemned 'the impassable *color line*, as they call it in this country, that prevents blacks and whites from travelling in the same railway carriage, or from eating at the same table in a restaurant, in the former slave states.' Yet, in the same breath, he noted that 'the

Black race is an inferior race, and it is utterly fanciful to believe that it would be possible for the Negro, given the same conditions as a white person, to achieve the intellectual level of the latter.'[2] Imperialists shared Huot's dilemma. 'If anything,' wrote Beckles Willson in *The New America: A Study of the Imperial Republic* (1903), 'my sympathies are with the people of the South, but no one can sympathize with intolerance, overbearance, and narrow-mindedness.' However, Willson, who had been the New York *Herald*'s correspondent in Georgia in 1889 and had subsequently founded a newspaper in Atlanta, was not in any way implying that Southern Blacks deserved to be placed on an equal footing with their white fellow citizens. To emphasize this point, he concluded his chapter on 'the Negro problem' by quoting Abraham Lincoln: 'There is a physical difference between the white and the black races which will for ever forbid the two races living together on terms of social and political equality. And inasmuch as they cannot so live, while they do remain together there must be the position of superior and inferior.'[3] Indeed, though conservatives around the turn of the twentieth century frequently denounced segregation, they rarely condemned the political disenfranchisement of Southern Blacks.

The overt racism found in many early anti-American texts would diminish during the interwar years. Yet ingrained prejudices continued to affect conservative assessments of America's racial problems. Harry Bernard, for instance, praised the advancement of African Americans in a 1942 article, but remained condescending towards Blacks: 'A good number are primitive, illiterate or little educated; they are persecuted by shameful or degenerate whites, and they acquire, in certain regions, what the Americans call an inferiority complex. They seem to be timid and evasive, obsequious, servile [and] their morals often reach quite a low level.'[4] In the early 1940s, Bernard travelled extensively in the American South while preparing a doctoral dissertation at the Université de Montréal on 'Le roman régionaliste aux États-Unis (1913–1940).' His doctoral research brought him into contact with the leading figures of literary regionalism in the United States.

When dealing with racial issues, the line between anti-American and continentalist sentiment often became blurred. The Canadian right, to be sure, has never held a monopoly on racial prejudice. What really distinguished conservative and liberal writing on race and ethnicity in the United States was the conclusions they drew from their assertions. Indeed, unlike their anti-American adversaries, continentalists did not see the republic's racial problems as a mark of inferiority. Goldwin Smith's writing on American race relations offers a good illustration of this perspective. In his youth, Smith had been an ardent abolitionist – the appearance of slavery in America, he later wrote, 'opened a new chapter of evil' – but as was the case with many of his contemporaries, Smith's abolitionism was not accompanied by any degree of racial tolerance. The African American, indeed, was a blot on American society, Smith argued in *The United States: An Outline of Political History* (1893): 'In the United States the white man has a burden, such perhaps as no other nation has been called upon to bear. It would be hard, at least, to find any instance of a problem so arduous as that of the two races in the South.'[5] Smith's commentary on race relations translated his contempt for Southern society – its aristocratism, he believed, was contrary to republican values – but did not dampen his zeal for continental union. Like Smith, many continentalists saw America's racial problems as an opportunity to criticize or isolate the South. There was something distinctly un-American about the South. It was a reactionary fragment in an otherwise progressive nation.

By the interwar years, racial prejudice was less prevalent in continentalist writing. Some observers, however, continued to insinuate that Blacks were a vaguely primitive people. Among them, William Arthur Deacon had perhaps the most unusual take on America's racial problem. Born in Pembroke, Ontario, Deacon received a law degree from the University of Manitoba and practised law in Winnipeg before becoming the literary editor of the *Winnipeg Free Press* and, later, of Toronto's *Saturday Night*. 'The black man was brought to the United States to labor gratis for the white,' he wrote in *My Vision of Canada* (1933), 'but it is a law of life that one may not labor for another without recompense; and that spiritual law's unescapable [*sic*] punishment looms over the United States.' According to Deacon, America's punishment would be miscegenation – 'the merging of white and black through marriage.' Indeed, he predicted, 'we are due to see within a few generations at most in the United States a new, hybrid race, distinct in color, and homogeneous in culture.' This, of course, could only be detrimental to the United States. 'The Negroes are nice people of considerable ability,' Deacon conceded, 'but they are undoubtedly primitive compared to Europeans.' As a result, 'there will exist south of us a people so much more child-like in their attitude towards life that ... the national distinctions will still be as wide as, say, that between a contemporary white

American and a Mexican.' Yet if Canada and the United States were bound to drift apart racially, the two nations would nonetheless conserve a strong bond: 'International friendship will not be jeopardized but enhanced as the fusion of races leaves us to deal with a government of brownish colored men, who will be instinctively courteous, who will respect us and like us.' Moreover, Deacon insisted, 'as the black blood interpenetrates with the white in the Republic, its people will turn increasingly to us, as the one confirmed friendly power, for intellectual and political guidance and leadership.'[6] The United States, it seemed, was destined to become Canada's white man's burden.

Intellectuals of all persuasions were often quick to point out that Blacks had historically received better treatment in Canada than in the United States and stories of the Underground Railroad abounded in Canadian commentary. Above all, noted William Arthur Deacon in 1933, 'Canada has always given the Negro rights of citizenship, fair treatment generally, and justice in the courts. We have no Negro problem to face.'[7] Canadian intellectuals took a similarly self-congratulatory tone when dealing with America's Native policy, which in Canada was widely condemned as genocidal. 'Canada has managed a large Indian population with little serious difficulty,' remarked George R. Parkin in his 1892 study of the British Empire. Meanwhile, 'her neighbours during the same years have been engaged in a series of wars of extermination, apparently the outcome for the most part of maladministration in Indian affairs.'[8] British and Canadian paternalism had worked where American aggressiveness had failed. And later improvements in U.S. policy following the Great War had little or no effect on Canadian commentary, because both continentalist and anti-American intellectuals tended to approach the problem from a historical standpoint.

In Quebec, it was frequently suggested that Canada's softer approach to Native issues was in keeping with the French and Catholic tradition. To this effect, A.D. DeCelles noted in 1896 that 'despite the difference that separates the White from the Redskin, the Frenchman befriended him, made him a companion on his excursions, and this relationship led him as far as marriage with indigenous women ... Such condescension won the aboriginal's heart, and the prestige of a French name was used by trappers to ensure safe passage ... while the Puritan, hateful to children of the forest, dared not venture alone outside his dwelling.'[9] This viewpoint was shared by some English Canadian writers. John Bartlet Brebner, for instance, told the Canadian Historical Association in 1931 that 'the French in North America had on the whole a very different record in their dealings with the Indians from that of the English. Unquestionably in this difference religion played a large part.'[10]

From the late nineteenth century to the 1920s, massive immigration fundamentally altered the American experience. The change was most evident in northern cities, where many immigrants found work in the country's expanding industries. Canadian intellectuals showed a great deal of interest in America's rising multiculturalism. From the 1890s to the 1920s, Canada also experienced large-scale immigration and, predictably, Canadian thinkers looked south for a glimpse of what the future might hold for their country. Reactions were mixed. In Quebec, multiculturalism was often hailed as a boon for the United States. Many intellectuals welcomed the dilution of the nation's Anglo-Saxon and Protestant stock and eagerly chronicled the rise of American Catholicism. More often than not, however, these writers held something of a hidden agenda. Indeed, the French Canadian perspective was largely conditioned by the important Franco-American population in the United States. Quebec had contributed to America's cultural mosaic in a significant way and assimilationist policies threatened Franco-American cultural survival. As a result, even intellectuals who were normally hostile to large-scale immigration in Canada regularly praised American multiculturalism in the abstract. For abbé Lionel Groulx, whose concern for Franco-American *survivance* was expressed in a number of conferences and articles, immigration and ethnic diversity were a source of wealth and strength for the United States:

> In a political state it is usually considered a point of weakness to have people of multiple races and origins. However, history will perhaps show that the strongest states and empires, and consequently the longest-lived ones, were precisely those with a composite structure, as if the balance of diverse minds made them more flexible in managing their destiny, and protected them better against thoughtless fury and catastrophic adventures. The most cultured Americans know full well that the demands of international life forbid any great population to deprive itself, at the present time, of one or the other of the great human cultures, especially French culture.[11]

American nativism was regularly denounced in Quebec, particularly in the 1920s, when a number of states enacted legislation to curb foreign-language instruction. These measures directly affected the large number of Franco-American children who attended French-language parochial schools. In a 1919 open letter to the governor of Connecticut, abbé Henri d'Arles denounced nativistic legislation that sought to hasten assimilation by suppressing foreign-language instruction in the state's schools: 'Is the linguistic unification that you advocate advantageous from any point of view? It would weaken the various races that proliferate here, and consequently weaken the national assets, if I can put it like that; attack the basic reserves on which our greatest destinies rest.'[12]

Imperialists had a very different take on the immigrant's impact on the United States. Cosmopolitanism, as they saw it, was yet another blemish on American society. By and large, imperialists argued that large-scale non-British immigration was rapidly weakening the nation's already diluted Anglo-Saxon stock. And the English-speaking race, they believed, was the last remaining pillar of civilization in the United States. 'America has revelled for nearly half a century in a carnival of miscegenation. Hers is the most mongrel race on earth,' warned Beckles Willson in 1903.[13] In an era when racial purity – in particular Anglo-Saxon purity – was generally viewed as a virtue, this was a serious indictment. But non-British immigrants were not only weakening the United States from a racial standpoint, they were also dangerous agents of political corruption, industrial strife, and revolution. The president of Victoria College, Nathanael Burwash (1839–1918), argued that immigrants were naturally drawn to revolutionism. Born in St Andrews, Lower Canada, Burwash was a Methodist minister and a moderate imperialist. In a 1901 address to the United Empire Loyalists' Association of Ontario, he warned that large-scale immigration would deepen the fundamental instability that characterized American society: 'The immigrant element is always the opposite of conservative … The millions who have crowded to the United States have been of the restless, progressive class, the class who are ever forgetting the old and seeking the new. They have intensified rather than moderated the revolutionary spirit of the founders of that nation.'[14] Inassimilable immigrants were destabilizing American society: they were responsible for spiralling criminality, they threatened the livelihood of native-born Americans, and they crowded into cities, thereby upsetting America's rural/urban balance.

English Canadian continentalists were not necessarily favourable to large-scale immigration. At the turn of the twentieth century, more than a few continentalists also saw the phenomenon as a serious threat to American civilization. Speaking before the Canadian Club of Montreal in 1912, Reverend James A. Macdonald insisted that Canada and the United States 'are at this moment endangered by the incoming of great masses of aliens, who are a danger to both our civilization and our ideals of government.'[15] Like many of their anti-American rivals, various continentalists considered the immigrant to be a likely source of crime and political corruption. These xenophobic continentalists, however, were usually quick to relativize the danger posed by non-British immigration to the United States. For his part, Goldwin Smith suggested in an 1891 address to the Young Men's Liberal Club of Toronto that America's alien population was, as far as burdens go, no worse than Quebec: 'The foreign element is unquestionably a source of danger and the Americans themselves, by their legislative restrictions which they are imposing on immigration, show that they are alive to the fact. But is the influence of the foreign element on the councils of the American commonwealth more alien in its character or more sinister than the influence of the French element on ours?'[16]

A number of later continentalists were far less hostile to large-scale immigration in the United States. William Bennett Munro, for instance, regularly refuted claims that immigrants were corrupting the American political system. Though he acknowledged that they were frequently involved in electoral fraud, Munro did not believe that 'the alien element is wholly or even mainly responsible for the fact that the government of great cities is America's "one conspicuous failure."' In fact, he argued that immigrants were systematically manipulated by corrupt native-born politicians who preyed on their naivety and inexperience. In *The Government of the United States*, published in 1919, Munro described how the immigrant's plight made him an easy target for crooked politicians:

All too soon after an immigrant passes the Statue of Liberty he is likely to be disillusioned. He came to America as to a land of promise, of political liberty, of social equality, and of economic fraternity. What he usually finds is hard labor at two dollars a day, a two-room home in a tenement, a foreman who bullies him at work, a walking-delegate who tells him to strike, and a politician who dictates how he shall vote. It is hard for the new arrival to discern the principles of liberty, equality, and fraternity in all this. Thus disillusioned and exploited the immigrant often becomes a malcontent and quite naturally becomes the prey of demagogues who use him solely for their own advantage.[17]

Being on the wrong side of Anglo-French conformity appears to have predisposed many immigrants from continental Europe to continentalism. This tendency was particularly pronounced in the work of German-born author Frederick Philip Grove, whose semi-autobiographical novel, *A Search for America*, published in 1927, explored the immigrant's plight and the promise of the New World. The novel was a commercial success and propelled the émigré writer to the forefront of Canada's interwar literary scene.

In Canadian commentary, some immigrant groups generated far more prose than did others. German-Americans, for instance, were the targets of a great deal of abuse during the two world wars. But in commentary published before the Second World War, Irish Catholics were undoubtedly the immigrant group that was most consistently slandered. Anti-Irish sentiment was widespread in Canada – more widespread, perhaps, than anti-American sentiment – and it coloured Canadian writing on the United States. Hostility to Irish-Americans was strongest among imperialists before the Great War, but it was present in the writing of a variety of intellectuals throughout the period under study.

Time and again, English Canadian intellectuals linked Irish immigration to crime and political corruption in the United States. Indeed, the corrupt Irish-American politician became a bit of a cliché in Canadian prose. For instance, one of Robert Barr's more successful novels, *The Victors* (1901), followed the rise of an illiterate Irish-American peddler, Patrick Maguire, from the gutter to Tammany Hall. Barr's character was a loose collection of anti-Irish stereotypes: Maguire drank, fought, stole, cursed, and cheated; he practised and celebrated political corruption. Barr's novel was not anti-American per se. It did imply, however, that Irish Catholics were a corrupting influence in U.S. politics. Similarly, in 1892, George R. Parkin suggested that Irish-American corruption was a serious impediment to American democracy: 'I lately heard a representative American writer and thinker in England say that in his judgement the Irish question was becoming a more disturbing factor in American politics and a more difficult one to deal with, than it has been for Great Britain ... We know that a split in Tammany may practically decide a Presidential election, and a Canadian may fairly think that any problem of race or creed with which he has to deal is not more perplexing.'[18]

Anti-Irish sentiment was, of course, tied to anti-Catholic prejudice. Roman Catholicism, many Protestants believed, invariably led to poverty, ignorance, and a disregard for political freedom. At the turn of the century, few Canadian intellectuals were more hostile to the Irish and to the Roman Catholic Church than Goldwin Smith. Though a fervent anti-imperialist, Smith had long opposed home rule for the Irish, whom he considered unfit to assume the burden of political autonomy. In his 1893 monograph on American history, Smith heaped scorn on Irish immigration: 'These people of a hapless land and a sad history, ignorant, superstitious, priest-ridden, nurtured in squalid poverty, untrained in constitutional government, trained only in conspiracy and insurrection, were a useful addition to the labour of their adopted country; of its politics they could only be the bane.' 'Clannish still in their instincts,' he continued, 'herding clannishly together in the great cities and blindly following leaders whom they accepted as chiefs, and in choosing whom they were led more by blatant energy than by merit, they were soon trained to the pursuit of political spoils and filled elections with turbulence, fraud, and corruption.'[19]

Imperialists regularly denounced the impact of Irish-American voters on the course of Anglo-American relations. Irish Catholics, it was argued, were propagating anti-British sentiment in America's body politic: Fenian terrorists had tried to foment an Anglo-American war in the nineteenth century, and later on, many Irish-American leaders had opposed America's entry into the First World War. A number of continentalists also deplored the Irish-American lobby's impact on both Anglo-American and Canadian-American relations. In 1942, John Mac-Cormac, though of Irish Catholic extraction himself, argued that Irish-American chauvinism was impeding wartime cooperation: 'The Irish ... brought with them, in their half-starved bodies, souls burning with hatred of England and thus imported into Anglo-American relations a note of discord that has sounded until this day.'[20] Irish immigrants were also occasionally blamed for American isolationism, a policy that upset a number of interwar continentalists.

In Quebec, anti-Irish sentiment was also widespread among intellectuals. Indeed, though many French Canadian writers praised American multiculturalism in the abstract, they sometimes heaped scorn on selected immigrant groups, and the Irish were their principal target. Elite hostility frequently revolved around ethnic tensions in the Roman Catholic Church. Many French Canadian intellectuals accused the Irish-American episcopate of dominating the American Church and of trying to assimilate Franco-Americans. Under the editorial direction of J.L.K. Laflamme (1872–1944), *La Revue franco-américaine* regularly disparaged Irish-Americans. 'Since its arrival in the United States,' Laflamme wrote in 1908, 'the Irish element ... has above all been an element of opposition ... today it is the soul of the Democratic party, which has given birth to the four or five radical parties that exist in the Republic.' The Irish were, he believed, a violent and disruptive group: 'The abundance of liberty that they find when they arrive in America causes them to tyrannize those who surround them and who don't have the advantage of being the most numerous group.' And this tyranny, Laflamme maintained, was aimed squarely at Franco-Americans and at other Catholic immigrants. Irish-American bishops 'want to prevent Catholics from different countries from forming compact national groups in America: German, Italian, Polish, Czech, Hungarian, French-Canadian. The bishops, following the example of Monsignor Ireland, want to Americanize them, with the result that the Church has become an instrument of Americanization.'[21] Born in Sainte-Marguerite, Quebec, Laflamme founded the *Revue franco-américaine* in 1908. Published in Quebec City, where Laflamme also worked as the editor-in-chief of *L'Action sociale catholique*, the review focused on issues related to Franco-American *survivance*. Laflamme had previously worked as the editor of *L'Indépendant* of Fall River, Massachusetts. His father-in-law, Jean-Baptiste Rouilliard, was a prominent figure in Franco-American journalism.

In Canada, a definite correlation existed between anti-Semitism and anti-Americanism. Jews were often portrayed as a subversive element in American industry, and in the perverse logic of the anti-Semite, they could embody the contradictory stereotypes of revolutionary subversion and capitalist greed. Before the Second World War, these stereotypes were widespread in Canada and, like all forms of prejudice, they found their way into the nation's literature. In 1901, for instance, James Algie, who practised medicine in Toronto, published *Bergen Worth*, an anti-American novel filled with violent Irishmen and unscrupulous Jews. Set during Chicago's great Pullman Strike of 1894, the book plays on two conventional anti-Semitic stereotypes: Jews are accused both of spreading radicalism and of debasing business practices. The story's Jewish character, 'the famous miser and money-lender' Isaac Dorenwein, is involved in a plot to extend the strike in order to profit from the purchase of depreciated Pullman stock.[22] Published under the pseudonym of Wallace Lloyd, Algie's novel was serialized in 1905–06 by *Canada First*, the organ of the ultra-protectionist Canadian Preference League.

In Quebec, anti-Americanism and anti-Semitism intersected along similar lines. For instance, Harry Bernard's 1924 critique of American cinema quickly degenerated into on attack on Jews. In *L'Action française*, he argued that the American movie industry was controlled by Jews – 'the films that we watch are, with very few exceptions, of American origin, or, more precisely, Jewish-American origin' – and that Jewish movie moguls were promoting immorality and subversion:

> In addition to the goal of dechristianisation that is attributed to them, the main aim of the Jews is to make money and lay their hands on the world's finances. In taking over the cinema, they dream not so much of making art as of carrying off wealth. To reach their ends, nothing is too trivial or too base; they will exploit passion in any shape and flatter instincts. They have no concern for moral or order, and the marvellous medium of education that is the cinema will become in their hands, thanks to their thirst for gold and their passion for domination, a tool of depravity, a school of corruption and revolution. If they can see a way to attract crowds and fill the till, they will propagate anti-social ideas, becoming the champions of divorce or free love, and even Malthusian practices on occasion. Natural enemies of order, they benevolently support the most destructive socialism. For them, nothing matters except the takings.[23]

The continentalist tradition was hardly devoid of anti-Semitic sentiment – Goldwin Smith was a notorious anti-Semite – but Jews usually received a fairer treatment in continentalist writing than in anti-American prose. Continentalist sentiment appears to have been strong among Canada's Jewish intellectuals, and positive depictions of American Jews could be found in continentalist literature. Merrill Denison, for instance, authored a radio play denouncing anti-Semitism as un-American. *An American Father Talks to His Son* was broadcast by CBS in mid-1939. Furthermore, one of the first works of fiction to deal with the Holocaust was written by a Canadian. In *Solomon Levi* (1935), Claudius Gregory (1889–1944) chronicled the life of an American Jew and his terrifying internment in a Nazi concentration camp. The novel is a powerful indictment of anti-Semitism and Nazism. Born in England, Gregory arrived in Canada at the age of seventeen. He spent most of his career working in journalism and advertising, first in Toronto, then in Hamilton, Ontario. According to Desmond Pacey, Gregory was one of the few Canadian novelists of his generation to seriously deal with the social problems of the 1930s.[24]

Unlike ethnic pluralism, the transformation of gender relations is integral to the modern ethos. Modernity is ultimately corrosive to traditional notions of femininity and masculinity. The industrial revolution, for instance, brought an increasing number of women into the paid labour force and urbanization forever altered the North American family. The early twentieth century, moreover, saw most Canadian and American women receive the vote. Whether gender relations in the United States before the First World War were marked by a greater degree of equality than in Canada is open to debate, but many Canadian intellectuals believed that they were.

Issues related to gender arose somewhat less frequently in Canadian writing on the United States than issues tied to race and ethnicity. Nevertheless, Canadian intellectuals had much to say about gender relations in the United States. Sara Jeannette Duncan was among the most prominent Canadian writers to look upon American gender relations with approval. Her novels often portrayed the United States as a society where women were freer than in Britain. In Duncan's most popular work of fiction, *An American Girl in London*, published in 1891, the American heroine and narrator, Mamie Wick, explains her situation in the novel's first sentence: 'I am an American girl. Therefore, perhaps, you will not be surprised at anything further I may have to say for myself. I have observed, since I came to England, that this statement, made by a third person in connection with any question of my conduct, is always broadly explanatory.'[25] In Duncan's novels, American women are plucky and uninhibited – Mamie Wick basically goes about scandalizing upper-class Londoners for three hundred pages – and are the product of a freer and less conventional society. Born in Brantford, Canada West, Duncan was educated at the Toronto Normal School, but soon abandoned teaching for journalism. She wrote for the Washington *Post*, the Toronto *Globe*, the Montreal *Star*, and the *Week*. In September 1888 she set off on a round-the-world tour and met her future husband, museum curator and journalist Everard Cotes, in Calcutta. She married him in December 1890 and spent most of the next three decades in India. In many ways, Duncan's continentalism was an expression of her aversion to imperialism, which she explored in a number of her novels, including her most brilliant work of fiction, *The Imperialist*, published in 1904.

In continentalist writing, the discussion of gender in the United States was frequently centred on political issues. Indeed, by the outbreak of the First World War, a handful of American states had granted women the right to vote, and Canadian intellectuals closely followed this experiment. William Bennett Munro, for instance, predicted that women's suffrage would not have a detrimental effect on U.S. politics and government. Contrary to popular wisdom, he noted in 1919, women's voting behaviour was not significantly different from that of men: 'The granting of voting rights to women in a dozen states of the Union has not demoralized domestic life in any of them, nor, on the other hand, has it had noticeably effective results in the way of securing these states a priority over the others in the humanitarianism of their laws. The chief merit of woman suffrage in these communities has been that of rendering content a large group of citizens without in any perceptible measure impairing the economic, social, or political order.'[26]

Later, Anne Anderson Perry, a vocal advocate of women's rights who began her career in journalism at the *Western Woman's Weekly*, expressed a great deal of satisfaction at the number of women appointed to key positions by President Franklin D. Roosevelt. 'In Canada,' she wrote in a 1933 article published in *Canadian Comment*, 'where one lone woman has had to carry the banners of her sex in the House of Commons and one in the Senate, where almost none of the high offices of State or even the ordinary political or partisan plums have come to women, save in the most meagre measure, the situation now revealed across the border gives to furious thinking as well as to cool reflection.'[27] In Perry's mind, Canadian women clearly had some catching up to do. It would be a mistake, however, to assume that the continentalist ethos was united in its support for women's rights. Many continentalists had little to say about gender relations in the United States, and some early pro-American writers would undoubtedly have agreed with their anti-American opponents when they asserted that gender relations were off balance south of the border.

Anti-American rhetoric contained significant gendered messages, and there existed a definite correlation between anti-Americanism and antifeminism in Canada. Both of these negative faiths were usually the expression of a deeper conservative ethos. Many Canadian conservatives were concerned by what they saw as rising gender equality in the United States, which they viewed as an affront to traditional notions of the complementarity of the sexes. American women were abandoning their established role as wives and mothers; they were invading the public sphere and, worse still, were given to promiscuity. The implication was clear: modernity was corrosive to traditional gender relations. To Andrew Macphail, whose idealization of traditional gender roles appears to have intensified after the untimely loss of his wife Georgina in 1902, the 'American woman' was insubordinate, sterile, vain, and idle.

Her rebelliousness, morevover, was quintessentially American: 'The United States began with an act of lawlessness and their conduct ever since has been marked by that spirit. Now this spirit of lawlessness has seized upon the women. It would be too large a matter to demonstrate how it has broken up the family life and disorganized the social relation, how it has instigated rebellion against the marriage tie and defeated the intent of all created beings that they should be fruitful and multiply.'[28]

Negative commentary on gender relations in the United States was most common in French Canadian writing. The evolution of anti-American sentiment contributed to this trend. Indeed, French Canadian nationalists were most critical of the United States during the interwar years, which to some extent can be viewed as a period of sexual revolution in America. More significantly, however, Quebec's conservatives placed a great deal of importance on the traditional role of women in *la survivance*, and perceived American attitudes towards gender equality were viewed as a threat to the nation. On occasion, the issue would surface in French Canadian literature. In his best-selling regionalist novel, *La campagne canadienne*, published in 1925, Jesuit Adélard Dugré (1881–1970) contrasted gender relations in the United States and Canada and warned his readers against emigration and mixed marriages. During a trip to rural Quebec, the novel's protagonist, Franco-American physician François Barré, is awakened to the harsh reality of his family's degeneracy:

> Before these men who were clearly masters of their household, who had such a clear and firm idea of what a family should be, the American doctor felt humiliated by the anarchy that reigned in his home. His wife really had too much control. If she had a dominant voice when it came to things in her domain, fine. If she alone took charge of furnishing the house, of hiring and firing servants, even if she went as far as deciding how to spend their free evenings, the destination and itinerary of their holidays, that was fine too; but taking charge of the direction of her husband's career, choosing his clients, and dictating his source of income – that was too much. In that area it was he, François, who should be the supreme judge and sovereign master. It was time Fanny learned and accepted that. There are cases of absolute necessity where a wife must obey and keep silent, if she cannot approve and be delighted.[29]

In Dugré's novel, François Barré's son is out of control and his wife is disobedient, domineering, irreligious, and immodest. The Barrés were, it seemed, a typical American family. Re-issued numerous times, including once in comic book form, *La campagne canadienne* was serialized by several Quebec newspapers.

French Canadian novelists often portrayed American women as alluring temptresses given to *l'amour libre*. Ringuet (Philippe Panneton, 1895–1960), for instance, filled his landmark 1938 novel, *30 arpents*, with sensuous and immoral American women. But the attractiveness of American women masked their inner torment. Indeed, as Ernestine Pineault-Léveillé (1898–1980) noted in 1936, American women led an empty, unfulfilling life: 'The humiliated American woman, lowered by divorce, the practice of trying to prevent conception, and birth control, has no children. She keeps doggies, leaving them everything when she dies: fortune, palace and cemetery.'[30] Born in Saint-Denis-sur-Richelieu, Quebec, Pineault-Léveillé was one of Canada's first women psychiatrists. She specialized in the treatment of children and authored two children's books, *Dollard. L'épopée de 1660 racontée aux enfants*, published in 1921, and *Comment ils ont grandi*, published in 1922. Both these volumes dealt with nationalist themes and were published by the militant Bibliothèque de l'Action française. Pineault-Léveillé was active in Quebec's interwar nationalist circles and was a friend and admirer of abbé Lionel Groulx.

As went the American woman, so too went the American family. Canadian conservatives believed that society's basic unit, the family, was under assault in the United States. Modern notions of equality, sexuality, and matrimony were dissolving the American family, and American society itself, it was predicted, would implode when its basic unit vanished. The disintegration of the family unit in the United States was attributed to a number of causes. According to abbé Georges-Marie Bilodeau, who taught at Quebec's only classical college devoted to adult education, the Séminaire des vocations tardives de Saint-Victor-de-Beauce, the American family was threatened by birth control, a practice which shocked many nationalists and was usually attributed to religious indifference in the United States. In America, Bilodeau argued in a 1926 monograph denouncing French Canadian emigration, 'Malthusianism, not to mention onanism, which in practice is the same thing, is the scourge of marriage, not only between Protestants and non-believers, but also between Christians.'[31] For the Roman Catholic clergy, the sorry state of the American family was yet another argument against emigration.

At its core, noted many nationalists, the American family was weakened by irreligion. 'The thing that excites admiration is the material progress of our neighbour,' wrote Hermas Bastien in 1933. 'The thing that horrifies,' he continued, 'is the neo-paganism of the great mass of Americans. Religious ideas, spiritualist doctrines, family solidity, these bases of Christian nations are, in America, undermined by sterilizing divorce, utilitarian pragmatism, and mystical pantheism.'[32] Denouncing the divorce rate in the United States was an anti-American staple. In 1893, John Castell Hopkins, a devout Anglican, deplored the 'looseness of the marriage-tie in the great Republic.' 'Between 1867 and 1886,' he noted in an American magazine, 'two hundred thousand divorces were granted in the United States, as compared with one hundred and sixteen given in Canada. The trouble, of course, is caused largely by a difference in the laws of the various States, which permit the anomalous and disgraceful condition of a man or a woman's being married in one state and single in another.'[33] For Hopkins, who was born of English parents in Dyersville, Iowa, and immigrated to Canada as a child, discussing the state of the American family was an opportunity both to denounce constitutional decentralization and to idealize Canadian society.

Continentalists usually put the issue of divorce into perspective. The American family was not disintegrating, they argued, and the vast majority of the states had perfectly acceptable divorce legislation. Reacting to incessant imperialist criticism of American divorce rates, Goldwin Smith acknowledged in 1891 that some states suffered from lax divorce legislation, but refused to see this as a specifically American problem or an impediment to continental integration. 'The increasing frequency of divorce,' he wrote, 'like the unsettlement of the relations between the sexes generally, is the malady of all countries; though at present in different degrees.' Besides, Smith continued, 'the tendency of American legislatures of late, I believe, has been against increased facility of divorce. At any rate we may maintain friendly relations and trade with our neighbours without adopting their divorce laws, or the theories which some of them may have embraced about the character and the proper functions of woman.'[34] In fact, Smith believed that Canada, not the United States, possessed the real divorce problem. 'The French Catholics will not allow the Dominion to have a regular Divorce Court,' he complained in *Canada and the Canadian Question.*[35]

Most continentalists also refused to see the American family as essentially dysfunctional. In *Those Delightful Americans* (1902), a novel that reversed the popular premise of *An American Girl in London*, Sara Jean-nette Duncan again contrasted gender and family relations in America and Britain. After arriving in the United States, the novel's English nar-rator and heroine, Carrie Kemball, notes approvingly that the family, as an institution, is more egalitarian and less stifling in America: 'There never has been anything feudal in the relations of American young people to their elders – they begin early to breathe, on the contrary, the equal privilege of the republic. No doubt there is some parental inquiry; but a certain calm acceptance is the usual thing.' Indeed, she continued, 'the yoke of family connection sits more lightly there than in England; the fact that a person who happens to be your second cousin married another person is no reason why you should call upon her, es-pecially if you belong to different denominations. You take no responsi-bility and she makes no claim; it must be less cramping, certainly.'[36] As far as Duncan was concerned, the family unit in the United States was essentially sound. It was less oppressive than in Britain and, as a result, it produced more autonomous women.

In the late nineteenth and early twentieth centuries, gender relations and the state of the family were significant issues in Canadian thought and writing. This ensured that these subjects would invariably find their way into commentary on American life. Conservatives believed that gender and family relations in the United States were unstable and, to illustrate their point, they often cited endless rows of divorce statis-tics. These figures served both to highlight Canadian-American differ-entialism and to emphasize modernity's caustic effect on marriage and gender relations.

Issues related to immigration and race relations in the United States also generated a fair amount of conservative commentary. America's treatment of its Black and Aboriginal population was often viewed as a repudiation of traditional notions of paternalism. However, if segrega-tion was criticized, racial equality was also frowned upon. A similar contradiction could be found in *nationaliste* writing on immigration, where American multiculturalism was often praised in the abstract while selected immigrant groups were simultaneously denigrated. Im-perialist writing was perhaps more coherent on this issue: large-scale non-British immigration was usually presented as a blot on American society.

Continentalist and anti-American rhetoric periodically intersected when it came to race and gender and also, as we shall see in the next chapter, on issues related to crime and industry in the United States. This tendency was most pronounced before the Great War, when the continentalist ethos was dominated by classical liberals like Goldwin Smith. However, even in the 1890s, conservative and liberal writing on the United States was usually distinguished by the conclusions drawn from the assertions made. Unlike their anti-American adversaries, continentalists did not generally see the republic's problems as a mark of inferiority, nor did they cause them to seriously reconsider their support for continental integration.

5 The Perils of Prosperity and the Search for Order

Industrialization and urbanization are integral to the modern ethos, and in the early 1900s, many Canadian intellectuals believed that industrial modernity had reached its paroxysm in the United States. Indeed, since the late nineteenth century, America had been increasingly identified with a specific economic system: industrial capitalism. Canadian conservatives, like their European counterparts, were very much in favour of free enterprise. Nevertheless, they often denounced massive urbanization, industrial gigantism, and monopolistic capitalism as threats to traditional modes of production and social organization. The right tended to prefer a system where industry was more decentralized, both in terms of its ownership and of its location.

American industry generated a great deal of commentary in Quebec, where rurality was perhaps more important to the conservative ethos. As French Canadian nationalists saw it, the United States was an industrial civilization whose capital investment was hastening the pace of Quebec's industrialization. For the *nationaliste*, the countryside was not only a reservoir of moral virtue, it was also a bastion of *survivance*. Indeed, with large-scale industry dominated by outsiders, *la terre* appeared to offer a viable alternative to urban exploitation and assimilation. In both Quebec and France, conservative anxiety regarding mass production peaked during the 1930s. The Great Depression confirmed nationalist apprehensions regarding massive industrialization and laissez-faire capitalism. Paul-Henri Guimont (b. 1906), for instance, blamed the Great Depression on American industrial gigantism. A rising star at Montreal's hotbed of Catholic economic thought, the École des Hautes Études commerciales, Guimont argued in 1935 that the United States had broken the natural balance between agriculture and industry.

Indeed, an overreliance on massive and heavily standardized industrial production had proved its undoing: 'In the formation of her economy, America held extravagant and insatiable ambitions on the new and crude system of industrial standardization. She despised the creative and conservative genuis of old Europe. Originality in design was unknown to her. She gave herself an excessive industrial superstructure, which corresponded to a too-small population.'[1] Stability, French Canadian nationalists believed, was the preserve of societies with a solid rural and agricultural base. Large-scale industry was inherently unsteady; it was driven by speculation and governed by the harsh laws of supply and demand in a way that agriculture was not.

Concerns surrounding industrialism were not confined to *nationaliste* discourse. Some imperialists were also troubled by the scope of industry in the United States, though generally to a lesser extent. Andrew Macphail, for instance, suggested that industrialization, in particular the mass production of processed food, was disintegrating the American family 'by destroying the multifarious occupation of every member of it.' 'In America,' he wrote in 1910, 'industrial change has been remarkably rapid, and there are women living in idleness to-day, who in their youth took the sheaf from the field and had the evening meal prepared from it before the night fell.' Accustomed to indolence, American women were refusing to shoulder the burdens of motherhood; they were making a sham of the institution of marriage. 'The country has grown rich,' Macphail concluded, 'but the family is destroyed.'[2]

Massive industrialization was seen as something of a ticking time bomb by many conservative intellectuals. Indeed, with industry came the proletariat, a dangerous class of propertyless malcontents who, many conservatives feared, would eventually be seduced by revolutionary agitators. These subversive forces were at work in the United States. Throughout the late nineteenth and early twentieth centuries, anti-American observers relentlessly chronicled industrial disturbances and the rise of radical unionism in the United States. Industrial strife clearly struck fear in the conservative heart. James Algie, for instance, began his 1901 novel, *Bergen Worth*, with a near-apocalyptic paragraph: 'The great railway strike of 1894 was going on at Chicago; the Pullman car riots were at their height. Apostles of discontent had aroused the masses. Loud-voiced agitators had unchained the tiger of irresponsibility and goaded to madness the wolf of want. The flag of anarchy was unfurled and "down with everything that's up" became the watchword of the hour.'[3] The founding president of the United Empire Loyalists'

Association of Ontario, George Sterling Ryerson, was equally appalled by industrial strife in the United States. Born into a prominent Toronto family – his uncle, Egerton Ryerson, was instrumental in establishing Ontario's school system – G.S. Ryerson was a medical doctor and major-general in the Canadian Militia. Like many Loyalist mythmakers, he linked American labour unrest with the nation's original sin: the revolution. Class conflict, Ryerson argued in *The After-Math of a Revolution*, published in 1896, was the result of the American Revolution's legacy of violence and disorder: 'A painful feature of the strikes and lockouts is the resort to force, attended in many instances by serious loss of life and destruction of property. But did not the Revolution teach Americans that if your neighbor does not agree with you, you may shoot him, confiscate his property, and injure him to the utmost of your ability?'[4]

The condemnation of American industrial agitation was not confined to conservative writing. A number of Canadian liberals at the turn of the twentieth century were equally appalled by labour unrest in the United States. Intellectuals like Goldwin Smith or A.D. DeCelles shared many conservative concerns regarding the revolutionary threat posed by the proletariat. 'Nowhere,' DeCelles wrote in 1896, 'have conflicts between bosses and workers been more bitter, more dangerous than in the United States; nowhere have strikes been more menacing to public order than in Pittsburg [*sic*], Baltimore and Chicago. They were, in their limited scope, like the early engagements of a social war.' Unlike Quebec's nationalists, however, DeCelles did not see industrialization itself as the root cause of labour unrest. 'Several causes have provoked anti-capitalist struggle, he noted in *Les États-Unis. Origine, institutions, développement*, 'the influence of Europe consumed by socialism, an influence caused by the propaganda of the numerous down-and-outs that immigration drags with it and who, by their revolutionary discourse, stir up discord and envenom conflict; the rapid concentration into a few hands of enormous fortunes that are more or less reputable, and consequently of a nature to exasperate the honest worker.'[5]

For most continentalists, resisting industrialization was seen as both pointless and counterproductive. Liberals and socialists before the Second World War understood the rise of modern industry, in America or elsewhere, to be both inevitable and intrinsically progressive. Conversely, they believed that societies that rejected industrialization were courting disaster. To this effect, the general manager of the Banque canadienne nationale, Beaudry Leman, warned Montreal's Cercle universitaire in 1928 that Quebec had little choice but to adapt itself to American *machinisme*:

> Must we adapt to the American situation? It seems to me that our reply must be: Yes, in terms of economics. Much as one might regret or even deplore the increasingly marked tendency towards standardization, and towards the disappearance of small specialized industry and individual work, which is both creative and innovative at the same time, this is understandable, but might I be permitted to suggest that this type of industrial activity is not the best adapted to our condition and needs? Moreover, in this regard, Europe is becoming rapidly Americanized and does not live solely from small industry. Europe has, just like America, some very big industries, and relatively speaking it uses methods that ensure the best return. Everyone is inclined, according to their sympathies, to generalize praise or blame. Not everything about standardization, which has produced some extraordinary results, is condemnable.

Trained as a civil engineer, Leman was a leading figure in Quebec business circles. Mass production, he believed, was not a threat to French Canadian *survivance*: 'I cannot conceive that our Latin culture and our humanism are seriously threatened by the fact that we will have at our disposal fewer shapes of bottles, fewer types of car wheels, and fewer types of tires.'[6] On the whole, though Leman was hardly a revolutionary figure, his ideas challenged many of the ruralist platitudes that were intrinsic to interwar French Canadian nationalism.

Ruralism was fairly common in prewar Canadian thought. To many conservatives, the United States was an essentially urban civilization. As Hermas Bastien noted in 1929, America evoked 'dizzying cities, polluted quays, provocative skyscrapers, tentacular factories, and burlesque vaudevilles.'[7] U.S. cities, in particular New York and Chicago, offended ruralist sensibilities. They were soulless cosmopolitan agglomerations where crime, corruption, and disease were rampant. Ruralism, however, was not exclusive to the conservative ethos. Many nineteenth-century liberals, including Erastus Wiman, were ruralists in the Jeffersonian tradition. 'One thing seems quite evident,' Wiman wrote in *Chances of Success*, a rambling 1893 collection of essays advocating commercial union and rugged individualism, 'that the growth of [American] cities, which in the last decade was sixty percent, as compared with the growth of the farms, which was but fifteen percent, will have to be reversed if any permanent prosperity is to exist in this country.' Born in Churchville, Upper Canada, Wiman entered the world of journalism at the age of sixteen when his cousin, William McDougall, the managing editor of the *North American*, hired him as a printer's apprentice. When the *North American* amalgamated with the Toronto *Globe* in 1855, Wiman became the paper's commercial editor. He joined the staff of R.G. Dunn and Co.'s mercantile agency in 1860 and would later become the New York firm's general manager. Like Thomas Jefferson, Wiman saw the independent farmer as the backbone of American freedom, prosperity, and stability. Massive urbanization, he surmised, threatened American society: 'In no country has the "hope of property" so stimulated the aims of humanity as in America, and that hope, encouraged and rewarded, is a powerful element underlying the prosperity of the nation. Diminish that hope, lessen it as in crowded cities, where property to the poor is an impossibility, and citizenship declines, manhood deteriorates and civilization sinks back.'[8]

Most twentieth-century continentalists did not share Wiman's misgivings regarding urbanization. They generally viewed the phenomenon as both inevitable and desirable. The American city was a source of great inspiration to poet and novelist Robert Choquette. Born in Manchester, New Hampshire, and educated at Montreal's Loyola College, Choquette saw great promise in New York City's cosmopolitan energy. His 1931 epic poem *Metropolitan Museum* introduced the theme of urbanism into French Canadian poetry.[9] For his part, the director of Harvard's Bureau of Municipal Research, William Bennett Munro, consistently defended the American city. Unlike many of his conservative contemporaries, he often stressed the American city's vitality and its ability to reform. 'The modern metropolis,' he wrote in 1912, 'is neither an Athens nor a Gomorrah; it is both rolled into one. In the rural community, which has the features of neither one nor the other, the problem of maintaining a reasonable standard of ideals and achievements is easier than in the city, where these things must be determined by the might of the stronger among its modern Helenes and Philistines.'[10]

The late nineteenth century saw the rise of mammoth corporations and an unprecedented concentration of wealth in the United States. Distrust of American capitalism was widespread among Canadian intellectuals and generally centred on the dangers of concentrated wealth. The concentration of wealth, conservatives believed, was destroying traditional notions of deference and status. For conservatives, the rise of the 'robber baron' seemed to signal a new era of unbridled materialism. The obscene concentration of wealth was, many conservatives believed, engendering a status revolution in America. The public stature of the 'robber baron' was growing and, as a result, spiritual and intellectual endeavours were becoming increasingly discounted. Material success, in turn, was being held up as the pinnacle of achievement. For many elites whose power and prestige rested on premodern notions of defer- ence and spiritualism – aside from Goldwin Smith and Vincent Massey, few of the intellectuals whose work is examined in this study would have been considered wealthy – the rise of American plutocracy fore- shadowed harmful social change for Canada.

Canadian intellectuals were aware that the United States was under- going – indeed exporting – a status revolution, and conservative critics were appalled by its implications. One of Quebec's leading conserva- tive women writers, Ernestine Pineault-Léveillé, insisted that the status revolution was marginalizing women of talent and standing and neu- tralizing their influence over society. In the United States, she warned the readers of the *Revue dominicaine* in 1936, 'the woman of the world is no longer the woman of higher social standing, with a careful edu- cation and extensively cultured. Self-interest and money have levelled everything, with several degrees of equality according to the capacity for receiving and adapting to one another. Often someone is little more than a rich woman, or merely an anonymous, colourless member, wi- thout influence in society.'[11]

The status revolution had perhaps no greater Canadian critic than Stephen Leacock. He regularly condemned 'the distinct bias of our whole American life towards commercialism.' In the United States, Leacock noted in a 1909 article published in the *University Magazine*, everything 'is "run" on business lines from a primary election to a prayer meeting. Thus business, and the business code, and business principles become everything. Smartness is the quality most desired, pecuniary success the goal to be achieved. Hence all less tangible and proveable [*sic*] forms of human merit, and less tangible aspirations of the human mind are rudely shouldered aside by business ability and commercial success.'[12]

A visceral aversion to plutocracy made Quebec's conservatives vocal critics of laissez-faire. Jules-Paul Tardivel, for instance, railed against the rise of monopoly capitalism in 1900: 'The railway companies, the powerful and monopolistic syndicates, the trusts of every sort, the com- bines – institutions that did not exist in the first days of the Republic – today exercise an influence that is as great as it is harmful on legislation, on the management of public affairs, on the national destiny.'[13] This critique would only intensify with time. Haunted by the spectre of revolution, most interwar *nationalistes* saw capitalism's inevitable by-products – poverty and exploitation – as the building blocks of revolutionism.

Laissez-faire capitalism and the concentration of wealth in the United States also worried a number of continentalists. Their critique, however, was somewhat different from that which emanated from conservative writing. Liberals and socialists were not overly concerned by the status revolution. They were nonetheless worried by the rise of plutocracy and its impact on American democracy. 'Nowhere has plutocracy been so unbridled or so ruthless as in the United States,' wrote O.D. Skelton in 1912. 'The trust millionaire has made the demagogue inevitable, and a spirit has been created in which all wealth, honest or dishonest, is under deep suspicion.'[14] Liberals like Skelton were very much in favour of free enterprise, but their faith in laissez-faire did have its limits, and they could not countenance plutocracy. Edmond de Nevers also worried about the growth of trusts and the concentration of wealth in America. Yet, like Tocqueville, de Nevers had great faith in America's inherent stability and resilience. As a result, he believed that the nation would eventually reform its economic system. 'I believe that the United States is destined to resolve the great social problems, because it is there that the struggle between capital and labour will take place first, at its height,' de Nevers wrote in 1904. 'The worker is not, in our neighbouring republic, the enslaved, pressurized, embittered man of the great European centres; he is a free man, aware of his dignity and used to constitutional processes. When the capitalist regime has given everything it can give, it will come to an agreement with the worker element. And I sense that the reform that will be inaugurated will be an inspired deed that the rest of the world will imitate.'[15]

Continentalists did not necessarily assume that laissez-faire capitalism was an affliction particular to the United States or that industrialism was a threat to American society. Capitalism, after all, was international in its scope, and the future of Western society, they believed, lay in industrial development. Besides, by the 1930s, the United States had taken concrete steps to correct the most flagrant abuses of laissez-faire industrialism. The New Deal had apparently dethroned laissez-faire and many progressive Canadians looked to the United States for economic guidance. America, they believed, had cleaned up its act while Canada, meanwhile, continued to cling to laissez-faire orthodoxy, and was consequently beset by irresponsible monopolies. In a 1941 pamphlet devoted to Canadian-American relations, F.R. Scott noted that Canada lagged behind the United States when it came to curbing the power of trusts and combines:

> In the sphere of economics, both countries are seen to have passed through the same stages of capitalist growth and change. The period of small-scale industry is over and politics and economics are becoming more and more interrelated. Power production, the large industrial unit, concentration of ownership and control are to be found in marked degree on both sides of the border. In some respects the process has proceeded further in Canada, where the smaller size of the economy and a less active public opposition to trusts and combines have resulted in an even more centralized economic grouping.[16]

Born in Quebec City, Scott studied at Bishop's College, in Lennoxville, Quebec, before attending Magdalen College, Oxford, as a Rhodes Scholar. He returned to Canada in 1923 and taught briefly at Montreal's Lower Canada College before enrolling in McGill University's Faculty of Law. Influenced by English-born Professor H.A. Smith, Scott took a keen interest in constitutional law. It was during this time that he founded the *McGill Fortnightly Review* with fellow poet and literary critic A.J.M. Smith and began to introduce his poetry to a wider audience. After graduating from McGill, Scott practised law in Montreal for a time and helped found the *Canadian Mercury*, the *McGill Fortnightly Review*'s ephemeral successor. He joined McGill's law faculty in 1928 and became its dean in 1961. He would remain at McGill until his retirement in 1964. Like Frank Underhill, Scott played an active role in the founding of both the League for Social Reconstruction and the Co-operative Commonwealth Federation. He was the CCF's national chairman from 1942 to 1950.

During the period under study, conservative anxieties regarding the impact of industrial capitalism blended with more traditional concerns regarding the violent nature of American society and its apparently defective system of justice. The issue of order was indeed at the heart of anti-American rhetoric. Conservatives believed that most aspects of American society were marked by disorder: the U.S. political system was unstable, the nation's approach to education was unbalanced, and its race relations were anarchic. However, violence and criminality were perhaps the most tangible signs of American disorder. The United States possessed an ineffective judicial system and was beset by crime and vigilantism. The issue of law and order was most preoccupying to imperialists. Notions of 'peace, order, and good government' appear to have played a much stronger role in the formation of identity and distinctiveness in English Canada than they would in Quebec, where American criminality was also viewed with some alarm, but did not generate nearly as much prose. The discussion of capital punishment and firearms, though an anti-American staple today, was scarcely present in commentary before the Second World War. Neither issue appears to have been the object of any significant Canadian-American differentialism or moral posturing.

In conservative commentary, violence and criminality were seen as intrinsic to the American experience. Andrew Macphail, for instance, spoke of a 'reign of lawlessness' in the United States and argued in 1909 that 'life is safer in a Yukon dance hall than in Madison Square Garden.'[17] American criminality was attributed to a number of causes. Immigrants and African Americans were regularly blamed for crime and violence in the United States. Most Tories, however, saw American disorderliness as a more deep-seated phenomenon. For some, it was a result of the nation's frontier experience. Western lawlessness, they argued, had left a permanent imprint on the American soul; it had taught Americans to rely on vigilantism – lynching, in particular, horrified Canadian observers – and to solve their problems with violence. Robert Falconer, for instance, saw the Ku Klux Klan's interwar reign of terror as a manifestation of pioneer vigilantism: 'Its power is due partly to the people having lost faith in their politicians; the machine is beyond their control, law is broken, they feel themselves isolated and betrayed; so they call up their old pioneering instincts, take the law into their own hands and in a rough and ready way mete out decisions according to the prevailing sentiment of the community in respect to good citizenship.'[18] For others, violence and lawlessness were the sombre legacy of the American Revolution. In his 1904 presidential address to the Royal Society of Canada, of which he was a founding member, Colonel George T. Denison suggested that the revolution had purged the early republic of its most law-abiding citizens, the Loyalists, and had taught Americans to disregard authority and solve their problems through violence:

On the other side of the line the lawless elements had got control. They had set law and order and government and constitution at defiance. The rights of property were set at naught ... This spirit has affected the nation ever since. The murders per annum in proportion to the population, being many times more than in other countries of the world. The number of lynchings are about equal to the number of legal executions, and are more often accompanied by the most barbarous scenes. Yet they seem to be accepted by public opinion as an unavoidable evil.[19]

Born into a prominent military family in Toronto, Denison was educated at Upper Canada College and the University of Toronto. As the commanding officer of the Governor General's Body Guard, he saw action during the Fenian raids and the North-West Rebellion. From 1877 to 1923, he was Toronto's senior police magistrate. An ardent imperialist and a rabid anti-American, Denison's conceptual universe was dominated by two fundamental ideals: loyalty and order. As a nation born of revolution, the United States of America was the negation of both these ideals.

In Quebec, it was sometimes suggested that criminality was reinforced by American mass culture, which glorified violence and criminality. Indeed, American society was not only violent, it revelled in violence. In his contribution to the *Revue dominicaine*'s 1936 inquiry into 'Notre américanisation,' the editor of Montreal's *Le Devoir*, Georges Pelletier (1882–1947), condemned the American yellow press' glorification of crime and immorality: 'The misbehaviour of a whole category of American society, the criminals and the gangsters inevitably victorious over the police, the repeated divorces of actors and cinema stars, industry moguls, leading financiers, stars of theatre and professional sport: all this, with the stories of love nests and the exploits of gunmen, appear on the front pages of this type of newspaper.'[20]

Conservatives tended to believe that in the United States the judiciary suffered, like every other branch of American government, from an excessive faith in democracy. Indeed, the American practice of electing certain magistrates was almost universally condemned in Canada. Even A.D. DeCelles, whose assessment of American institutions was fundamentally positive, could not countenance an elected judiciary. 'This is the most dangerous of democracy's innovations, exposing justice to the darkest suspicions,' he wrote in 1896. Without a doubt, 'the independence of the magistrature, which is the first safeguard of its honesty, received a fatal blow the day it became an elective function. It is difficult to understand how the Americans, who never dare bank on human probity, have consented to accept a principle that is the most certain destroyer of it.'[21]

Continentalists had some difficulty in countering the torrent of anti-American prose centred on crime and violence. Crime rates, after all, were higher in the United States than they were in Canada. As a result, most continentalists merely accepted the fact that America was a more violent society. This Canadian-American divergence was credited to several factors. In *My Vision of Canada*, published in 1933, William Arthur Deacon attributed American violence to the nation's youthful exuberance: 'Their lawlessness, lynchings and instinct for "direct action" in general is really exuberance, uncontrolled high spirits, the same lack of forethought and responsibility as you would find in a ten-year-old boy. Their apparent hypocrisy in matters like prohibition and prostitution is mostly youthful thoughtlessness.'[22] More often, however, American turbulence was viewed as a legacy of the frontier. S.D. Clark, whose pioneering work in Canadian sociology explored the impact of the frontier on the nation's development, noted that 'all frontier situations tended to produce a type of society in which little respect was paid to the institutions of law and order.' Born on a farm near Lloydminster, Alberta, Clark studied history and sociology at the University of Saskatchewan, the London School of Economics, McGill, and the University of Toronto. He joined the University of Toronto's Department of Political Economy in 1938. 'The frontiersman,' Clark wrote in 1944, 'tended to take the law into his own hands, and the authority of the policeman and judge was disputed by that of the gang and vigilante committee.' This was particularly the case in 'the frontier society in the United States,' where, unlike in 'the Canadian frontier community,' 'traditional and constituted authority' exerted a lesser degree of control.[23] Over time, this would leave a permanent imprint on American society.

Continentalists, however, rejected the notion that American society was in a state of near anarchy and refused to consider the disparity between Canadian and American crime rates to be a significant issue. For instance, in a 1931 collection of essays, Toronto *Daily Star* reporter Roy Greenaway (1891–1972) showed irritation with sanctimonious Canadian judgments on American criminality: 'In our attitudes towards the crime records of the United States we Canadians are fast developing a pharisaical superiority complex that is irritatingly comic.' Canada was hardly a heaven of law and order, Greenaway insisted. Chicago, for instance, had Al Capone, but Hamilton, Ontario, had Rocco Perri, the 'King of the Bootleggers.' Besides, as Greenaway, who had studied at Victoria College and Harvard, went on to point out, crime statistics in the United States were inflated because Americans considered 'not only minor breaches of the traffic and liquor laws as criminal offences, but also trivial assaults, which in the eyes of the general public are not, and perhaps, never will be so regarded.'[24] The United States was not rife with lawlessness; it was simply enforcing laws which, like prohibition, did not exist in many Canadian jurisdictions.[25]

American plutocracy, vigilantism, and criminality worried both liberals and socialists. Yet their critique of these phenomena was essentially punctual. They understood that the United States embodied a new era in human development – the mass age – which, in spite of its faults, contained great promise. Industrialization and urbanization were the way of the future; they were inevitable and ultimately desirable. In this sense, plutocracy, labour unrest, and crime were merely bumps in the road. For many conservatives, however, these problems were among the very hallmarks of American life. Violence and disorder were a fundamental part of the American experience; they were, for some imperialists, a legacy of the nation's revolutionary birth. Moreover, in the United States, both the concentration of wealth and the rise of the proletariat were engendering a most unfortunate status revolution. To conservative intellectuals, who placed a great deal of importance on order and stability, the United States offered a chaotic glimpse into Canada's not-so-distant future. Like all Canadian intellectuals, imperialists and nationalists dissected American society because it was pertinent to their own national experience. Canadian assessments of American politics, culture, or business indeed served a higher purpose: they allowed Canada's intellectuals to define their national experience and to suggest what its relationship with the wider world should be.

6 Canadian Identity and America

Anti-American sentiment, nationalism, and the politics of Canadian identity have often shared a deep intimacy. During the period under study, these elements, along with a specifically anti-American reading of Canada's physiography known as the Laurentian thesis, were tied to a wider discussion related to the modern ethos. Conservatives, particularly in English Canada, were eager to show that their nation, unlike the United States, was founded on the bedrock of tradition. Anti-Americanism has historically been the principal negative expression of the English Canadian identity. A defensive reaction generated by a people who share much in common with their American neighbours, it has served as a foil to define what Canada is not, and was used, to a certain extent, as a rallying point for a nation deeply divided along regional, religious, and ethnic lines. Indeed, exacerbated differentialism – an element integral to the anti-American ethos – has long served as a unifying force in the politics of Canadian identity. Ideology and utopianism have traditionally played a key role in the construction of identity in the New World. Not surprisingly therefore, anti-Americanism has traditionally played a similar role in English Canada to anti-British sentiment in nineteenth-century America. Both served to affirm the fundamental ideological distinctions between two largely English-speaking societies.[1]

For the English Canadian imperialist, the survival and basic identity of the Canadian nation was tied to conservatism, and the United States was consistently depicted as the antithesis of Canadian society. The Canadian-American border, indeed, was not merely an adminstrative line, it marked the divide between two fundamentally different societies. The Dominion of Canada was everything the United States was not: a stable, organic society built on continuity and the rejection of revolutionism. Similar, though generally non-political, arguments would also be used to distinguish Quebec from its American neighbour. *Nationaliste* differentialism was primarily ethno-religious in nature; French Canada, it was argued, was a Catholic and Latin society. It was therefore the racial and spiritual antithesis of both the United States and English Canada. In the end, however, anti-Americanism was far less important to the construction of French Canadian identity, whose differentialism was far less focused on the United States.

Imperialists and nationalists also insisted on the conservative nature of Canadian society to consolidate their power and influence. According to Patricia K. Wood, they 'sought sole ownership of the power to define "Canadian," and paradoxically externalized their Canadian opponents by presenting them as a foreign enemy.'[2] If Canada was a conservative nation, then conservatives should speak for Canada. Continentalists, it was argued, were unfit for leadership; their core values were un-Canadian (i.e., radical).

Anti-Americanism was a key ingredient in the imperialist creation myth. Canada's birth, indeed, could be traced to an anti-American saga: the Loyalist migration. 'Canada is one of the oldest colonies,' wrote Colonel George T. Denison in 1895, 'and yet her history can only be said to fairly commence with the migration of the United Empire Loyalists at the close of the American Revolution in 1783.'[3] Imperialists frequently recounted the Loyalist migration in tones that evoked the Book of Exodus. The Loyalists had suffered for their loyalty; they were anti-American and conservative heroes; and their faith in a united empire was unshakable. In their rejection of republicanism they had given birth to a fundamentally ordered, conservative nation. In short, Canada would never have become a British dominion without the Loyalists. For their descendants, this narrative had an added attraction. As Norman Knowles notes, it allowed individuals like Colonel Denison to affirm their 'patriotic and genealogical superiority and assert their claims to influence.'[4]

According to the imperialist narrative, the Loyalists had founded a nation on the bedrock of continuity. Consequently, noted R.G. Trotter in a 1933 article, 'Canada holds a distinctive place on this continent inasmuch as she has never broken with the old world politically, but instead has been able to develop her autonomy and acquire her nationhood while still retaining an organic association and common loyalties with the mother country and the rest of the Empire.'[5] This sort of statement, however, did not merely assert Canada's conservative and non-American nature, it also contained insidious racial and ethnic cues which affirmed the social and political pre-eminence of British Canadians.[6] Indeed, if Canada was a British nation, then Canadians of British ancestry were its natural leaders. Not surprisingly, therefore, outside of French Canada, anti-American sentiment was most prevalent among intellectuals of British – particularly English – birth or heritage.

Canada's distinctiveness – and superiority – lay in its essentially British and conservative nature. The Canadian political system lay at the heart of imperialist differentialism. Constitutional monarchy and the imperial bond, it was argued, bred order and deference. Moreover, Canada's political stability underpinned its moral order. For some imperialists, including Colonel Denison, Canadian distinctiveness was also fundamentally racial. The Dominion of Canada was not only constitutionally British, it was also far more Anglo-Saxon than the United States, a nation whose racial integrity had been weakened by slavery and massive non-British immigration. A number of more moderate imperialists, however, considered the United States to be an essentially Anglo-Saxon nation and did not see race as central to Canadian-American differentialism. They insisted that the American Revolution had not sundered the racial bond that united all Anglo-Saxons.

In spite of its anti-American proclivities, imperialist rhetoric did possess a certain willingness to acknowledge aspects of Canada's Americanness. This tendency became more pronounced after the Great War. 'Canada is British and American, economically more American than British, spiritually more British than American,' insisted the imperialist *Round Table*'s anonymous Canadian correspondent in 1925.[7] Canadian-American similarities were often attributed to a shared British heritage.

Prior to the First World War, few imperialists questioned Canadian anti-Americanism. Those who did generally viewed the phenomenon as a consequence of American hostility to Canada and, in particular, as a legacy of the revolutionary republic's mistreatment of the United Empire Loyalists. America, they claimed, had offended Canadian sensibilities with a variety of affronts ranging from invasion to protectionism and deserved to be chastised. Anti-Americanism, indeed, was historically justifiable. Besides, it inhibited continentalism and helped to preserve Canada's distinct identity. By the interwar years, however, some Tories became increasingly uncomfortable with overt anti-Americanism. R.G. Trotter, who received a doctorate from Harvard University, argued in a 1933 article that 'our national life will be elevated by concentrating attention on positive values rather than by spending our best energy in negations.'[8] Like many Tories born in the 1880s and 1890s, Trotter's anti-Americanism was relatively subdued.

French Canada was also viewed by many imperialists as an element of national distinctiveness and an asset in the struggle against both annexation and Americanization. It was an antimodern – and somewhat reactionary – fragment. Quebec, wrote Robert Falconer in 1925, 'is out of sympathy with American democracy. Even American Catholicism is too liberal for the Quebec ecclesiastic. Nor does the sentimental affinity of the educated American for modern France win over the French Canadian, for he disapproves the very ideals of France which America admires. The American glories in his progressiveness, the French-Canadian lives on the authority of tradition.'[9] In the end, though many imperialists might not have been well disposed towards French Canadian demands for equality, they nevertheless recognized that Quebec played a role in Canadian distinctiveness.

Like Falconer, French Canadian nationalists saw Quebec and the United States as fundamentally antithetical entities. For Father Adélard Dugré, who taught theology at Montreal's Scolasticat de l'Immaculée Conception from 1919 to 1932 and was appointed the Society of Jesus' assistant general superior for the British Empire and Belgium in 1936, the contrast between Quebec and the United States was evident: French Canadian society was 'simple, patriarchal, essentially Catholic and conservative,' while American society was 'dazzling and showy, Protestant and materialistic.' Quebec, as the inheritor of pre-revolutionary France, was the embodiment of Catholic tradition, while the United States was the quintessence of both Protestantism and modernity. Accordingly, Dugré began La Campagne canadienne, a novel that explored the differences between French Canadian and American society through the tale of a Franco-American family torn between its rural French Canadian roots and its urban Midwestern American home, with the following preface:

> There currently exist in North America two completely different civilizations: one is represented by a hundred million Anglo-Saxons, the other by three or four million Canadians of French origin. What distinguishes these two unequal groups is not only the language that they speak or the religious faith of the vast majority, but also the diversity of their ways of behaving, their different ways of seeing life, its pleasures and its duties. In French Canada, the temperament and traditions of seventeenth-century Catholic France have been inherited; in Anglo-Saxon America, free

interpretation of the Bible and the utilitarian spirit of Elizabethan England have been inherited ... This opposition in the character of the two ethnic groups is constantly revealed in everyday life: religious practice, family customs, education, literature, business and advertising, electoral processes, popular holidays, everything reveals to the least attentive observer the profound differences that distinguish the unassimilated French Canadian from the typical American.[10]

But French Canadian distinctiveness was not only based on Catholicism and French language and culture, it was also racial. Americans (and English Canadians), it was argued, were Anglo-Saxons, and French Canadians, as Latins, were their racial antipodes. The two races, indeed, possessed fundamentally different characteristics. As Father Édouard Hamon noted in one the first books devoted to emigration and Franco-American affairs, *Les Canadiens-Français de la Nouvelle-Angleterre,* published in 1891: 'the French character is the total opposite of the Anglo-Saxon American character. As much as the one is cheerful, expansive, unworried, commiserative, ready to make the most generous sacrifices, the other is cold, focused, calculating, and egotistical.'[11] These racial differences would inevitably spawn two fundamentally different societies. The French-born Jesuit was not the only *nationaliste* to embrace various prevailing notions regarding *la psychologie des peuples.* William Chapman (1850–1917), for instance, saw the Spanish-American War as a clash between two antithetical races. In the preface to an 1898 poem dedicated to the Queen of Spain, the erstwhile civil servant – Chapman had lost his job with the office of the attorney general of Quebec after the 1897 provincial election removed the Conservative party from power – noted that Quebec and the United States shared little more than geography. Spain and French Canada, by contrast, shared a deep spiritual and racial bond: 'Today the American eagle does not have our sympathy, much less our love. Our love! We give it to Spain ... The Spanish are, so to speak, our brothers; like us they feel the unalterable Latin blood flowing through their veins, their language resembles our own just as marble from Paros resembles marble from Carrara, and their Catholic faith is the star that guides the ship carrying our national and religious destinies.'[12]

There was, however, a certain *américanité* to nationalist prose. French Canadians, wrote abbé Lionel Groulx in 1935, 'number ... among the oldest Americans.' Indeed, he continued, 'nobody is more firmly rooted than us in this America, nor more identified with this continent.'[13] But this sort of statement rarely led to a real assessment of Quebec's essential continentalism. On the contrary, many French Canadian conservatives would only readily acknowledge an Americanness of negative traits. For instance, in 1937, the head of the Public Archives of Canada, Gustave Lanctot, insisted that 'the average Quebecer, equally liberated from European inhibitions, resembles the average American in his political democratism, his social egalitarianism, his intellectual incuriosity, his unflagging benevolence and his adventurous tastes.'[14]

By contrast, the continentalist ethos was passionate about *américanité*. Intellectuals like Goldwin Smith and Frank Underhill insisted on Canada's essentially continental nature because they hoped to identify their nation as an essentially modern and North American entity. And Canada's Americanness was not fundamentally the result of Americanization. On the contrary, the Canadian experience was innately 'American.' John W. Dafoe, for instance, repeatedly argued that Canada had been an American nation from its inception. Speaking before an English audience in 1930, the editor of the *Winnipeg Free Press* insisted that even the Loyalists were fundamentally American in their culture and ideals: 'The people who were driven into exile were called Tories by the Americans, but that term was true of only a very small element. The great bulk of these people were of precisely the same type as the men in the American armies, but they did not think that the situation which had arisen between the colonies and Great Britain was one which could be profitably settled by an appeal to the sword.[15] Born in Combermere, Canada West, Dafoe was himself of Loyalist descent. However, unlike Colonel Denison or George Sterling Ryerson, he did not mythologize his Loyalist forbears. A staunch liberal, Dafoe understood that the memory of the United Empire Loyalists was being used to further a Conservative political and social agenda. He occasionally sought to undermine this agenda by emphasizing the fundamentally American nature of the Loyalist experience.

Race and ancestry played an important role in continentalist attempts to define Canada's essentially American nature. But equally important, particularly to interwar continentalists, was the homogenizing force exerted by the frontier and the environment on North American society. F.R. Scott saw Canadian-American similarities as the result of both a common ancestry and a shared environment: 'It would be wrong to attribute all the American characteristics of Canadian life to the influence of the United States. Men and women, whether north or south of the American boundary, derive from the same racial stocks, live on the same continent, and have to abstract a living from a very similar physical environment; it is not surprising that in the process of time their social and economic institutions have come to have great similarities.'[16]

Nonetheless, continentalists recognized that there were noteworthy differences between Canada and the United States. P.E. Corbett, for instance, wrote in a 1931 article published in London's *Contemporary Review* that Canada 'has still the upper hand on crime' and that 'in spite of New York's dictation of fashions and the more superficial morals, we shall probably continue as a people to attach more sanctity to marriage and the family than do our neighbours.'[17] That said, most continentalists would likely have agreed with S.D. Clark when he argued in 1938 that Canada's distinctiveness was essentially a regional variation of a wider North American culture: 'The preponderance of settlers from the British Isles, a large French-Canadian population, and the more rural character of Canadian life combine to give a certain individuality to Canadian culture, but hardly a greater individuality than regional communities within a single nation may possess.'[18]

Continentalist differentialism was largely aimed at Europe. Nevertheless, continentalists diverged on just how distinct European and North American society really were. North American isolationists like William Arthur Deacon and Frank Underhill saw Europe and North America as essentially separate and, to a large extent, antithetical entities. Europe was portrayed as hopelessly corrupted by inequality, hatred, and militarism, while North American society was presented as fundamentally tolerant, peaceful, and free. Most continentalists were not as passionately anti-European as Underhill and Deacon. Intellectuals like John W. Dafoe and Arthur Lower readily acknowledged that both Canada and the United States shared a wider British heritage. Canadians were in many ways British, but so were Americans, though to a lesser extent. 'The United States is of the European world but not in it,' wrote Arthur Lower in 1939. Canada, on the other hand, 'is in the American world but not exactly of it. She has a foot in both continents and if sentiment and tradition draw her to Britain, her daily bread draws her to the rest of America.'[19] One of Canada's foremost historians, Lower spent most of his career at United College, Winnipeg, where he chaired the Department of History for eighteen years, and at Queen's. He was keenly interested in the staples trade and in Canadian-American relations. In 1938, he contributed a volume entitled *The North American Assault on the Canadian Forest* to the Carnegie series on Canadian-American relations.

In English Canada, continentalist attitudes towards Quebec's Americanness evolved over time. For many early continentalists, including Goldwin Smith, French Canada was an un-American backwater. In 1891, the notorious Francophobe asserted that Quebec, like the American South, was a reactionary fragment. 'Quebec is a theocracy,' he wrote, 'its character had been perpetuated by isolation like the form of an antediluvian animal preserved in Siberian ice.'[20] Smith believed that only assimilation could bring French Canada up to the North American standard. By the interwar years, however, many continentalists were inclined to view French Canadian society as inherently North American. Attitudes towards Quebec had evolved, and while a degree of Francophobia certainly persisted in continentalist prose, it was now generally assumed that Catholicism and the French language did not necessarily alienate Quebec from the wider North American ethos. John Bartlet Brebner, for instance, claimed in 1931 that 'Canadians are not a Franco-British people, they are two kinds of North Americans.'[21]

Continentalists were united in their distaste for anti-Americanism. They firmly believed that anti-American sentiment hampered the emergence of both a modern national identity and a continental frame of reference. Canadians, they hoped, were sufficiently mature to found their national identity on something other than the repudiation of their neighbours. In this spirit, P.E. Corbett concluded his landmark 1930 article on anti-American sentiment with the following warning:

> There are those among us who proceed on the theory that our autonomy and our British allegiance can be preserved by fostering anti-Americanism. That is a bad policy for ourselves, and a bad policy for the Commonwealth. In addition to impeding our own social and economic development, it would impair our real usefulness in the somewhat over-vaunted rôle of 'interpreters.' Worst of all, it is lamentable stuff to weave into the texture of a forming national spirit and make a part of Canadianism.[22]

Like many young men of his generation, Corbett served in the Great War. Severely injured at the Battle of the Somme, he was awarded the Military Cross in 1918. After the war he resumed his studies at Oxford University and served as an assistant legal adviser to the League of Nation's International Labour Office. In 1924, he was appointed professor of Roman law at McGill's Faculty of Law. Corbett served as the faculty's dean from 1928 to 1936. Under his direction, the Faculty of Law recruited both F.R. Scott and John P. Humphrey and became something of a hotbed of continentalist sentiment. Serving briefly as McGill's acting principal, Corbett continued to teach Roman and international law until 1942, when he left Canada and joined the faculty of Yale University. He became an American citizen in 1947.

Rather than explaining away anti-Americanism by reciting the endless list of indignities suffered by the Dominion of Canada at the hands of the United States, continentalists generally looked inwards for its causes. They argued that anti-Americanism had little to do with American actions or policy. For instance, though P.E. Corbett cited the American Revolution and a succession of diplomatic irritants as contributing to anti-American sentiment, he attributed the phenomenon principally to the Dominion's latent inferiority complex.[23] Western Canada's leading intellectual, John W. Dafoe, added another piece to the puzzle: he also acknowledged that American hostility to Canada had fostered anti-Americanism, but saw the phenomenon as largely instrumental. Above all, he argued in 1935, anti-American sentiment was a political tool used time and again by the Conservative party to manipulate the Canadian people: 'For at least a century, first in Canada and afterwards in the Dominion, no general election was ever fought without at least an attempt being made by the Party of the Right to make political use of this anti-American sentiment. The formula was simple. In its earlier form the Party of the Left was charged with disloyal sentiments and separatist tendencies, its fell purpose being to transfer the country to the United States.' During the reciprocity campaigns of 1891 and 1911, he continued, 'what looked like certain victory for the Liberals was turned into defeat by a resurgence of ultra-Imperialistic and anti-American feeling.'[24] A quarter-century after the 1911 election, Dafoe was still deeply embittered by the Liberal party's defeat. In his mind, anti-Americanism was nothing more than a contrivance used by the 'Party of the Right' to stifle progress.

On the issue of identity, French Canadian continentalism diverged significantly from its English Canadian counterpart. Leading continentalist intellectuals like Sylva Clapin, Edmond de Nevers, Errol Bouchette, and Jean-Charles Harvey regularly argued that Quebec and the United States were essentially different societies. Bouchette, for instance, insisted in 1905 that the French Canadian soul and mission were unlike those of the United States: 'The United States forms a great and noble people, an eminently civilizing people, and among whom the social question has already found solutions on several points. We must admire their virtues and seek their friendship. But never will we be able to merge ourselves with them because we are different, our soul is not their soul, and because Providence is clearly setting aside another mission, no less noble, for us.'[25]

In Quebec, what really distinguished continentalist and anti-American views on identity was the willingness of intellectuals like Errol Bouchette to celebrate the province's Americanness and to promote closer relations with its southern neighbour. Continentalists understood that a wider ethos of rupture with Europe united the various nations of the New World. 'It is not accurate to say that Spain is found in Mexico, a rejuvenated England in the United States, a new France on the banks of the St Lawrence,' Bouchette wrote in the *Revue canadienne*. 'Even if these people speak Spanish, English, French, and even if they conserve much from the mother country, it does not stop them from being different people.'[26] Called to the Quebec bar in 1885, Bouchette quickly turned his attention to journalism, moving back and forth between Quebec City, Montreal, and Toronto over the next several years, and contributing articles to a number of Liberal newspapers, including *L'Étendard* of Montreal, *L'Électeur* of Quebec, the Montreal *Herald*, and the Toronto *Globe*. In 1890, he became the private secretary of Quebec's Minister of Public Works, Pierre Garneau. Three years later, he returned to his original occupation and resumed practising law in Montreal. Moving to Ottawa in 1898, he served for two years as the private secretary to Canada's Minister of Revenue, Sir Henri-Gustave Joly de Lotbinière, and was appointed assistant librarian of the Library of Parliament in 1903. He would hold this position until his untimely death in 1912.

In many ways, geography lends itself to subjective reasoning: talk of disputed territory or 'historical' borders is often tied to wider issues of identity and memory. Canada has not escaped this type of discussion. During the period under study, there was a great deal of discussion regarding whether Canada's natural fault lines ran along a north-south or an east-west axis. For continentalists, North America's basic geography followed a north-south orientation and the Canadian-American border was viewed as a somewhat arbitrary line. The Dominion of Canada, therefore, was an inherently regionalized nation whose physiography was tied to that of its southern neighbour. Indeed, despite a tendency to homogenize the North American experience, the continentalist ethos readily accepted Canada's essential regionalism. The basic premise of continentalist regionalism was formulated by Goldwin Smith in the introduction to *Canada and the Canadian Question*:

Whoever wishes to know what Canada is, and to understand the Canadian question, should begin by turning from the political to the natural map. The political map displays a vast and unbroken area of territory, extending from the boundary of the United States up to the North Pole, and equalling or surpassing the United States in magnitude. The physical map displays four separate projections of the cultivable and habitable part of the Continent into arctic waste. The four vary greatly in size, and one of them is very large. They are, beginning from the east, the Maritime Provinces – Nova Scotia, New Brunswick, and Prince Edward Island; Old Canada, comprising the present Provinces of Quebec and Ontario; the newly-opened region of the North-West, comprising the Province of Manitoba and the districts of Alberta, Athabasca, Assiniboia, and Saskatchewan; and British Columbia ... Between the divisions of the Dominion there is hardly any natural trade, and but little even of forced trade has been called into existence under a stringent system of protection ... Each of the blocks, on the other hand, is closely connected by nature, physically and economically, with that portion of the habitable and cultivable continent to the south of which it immediately adjoins, and in which are its natural markets.[27]

Smith's ideas regarding Canada's fundamental geographic orientation would spark an intense and decades-long debate in Canada. He believed that Canada's regionalism was an insurmountable obstacle to unity and would inexorably lead to continental union. Canada was a geographic, economic, and ethnic absurdity in which 'the advance of commerce and civilisation ... is paralysed by geographical dispersion, commercial isolation, and the separatist nationality of French Quebec.'[28] Nearly all subsequent continentalists rejected Smith's pessimism. They argued instead that regionalism made nation-building and free trade imperative. John W. Dafoe, for instance, took Smith to task in a 1927 lecture given at the University of Chicago: 'Goldwin Smith used to say that Canada was an attempt to defy geography, and he predicted that the laws of nature would override the will of man. There was a time when it looked as though this pessimist was right; but these doubts no longer assail us. Canada is an exhibit against the theory of economic determinism as the arbiter of the fate of nations.'[29] Yet Dafoe and others did not challenge Smith's basic contention: that the continent's natural divisions ran along a north-south axis and that each of Canada's regions was in many ways the prolongation of a contiguous American region. The essence of what is now referred to as the borderlands concept could indeed be found in early continentalist discourse.[30]

To the Canadian imperialist, the very idea that the Dominion of Canada was a fractured country whose regions had less in common with each other than with adjoining regions in the United States was abhorrent. Centralism was intrinsic to the imperialist ethos and imperialists tended to underline the fundamental unity of the Canadian experience. Canada, they believed, was united by its common adherence to British tradition and its rejection of American values. 'Nothing but a powerful common purpose could have enabled Canadians to triumph over geography as they have done,' wrote Robert Falconer in 1925. He was indeed confident in the strength of Canadian unity:

> In Canada or in Europe the American is known at once, whether he comes from Maine or from California, from Wisconsin or from Georgia. So also the term 'Canadian' is employed as expressive of a unified national sentiment among the provinces of the Dominion. That such a sentiment exists is obvious to any one who has lived long enough in the different provinces to understand the life of their several communities. Halifax is more like Victoria than the former is like Portland, Maine, or the latter like Portland, Oregon. Toronto resembles Winnipeg more than the former resembles Buffalo or the latter Minneapolis. And in spite of difference of language and social and religious institutions the province of Quebec is closer in spirit to the Maritime provinces or to Ontario than to any of the United States.[31]

For several decades, Canadian Tories would put forward various arguments to counter Goldwin Smith's vision of Canada's physiography and its implications regarding continental integration. In a scathing review of *Canada and the Canadian Question*, the elder statesman of Canadian imperialism, George Monro Grant, acknowledged that geography had hampered Canadian growth, but countered that 'geography is not the sole or even the primary factor in the formation of nations.' 'Man triumphs continually over geography or nature in any form,' he asserted. 'Every trans-continental railway is such a triumph.' In the end, Grant was convinced that the strength of British tradition and the 'triumph of science' would easily allow the Dominion of Canada to overcome its geographic dispersion.[32] For his part, the associate editor of the Toronto *Daily Empire*, John Castell Hopkins, put forward a more geographic argument to counter Smith's thesis. Hopkins claimed in 1893 that the 'brilliant but intensely unpopular Englishman' had misread the orientation of Canada's geography and communications. The Dominion's 'commerce, railways, steamship lines, cable projects, and waterways all converge, east and west, toward Britain and British countries, instead of south to the United States,' he wrote in an American magazine.[33] Canada was built along an east-west axis, and both the nation's separateness and the imperial bond were inscribed in its infrastructure and basic geography.

Hopkins had articulated one of the core tenets of what would later be known as the Laurentian thesis. The thesis was partly derived from the staples theory of Harold Innis, an economist at the University of Toronto. In a 1930 monograph entitled *The Fur Trade in Canada*, Innis argued that Canada was not a geographic absurdity; its unity and physiographic coherence were founded on the St Lawrence–Great Lakes system and on the development of a succession of economic staples. 'Penetration of the continent by the St Lawrence,' he later wrote, 'facilitated development of trade from Europe in staple products beginning with the fur trade and continuing with the timber trade, and, after 1850 and the construction of railways, with livestock products and wheat.'[34] The nation's geography and economic structure ran primarily along an east-west axis, linking Canada to Europe.

Tory intellectuals instantly seized upon Innis' ideas, which they understood to be implicitly anti-American and centralist. If Canada was a northern nation built along an east-west axis, then continental integration and the sundering of the imperial bond would lead to disaster. Furthermore, the maintenance of the east-west axis required a strong central government. Donald Creighton was Innis' most fervent disciple. Born in Toronto, Creighton was the most prominent English Canadian historian of his generation. He joined the University of Toronto's Department of History shortly after completing his studies at Balliol College, Oxford, and would remain there until his retirement. In *The Commercial Empire of the St Lawrence, 1760–1850*, an influential monograph published in 1937, Creighton worked Innis' staples theory into the overtly anti-American Laurentian thesis, arguing that Canada's struggle against continentalism was rooted in geography and economics. Canada's basic essence, it seemed, was anti-American.

The Laurentian thesis was not terribly popular in Quebec: its implications regarding the imperial bond and constitutional centralization were not likely to elicit a great deal of sympathy in a province where anti-imperialism and the compact theory rallied a significant proportion

of the population. Goldwin Smith's conception of a fractured, regionalized, and artificial Canada, however, did appeal to many French Canadian nationalists. Indeed, in spite of his Francophobic rantings, Smith's
influence could be felt in Quebec's intellectual circles. He even attracted
a key ally in the province: Henri Bourassa. The unlikely duo found common ground in their fervent opposition to British imperialism, most notably during the South African War. Bourassa, like Smith, understood
that the continent's natural divisions ran along a north-south axis, and
he lambasted imperialists for refusing to acknowledge this basic fact.
'It is inconceivable that sensible and practical men should so completely live outside the sphere of reality,' he wrote in 1911. 'They seemingly
ignore the elements of Northern America [sic] geography, and forget
that the political division of this continent has been made with an entire disregard for the laws of nature.'[35] Bourassa also briefly accepted
Smith's contention that 'the extension of the Dominion to the Pacific'
had destroyed every last vestige of the nation's 'material unity.'[36] In the
wake of the Conscription Crisis and the divisive federal election of 1921,
Bourassa openly mused that Confederation's days were numbered.[37]

Bourassa quickly recanted this position. In the end, his faith in Canada prevailed. Bourassa's disciples, however, were not as optimistic. In
a 1922 inquiry into 'Notre avenir politique,' L'Action française suggested
that Canada's disintegration was at hand and that the time had come to
prepare for the birth of an État français. The review's editor, abbé Lionel
Groulx, fully embraced Goldwin Smith's vision of the Canada as a geographic, economic, and ethnic absurdity. Groulx was not a separatist,
but he did believe that the Canadian nation contained the seeds of its
own dissolution. One of the inquiry's contributors, Father Rodrigue Villeneuve (1883–1947), an Oblate who taught philosophy at the Scolasticat
d'Ottawa from 1907 to 1930, expanded on this theme:

> Between the east and the west, there is a *hostile distance*. In vain have we
> hoped to erase this estrangement that gives our country the expanse of
> an empire by constructing interminable and costly railways. The country
> would have made itself bankrupt by it unless the provinces who could get
> no use out of them paid for those who would; which is hardly a distribu-
> tion likely to cement unity. Besides, the natural divisions, in a territory
> that is, as has been said, *a geographical absurdity*, clearly diverge in interest,
> imposing free trade there, calling for tariff protection here. I well know
> that *human geography* is not inevitably measured by rivers or mountains,
> and that the political borders that last are those created by national spirit

rather than by surveying plans. But it is by a national solidarity of interests and common spirit that geographical gaps can be filled in. In the case in point, this is precisely what is most lacking.[38]

Later, after becoming the Archbishop of Quebec and primate of the Canadian Church, Villeneuve would disavow his 1922 contribution to 'Notre avenir politique.'

The pessimism of the 1922 inquiry's conclusions did not stand the test of time. Yet the belief that Canada existed in defiance of geography and that the North American continent was organized along a north-south axis would remain significant to the intellectual geography of French Canadian nationalism. In English Canada, Goldwin Smith's ideas regarding the north-south pull of North American geography and the essential regionalism of the Canadian nation were generally used as an argument in favour of free trade. They served a very different purpose in Quebec. For many leading French Canadian nationalists, North America's physical geography legitimized a more decentralized federal structure. Canada's basic geography, they argued, made constitutional centralization impractical.

A general acceptance of the continent's north-south axis did not prevent many *nationalistes* from viewing climate and geography as elements of Canadian-American differentialism. Canada and the United States, it was argued, were almost in separate hemispheres. Canada was unquestionably a nation of the northern hemisphere, and French Canadians were an inherently northern people. The United States, on the other hand, was a southerly nation, and its people were accustomed to the comforts of living in a temperate climate. American life was easy: snowfall was sparse and crops grew faster and longer. This, in turn, helped breed a lazy and materialistic society. By contrast, argued Father Adélard Dugré in 1925, the rigours of the northern climate had reinforced French Canadian vigour and spiritualism: 'A cold climate, a calm nature, difficult economic conditions, robust religious faith have developed among the French Canadians endurance in difficult work and the facility of contentment; a temperate climate, a generous nature, an abundance of riches have developed in the Americans a taste for living and an attachment to worldly goods, whereas the mysticism of the Puritan pioneers gave way among them to an increasingly notable religious indifference.'[39]

At the turn of the twentieth century, this type of argument was also present in imperialist prose. The North captured the imagination of imperialists and *nationalistes* alike, and climate and nordicity were seen as key elements of Canadian distinctiveness by men of science like Andrew Macphail or William Osler. Talk of Canadian nordicity was usually tied to racialism. William Osler, who had left Canada in 1884 to teach clinical medicine at the University of Pennsylvania and would later join the faculty of Johns Hopkins University, pondered the racial advantages of a cold climate in a 1904 speech delivered before the Canadian Club of Toronto: 'We often hear it spoken of as a disadvantage to this country that it is situated so far north. There has rarely been in the history of the world a very strong nation not situated in the north and it is very much to our advantage that we have a rigorous winter and that the climate is a bit hard at times. It is very much to the advantage of the race, and it is likely to produce in the coming ages a stronger race than on any other part of the continent.'[40]

But the Canadian climate not only virilized Anglo-Saxons, it also repelled darker races. George R. Parkin was among the most vocal proponents of this idea. Born in Salisbury, New Brunswick, and educated at the University of New Brunswick, Parkin was the headmaster of the Bathurst Grammar School from 1868 to 1872 and of Fredericton's Collegiate School from 1874 to 1889. In 1889, at the request of the Imperial Federation League, he embarked on a lecture tour of the British Empire to promote imperial unity. Parkin served as the headmaster of Upper Canada College from 1895 to 1902, when he was appointed the organizing representative of the Rhodes Scholarship Trust in England. In 1908, he informed the Empire Club of Canada that climate was one of Canada's greatest assets: 'We have the most prodigious advantages on this northern side of the line; advantages of various kinds. And first and foremost among these I am inclined to place the thing of which some Canadians have been ashamed, but in which I glory; and that is that we are the "Lady of the Snows" and that we have a 30 to 40 below zero climate.' 'Look at what it sets us free from,' Parkin exclaimed. 'What is the incubus that rests upon the United States to-day, and for which the most thinking men have found it impossible to find a solution? It is the great colour problem. We never can have a problem of that kind in this country; it is impossible.'[41]

The corollary to all this talk of northern virility and natural selection was clear: the United States was a nation whose racial stock had been degenerated by the interrelated evils of heat, slavery, and immigration. And these problems were not confined to the southern states. Andrew Macphail, for instance, argued that the near-tropical climate of the American South was contaminating the nation's more temperate regions. With regard to the practice of lynching, the founding editor of the *Canadian Medical Association Journal* noted in 1910 that 'infection spreads. The peculiar diversion which the inhabitants of Alabama employ to relieve the tedium of life in a sub-tropical climate soon comes to be practised in Illinois.'[42]

While not all imperialists were inclined to view America's racial stock as inherently inferior, they tended to agree that it lacked the higher degree of natural selection associated with a northern climate. This belief, however, was not confined to the right. Until well into the twentieth century, it was widely assumed that Blacks and southern Europeans were biologically ill-equipped to cope with the rigours of the Canadian climate. As a result, a number of continentalists also saw Canada's weather as a source of racial strength. Reverend James A. Macdonald, for instance, argued in 1915 that the northern climate had prevented runaway American slaves from settling permanently in nineteenth-century Canada: 'To the slaves Canada was Goshen, not Canaan. Many of them grew to comfort and prospered. But Emancipation Day was the day of their deliverance. From that day on they began to set their faces again to the warm southland. Canada never would have had the negro or a negro problem had it not been for slavery. It is not a matter of law, but of latitude. In the northern zone the thermometer is on the side of the white man.[43]

Racial prejudice was common in early continentalist prose. It did not seriously deter continentalists, however, from promoting closer relations with the United States. They argued that Canada's very geography made continental integration necessary and inevitable, and were correspondingly sceptical of conservative theories like the Laurentian thesis. Often dismissed as un-Canadian by the conservative intellectuals who claimed to be the guardians and unique spokesmen for the nation, continentalists tried to brand Canada as an essentially modern, North American nation. As we shall see in the next chapter, however, they were continuously hampered in this endeavour by the twin spectres of annexation and Americanization, which the intellectual right often conjured in order to denigrate continental integration and Canadian-American cultural convergence.

In the late nineteenth and early twentieth centuries, conservative talk of climate and geography regularly expressed a desire to affirm Canada's anti-American distinctiveness. For imperialists, the nation's nordicity and its east-west axis reinforced its conservative, British, and antimodern essence. The imperial bond, along with British continuity and tradition, were inscribed in Canada's basic physiography. French Canadian nationalists balked at this suggestion. Like the continentalists, they often embraced the idea of a regionalized country whose natural faultlines ran north and south. They did not, however, insist that French Canada was an essentially modern entity that shared a wider ethos of rupture with the United States. They argued instead that their nation was spiritually, racially, culturally, and linguistically distinct from the United States.

7 Twin Perils: Annexation and Americanization

The twin spectres of annexation and Americanization have long cast a shadow over the discussion of Canadian-American relations. Annexation, in particular, has been a recurring theme in Canadian political and intellectual debate. Generally speaking, the spectre of annexation is evoked when Canadians debate the merits of continental integration. However, in the nineteenth century, annexation was seriously discussed and debated on several occasions, particularly during periods of economic despair. Some Victorian intellectuals believed that the solution to Canada's problems lay in continental union. Their ideas were well received in certain circles, and annexation was not far from being a legitimate political option in nineteenth-century Canada. By about 1900, however, intellectual annexationism had basically disappeared from Canadian discourse. The return of prosperity had put an end to annexationist self-doubt. Talk of continental union persisted nonetheless. Indeed, Tories continued to use the spectre of annexation to tarnish their continentalist adversaries. Annexation, it was argued, would be the ultimate consequence of continental integration. That nearly all continentalists were viscerally opposed to annexation was irrelevant; annexation was a bogey.

Annexationists believed that continental union was the only way to permanently ensure Canadian prosperity. Annexation would also bring greater freedom and democracy to Canada, argued Goldwin Smith, whose ideas formed the intellectual core of annexationism's last gasp in the late 1880s and early 1890s. Yet Smith disliked being labelled an 'annexationist.' 'Annexation is an ugly word,' he wrote in his magnum opus, *Canada and the Canadian Question*. 'It seems to convey the idea of force or pressure applied to the smaller state, not of free, equal and honourable union, like that between England and Scotland.'[1] Smith dreamed of a 'continental union' between consenting partners. Canada was not to be 'annexed' by the United States; its provinces were to enter the union freely as equal partners in the American commonwealth.

Goldwin Smith had not always believed that Canada's destiny lay in continental union with the United States. Shortly after settling in Toronto, in 1871, he became active in the fledgling Canada First movement, which sought to promote the political and cultural development of the nascent Dominion. However, the movement collapsed in the mid-1870s and Smith grew increasingly convinced that the new nation was destined to fail. By 1877, when his first article advocating continental union was published in London's *Fortnightly Review*, Smith had become an ardent annexationist. His arguments are well known: the Canadian nation, he believed, was a profound absurdity. Its indefensible borders ran counter to the continent's physical geography and its economy was based on artificial tariff barriers. Economic arguments indeed dominated annexationist rhetoric in the nineteenth century. For Smith, Canadian prosperity simply required annexation. To continue to resist continental union was to perpetuate economic marasmus and massive out-migration. Only a small minority of Canadians, Smith argued, benefited from economic protectionism: 'For the few who profit by the system there may be large fortunes and baronial mansions in England, where they will win titles and social consequence by making Canada move, or pretending to make her move, in conformity with the interests of an aristocratic party in Great Britain. For the people at large there will be the inevitable fate of a country kept by artificial separation and restriction below the level of its continent in commercial prosperity and in the rewards held out to industry.'[2]

Goldwin Smith's case for continental union was not limited to economic arguments. Canada's problems, to be sure, were also political and ethnic. Smith was haunted by the spectre of French and Catholic domination, and could only envisage one solution to the French Canadian question: assimilation. There was, however, a major obstacle to the assimilation of French Canada: 'The forces of Canada alone are not sufficient to assimilate the French element or even to prevent the indefinite consolidation and growth of a French nation.'[3] Only annexation could guarantee assimilation. Continental union would also bring an end to British colonialism on the North American continent. Without Britain meddling in her affairs, Canada could finally assume her democratic and continental destiny. Moreover, Smith argued that with the Canadian irritant removed from Anglo-American relations, a significant source of transatlantic discord would disappear. Annexation, in this sense, would accomplish a significant step towards the moral reunion of the Anglo-Saxon people.

Even in his heyday, Smith was a relatively unpopular figure. Yet he was not devoid of followers. As he noted in *Canada and the Canadian Question*, 'the English inquirer had better be cautious in receiving the confident reports of official persons, or listening to public professions of any kind. The very anxiety shown to gag opinion by incessant cries of disloyalty and treason shows that there is an opinion which needs to be gagged.'[4] Smith's followers were a diverse lot. They embraced his indictment of the Dominion, but often opted for a more proactive approach to annexation. For instance, in an 1891 pamphlet published shortly after *Canada and the Canadian Question*, Samuel R. Clarke argued that the Liberal party needed to adopt annexation as its platform. 'So far as the progressive Reform party is concerned, it must be either annexation or retrogression,' he wrote. 'My own idea is the Reform party will advance. They seem clearly to be fighting the annexation battle under cover of the "unrestricted reciprocity" colours for the present.'[5] Goldwin Smith, for his part, was content to see the Liberal party take up free trade as its warhorse. Once it was enacted, the two nations would inevitably coalesce. Continental union was more a matter of destiny than of politics.

Continental union also had its supporters in Quebec. In the late nineteenth century, the province's annexation movement was mainly composed of impenitent *rouges* like Louis-Honoré Fréchette and Jean-Baptiste Rouilliard. Fréchette was a prominent figure in late nineteenth century Quebec's intellectual circles. His poetry was intensely patriotic and liberal, and he frequently crossed swords with the province's conservative and clerical elite. Fréchette served as the Member of Parliament for Lévis, from 1874 to 1878, and was appointed clerk of Quebec's Legislative Council by Premier Honoré Mercier in 1889. Rouilliard, who founded and edited several Quebec newspapers in support of Mercier's Parti national, also benefited from the premier's largesse: he served as the inspector general of Quebec's mines in the late 1880s and early 1890s. Shortly thereafter, Rouilliard settled permanently in New England. Over the next several years, he would found a number of short-lived Franco-American newspapers, including *L'Aigle* (Salem, Massachusetts), *L'Amérique* (Biddeford, Maine), and *La République* (Lewiston, Maine).

Unlike Wilfrid Laurier, their Liberal contemporary, Fréchette and Rouilliard never came to embrace Confederation. Instead, they believed that the solution to most of French Canada's problems lay in continental union. Annexation would bring an end to such nagging problems as economic marasmus and massive emigration. 'Continental union, by annexation to the United States, would ensure a uniform tariff, a high protective tariff against the transatlantic countries, and free trade with the peoples of the Americas,' Jean-Baptiste Rouilliard argued before Montreal's Club National in 1893.[6] Continental union, it was also claimed, would free Quebec from the twin evils of British colonialism and Anglo-Canadian domination, and would herald a democratic and secular millennium for the French Canadian nation. In 1893, Louis-Honoré Fréchette insisted that annexation was a veritable panacea for Quebec's problems:

> In fact, alliance with the States of the Union would with one sweep of the pen settle all those thorny questions which now embarrass us. At one stroke we should benefit by all the progress of our neighbors up to this point; we should enter into free commercial relations with a country of seventy millions of inhabitants; the lines uncomfortably strained which hold us in the wake of another people would be thrown off; we should have no more hatred or rivalry of faith or race; no longer conquerors ever looking upon us as the conquered; no longer any joint responsibility with any European nation; no longer any frontiers; no longer any possible wars; a single flag over the whole of North America, which then would be, not the holding of any particular nation, but the home of Humanity itself, the Empire of Peace, the richest and most powerful dominion of the earth, under a democratic government having as its leading principle the recognition of the same rights and the imposition of the same duties among all its subjects, without question of the blood which flows in their veins or of the form in which they may choose to worship God.[7]

Rouilliard and Fréchette were convinced that the sovereignty vested in U.S. states would be sufficient to guarantee French Canadian *survivance*. In contrast, the Dominion's constitutional centralism and constant talk of imperial federation did not bode well for the French Canadian nation. By 1893, Fréchette was convinced that annexation enjoyed broad support in Quebec: 'The idea of Annexation has, during the last few years, made rapid progress with Canadians of French origin; the fact is that, even to-day, were they consulted on the question under conditions of absolute freedom, without any moral pressure from either side, I am certain that a considerable majority of Annexationists would result from the ballot.'[8]

Continental union did not, in fact, enjoy broad support in Quebec. It failed to rally the support of most of the province's liberal intellectuals, and most French-speaking annexationists, in fact, were Franco-Americans. The *petits Canadas* of New England were breeding grounds for annexationism. Fréchette and Rouilliard had both lived in the United States, as had Quebec's most brilliant annexationist, Edmond de Nevers. Unlike Rouilliard and Fréchette, however, de Nevers was no *rouge*. In the 1890s, he professed a passive and almost conservative form of annexationism that differed in many ways from the militant and republican ideals of Rouilliard and Fréchette. Edmond de Nevers' annexationism was born of cold realism. As he saw it, imperial federation was both unfeasible and undesirable, and Canadian independence was (regrettably) unattainable. This left only one realistic option for Quebec: annexation. But continental union would open new possibilities for French Canada: 'We know, in short, that the day will come when the border that separates Canada from the United States will disappear, when North America will form but one vast republic, and we aspire to build in the east a centre of French civilization, which will make a contribution to the intellectual progress, to the morality and to the diversity of the Union.'[9] The new America would be a loose confederation of ethnic blocs, and a French Canadian state would ultimately come to dominate the northeast.[10] Like Fréchette and Rouilliard, de Nevers argued that annexation would allow Quebec to finally assume her North American destiny. 'When the hour has sounded for the definitive separation of the Old World from the New, destiny will be realized, peaceful and solemn, and nothing will disturb the tranquillity of the universe,' de Nevers wrote in *L'avenir du peuple canadien-français.*[11]

In the late nineteenth century, annexationism worried many Canadians. Imperialists were particularly concerned. Annexation threatened to eliminate Canada as a disctinct and British political entity. Moreover, the annexation movement, though relatively small, attracted a reasonable amount of attention in Britain and the United States. Goldwin Smith was one of only a handful of Canadian authors known outside the Dominion of Canada, and British and American periodicals frequently asked him to comment on Canadian affairs. As a result, a significant portion of the debate surrounding annexation was conducted in foreign publications. Anglo-American opinion, it seemed, was at stake. Imperialists accused Smith of misrepresenting Canadian opinion, of underestimating the nation's potential, and of inflating its problems. Smith was undermining Canada's reputation abroad: his prose encouraged Americans to believe that their nation would someday annex Canada and it weakened support for imperial federation in Britain.

In the late nineteenth century, the imperialist riposte to annexationism was above all an attack on the person of Goldwin Smith. Smith, it was argued, did not understand Canada, nor did he speak for Canadians. The chief clerk of the House of Commons, John G. Bourinot, described Smith in 1895 as 'that tall, gloomy figure, isolated from the people of Canada, who admire his abilities but pay no heed to his opinions.'[12] Imperialists continuously externalized their opponent. Smith, they insisted, was not a real Canadian. George Monro Grant, who served as the principal of Queen's University for twenty-five years, saw the old professor as a prime example of the complete ignorance of Canadian affairs that existed at even the highest levels of British society: 'For all that he knows of the deeper feelings and convictions of Canadians, he might have lived for the last twenty or thirty years in an English cathedral close; and he is therefore continually rasping the thin-skinned among them by oracular declarations which would be considered insulting were they not ascribed to dyspepsia or disappointment. Yet he is about the only writer on Canadian topics who ever reaches the British politician!'[13]

Annexation, imperialists insisted, was a fringe solution that only rallied a handful of malcontents. In *The Great Dominion*, an 1895 treatise written largely for a British public, George R. Parkin dispelled the notion that annexationism was all the rage in Canada: 'It may be questioned whether there is in Canada to-day, from Atlantic to Pacific, any political passion so strong as opposition to absorption into the United States. It is practically accurate to say that no avowed annexationist could be elected to the Dominion Parliament. If any believer in annexation gets a seat there, it is by concealing his views.'[14] Imperialists repeatedly insisted that the evident superiority of Canadian society forever condemned annexationism to the political fringe. To this effect, John Castell Hopkins claimed in 1893 that 'the defects in American national life have long been keenly studied and criticised in Canada, and the most enthusiastic advocate of annexation knows that this belief in the superiority of Canadian institutions, laws, politics and even morals, is ingrained in the heart of the average citizen whom he endeavours to convert.'[15] Even protracted economic marasmus would not convince

Canadians to opt for continental union. In a widely read review of *Canada and the Canadian Question*, George Monro Grant, who was ordained a Presbyterian minister in 1860, argued that 'the present book, in its perpetual insistence on the material prosperity that union would bring, appeals far too much to the baser side of human nature. Surely the lessons that history teaches are that wealth is not the one thing indispensable to a people.'[16]

Smith had even misunderstood the dynamic of Anglo-American relations. Indeed, imperialists repeatedly insisted that annexation would not improve Anglo-American relations or hasten the moral reunion of the Anglo-Saxon race. On the contrary, in 1891, Grant warned that annexation would be akin to trying to 'appease a tiger by giving it blood.' American jingoes would exult that they had 'driven the British flag from this Continent' and would be encouraged to continue twisting the lion's tail. Grant, who emerged as Smith's most prominent critic in the 1890s, was 'convinced that the best way to gain the friendship of the United States – and we all wish to gain it – is by preserving our own self-respect and maintaining our own rights.'[17] In the end, he and others believed that the moral union of the English-speaking peoples would be accomplished through some form of imperial federation, and not through annexation.

Many continentalists at the end of the nineteenth century were also opposed to annexation. Chief among them was Erastus Wiman, the indefatigable promoter of commercial union between the United States and Canada. Wiman, who became an American citizen in 1897, saw annexation as both undesirable and impossible. 'There are only three ways in which a political alliance could be achieved between the two nations of North America,' he told the Union League Club of Brooklyn, New York, in 1891. 'These three means are Revolution, Conquest or Purchase.' And all three options, he assured his audience, were unthinkable.[18] Besides, Wiman insisted, annexation was thoroughly unnecessary since all of its benefits (and none of its drawbacks) could be acquired through a North American customs union.

Fatally weakened by the return of prosperity in the mid-1890s, the annexation movement died with Goldwin Smith. Still, the old man has haunted Canadian continentalism since the rainy June day when he was laid to rest. Early twentieth-century conservatives, indeed, frequently conjured the spectre of annexation, which has always provided anti-Americans with a bogey to use against their continentalist opponents. Continental integration, it was argued, would ultimately lead to annexation. Moreover, imperialists regularly externalized their opponents by presenting them as un-Canadian. Mainstream continentalists, many argued, were little more than closet annexationists who secretly yearned to be American. During the 1911 federal election, for instance, Canadians were repeatedly warned that reciprocity would put Canada on the road to continental union and that continentalists were unfit for national leadership. By the 1930s, however, there was relatively little talk of annexation in imperialist circles. The Depression, and later, the Second World War, made a certain degree of continental integration appear indispensable to Canadian prosperity and security. This attitude did not last. By the war's end, conservative intellectuals like George Grant were again warning Canadians about the peril of continental union.

Twentieth-century continentalists were usually quick to react to any suggestion that their ideas, if applied, would ultimately lead to Canada's demise. O.D. Skelton, for instance, mocked voters who believed that 'when a Canadian farmer sells a bag of potatoes to a New Yorker he throws in his country to boot.' Indeed, he asked in the lead-up to the 1911 reciprocity election, 'if trade intercourse involves political union, how is it that the twenty years in which our imports from the United States have doubled each decade are precisely the twenty years when national and imperial sentiment has been mounting highest?'[19] Reciprocity and independence, as continentalists saw it, were Canada's best protection against annexation. Besides, insisted many interwar continentalists, the United States did not even want to annex Canada. The terrible sacrifice made by Canadians during the Great War and Canada's entrance onto the world stage had apparently convinced the American people that Canada was a real nation whose sovereignty and national aspirations deserved respect. In a 1941 article dealing with Canada's place in the inter-American community, P.E. Corbett argued that annexation was a complete dead letter: 'The bogey of annexation that stalked so fiercely thirty years ago is dead. Its burial has enabled Canadians to approach more dispassionately the problems of practical adjustment to their American environment.'[20]

Annexation was not generally viewed as a serious menace in early twentieth-century Quebec. Nevertheless, French Canadian nationalists occasionally speculated that continental union might be brought about by the Canada's geographic, ethnic, and economic incongruities. Talk of annexation was often tied to a wider discussion of Quebec's place within Canada. In 1912, for instance, Henri Bourassa argued that French Canadian rights had become so eroded in the Dominion of Canada that annexation would make little difference to *la survivance*. French Canadians, he wrote in a pamphlet aimed at an English-speaking audience,

> have been brought, through a long succession of checks and humiliations, whose end is not yet in sight, to realise that outside their Quebec 'reserve,' they possess no more and no fewer privileges than they would enjoy in the United States; and that they are treated, by their English-speaking Canadian brothers, with infinitely less regard than are their compatriots in the United States by the descendants of the *Bostonnais* – the traditional enemy against whom they defended, for a century, the integrity of the Canadian territory, and later on the honour of the British flag.

Bourassa argued moreover that the 'the Province of Quebec and its legislature would enjoy a much larger measure of autonomy in the American Union than under the constitution of Canada.' Bourassa, of course, was no annexationist; he was merely making a point. *Le Devoir*'s fiery editor was tired of 'the bug-bear of Annexation' being used to frighten 'the babes of Canada … into the grip of extreme imperialism.'[21] Imperialism, not annexation, was the real threat to Canadian society. Imperialist rhetoric and actions were eroding French Canadian rights from coast to coast; and they were impeding Canada's march towards independence. What is more, Bourassa insisted, they were wearing down Quebec's faith in the Canadian nation. This, in turn, would likely weaken the province's historical opposition to annexation. The best antidote to continental union, therefore, lay in granting rights to the French Canadian minority and in Canadian independence.

In nationalist prose, Quebec was frequently portrayed as a bulwark against annexation. Despite Canada's internal weaknesses, the nation's separateness had been maintained by French Canada's repeated refusal to accept continental union. By contrast, argued Lionel Groulx, English Canadians had shown a great degree of inconsistency when it came to annexation. The abbé noted with some satisfaction that the 1849 Annexation Manifesto had, for the most part, been the work of so-called loyalists: 'In the forefront of signatories to the document figured a good number of English leaders from Montreal's financial and political worlds. Every group – conservatives, reformists, *rouges* – were represented, with the delightful characteristic, however, that the Tory element dominated.'[22]

French Canadian conservatives were more inclined to discuss the effects of annexation than their English Canadian contemporaries. For the imperialist, the rupture of the imperial bond and the destruction of Canada's political system would immediately wipe out the Canadian nation. Quebec's nationalists, for their part, did not believe that the French Canadian nation could simply disappear overnight. 'Annexation might change political allegiances and some administrative conventions, but they cannot directly affect the existence of the nation,' wrote Lionel Groulx in 1928.[23] In French Canada, absorption implied far more than the loss of political sovereignty; it supposed the extinction of Roman Catholicism and the French language and culture in Quebec – *l'annexion morale*. Nevertheless, it was assumed that political union would slowly poison French Canada's traditional social order. For Father Jacques Cousineau (1905–1982), a Jesuit who spent a number of years working with Quebec's Catholic labour unions, annexation would spell disaster for French Canada's religious faith: 'Annexation … would tend to disturb for a long time the religious metabolism of the French Canadian individual. The part of the bourgeoisie that has stayed with the Church because of social conformity rather than personal adherence would leave more or less slowly … The rural tone and solid continuity of our Christian life would see themselves further watered down by the growing attraction to cities and by the alarming preponderance that urban customs of piety would take on.'[24]

Annexation would not only devastate Quebec's spiritual order, it would also deepen the economic marginalization of Canada's French-speaking population. In 1941, François-Albert Angers (1909–2003), an economist at Montreal's École des Hautes Études commerciales, warned the readers of *L'Action nationale* that continental union would be an economic disaster for Quebec. With the disappearance of protective tariffs, the province would lose a significant portion of its industrial base and be relegated to the level of a resource hinterland: 'Quebec would then become, in the great republic, a state of farmers, lumberjacks, miners, and electricty power stations, no doubt with a minimum of industrialization arranged right here in case the raw-materials factor gave it the upper hand over everywhere else for its location. In these conditions, Quebec could stay French, but without any hope of maintaining its population growth.'[25] Like most of the *nationalistes* of his generation, Angers was a moderate ruralist. He feared that large-scale, rapid, and centralized industrialization would destroy Quebec's economic and social order, but he also believed that an over-reliance on agricultural production and simple resource extraction was a recipe for economic marasmus, underdevelopment, and massive out-migration.

Instead, Angers argued for a cautious and decentralized program of industrial development. Medium-size, regionally based industry tied to agriculture or resource extraction was the best way to ensure the overall stability and prosperity of French Canadian society.

Americanization – the process of adopting American values and practices – was seen as a form of annexationism in Quebec. Invariably described as pernicious, Americanization was assimilation writ large, but with a modern twist. For nationalist intellectuals, Americanization entailed the gradual suffocation of traditional society. Religious indifference would become generalized, the family would slowly disintegrate, and the French language and culture would progressively disappear; French Canada would cease to exist. Unlike annexation, Americanization was a major source of concern in Quebec. This was particularly true during the interwar years, when *nationaliste* intellectuals were alarmed by the rapid spread of American popular culture in Quebec. During the period under study, the intellectual struggle against *l'annexion morale* reached its zenith in 1936, when the *Revue dominicaine* published a series of articles denouncing 'Notre américanisation.' Americanization, it was argued, was a sly form of assimilation precisely because it relied on seemingly benign (i.e., cultural) means of propagation. Indeed, as Victor Barbeau, who had served in the Royal Air Force during the First World War, noted in 1922, while Britain's attempts to assimilate French Canada through violence and legislation had failed, American efforts to weaken French Canadian *survivance* with movies, jazz, chewing gum, comics, soft drinks, chorus girls, and baseball were succeeding:

> These are what, in any case, the Americans use here. The country is infested with them from coast to coast. An economic vassal of the United States, Canada is poised to become its spiritual vassal as well. English Canadians and French Canadians think, live, and judge by their neighbours alone. At all levels of society, American influence penetrates and develops. We go to the cinema only to glorify their prowess, admire the ingeniosity, applaud their flag. We read their newspapers and their reviews only to learn their latest exploits or their greatest political and sporting accomplishments. They are erasing our national life. We seem to exist only to congratulate ourselves for having them as our neighbours, and apply ourselves to resembling them as much as possible.[26]

Tourism, international labour unions, and American investment were viewed as key vectors of Canadian-American convergence. Women were also cited as possible agents of Americanization. 'Women are one of the biggest factors responsible for Americanization in Canada,' wrote Ernestine Pineault-Léveillé in 1936. 'Americanization,' she continued, 'has unhinged women. By proposing every liberty to them, by bringing them out of the home where they are queen and natural mistress, by clouding their consciousness and disturbing their faith, it has with the same stroke broken the family, worsened the economic problem and dishonoured society.'[27]

However, despite all the doom and gloom surrounding 'notre américanisation,' most writers insisted that Quebec had yet to succumb to *l'annexion morale*. 'It must be noted that this infiltration is mainly happening in large towns, and is penetrating infinitely less and only indirectly in the countryside, so that really it has only reached half the population,' Gustave Lanctot wrote in *Les Canadiens français et leurs voisins du sud*, published in 1941, the only French-language tome in the series of twenty-five volumes sponsored by the Carnegie Endowment for International Peace.[28] But Quebec could not simply rely on her rurality to counter Americanization. Cultural survival required a plan. Censorship and cultural protectionism were occasionally touted as means to offset *l'annexion morale*, but most intellectuals saw these measures as wholly inadequate. To survive, Quebec would have to create viable alternatives to American mass culture. As Jean Bruchési noted regarding American magazines, 'if we want to counter, as far as this is possible, the junk literature that comes to us from the United States let us at least have, for the masses, a magazine that is done well, lively, presented with taste, whose range of subjects equals the excellent quality of its literary form, and which gives prominence to things and people from our country.'[29] Cultural resistance would also require a strong sense of national pride among French Canadians. Achieving this nationalist renaissance would, in turn, necessitate both education and agitation. Father M.A. Lamarche, for instance, concluded the *Revue dominicaine*'s inquiry into 'Notre américanisation' by insisting that 'an anti-Americanization education campaign, both scholarly and popular ... is of vital urgency.' As he saw it, anti-American rhetoric would have to play a key role in the nationalist resurgence that was occuring in 1930s Quebec: 'It is contradictory and vain to claim to awaken national sentiment in young people as in old people (I am speaking of a reasoned feeling, experienced through the Catholic doctrine), without at the same time warning and guarding them against what we call American moral annexation.'[30]

Quebec was frequently presented as a bulwark against the Dominion's Americanization. 'Because it remains faithful to its traditions,' Gustave Lanctot told the Royal Society of Canada in 1937, 'Quebec plays the role of a barrier against Americanization, as it did in 1775, 1849, and 1887, a barrier that forces the country to stop and reflect before jumping into the unknown of American assimilation. In this way it carries out a national work, all the while pursuing its own particular goal, which is the integral preservation of its language, its religion, and the institutions handed down from its ancestors.'[31] Born in Saint-Constant, Quebec, Lanctot was awarded a Rhodes Scholarship in 1909 and was appointed to the staff of the Public Archives of Canada in 1912. Soon after the outbreak of the Great War, he enrolled as an officer in the Canadian Expeditionary Force and served overseas as the assistant director of war trophies. Demobilized in 1918, he was awarded a doctorate from the Université de Paris in 1919 for his dissertation entitled 'L'administration de la Nouvelle-France.' Upon his return to Canada, he became the director of the Public Archive's French Section. An admirer of British institutions, Lanctot was one of the leading figures of twentieth-century French Canadian loyalism. He was thus eager to show that Quebec had remained loyal to Britain since the late eighteenth century and that this loyalty had ensured Canada's survival as a separate – and British – political entity.

A number of *nationaliste* intellectuals used the province's historical opposition to annexation and Americanization as an argument in favour of French Canadian rights. For instance, in his 1941 *Reflets d'Amérique*, Édouard Montpetit's condemnation of Americanization quickly morphed into an appeal for biculturalism: 'If we cannot reconcile ourselves to a national standpoint that reflects Anglo-French culture, the influence of American civilization, which is very close and armed with powerful means of penetration, will spread.'[32] Nevertheless, when it came to the issue of Americanization, English Canadians were often portrayed as lost causes. Their society, argued Father Rodrigue Villeneuve in 1922, was thoroughly Americanized: 'In the country of Canada, whole provinces are already completely Americanized, not only by their common language but also by their ideas, feelings and tastes; by their interests, their businesses, their entertainment; by religion, education, the theatre, magazines and daily newspapers; by similar moral licentiousness, religious indifference, divorce, Malthusianism, feminism, liberal democracy, and social egalitarianism.'[33]

Imperialists would have balked at Villeneuve's suggestion that English-speaking Canadians were thoroughly Americanized. Still, the progressive Americanization of Canada was a source of concern to Tory intellectuals. They warned that cultural Americanization would eventually lead to Canada's political and spiritual domination. As Canadians adopted American values and practices, they would gradually lose faith in the Dominion and the Empire. The imperial bond would eventually be broken and Canada would inexorably drift towards continental union. As in Quebec, the bulk of English Canadian commentary regarding Americanization was published during the interwar years. However, since these years coincided with a decline in imperialist sentiment, the English Canadian response to Americanization was somewhat muted. A few prominent Tories did not even take the issue seriously. For instance, in the 1930s, Stephen Leacock poked fun at British anxieties regarding Canada's progressive Americanization: 'Every now and then ... English newspapers break out into a discussion of what is called the "Americanization of Canada." The basis of the discussion is always a sort of underlying fear that Canada is getting a little too close to the United States. It is the same sort of apprehension as is felt on a respectable farm when the daughter of the family is going out too much with the hired man. The idea is that you can't tell what may happen.' The Dominion of Canada, Leacock insisted, was strong enough to resist Americanizing influences. 'That this relationship is likely to end in, or even move towards, a political union, is just a forgotten dream,' he wrote in 1936.[34]

Most imperialists were not so flippant when it came to Americanization. In an oft-quoted 1920 article for the *Canadian Historical Review*, Archibald MacMechan (1862–1933), a professor of English at Dalhousie University in Halifax, warned that Canada was slowly becoming a 'vassal state.' Though outright annexation was no longer a likely scenario, MacMechan insisted that 'the danger is far more subtle and far more deeply to be dreaded. It lies in gradual assimilation, in peaceful penetration, in spiritual bondage – the subjection of the Canadian nation's mind and soul to the mind and soul of the United States.' Of all the vectors of Americanization, which included sports, schoolbooks, and movies, MacMechan argued that the press was the most pernicious: 'Not only is the Canadian newspaper built along American lines, but it is crammed with American "boiler plate" of all kinds, American illustrations, American comic supplements. American magazines, some of them distinctly anti-British in tone and tendency, flood our shops and book-stalls. Every new Canadian magazine is on an American model, some of them borrowing an American title and changing only the national adjective.'[35]

Though American radio and movies were often singled out as vectors of Americanization, the imperialist right was particularly concerned by the popularity of various American magazines in Canada. American magazines contributed to the propagation of American values in Canada, but they also competed with Canadian magazines for subscribers and advertisers. Imperialists often contended that Americanization could be curbed with state intervention. Tariffs, censorship, subsidies, and the creation of national cultural institutions such as the Canadian Broadcasting Corporation were usually applauded in imperialist circles. British immigration and the expansion of Anglo-Canadian trade were also cited as effective barriers to Americanization.

American popular culture was sometimes criticized in interwar continentalist circles. 'We draw our cultural importations from the bottom, not the top,' lamented Douglas Bush in 1929, 'we take our color from the *Saturday Evening Post* rather than the *Yale Review*.' Nevertheless, he continued, 'it is not quite fair to rail at the vulgarity of such American products as cheap magazines, movies, and chewing-gum when we import such things in enormous quantities; our taste would seem to be the same.'[36] In the end, Americanization did not really alarm English Canadian continentalists. Most saw Canadian-American cultural convergence as proof that both nations shared a wider North American ethos. It was not, as conservatives claimed, a prelude to moral or political assimilation. On the contrary, insisted H. Carl Goldenberg (1907–1996) in 1936, the whole concept of Americanization was something of a sophism: 'It is too often forgotten, however, that Canada does not have to be "Americanized," because Canada *is* a North American nation. We can neither deny nor avoid the facts of geography. The three thousand miles of boundary which separate Canada from the United States are a purely imaginary line. The people on each side of this line, in the main, speak the same language, have the same habits and ways of thought, and dress in similar fashions.'[37] A graduate of McGill University, Goldenberg was called to the Quebec bar in 1932. He practised law in Montreal and frequently acted as an adviser on industrial relations and constitutional matters to various governments in Canada and abroad. From 1968 to 1971, he served as a special counsel on constitutional affairs to Prime Minister Pierre Trudeau. Like many Jewish-Canadian intellectuals, Goldenberg was uncomfortable with the Anglo-conformity and anti-Americanism associated with Canadian imperialism.

In 1939, Lionel Gelber (1907–1989), a University of Toronto professor of international relations whose family had left Eastern Europe for Canada in the late nineteenth century, argued that 'Americanization' was simply a code word for 'modernization,' a phenomenon which was associated with the United States because that is where it had reached its paroxysm: 'It is the paradox of Americanization that it has not really been Americanization in any deliberate propagandist sense. Rather, it is the spread of a social system the name of which happens to be derived from its largest and most famous exemplar – one that springs from a common environment and that answers a common need.'[38] Besides, noted John Bartlet Brebner in 1931, Canadians had played a key role in crafting North America's wider culture. Cultural exchange, he reminded the Canadian Historical Association, was a two-way street: 'It is worth recalling that Canada and Canadians have played probably somewhat more than their proportionate part in designing the continental pattern of life. Scientists and inventors from Quebec to California sell their ideas, whether they be of ginger ale or preventive medicine, in New York or Pittsburgh or Chicago. The same thing can be said of many painters and writers and professional men.'[39]

The measures proposed by conservative Canadians to counter Americanization – protectionism, cultural nationalism, and imperialism – were often viewed as inherently regressive by continentalists. 'We cannot escape the fact that for good or for bad we are located in North America,' Frank Underhill wrote in 1929. 'English culture is a plant which is too delicate to survive for long the process of being transplanted across the Atlantic. Those colonially-minded persons who think to save us from the flood of Americanism by appealing to English traditions may as well start a campaign to bring back the horse and buggy.'[40] In the end, few continentalists were worried about Americanization, which many dismissed as a sophism, or by continental union, which – annexationists aside – they believed was a conservative bugbear.

For their part, imperialists and French Canadian nationalists believed that Americanization was toxic to Canadian tradition, and they repeatedly warned Canadians that cultural convergence was a serious threat to Canada. To this end, imperialists were usually quick to evoke the spectre of annexation and, with it, to vilify their continentalist opponents. In Quebec, the spectre of assimilation, of moral annexation, served a similar purpose. Both imperialists and French Canadian nationalists sought to assert the antimodern integrity of their nation and, as we shall see in the following pages, their antimodern struggle would often express itself in the discussion of Canadian-American relations.

8 Canadian-American Relations and American Foreign Policy

During most of the period under study, the Canadian-American relationship was not fundamentally bilateral. British diplomats played a role in Canadian foreign affairs until the 1920s, and even after the 1931 Statute of Westminster, the Dominion of Canada's ties to Great Britain continued to affect the course of Canadian-American relations. Canadian commentary regarding the Dominion's relationship with its southern neighbour reflected this. To discuss Canadian-American relations, indeed, was also to discuss Canada's connection to Britain. In the late nineteenth and early twentieth centuries, Britain and the United States were often understood to be antithetical entities; to draw closer to one was to drift away from the other. And this opposition was not merely intellectual and spiritual, it was also economic and geopolitical. For instance, many Canadians believed that an increase in the volume of Canadian-American trade would engender a corresponding decrease in the volume of Anglo-Canadian trade. This, in turn, would invariably lead to the loosening of the imperial bond, a possibility that was viewed with alarm in certain circles, and with some satisfaction in others.

Late nineteenth- and early twentieth-century imperialists were undoubtedly the nation's most cautious observers when it came to the Canadian-American relationship. They hoped to see the Dominion of Canada maintain cordial relations with the United States without sacrificing Canadian sovereignty or endangering imperial unity. Continental integration, to be sure, was more or less out of the question. To draw closer to the United States, many believed, was to risk absorption. To this effect, Colonel George T. Denison issued the following warning in the final paragraph of his 1909 autobiography: 'We must not forget, that with a powerful neighbour alongside of Canada, speaking the same language, and with the necessarily intimate commercial intercourse, an agitation for closer relations, leading to ultimate absorption, is easy to kindle, and being so plausible, might spread with dangerous rapidity.' 'This is a danger,' he continued, 'that those both in Canada and Great Britain, who are concerned in the future of the British Empire, would do well to take to heart, and by strengthening the bonds of Empire avert such dangers for the future.'[1]

Nevertheless, though imperialists at the turn of the twentieth century generally balked at continental integration, they were usually quick to approve of any move towards Anglo-American rapprochement. Anglo-American concord, they believed, would strengthen the Dominion of Canada's overall stability and prosperity. Moreover, several imperialists, including George R. Parkin, fancied that Canada could act as an interpreter in the Anglo-American relationship, thereby reinforcing her position within the British Empire and healing the great schism of 1776: 'Canada, in the middle ground that it occupies, will prove to be the solvent which will unite in sympathy and on honourable terms the two great nations with which she is allied in race and language.'[2] An Anglo-American rapprochement sponsored by Canada was seen as a first step towards an Anglo-Saxon millennium. Anglo-Saxon unity, indeed, was the professed goal of Canadian imperialists. It was integral to the imperialist sense of mission, which Beckles Willson defined as 'a belief in the common mission of the English-speaking race to ameliorate human conditions which might otherwise never be ameliorated.'[3] Nevertheless, as hazy concepts went, 'Anglo-Saxon unity' was even hazier than 'imperial unity.' For John G. Bourinot, who was awarded a knighthood by Queen Victoria in 1898, this nebulous chimera would be centred on a defence alliance between the United States and the British Empire: 'Although a federation of the world must ever remain a poet's dream, an alliance of all English-speaking communities for common defence would assuredly be a guarantee not only for the security of this continent, but also for the peace and happiness of all civilized nations.'[4]

In the end, however, anti-American assumptions were scarcely undermined by Anglo-Saxon rhetoric, which generally amounted to little more than a series of bland pleasantries. At the turn of the twentieth century, imperialists tended to view Canadian-American relations in terms of tensions and enmity. By and large, these tensions could not be attributed to British and Canadian policy, they argued, because both nations had generally acted in good faith when dealing with the United States. Imperialists reasoned that Canadian-American disputes were usually the result of American policy and opinion. 'Most Canadians believe to-day that the United States has shown a steady, deliberate dislike of their country and has pursued a policy more or less injurious to their interests,' wrote John Castell Hopkins in 1893.[5] The United States had consistently hampered Canadian growth and expansion since the late eighteenth century. It had acquired territory at Canada's expense in Maine, the Ohio Valley, and the Pacific Northwest, and had conspired to acquire even more. In fact, a few imperialists before the Great War, including Colonel Denison, were convinced that the United States constituted a serious military threat to the Dominion.

Imperialists repeatedly pointed out that American opinion was often openly hostile to Britain and the Empire. To this effect, Arthur Johnston reminded the readers of his 1908 monograph on the American Revolution that a 'distrust of, and a latent antipathy to, England and Englishmen is the inheritance of every citizen of the great Republic born or educated on its soil. Their minds are so filled and obsessed by the absurd and mendacious American school histories and traditions that they are incapable of dissociating Englishmen of the present generation from those who participated in the scenes enacted in the early history of their country.'[6] Worse still, the average American was utterly ignorant of Canadian affairs and had little or no respect for Canadian nationhood. 'The statesmen and people generally of that country have been always remarkably ignorant, not only of the history, but of the political institutions and of the political sentiments of the Canadians,' wrote John G. Bourinot in 1898. 'They have never appreciated the tendency of this political development, which is in the direction of a new nationality, not inferior to the United States in many elements of a people's greatness.'[7] Moreover, it was claimed that American diplomats had no sense of fair play, and that the U.S. political system, with its checks and balances, made diplomatic negotiations particularly arduous.

Imperialists saw Britain as the champion of Canadian nationhood and, furthermore, as the guarantor of Canada's power and prestige. They argued that the Canadian nation would not have survived the nineteenth century without British protection, and believed that continentalist and *nationaliste* calls for complete Canadian independence were largely misguided. Canada needed the imperial connection. 'Independent, we could not survive a decade,' wrote Stephen Leacock in 'Greater Canada: An Appeal,' a 1907 article published in the *University Magazine*. 'Those of us who know our country realize that beneath its surface smoulder still the embers of racial feud and religious bitterness. Twice in our generation has the sudden alarm of conflict broken upon the quiet of our prosperity with the sound of a fire bell in the night. Not thus our path. Let us compose the feud and still the strife of races, not in the artificial partnership of an Independent Canada, but in the greatness of a common destiny.'[8] In 1911, Leacock's celebrated article was reprinted and widely distributed by interests opposed to reciprocity.

Though many imperialists were genuinely upset by what they saw as repeated British indifference to Canadian interests – Colonel Denison and many others believed that only imperial federation would ensure that British diplomats would protect Canadian interests – most also took issue with the widely held belief that Great Britain had repeatedly purchased Anglo-American peace by sacrificing Canadian interests. On the contrary, argued Queen's professor of colonial history, William Lawson Grant, in a 1913 article published in London's *Round Table*, British power was the historical key to Canadian survival and expansion. 'If British diplomacy has been one long series of surrenders,' Grant asked, how is it that 'Canada is to-day a puissant young nation, extending from Atlantic to Pacific?' The answer lay in British power and realpolitik: 'Whether we look at the general results of British diplomacy, or consider individual instances, we find that, whereas France and Spain have been squeezed out of the New World by the United States, Great Britain has always been strong enough to enforce at least a compromise.' Britain had sacrificed vast tracts of land to appease the United States, but she had saved the farm. 'British diplomacy has other interests to consider as well as those of Canada,' Grant wrote, 'but if it be argued that for this very reason Canada would do better to stand alone, the answer is easy. She is in the world, and she cannot get out of it. If, in the world situation at any particular time, she had endeavoured to stand alone, how would she have fared? Granted, that to be part of an Empire, and thus at times to be considered only a part, has its disadvantages. What would have been her fate had she fronted the billows unaided?'[9]

By the interwar years, the imperialist outlook on Canadian-American relations had noticeably softened. Americans, it seemed, had acquired a new respect for their northern neighbours. Indeed, argued Robert Falconer in 1925, Canada's terrible sacrifice in the Great War had awoken America to the Dominion's strength and promise: 'England regards Canada with the pride of a first-born; in the Empire she holds the prestige of age and position. The United States no longer looks upon her as an intruding colony on the continent, but respects her as a nation within the British Commonwealth and as a neighbour who will take her own way to success. The Dominion, therefore, may now play a new part. No longer thought of as factious she may become an interpreter.'[10] Present in imperialist rhetoric before the Great War, the idea of Canada as an Anglo-American interpreter intensified during the interwar years, while bland pleasantries regarding the unguarded frontier, which were relatively infrequent in early imperialist writing, became more common. Moreover, by the 1930s, the idea that the United States might constitute a military threat to the Dominion of Canada had become the object of some ridicule.

As Tory anti-Americanism eased up, so too did conservative apprehensions regarding continental integration. This was particularly the case during the Second World War, when fear, realism, and indeed loyalty to Britain brought many staunch imperialists to support wartime cooperation and integration with the United States. The Ogdensburg and Hyde Park agreements, it was argued, aided Britain in her darkest hour. To refuse wartime integration and cooperation, therefore, was to jeopardize British defence. 'It will be a poor kind of loyalty to the British if we insist upon being more British than they are, to the extent of being more anti-American,' the English-born editor of Toronto's *Saturday Night*, B.K. Sandwell (1876–1954), told Dalhousie's Institute of Public Affairs in 1941.[11] Nonetheless, Tory intellectuals held some reservations regarding wartime continental integration. Some worried that Canada might become an American dependency if Canadians took a careless attitude towards the new defence relationship.

Earlier imperialist ideas, to be sure, had survived the Great War, albeit in a watered-down form. Indeed, though imperial federation's day had passed, the idea of a powerful Commonwealth of freely associated states now galvanized Tories. R.G. Trotter, for instance, insisted in 1938 that Canada's ties to the British Commonwealth buttressed Canadian nationhood: 'Canada needs and will continue to need the prestige and strength of the Commonwealth association if she is to preserve not merely the professed friendship of her neighbour but the latter's respectful recognition and acceptance, in practice, of the realities of the Dominion's national independence.'[12] B.K. Sandwell, for his part, warned Canadians in a 1939 pamphlet that continentalist assurances that North American integration would free Canada from residual British domination were missing the mark: 'For Canada to accept the leading-strings of the United States would be to reduce herself from the rank of a completely self-governing nation to that of a protectorate. It would be to place in the hands of another nation the control of the most important decisions affecting Canadian national existence, without conferring on Canadians any share in, or any influence upon, the political life of that nation.'[13]

In the late 1930s and early 1940s, Tory resistance to continental integration often expressed itself through a rejection of pan-Americanism. Indeed, with continental Europe essentially closed to Canadian goods, many continentalists began to argue that the time had come for Canada to join the Pan-American Union and rethink its relationship with Latin America. R.G. Trotter led the conservative charge against the pan-American ideal. To join the Pan-American Union, he warned in 1939, was to subject Canada to American domination. 'Canada has some interests in the Western Hemisphere, it is true, which might appropriately be reflected in some formal association with other powers in this hemisphere,' Trotter admitted, 'but it may be questioned whether those interests are of the kind to make it appropriate for us to be one of the large group of minor powers associated under the leadership of the United States, in a bureau which an American friend of mine, a specialist in international problems and institutions, recently called an appendage of the State Department.' Joining the Pan-American Union, moreover, would 'mean lining ourselves up with a tradition involving a repudiation of our own essential character as a nation. For the framework and the philosophy of Pan-Americanism itself, whatever the use that some American states might now like to make of it, are still essentially defensive and ingrowing.' Pan-Americanism was viewed as a dressed-up version of isolationism. 'Its unifying spirit is the tradition of an independence of Europe won through revolutionary conflict that furnishes in each republic the cherished core of national pride.' 'Canada's national position has not been reached thus,' Trotter continued, 'and to do anything that attempts to assimilate Canadian tradition to that aspect of the tradition of the American republics is to nullify the inherent advantages that result for ourselves and for a wider international comity, from Canada's realization of political nationality without such a core of traditional antagonisms to the non-American world.'[14] In the end, Trotter rejected the Pan-American ethos because he saw it as inimical to Canada's tradition of British continuity. To enter the Pan-American Union, he believed, was to sunder the bond that linked Canada with Britain and the Commonwealth, and furthermore, to imperil the British and conservative essence of Canadian nationhood.

Besides, remarked several prominent Tories, Canada had little or nothing in common with the nations of Latin America. By and large, the South American republics were viewed as undemocratic and under-developed backwaters; their Catholic inhabitants spoke Spanish and Portuguese and were, for the most part, not of European ancestry. Some conservative intellectuals, including George Grant, also believed that it would be geographically absurd for Canada to join the Pan-American Union. The whole concept of pan-Americanism, Grant argued in 1945, ran counter to Canada's fundamental nordicity: 'If it ever comes to a choice between the Commonwealth and the Pan-American Union, the former is of vastly greater importance to us as a nation than the latter. For what the believers in the western hemisphere forget is geography. Canada is even more intimately bound up with the northern hemi-sphere than with the western hemisphere.'[15]

In the end, Canada did not join the Pan-American Union – renamed the Organization of American States – until 1989. Indeed, though war-time support for continental integration ran high, Prime Minister Mac-kenzie King did not press his luck with further changes to the Canada's geopolitical position. Significant popular support for continental inte-gration, he surmised, would be fleeting. Few continentalist intellectuals were quite so pessimistic. By the late 1930s and early 1940s, continental integration appeared to be an idea whose time had finally come. Dur-ing those years, continentalism, though basically constant in its ideas, became less defensive and more self-assured in its assumptions.

First among these assumptions was the idea that the Canadian-American relationship had been primarily characterized by peace and friendship. Indeed, unlike their anti-American adversaries, continental-ists – annexationists aside – continuously played down elements of fric-tion in Canadian-American relations. For instance, in the introduction to his 1942 study entitled *The Unguarded Frontier*, Edgar McInnis argued that the Canadian-American relationship, though at times turbulent, was essentially sound. 'If the factors which make for antagonism have been real,' he wrote, 'the factors which dictate a serious effort at har-mony and co-operation have been far more powerful and persistent. At the root of the relations between Canada and the United States has been a firm desire to share the North American continent in amity and without strife.'[16]

Continentalists did not view American might as a threat to Canadian nationhood. Even in the late nineteenth century, writers like Erastus Wiman considered the very idea of an Anglo-American war fought on

Canadian soil to be absurd. American power, Wiman and others insisted, actually protected Canada from outside threats. Continentalists generally downplayed annexationist and anti-British sentiment in the United States, and they often blamed Britain for the disputes and tensions that periodically arose between Canada and the United States. On the whole, it was argued that Americans respected Canadian independence. In fact, remarked Frank Underhill in 1929, 'the real danger of Canadian-American relations is not, as some of our professional patriots would like us to believe, that the Yankees are plotting daily against us, but that they are not thinking about us at all.'[17]

Continentalists sought to achieve Canadian-American integration and cooperation without sacrificing Canada's separate political identity. Continental integration was seen as an essentially economic endeavour, and would be primarily realized through reciprocity or, some argued, through a North American customs union. Canadian-American cooperation, for its part, would be achieved through the creation of bilateral bodies to deal with issues ranging from trade to defence. The International Joint Commission, which was created in 1909 to regulate Canadian-American boundary waters, was viewed as a model in this regard.

For many continentalists, Canadian-American integration was seen as a step towards the creation of a wider North Atlantic, Pan-American, or international community. As a result, relatively few pro-American intellectuals wanted Canada to withdraw from the Commonwealth or the League of Nations. Canada's position in the Commonwealth, for instance, was often understood to provide the nation with an opportunity to act as the linchpin of Anglo-American relations. Indeed, though continentalists occasionally made light of Canada's much touted role as an interpreter in the Anglo-American relationship, most also firmly believed that Canada could and should assume such a role. For instance, in July 1939, Arthur Lower, who had served as an officer in the Royal Navy during the Great War, insisted that 'Canada's position qualifies her well for what has often been said to be her destined role, that of interpreter between the two great branches of the English-speaking world. She can understand, for example, the Englishman's touchiness on the subject of sea supremacy and can also appreciate America's desire for freedom of the seas, for in wartime her commercial interests would be identical with those of America.'[18]

However, the continentalist sense of mission was not limited to Anglo-American relations. On the contrary, continentalist intellectuals

believed that North American peace and prosperity contained enduring lessons for all of mankind. After all, Canada and the United States
shared the world's longest undefended border and had managed to
avoid going to war against each other since 1814. For his part, Reverend James A. Macdonald, who played an important role in the establishment of the World Peace Foundation, eulogized the undefended
border with evangelical zeal. It was, he exclaimed in 1917, a beacon
of Christian virtue: 'There you have it! More than five thousand miles
of North America's international boundary between the United States
and Canada! ... More than five thousand miles, with never a fortress! ...
More than five thousand miles of civilized and Christianized internationalism! God's shining sun in all his circling round lights up no such
track of international peace, and crosses no such line of international
power, anywhere else in the world.'[19]

Though exceptional, the Canadian-American model was also seen
as exportable. In 1934, James T. Shotwell convinced the Carnegie Endowment for International Peace to sponsor the publication of a series
of studies on Canadian-American relations because he believed that
'statesmanship and common sense have ultimately built up a technique
for the settlement of disputes between Canada and the United States
which can and should furnish a model to all the world.'[20] Profoundly
influenced by his father's Quakerism, Shotwell's interest in international affairs was an extension of his lifelong commitment to the cause
of international peace and disarmament. He and others were convinced
that Canadian-American harmony proved that the formula for international peace could be found in the arbitration of disputes, trade, and
the free exchange of population. Legalists, including P.E. Corbett, were
particularly intent on demonstrating that arbitration and respect for the
rule of law were the basis for Canadian-American concord. In *The Settlement of Canadian-American Disputes*, published in 1937, Corbett insisted that 'the remarkable success of arbitration between Canada and the
United States is due to the fact that these two countries have sufficient
respect for judicial methods and their common legal tradition to endow
their joint tribunals with the power of deciding according to "law and
equity," and then to accept, in the main with no more discontent than
the losing litigant may be expected to manifest, a liberal interpretation
by the arbiters of what constitutes equity in the matter at issue.'[21]

There were, of course, some clouds on the horizon. For instance,
many continentalist intellectuals were convinced that American ignorance of Canadian affairs hindered Canadian-American harmony.

British involvement in Canadian-American relations also tended to be viewed with concern by intellectuals, including John Bartlet Brebner, whose continentalism was tied to a wider Atlanticism. Many continentalists believed that the main threat to Canada's sovereignty was not American imperialism, but British paternalism. They hoped to draw Canada closer to the United States in part because they wished to affirm Canada's independence from Britain. Indeed, though the continentalist ethos was not anti-British per se, it did provide, for some intellectuals, notes Graham Carr, 'a safety-valve for releasing pent-up colonial hostility toward imperial Britain.'[22] In a 1933 essay, William Arthur Deacon, the outspoken literary editor of the Toronto *Mail and Empire*, dismissed the idea that British power and diplomacy had protected Canada from American expansionism: 'Consistently, each and every time Canada's interests have been entrusted to Great Britain in connection with a dispute with the United States, Canada has lost through the English arbitrator siding with the advocates of the United States' claim.' Deacon argued that American indifference, not the British connection, had saved Canada from annexation: 'The United States did not want Canada, partly from ignorance of its value, but chiefly because she was busy filling her own empty spaces and exploiting her own resources. Until the end of the 19th century, the United States was the most insular of the great powers, sublimely indifferent to the world beyond her borders. Therein lay Canada's early safety – to the credit of neither nation, but to our own lasting advantage.'[23]

Continentalist intellectuals were early and enthusiastic supporters of Canadian-American military cooperation and integration. For instance, English Canada's most prominent pre–First World War advocate of Canadian independence, John S. Ewart, had called for a North American defence pact decades before the Ogdensburg Agreement was signed.[24] Canada and the United States shared the same strategic interests, continentalists insisted. Besides, by the late interwar years, it had become clear to most continentalist intellectuals – and to most Canadians – that Britain could no longer guarantee Canada's security. 'A distant country may make a good market in time of peace,' F.R. Scott wrote in 1941, 'but it may make a poor base for defense in time of war. Strategically, Canada is and must be an integral part of North American, and hence of hemispheric, defense.'[25] Continentalist intellectuals accordingly hailed the signing of the Ogdensburg and Hyde Park agreements. Moreover, socialists like Scott believed that wartime economic cooperation had the added attraction of getting Canadians accustomed to statism and economic planning. Continentalists were nevertheless conscious of the pitfalls of strategic integration. Canada would need to be an active partner in defence integration, many argued. Otherwise, the nation would simply become a satellite of the United States.

By the late 1930s, a number of continentalist intellectuals began to argue that hemispheric integration was also integral to Canadian prosperity and security. During this time, Canada's leading proponent of pan-Americanism was McGill's John P. Humphrey. A liberal internationalist, Humphrey believed that regional associations like the Pan-American Union could form the building blocks for a new international organization and that hemispheric integration was the first step towards drawing the United States out of its isolation. Canada, he insisted, could not afford to continue snubbing the Pan-American Union. Membership in the Union would not require Canada to withdraw from the Commonwealth. 'As these two great international organizations are presently organized,' he wrote in a 1941 article published in the *Canadian Forum*, 'there would be no incompatibility, either legal or political, in Canada belonging to them both.' Besides, the Pan-American Union was no longer an instrument of American domination. Indeed, Humphrey claimed that Roosevelt's Good Neighbor Policy, which promised an end to American intervention in Latin America and the Caribbean, had fundamentally altered the dynamic of hemispheric relations. Canadian membership in the Pan-American Union would foster trade between the South American republics and Canada and, in the context of the Second World War, hemispheric integration was viewed as vital to Canadian security and defence.[26]

The *nationaliste* attitude towards Canadian-American relations was marked by some degree of ambivalence. A number of nationalists, including André Laurendeau, worried that continental integration might pave the way for annexation. Others, however, anticipated that any improvement in the Canadian-American relationship would result in a corresponding loosening of the imperial bond. A rapprochement between Canada and the United States, in this regard, was seen as an important step towards Canadian independence. For this reason, *Le Devoir*'s parliamentary correspondent, Léopold Richer, argued in 1941 that French Canadians should actively support Canadian-American cooperation:

Far from snubbing a policy of Canadian-American rapprochement, far from stopping at the dangers that a policy of independence represents, we must support it and encourage it with all our might, so that it might bear fruit at the end of the present conflict. For all nations, including the Canadian nation, independence is desirable in itself. Not an independence that looks down on the rights of other nations and that leads to the worst catastrophes: the neighbouring republic would prevent us from attempting any foolish adventure. But a true independence, which would be supported by a close and friendly collaboration with the United States. An independence, in short, that would free us from the present artificial links, in order to accept those shaped by geography, which consequently correspond to necessities.

'It is important,' Richer wrote, 'for us to become accustomed to the idea that Canada, while recognizing the obligations that her geographic and economic situation imposes, can live freely and prosper in collaboration with the United States.'[27]

British involvement in Canadian-American relations was often viewed with distaste in Quebec's intellectual circles. Henri Bourassa, for instance, regularly accused British diplomats of selling out Canadian interests. 'Thanks to the zeal, intelligence, and generosity displayed tirelessly by British statesmen and diplomats in serving American interests,' he wrote in a 1919 pamphlet, 'Canada has become a geographic incoherence, a string of regions without direct contact, separated by immense natural barriers, with each one separately attracted by the huge and growing force of attraction that emanates from the American republic, their only neighbour.' Bourassa was convinced that British policy had set the stage for annexation, and that only independence from Britain could prevent such a disaster. 'An independent Canada would be more sheltered from American greed than a Canada dependent on Britain,' he argued.[28]

During the Second World War, talk of Anglo-Saxon unity aroused a great deal of suspicion in Quebec. French Canadian intellectuals, to be sure, were more or less united in their opposition to British imperialism, and the very idea that Britain and the United States might combine their power to create a new world order was viewed with alarm. Invited to speak at a 1941 conference on Canadian-American affairs sponsored by the Carnegie Endowment for International Peace, François-Albert Angers criticized the other participants for their readiness to embrace Anglo-Saxon hegemony. He worried, 'as a Canadian of non-British origin, that a reorganization of the world' would be founded 'on the basis of a too-exclusive Anglo-Saxon brotherhood and pride – which has been too much, in my opinion, the theme of this conference since its beginning and which might be construed, by other nationalities in the British Empire and the United States, as an unbearable and an unjustifiable rebuff, and by other nations, as a tentative overture for an Anglo-Saxon domination of the world.' Trained at the École libre des Sciences politiques in Paris, Angers embraced a multilateral world view. He wished 'to make possible the organization of collaboration between the peoples of the world on an equal footing, with due respect to the traditions and social state of each, and with a view to giving every nation the possibility of attaining an economic standard acceptable in our times.'[29]

Nationaliste intellectuals were more enthusiastic when it came to pan-American relations. 'It is becoming clear to everyone,' warned Lionel Groulx in 1922, 'that a new classification of the regions of the world is under way, and that an upset in the balance of power will take place, to Europe's detriment.' The Western Hemisphere would play a central role in the emerging new world order, and Groulx believed that Canadians – in particular French Canadians – needed to get on the pan-American bandwagon. 'Only, it has to be said, our appalling happy-go-lucky attitude of a state in guardianship has allowed us to observe, without emotion, the vaste pan-American movement that has developed in the two Americas since 1914,' he lamented. To counter this indifference, Groulx endeavoured to include some discussion of Latin American affairs in the pages of *L'Action française*. French Canada was believed to share a great deal of religious and cultural affinities with Latin America and, as the abbé later noted in his memoirs, 'I have always believed that we ought to look in that direction for a counterweight to Washington's omnipotent influence.'[30]

Anti-Americans and continentalists in French Canada were usually on the same page when it came to Canadian independence and pan-Americanism. However, on the issue of continental integration, continentalists like the editor of Montreal's *Le Jour*, Jean-Charles Harvey, did not suffer from the ambivalence that affected some of their anti-American peers. On the eve of the Second World War, Harvey declared to an assembled group of Canadian and American scholars that 'it would be desirable if both Canada and the United States got together more closely to act as the natural arbiters of peace; they should abolish barriers between themselves and set up free trade, free migration, similar social and economic laws, and, on that basis, create a new world of love and justice.'[31] Like many continentalists, Harvey believed that Canadian-American integration would hasten the modernization of French Canadian society.

American foreign policy has always held a particular fascination for Canadian intellectuals. Indeed, to scrutinize America's relationship with the wider world is, in many ways, to ponder Canada's foreign policy options. During the period under study, the examination of American foreign policy allowed Canadian intellectuals to grapple with two key geopolitical sensibilities: imperialism and isolationism. The issue of American imperialism dominated Canadian discussions of American foreign policy from the late nineteenth century to 1914, while the question of isolationism was at the forefront of Canadian commentary from 1914 to the early 1940s.

On the whole, Canadian imperialists held a positive, though certainly not uncritical, view of American imperialism. Their penchant for colonial expansion and the uplifting of non-whites made them view the American acquisition of Puerto Rico or the Philippines in a positive light. America, for all its faults, was spreading the virtues of western civilization among the 'ignorant' and 'downtrodden' peoples of the southern hemisphere. The United States, it seemed, was finally emerging from its isolation and making a positive contribution to the civilizing mission of the Anglo-Saxon race.

No Canadian intellectual was a more enthusiastic supporter of American imperialism than Beckles Willson. He believed that the Spanish-American conflict would herald a new era of imperialist regeneration for the United States. 'The year 1898 was one of the epoch-marking years in the history of America,' Willson wrote in *The New America: A Study of the Imperial Republic*, a 1903 book written to celebrate nascent American imperialism and to promote Anglo-American cooperation. 'In that *annus mirabilis* was decided the momentous question whether the United States were to continue their policy of political isolation, or were, as a united State, to take up a position amongst the world-powers, and, in the language of one native writer, "assume the unselfish obligations and responsibilities demanded by the enlightened civilization of the age."' Willson, who had been the Boston *Globe*'s correspondent in Cuba in 1888, believed that imperialism was the answer to many of America's woes. Indeed, like most Canadian imperialists, he was convinced that colonial ventures uplifted both the colonizer and the colonized. As a result, American imperial expansion would not only benefit 'alien and distant races,' but would also help purify American politics and society. It would, for instance, unite America's various sections under the banner of imperialist expansion. Moreover, Willson argued that the denial of suffrage 'to the horde of dark-skinned Sandwich or Philippine islanders, or to the fanatical blacks of the Antilles' would 'operate as a powerful argument in favour of the restriction of the suffrage of negroes and illiterates at home.' Perhaps most importantly, however, imperialist expansion would fuel the growth of executive and federal power which, in turn, would strike a powerful blow against localism and political corruption: 'Since 1898 we observe a marked tendency to raise the whole tone of public life. Public interest has become centred on Imperial matters, in the upbuilding of international commerce, in the work of establishing peace and orderly government in the outlying portions of the Empire. It has less to spare for the local political crank with his petty programme, or the local boss in his wire pulling.'[32]

At the end of the day, however, Canadian imperialists only approved of American expansionism when it was directed at Spanish colonies or at remote islands in the South Pacific. They quickly changed their tune when expansion appeared to threaten Canada or the British Empire. Imperialists were more or less united in their opposition to the Monroe Doctrine, which they saw as both regressive and aggressive. Beckles Willson, for instance, firmly believed that the doctrine, which forbade the European powers from establishing new colonies in the Americas, was an obstacle to the progress of western civilization: 'It is opposing the principle of the "constantly increasing responsibility of the superior and competent nations and the constantly lessening sway, influence, and territory of the inferior and the incompetent," which is to-day one of the mightiest forces in the world.' European colonization, Willson argued, would uplift the 'semi-civilized' peoples of Latin America. 'Assuming that Germany, highly civilized, efficient, capable, and honest, desires to plant a German colony in the Southern Continent. Does any but a prating dunce or a parish bigot suppose that this would not redound to the advantage of the whole district where German institutions rose, German thrift spread, or German laws ran?' he asked. Indeed, though he would later serve as a senior officer in the Canadian Expeditionary Force, in 1903 Willson was not above preaching racial solidarity with Germany: 'The truth is, America herself would greatly benefit from Germany's colonizing labours in the Southern Continent. She has far more bond with a great cultured Protestant Germany than with the horde of semi-Spanish, semi-civilized Peruvians and Argentinians.'[33]

Stephen Leacock, for his part, denounced the Monroe Doctrine as an instrument of American domination. Americans believed that the Monroe Doctrine gave them the right to sever Canada's ties to Britain and turn the Dominion into an American protectorate. Moreover, Leacock scoffed at the idea that the Monroe Doctrine protected Canada against an attack by a European power. Britain, not America, was Canada's protector. Indeed, Leacock argued that the United States would not risk being dragged into a European war to defend a British dominion. 'Consider now a moment what would be the consequences, under present conditions of international politics, of the supposed axiom that Canada is protected by the United States,' he wrote in 1909. 'It could only mean that no matter what European power or combination of powers might be at war with Great Britain, no matter how the United States might otherwise be disposed towards that power, no matter what part Canada might be taking in the contest – that the United States would declare to the European power that Canadian territory, Canadian ships, and Canadian commerce were outside of the legitimate field of belligerent attack. The thing is absolute nonsense.[34]

Continentalists generally rejected the idea that the Monroe Doctrine was threatening, regressive, or imperialistic. John S. Ewart, who had acted as the chief counsel for Canada during the 1910 North Atlantic fisheries arbitration at The Hague, insisted in 1913 that the Monroe Doctrine's 'operation has been extremely beneficial' to both Canada and the wider pan-American community. The doctrine did not threaten Canada, quite the contrary, and it had 'never either led to war, or to participation in war by the United States. Its original enunciation for example, in 1823, *prevented* war.'[35]

Nevertheless, during the period under study, continentalist intellectuals were often more critical of American foreign policy than were their anti-American opponents. This pattern emerged in the late 1890s, when Washington acquired what amounted to colonies in the Caribbean and South Pacific. Many Canadian continentalists were unimpressed by America's nascent imperialism. An anti-imperialist current ran through continentalism, and its principal exponent at the turn of the twentieth century was Goldwin Smith. In 1902, he published *Commonwealth or Empire? A Bystander's View of the Question*, a short essay denouncing American imperialism. The United States, he insisted, had reached a fork in the road: 'Shall the American Republic be what it has hitherto been, follow its own destiny, and do what it can to fulfil the special hopes which humanity has founded on it; or shall it slide

into an imitation of European Imperialism, and be drawn, with the
military powers of Europe, into a career of conquest and domination
over subject races, with the political liabilities which such a career entails?'[36]

Imperialism, Smith argued, was a significant threat to America's republican institutions. He believed that the subjugation of 'half-civilized
races' would destroy the very principles of liberty and equality upon
which the American republic was founded. Imperialism bred barbar-
ity (in both the conquered and the conqueror) and Smith questioned
whether the American attempt to pacify the Philippines would leave
'the character of the conquerors ... untainted by this competition in
cruelty with a half-civilized race.' Smith was equally worried by the
growth of militarism that he believed had accompanied American imperial ventures. Like many nineteenth-century republicans, he had an
aversion to large standing armies, which he viewed as a threat to both
freedom and democracy. 'It is needless to say what is the relation of
Militarism to political liberty. It has been the same ever since the military power enslaved Rome,' he wrote in 1902. Smith's repeated refer-
ences to ancient Rome in *Commonwealth or Empire?* were significant.
Indeed, his reading of history had convinced him that empires were
essentially ephemeral. As a result, he believed that America's transition
from republic to empire, like that of ancient Rome, would eventually
lead to its disintegration.[37]

Two years earlier, another friend of the American republic, Edmond
de Nevers, urged the United States not to pursue overseas expansion,
which he viewed as a repudiation of 'the Constitution, the Declaration
of Independence, the teachings of Washington, Jefferson, and Monroe.'[38] Similarly – and despite being a decorated veteran of the Spanish-
American conflict – Sylva Clapin warned against the recent emergence
of 'a warlike spirit which can push people to the worst adventures.'
America's phenomenal growth in the nineteenth century, he believed,
could be found in the nation's repudiation of militarism. However,
Clapin noted in 1900 that 'militarism, which we thought impossible in
the United States, is starting to take hold among our neighbours.' This
martial spirit troubled the erstwhile editor of the *Courrier de Saint-Hyacinthe*: 'The regular army has today reached a considerable size, and
formidable armaments are continuing in all the navy yards. Moreover,
the annexation of Puerto Rico and the Philippine Islands has given
birth, especially among the Republicans, to a policy of expansion that
can be summed up in one word: imperialism.'[39]

During the period examined here, French Canadians tended to view themselves as the victims of imperialism, and liberals and conservatives alike regarded imperialist expansion and militarism with suspicion. The moral and spiritual uplifting of Africa and Asia, it was argued, could not be achieved at the point of a bayonet. To this effect, *nationaliste* poet William Chapman derided claims that a U.S. victory in the Spanish-American War would serve the higher interests of humanity. 'This war is ignominious,' he asserted in 1898, 'and what makes us find it even more criminal is the hypocritical declaration of the Americans who claim that they want to spill blood only to serve humanity.' Chapman believed that America was ill-placed to give the world lessons in uplifting humanity: 'We know the love Uncle Sam's children have for humanity; we know how they have treated and continue to treat the black race under their star-spangled flag; we have before our eyes the abominable example they have given to the civilized world in allowing polygamy in Utah, in letting Brigham Young humiliate thousands of civilized Christians to the level of veritable human beasts lost in the shadows of ignorance and perversity.'[40]

Later on, America's belated entry into the two world wars and her refusal to join the League of Nations caused a noteworthy shift in the tone and focus of Canadian commentary. In English Canada, the theme of American imperialism received little attention from 1914 until the early 1940s. During this period, the discussion of American foreign policy generally revolved around the issue of isolationism. As a strategic doctrine, isolation generated a great deal of criticism in Canada, far more, in fact, than American imperialism ever had. Quebec was an exception to this trend. French Canadian criticism of American foreign policy diminished during the interwar years. Unlike their English Canadian peers, French Canadian intellectuals were fairly ambivalent when it came to American isolation. On the one hand, they tended to approve of the League of Nations and, more generally, of multilateralism. American isolation, in this sense, was seen as detrimental to the new world order that had emerged from the Great War. To this effect, in 1935, Paul-Henri Guimont, who had recently received a master's degree in economics from Harvard University, urged President Roosevelt to embrace a more interventionist vision of foreign affairs: 'He must endorse Wilsonian policy and collaborate more closely and less sentimentally on the international front, which he has scarcely pursued yet, and which the American mind seems scarcely disposed to admit. The economic salvation of the American nation must not be left to the mercy of a people in disarray, a people still obsessed by its own borders. Participating in world affairs is a characteristic of a nation's virility.'[41]

On the other hand, most interwar French Canadian intellectuals dreaded foreign entanglements and were generally hostile to the idea of multilateral interventionism sponsored by the League of Nations. Indeed, in many ways, Quebec and the United States shared a similar world view during the 1920s and 1930s. Consequently, criticism of American isolationism was fairly rare in Quebec's intellectual circles, and many thinkers would have agreed with Lionel Roy (b. 1905), a lawyer and contributor to *Le Canada français*, when he noted in 1933 that the American 'participation in international life is neither more remarkable nor more onerous than that of other nations. Their policy is above all national.'[42]

The atmosphere in English Canada's interwar intellectual circles was not particularly congenial to American isolationism. Many continentalists embraced liberal internationalism and were correspondingly dismayed by America's refusal to join the League of Nations, which James T. Shotwell considered to be 'one of the greatest political mistakes the United States has made.'[43] A former foreign policy adviser to President Woodrow Wilson, Shotwell worked ceaselessly during the interwar years to counter American isolationism and to promote America's entry into the League of Nations, eventually becoming the president of the American League of Nations Association in 1935. John W. Dafoe, who played a key role in the founding of the Canadian Institute of International Affairs, was equally disappointed by America's refusal to embrace her international responsibilities. Drawing on his experience at the Paris Peace Conference of 1919, which he had attended as a member of the Canadian delegation, Dafoe scolded the Americans attending a 1935 symposium on Canadian-American relations for their nation's rejection of Wilsonian idealism. 'There was something to be seen at Paris that never happened in the world before,' he said. 'One country, at a great international conference, had the moral leadership of the world by universal consent; not by military leadership or leadership by the threat of force, but by the strength of a moral ideal. I want to say to you Americans that that was the hour of your power and your glory, – and you threw it away, with very serious consequences to yourselves and with consequences to the world far beyond calculation.'[44]

A majority of continentalists saw isolationism as a dangerous policy both for the United States and the wider world. In fact, by the end of the Second World War, relatively few Canadian intellectuals feared

America's status as an emerging superpower. On the contrary, once the conflict ended, many worried that the United States would again retreat from the world stage. Continentalists were particularly anxious to see the United States assume the mantle of postwar international leadership. American isolationism did have its apologists, however, and many continentalists, though critical of isolation, were also inclined to minimize or relativize its effects. For instance, Toronto *Globe* journalist Peter McArthur (1866–1924), whose weekly column on rural life was widely read, insisted that American isolation should not be confused with indifference. In *The Affable Stranger* (1920), a series of sketches of American life gathered while on a trip through the United States, he reasoned that America would eventually assume its international responsibilities: 'While I would not pretend to defend the United States for its present isolation ... I have a feeling that under this apparent indifference there is a blind, instinctive groping for the true solution of humanity's problem. I found the best people perplexed rather than defiant. They were raging at their own futility – futile because they could not yet see through the battle-smoke that still envelops the world.'[45] Many continentalists argued, moreover, that isolationist sentiment was hardly confined to the United States. 'The American world-outlook frequently appears to Canadians insular and selfish, although in many respects there is a striking similarity between it and their own,' wrote the University of British Columbia's future dean of graduate studies, Henry F. Angus (1891–1991) in 1938.[46]

Attempts to explain or excuse American isolation were rarer during the two world wars. Even so, a certain defence of American neutrality could be found in wartime continentalist circles. For instance, in July 1915, O.D. Skelton suggested that the United States might be more useful to the Allied cause as a neutral nation. Britain and France already possessed naval preponderance, and if America were to enter the conflict, 'it would simply mean that the stream of munitions now beginning to go to the Allies would be turned to the use of the United States forces, who would not be able to use them for many months later.'[47] Similarly, in July 1941, F.R. Scott insisted that the United States had become a quasi-belligerent whose support was vital to the Allied war effort. American neutrality, in fact, was little more than a façade. 'Now the principal fact about the United States is that its policy is one of all aid to Britain,' Scott wrote shortly after returning from Harvard University, where he had spent a year as a Guggenheim Fellow. 'Moreover, as the pressure in the Atlantic and the Mediterranean increases, opinion

in favor of increasing the amount of aid solidifies. The logic of the policy carries opinion along. If you have decided to help someone because
their existence is necessary for your defense, when they need more help
it seems natural to provide it.'[48]

F.R. Scott's defence of American neutrality was more than knee-jerk
pro-Americanism. Along with Frank Underhill, Scott was one of Canada's leading proponents of North American isolation in the 1930s. In
fact, many of the intellectuals involved in the League for Social Reconstruction rejected the liberal internationalism of Shotwell and Dafoe.
In a stinging review of Dafoe's influential *Canada: An American Nation*,
published in 1935, Underhill lashed out at the old man's 'vague expressions of faith in League ideals.' 'But what if the outside world per-
sists in going mad, as it has persisted since Mr Dafoe delivered these
lectures? Isn't it about time that we began to consider seriously this
possibility of North American isolation?' Underhill asked. 'American
journals have been full in recent months of discussion of this theme. But
in Canada there is a persistent silence; and in our circumstances, with
entanglements both in the League of Nations and in the British Empire,
silence really means casting your vote for Canadian participation in the
next European war. If we don't discuss possible alternatives before the
fever of war is sweeping over us, we shall have no alternative at the
critical moment but to succumb to the fever.'[49] The Great War deeply
embittered Underhill and, unlike fellow CCFer F.R. Scott, the University of Toronto's most controversial professor did not shy away from
the isolationist label.[50]

The most sweeping critique of American isolation did not come from
liberals like Dafoe or Shotwell, but rather from the intellectuals associated with Canada's Tory tradition. For Dafoe and Shotwell, isolation
squandered a good deal of America's moral authority. Imperialists, for
their part, saw isolationism as the logical consequence of America's
fundamental flaws. The republic's shortcomings could once again be
traced back to 1776, when Americans chose to forsake the imperial
bond. In the United States, wrote R.G. Trotter in 1924, 'violent sever-
ance of the imperial tie produced a natural pride in independence that
became a paramount trait, which, however fine in itself, bred inevitably a special sense of isolation from the world in general.' Conversely,
in Canada, 'attachment to the imperial link ... afforded a unique opportunity for realizing national aspirations without losing the sense,
or the reality, of being part of a larger whole.'[51] In imperialist prose,
the parochialism of the American mind was repeatedly contrasted with

Canadian outward-lookingness. It was argued that respect for tradition and continuity – the very essence of conservatism – led Canadians to repudiate isolationism.

Traditionalism was at the core of the conservative critique of the United States. However, though imperialist and *nationaliste* anti-Americanism possessed similar foundations, they diverged on a number of key issues, notably those surrounding Canadian-American relations and American foreign policy. Indeed, French Canadian hostility to imperialism made Quebec's nationalists far more open to a Canadian-American rapprochement and far less inclined to support American expansionism than their English Canadian counterparts were. French Canadian nationalists were persistent critics of American society, but their attitude towards Canada's relationship with the United States was, in many ways, ambivalent. In fact, it was similar to that of English Canadian continentalists, who tended to disapprove of nascent American imperialism and, in some instances, tacitly approved of isolationism. Continentalists saw Canadian-American integration as a normal and largely beneficial process and, consequently, were fervent in their support for the liberalization of Canadian-American trade.

9 Canadian-American Trade, Unionism, and Migration

Issues related to tariffs, trade, and investment have long been integral to the intellectual history of Canadian-American relations. In English Canada, for instance, the debate surrounding reciprocity has traditionally aroused a great deal of passion and has acted as a litmus test for anti-American sentiment. Canada's commercial relationship with the United States has generally been viewed as the paramount issue in Canadian-American relations. During the period under study, the free trade debate reached a fever pitch during the federal election of 1911, which was called by Wilfrid Laurier's Liberals to decide the fate of a reciprocity agreement negotiated with the Taft administration. By contrast, the 'free trade' election of 1891 had not aroused quite the same intensity of passion because it was centred on the abstract issue of 'unrestricted reciprocity' with the United States rather than on a concrete agreement.

In the late nineteenth and early twentieth centuries, Canadian imperialists were overwhelmingly hostile to the liberalization of Canadian-American trade.[1] Arguments against reciprocity generally revolved around its political implications, but imperialists also questioned its economic advantages. It was argued that the American and Canadian economies were not complementary, since both nations' exports were similar and competed with each other on international markets. The continent's basic geography had created two distinct economic spaces and the thrust of Canada's east-west axis commanded that the bulk of the Dominion's exports be directed towards Europe and, in particular, towards Britain. In *The Great Dominion: Studies of Canada*, published in 1895, George R. Parkin summarized the imperialist school's economic arguments against free trade. His line of reasoning contained elements of what would later be known as the Laurentian thesis:

What is the natural market for Canadian products? This is a question much debated in Canadian party politics; it is a question which should be studied closely in England, where it is often carelessly assumed that the contiguity of the United States creates for Canada an overwhelming interest in the market nearest at hand. Without detailed examination of the facts, this conclusion is a natural one. That 65,000,000 of people on its immediate borders should make a far greater demand on the products of the Dominion than 40,000,000 of people 3,000 miles away, seems, on first thought, a reasonable inference. It does not seem so reasonable when we reflect on the one simple fact that the staple products of Canada are, with one or two exceptions, staple products of the United States as well, and that, therefore, over a large range of industry, the two countries are natural rivals in markets where their surplus products are required. There is a physical fact, too, which must be once more specially noted in considering the question. Almost to the heart of the continent Canada enjoys the advantage of water carriage – a circumstance which beyond everything else minimizes for commercial purposes the effect of distance ... Keeping these considerations in view, it seems to me capable of demonstration that the great and dominant trading interests of Canada lie with Britain rather than with the United States – with the far market rather than with the near.[2]

Imperialists consistently argued that the potential of the American market paled before the vast possibilities of imperial trade. As a result, in the late nineteenth and early twentieth centuries, an imperial customs union was often viewed as the key to Canadian prosperity.

More often than not, however, Tory intellectuals sought to shift the debate regarding free trade away from economic issues. They relied primarily on political arguments to attack reciprocity. Political allegiance and sentiment, imperialists insisted, invariably followed trade. As a result, a significant diversion of Canada's international trade towards the United States would inexorably lead to the sundering of the imperial bond and, eventually, to annexation. This line of argument was used most fully during the 1911 election, when the issue of reciprocity was often presented as a clear-cut choice between the British connection and annexation to the United States. The founding editor of *The British News of Canada*, Arthur Hawkes (1871–1933), was particularly adept at exploiting this line of reasoning. Born in Kent, England, Hawkes had worked as a reporter for several British newspapers, including the Manchester *Guardian*, before emigrating to Canada in 1905.

As the general secretary of the Canadian National League, an anti-reciprocity front group, he contributed to the barrage of propaganda that
played a key role in the defeat of the 1911 reciprocity agreement. 'The
agreement proves that the time has come for Canada to choose, perhaps
finally, between remaining in the orbit of the Empire and achieving first
renown in the constellation of kindred British nations, and gravitating
to the lesser glories of the Republic,' Hawkes wrote in *An Appeal to the
British-Born*, a widely distributed 1911 pamphlet aimed at convincing
British-born Canadians to reject reciprocity. Indeed, he continued, President William Howard Taft 'has clearly indicated the strength of the
desire in the United States that the Reciprocity Agreement shall destroy
all possibility of a commercial unity within the British Empire. In the
United States there is no illusion as to the extent to which commercial
and political control may be interchangeable terms.' The agreement, to
be sure, 'would destroy the artery through which East and West live
a common, national life.'[3] Only protective tariffs, Hawkes reasoned,
could safeguard national unity and the imperial bond upon which Canadian nationhood rested.

Nevertheless, while most imperialist intellectuals opposed the liberalization of Canadian-American trade, many were also critical of American protectionism, which was viewed as an essentially hostile act. This
apparent contradiction scarcely bothered most imperialists, whose resistance to the idea of reciprocity would, at any rate, steadily decline in
the 1920s and 1930s. This evolution was most apparent in the writing
of Stephen Leacock, whose opposition to reciprocity had been a great
asset to the Conservative party in 1911. By the 1930s, however, Leacock
was regularly poking fun at his earlier antagonism to the liberalization
of Canadian-American trade.

A firm belief in the benefits of Canadian-American free trade united
continentalists of all stripes. It was indeed one of continentalism's core
tenets. Free trade with the United States would bring prosperity to the
Dominion, insisted intellectuals as ideologically distant as O.D. Skelton
and F.R. Scott. The Canadian and American economies were complementary, and if allowed to interact freely, they would generate both
wealth and employment. North America was a natural economic space,
and even robust protectionism would not ultimately halt the progress
of Canadian-American economic integration. 'A reciprocity treaty, pro-
viding for free trade in raw commodities, was in effect from 1854 to
1866,' wrote H. Carl Goldenberg in 1936. 'Even after its abrogation, and,
not withstanding the protectionist policies of both countries, their trade

continued to grow. Since 1883 the United States has steadily maintained its position as the principal source of Canada's imports, and from 1921 to 1932 it was also the principal market for Canada's exports.'[4]

Unlike their imperialist opponents, continentalists centred their arguments on economic issues. The National Policy, they insisted, was an abject failure. By hampering trade with Canada's natural trading partner, it had slowed the nation's economic growth and fostered underdevelopment. Continentalists viewed various schemes to achieve economic self-sufficiency or to create an imperial free-trade zone as little more than conservative chimeras. In *Canada and the Canadian Question*, Goldwin Smith, who supported reciprocity with the United States in part because he believed that it would hasten continental union, heaped ridicule on the whole idea of an imperial customs union:

> It has been proposed that rather than succumb to the force of nature, and allow Canada to secure her destined measure of prosperity by trading with her own continent, England should put back the shadow on the dial of economical history, institute an Imperial Zollverein, and restore to the Colonies their former protection against the foreigner in her market. It is hardly necessary to discuss a policy in which Great Britain would have to take the initiative, and which no British statesman has shown the slightest disposition to embrace. The trade, both of imports and exports, of England with the Colonies was, in 1889, £187,000,000; her total trade in the same year with foreign countries was £554,000,000. Is it likely that she will sacrifice a trade of £554,000,000 sterling to a trade of £187,000,000 sterling? The framers of an Imperial Zollverein, moreover, would have some lively work in reconciling the tendencies of strong Protectionist Colonies, such as Victoria and Canada, with the free trade tendencies of Great Britain and New South Wales. The Conservative Prime Minister of England, if he has been correctly reported, holds that the adoption of Protection, on which the Imperialists of Canada insist as a condition of any arrangement, would in England kindle a civil war.[5]

Continentalists also scorned the idea that Canadian and imperial unity rested on limited economic intercourse with the United States. Canadian nationhood, they insisted, was not fundamentally precarious and would undoubtedly benefit from free trade with its southern neighbour. 'Given permanence,' wrote O.D. Skelton in 1910, 'the closest of trade relations with the United States cannot but be beneficial; the Canadian national spirit, however weak it may have been a quarter century ago, is in these days of prosperity and expansion too strong and self-reliant to be endangered by close commercial intercourse with the republic.'[6] In fact, argued John W. Dafoe, it was the National Policy that threatened Canadian unity and nationhood. By fostering the concentration of industry in southwestern Quebec and southern Ontario, the policy had turned the rest of Canada into an underdeveloped resource hinterland. 'I am deeply concerned at the strains upon Confed- eration which arise from the fact that we have a large vested interest in secondary industries which today are essentially uneconomic and which, because they have to be maintained, are destroying the basis of prosperity in two-thirds of the provinces of Canada,' the West's most eloquent champion told a group of scholars in 1935.[7] As far as Dafoe was concerned, it was economic marasmus and regional disparity, not free trade that threatened the unity of the Canadian nation.

American protectionism irritated Canada's continentalist intellectuals, but it was Canadian scepticism regarding the benefits of free trade that really exasperated thinkers like Skelton and Dafoe. The defeat of reciprocity in 1911 was lamented for decades in continentalist circles. It was viewed as an irrational decision that would have long-term negative consequences on the Canadian economy. Speaking at a Liberal policy conference in 1933, P.E. Corbett argued that the defeat of reciprocity was yet another example of the deleterious impact of anti-Americanism on Canadian society: 'There is, it seems to me, a totally unnecessary amount of suspicion in our approach to problems connected with the joint Canadian-American exploitation of our North-American patrimony. Played upon by selfish interests in 1911, that suspicion rejected a reciprocity in trade which we had long coveted and have often coveted since.'[8]

Continentalists were inclined to blame the Depression and the growth of trusts and combines on protectionism. Tariffs, they argued, served special business interests and were a constant source of irritation in the Canadian-American relationship. By contrast, continentalists held that trade, in particular free trade, fostered international peace and understanding. In 1891, Erastus Wiman informed the readers of the *North American Review* that 'intimate trade relations' could help 'heal the great schism of the Anglo-Saxon race.'[9] Wiman was one of the few continentalists who actually stood to benefit personally from continental integration. He had made substantial investments in Canadian resources, and the North American customs union he tirelessly promoted would undoubtedly have benefited his investment portfolio.

'Yet in spite of these legitimate personal advantages,' writes Ian Grant, 'Wiman was more than just a self-interested businessman. Certainly one of his prime objectives in promoting commercial union was to attempt to extend to his fellow Canadians some of the immense prosperity which he had acquired. He firmly believed that the National Policy was unnecessarily forfeiting to Canadians a standard of living which was rightly theirs. It was estimated that he personally spent $30,000 to promote this grandiose scheme.' Above all, Grant insists that Wiman 'was a philanthropist in his own right and the promotion of the welfare of Canadians was part and parcel of a liberal ideology which he argued continuously between 1887 and 1893.'[10]

The issue of reciprocity did not generate intense passion in Quebec, and relatively few intellectuals appear to have viewed the liberalization of Canadian-American trade as a grave threat to French Canada. Continentalists supported the measure, as did a number of nationalists. They could see the economic benefits of reciprocity and, more significantly, they believed that it would weaken the imperial bond. Unlike imperialists, who feared that reciprocity would ultimately destroy the Canadian nation, most French Canadian intellectuals did not assume that the measure would seriously affect either Canada's sovereignty or Quebec's distinct society. Henri Bourassa was fairly representative of the dispassionate support for reciprocity that was common in Quebec. Though he fervently opposed Laurier's 1910 Naval Service Act and campaigned against the Liberal party during the subsequent federal election, the *nationaliste* leader saw little danger in the 1911 draft reciprocity agreement: 'A measure of reciprocity, both broad and prudent, between Canada and the United States, is natural; it is in conformity with the political traditions and the economical needs of Canada. Kept within proper limits, it affords great advantages to our agriculture and to all the industries derived from the exploitation of natural resources, without threatening our commercial independence, our political autonomy and our attachment to the Empire.' But reciprocity's main advantage did not lie in the economic sphere. 'It is certainly the most treacherous and effective blow which Sir Wilfrid Laurier has ever given to the cause of Imperialism, which he has heretofore so well served,' Bourassa wrote in an English-language pamphlet derived from a series of articles that had previously appeared in *Le Devoir*. Reciprocity would place 'an insuperable obstacle in the way of an Imperial customs union,' he concluded, 'and this is, in our eyes, the main reason for its adoption.'[11]

Unlike the liberalization of Canadian-American trade, the massive influx of American investment capital into Canadian industry was viewed with some alarm in Quebec's intellectual circles, particularly during the interwar years. The surge in American investment after the First World War coincided with the rise of a more militant and conservative form of French Canadian nationalism. In the 1920s, as the volume of British capital invested in Canadian industry sagged and the United States became Canada's chief source of foreign investment capital, a number of French Canadian thinkers feared that a hostile takeover of Canadian industry was in the works. Indeed, unlike the British, who favoured indirect, portfolio investment, American capitalists preferred to invest directly in Canadian industry. As a result, many intellectuals worried that Canada was quickly becoming a branch plant economy and that French Canadians would be permanently relegated to its lower echelons. American investment was deepening *l'infériorité économique des Canadiens français*.

Esdras Minville led the charge against interwar American investment. Born in Quebec's Gaspé Peninsula, he was educated at the Brothers of the Christian Schools' Pensionnat Saint-Laurent and at Montreal's École des Hautes Études commerciales. After obtaining his *license en sciences commericales* in 1922, Minville worked for a few years in the private sector, first at an insurance firm, then at a brokerage house. In 1927, he joined the faculty of the École des Hautes Études commerciales. He served as the school's principal from 1938 to 1962 and as the Université de Montréal's dean of social science from 1950 to 1957. In an era when concerns regarding the economic marginalization of French Canadians were at the forefront of nationalist discourse, Minville quickly rose to a position of prominence within Quebec's intelligentsia. His economic nationalism was intensely Catholic and conservative, and sought to empower French Canadians, in part, through co-operatism and corporatism.[12]

Minville understood the importance of foreign investment in the development of Canadian resources. However, he was also convinced that the influx of American capital after the Great War was too much, too fast. A moderate ruralist, Minville worried that massive American investment was fuelling industrial gigantism. 'The industrialization of Canada was effected without any method, and, in view of the size of our population, too quickly. Disturbances of the social and political order resulted from it,' he warned the readers of *L'Action française* in 1924. But American investment was not merely destabilizing the Dominion's sociopolitical structure, it was also deepening the economic marginalization of French Canadians. The French Canadian bourgeoisie, Minville argued, lacked the capital necessary to compete with American corporations. 'Every batch of foreign capital arriving in our province means the postponement of the day when our nation will at last shake off the economic yoke that today weighs so heavily on it,' he insisted.[13]

American investment was yet another agent of modernity. It not only accelerated Canada's urbanization and industrialization, but also brought moral decrepitude in its wake. Minville noted, for instance, that American capitalists often insisted that their French Canadian workers transgress the Lord's Day. Investment capital, moreover, was an instrument of American imperialism. 'The greatest democratic republic in the world is not without imperial pretensions,' Minville wrote in 1924, 'it obeys the tendencies of our time and imitates the example of the great European powers ... The dollar is their weapon, and the people that presently monopolize 48 percent of the world's gold reserves intend to use it to propagate their ideas and spread their influence.'[14] However, like most interwar French Canadian nationalists, Minville was reluctant to employ large-scale nationalization to solve the problem of foreign ownership. He insisted that the development of French Canadian enterprise and a more intelligent strategy regarding the concession of Quebec's natural resources were the best methods to prevent an American takeover of the province's industry and resources.

A number of French Canadian continentalists were also deeply concerned about the impact of American investment on Quebec's economic structure. In fact, it was Errol Bouchette, a liberal nationalist, who first sounded the alarm at the turn of the twentieth century. Bouchette's calls to 'Take over industry' deeply influenced the economic thought of both Esdras Minville and Jean-Charles Harvey. Like Minville, the anticlerical Harvey wanted French Canadians to harness their capital and develop Quebec's resources before it was too late. However, unlike the work of his conservative contemporary, Harvey's writing on American investment did not contain anti-American or anti-industrial undertones. 'The industrialization of the province of Quebec will inevitably continue, be it by French-Canadians or foreigners,' he wrote in 1920. 'It may be that it sometimes brings disadvantages, but in this case we will apply the proverb about choosing "the lesser of two evils." And it would be better that our riches become our property rather than that of our neighbours.'[15]

Harvey's interwar preoccupation with the American takeover of Quebec's industry produced a mildly risqué 1922 novel, *Marcel Faure*, which was inspired by the years he spent working as a publicist for the Machine agricole nationale, a failed French Canadian business venture. In the story, the hero, Marcel Faure, a young French Canadian entrepreneur, struggles against Anglo-American competitors to transform the fictional village of Valmont into a near-utopian industrial centre. The novel, which was not well received in clerical and conservative circles, contained descriptions of physical intimacy and placed most of the blame for the economic marginalization of French Canadians on Quebec's Catholic clergy and on the province's system of classical education. In one passage, the anticlerical Faure ponders the ill-effects of Catholic idealism: 'Convinced, by auto-suggestion, that our atavistic idealism should keep us above worldly goods, misled by our very education to look down on commercial nations, we have lived on the margins of material reality, leaving our concrete and practical neighbours to come into our house and set themselves up as masters.' In the long term, Harvey warned in a 1920 pamphlet, the American takeover of Quebec's industry would lead to national decrepitude: 'In their thousands, our workers are serfs under foreign control. The day will come, if it has not already, when our proletariat, conscious of its bondage, obeying only men who do not talk their language and know nothing of their traditions, will believe themselves to belong to an inferior race. From this apparent inferiority will come scorn towards their own people, and from this scorn, national apostasy.'[16]

Similarly, in 1928, Beaudry Leman warned Montreal's Cercle universitaire that 'economic enslavement generally brings political domination before long; if we further delay in fully qualifying ourselves to respond to our vocation of French Americans, we will cease to be good Canadians and we will be preparing ourselves to become ordinary Americans.' Like many French Canadian liberals, Leman was inclined to look inwards for the causes of French Canada's economic marginalization. 'The most serious threat is not the one that penetrates in the form of financial capital but the one represented by the moral and intellectual capital of men better prepared than us to take advantage of the natural wealth that Providence has put at our disposition and that we will have let slip through our clumsy or lazy hands, contenting ourselves with receiving a dish of lentils in exchange,' Leman wrote in the *Revue trimestrielle canadienne*.[17] He did not blame the takeover of Quebec's resources on American greed or imperialism. American capitalists, Leman surmised, were simply investing where there were profits to be made. If French Canadian entrepreneurs could not compete, then the problem obviously lay with French Canadian business practices and, more generally, with French Canadian *mentalités*. For this reason, French-speaking continentalists hoped to counter *l'infériorité économique des Canadiens français* by modernizing Quebec's education system and better harnessing the potential of French Canadian capital. The latter solution was particularly attractive to Leman, who ran the province's leading French Canadian bank. To be sure, continentalists like Leman and Harvey were even less inclined than their conservative adversaries to consider nationalization as an acceptable solution to the American takeover of Quebec's industry.

American investment did not generate a great deal of apprehension in English Canada until Walter Gordon issued his Royal Commission report on Canada's Economic Prospects in 1957. Indeed, during the period under study, few imperialists viewed American investment as a threat to Canadian sovereignty or nationhood. Until the First World War, British portfolio investment accounted for over two-thirds of all foreign investment in Canada, and the postwar surge in American investment coincided with the decline of Canadian imperialism. Interwar Tories like Robert Falconer saw little danger in massive American investment in Canadian industry. 'Mutterings of alarm have quite recently been heard in some eastern manufacturing centres lest the American is getting such a grip upon the Dominion that in a few decades by means of peaceful penetration Canada will be Americanized,' Falconer wrote in 1925. 'This is merely another form of the old cry of Goldwin Smith as to manifest destiny. Even those Americans who under protection have established branch institutions in Canada have nothing to gain by annexation.'[18]

Outside of Quebec, liberal intellectuals were enthusiastic supporters of American investment in Canadian industry. During the interwar years, the most compelling case for American investment was made by two Canadian economists, Herbert Marshall (b. 1887) and Kenneth W. Taylor (b. 1899). In 1936, they teamed up with an American colleague, Frank A. Southard, to author *Canadian-American Industry: A Study in International Investment*, the first volume in the Carnegie series. This influential monograph would serve as the standard text on American investment for the next two decades. Marshall and Taylor both served in the Canadian Expeditionary Force before entering the federal civil service. Marshall was appointed dominion statistician in

1945 and Taylor served as Canada's deputy minister of finance from 1953 to 1963. Staunch Liberals, they advised Prime Minister Mackenzie King on economic affairs and were enthusiastic supporters of continental integration. 'Geography and history have made it inevitable that the economic structures of Canada and the United States should become closely intertwined,' went the first sentence of their monograph. This basic assumption underpinned much of their work. Marshall and Taylor argued that even the most radically protectionist measures could not reverse the course of continental integration, since high tariffs merely fostered the creation of American branch plants. 'The very attempts on Canada's part to preserve an independent economy, through tariffs, through Imperial preference, through appeals to local patriotism, have not infrequently promoted the "American penetration" which they were designed to repel,' they noted in the introduction to their study.[19]

Marshall and Taylor insisted that Canadians had little reason to fear American investment. 'There is little evidence of political interference by foreign-controlled companies,' they wrote. 'Doubtless American-controlled companies, like most other companies, use such political pressure as they may be able to muster to further their economic interests. Doubtless, too, like other companies, they contribute to campaign funds of one or of all political parties. But their interest is almost invariably the interest of a particular company or industry and not in a large sense a pushing of "American" interests.' Besides, as the economists were quick to note, British investment, which was widely viewed as essentially benign, hardly came without strings attached: 'Pressure from foreign investment banking interests is more likely to be open and political than that from branch plants. But Canada has, hitherto at least, had more difficulties in this respect with London than with New York. Bitter pressure has been brought to bear by London financial groups on a number of occasions, notably in the long and still unsettled Grand Trunk securities issue.'[20]

American investment was essential to Canadian prosperity and development; it facilitated the transfer of technology and fostered better relations between Canada and the United States. Besides, as Marshall and Taylor pointed out, after the First World War, only the United States was in a position to provide the large-scale investment capital needed to develop the Dominion's resources. And the promise of long-term capital self-sufficiency rested on the development of Canadian resources. Moreover, as many interwar continentalists were quick to point out, Canadian investment in American industry was not insignificant. 'Every Canadian and every American who has any knowledge of the Canadian economy is aware of those hundreds of American-owned factories, mines, public utilities, or what not in the Dominion of Canada. But few Canadians and even fewer Americans realize that in proportion to Canada's wealth and population her direct investment in the United States is even larger,' wrote Marhall and Taylor. They noted that 'on a *per caput* basis, only two countries (Great Britain and the Netherlands) exceed Canada in importance of foreign investments.'[21]

Marshall and Taylor acknowledged, however, that Canada's dependency on American investment reduced the Dominion's policy options. For instance, radical economic reform, which neither Marshall nor Taylor approved of anyway, would be exceedingly difficult and potentially disastrous in an economy heavily dependent on foreign investment. 'If Canada, unaccompanied by the United States, were to move along novel economic paths which involved some reinterpretation of property rights, there is little doubt that international difficulties would arise,' they wrote.[22] Left-wing continentalists shared these concerns and were accordingly reluctant to praise American investment.[23] However, their infrequent criticism of American investment was in fact directed at capitalism, rather than at the United States. As Frank Underhill put it in 1929: 'There is no real difference, except in names, between being controlled by a Holt and being controlled by a Morgan. And nothing is more certain than that the Morgan of the next generation will gobble up the Holt of the next generation. The best defence of a distinct Canadian nationality is to make sure that these great strategic public services shall be owned and controlled by the people themselves.'[24]

In Canada, the history of trade unionism has been intimately linked to the American labour movement. Throughout the period examined here, a majority of Canada's unionized workers were members of international (i.e., American) unions. Indeed, as American capital flowed north, so too did organizations like the Knights of Labor, the American Federation of Labor (AFL) and, later, the Congress of Industrial Organizations (CIO). The growth of international unionism worried many on the anti-American right. International unions, it was claimed, fostered both Americanization and radicalism. Nevertheless, the penetration of American unions produced little more than sporadic criticism among Canada's imperialist intellectuals. This was perhaps because the alternatives to international unionism were viewed as even less attractive. Indeed, the British labour tradition was more radical than its American counterpart, as were many of the Canadian unions that drew their inspiration from Britain.

During the period under study, resistance to international unionism was strongest in Quebec. The province's Roman Catholic clergy viewed American unions as dangerous agents of secularism and assimilation, and saw itself as engaged in a crucial struggle with international unionism for the soul of Quebec's proletariat. As far as the Church was concerned, issues related to labour and industry were indissociable from religion. As a result, theological arguments dominated *nationaliste* criticism of international unionism. Henri Bourassa summed up the nationalist position in a 1919 pamphlet: 'International secular unionism is pernicious in itself and in every country, because it does not take into account, when seeking advantages for its members, of God, family, or country, the three fundamental foundations of Christian social order.' However, he coninued, 'the danger is incomparably greater here than anywhere else, because of the unique proximity of the United States. International unionism means, in Canada, the complete subjection of Canadian workers to the caprices and domination of American labour. It is one of the most complete and striking manifestations of the moral and economic conquest of Canada by the United States.'[25]

Nationaliste intellectuals refused to accept the notion that class solidarity could transcend borders and religious denominations, and they were fervently opposed to the establishment of a secular, American space within Quebec's proletariat. Secularism, indeed, was a veritable Pandora's box. 'Secularism has made American trade unionism favourable to the spread of errors (revolutionary, socialist),' wrote Catholic labour leader Alfred Charpentier in 1920, 'it does nothing but aspire ceaselessly to increasingly egalitarian reforms; in this way it is, more or less without knowing it, the precusor of socialism'[26] International unions, it was argued, had a penchant for strikes, violence, and ultimately, for subversion. Indeed, in nationalist prose, America itself was often viewed as a *terreau fertile* for radicalism.

For French Canadian nationalists, the antidote to international unionism could be found in the establishment of Catholic labour unions. Alfred Charpentier, a bricklayer who played a key role in the 1921 founding of the Confédération des travailleurs catholiques du Canada, argued that 'the workers' union does not have an economic function alone … it also has a social, and consequently a moral, function to fulfil.' Catholic unionism, therefore, 'was necessary to popularize and diffuse the higher principles of Catholic social morality, without which there is no real possible solution to economic problems.'[27] Charpentier hoped to bring about a new industrial order based on Catholic principles. As a result, he and others shunned the idea of class struggle and sought instead to foster collaboration between labour and capital.

Opposition to international unionism, however, was not confined to the right. During the interwar years an embryo of left-of-centre anti-Americanism could be found among the leaders of Canada's national unions. Their opposition to international unionism – they were particularly contemptuous of the American Federation of Labor's philosophy – was tied to a wider struggle for industrial unionism and political activism. Nationalism, indeed, was a very secondary consideration to men like William Thomas Burford (b. 1892), who served as the secretary-treasurer of the All-Canadian Congress of Labour and, later, of the Canadian Federation of Labour. Born in England, Burford was a veteran of the Great War and an electrician by trade. In a 1930 article for the *Canadian Forum*, he scoffed at the argument that since 'capital recognizes no boundaries, labour should organize on a continental rather than on a national scale, to resist a common exploitation.' In fact, as he pointed out, 'in the chief Canadian industrial undertakings which United States capital controls, the United States unions are barely represented.' American unions, Burford continued, 'organize by craft and not by the shop ... Their structure is primitive, and it is their aim to improve standards for an exclusive membership of craftsmen rather than to unite the working class for its general advancement.' As far as Burford was concerned, international unions were not sufficiently radical and the AFL's determination to shun partisan politics hindered the growth of an influential workers' party in Canada. 'Labour's political impotence in Canada is the logical consequence of an economic organization framed regardless of industrial and national circumstances,' he wrote.[28]

For the most part, continentalists approved of international unionism. The formation of international unions, argued the Canadian vice-chairman of the International Brotherhood of Electrical Workers, Ernest Ingles (b. 1897), was a logical and necessary response to continental integration: 'Capital flows across the imaginary boundary line in both directions with a mobility and fluidity truly remarkable. A great number of our industrial establishments are financed from across that line, and with such a great number of our industrial establishments mere branch houses of United States concerns, it is a natural development that there should be an international labour movement.'[29] Left-wing continentalists, including F.R. Scott, would not have rejected this analysis. Nevertheless, in 1938, Scott lamented 'the inability of most international trades unions to take part in politics.' This state of affairs, he insisted, was hampering the growth of the CCF.[30] Scott's criticism, however, was directed at the unions affiliated with the American Federation of Labor. Another international union, the more radical Congress of Industrial Organizations, did have his support.

The period under study witnessed significant population movement within North America. Principally attracted by better employment opportunities and higher wages, close to 1.5 million Canadians settled in the United States between 1890 and 1930. By 1930, when the United States essentially shut its doors to Canadian immigration, slightly over 9 per cent of its immigrants were born in Canada. Most Canadian immigrants settled in the northeastern and midwestern states, though California and the Pacific northwest also attracted a number of Canadians in search of opportunity. Roughly a third of all Canadian immigrants were French-speaking. This exodus slowed Canada's demographic growth, but did not prevent its population from more than doubling between 1890 and 1930.[31] Canada received large numbers of immigrants during these years, and though its balance of migration with the United States was negative, roughly 400,000 Americans settled in Canada between 1890 and 1930. By 1931, Americans were Canada's second-largest immigrant group after the British. American immigrants were often drawn to agriculture and white-collar occupations and were most heavily concentrated in Saskatchewan, Alberta, and British Columbia.[32]

In Quebec, emigration to the United States was widely viewed as a national disaster and was the object of a broad consensus among the intellectual elite – even the most continentalist thinkers were anxious to put an end to the exodus. Anti-American rhetoric played an important, though largely unsuccessful role in the *nationaliste* strategy to halt French Canadian emigration to the United States, and the *fièvre des États* that struck Quebec in the late nineteenth century compelled the clergy and its conservative allies to intensify their criticism of the United States. Unlike English Canada, which could count on immigration to maintain and expand its position within Confederation, French Canada could only rely on natural increase. Countering the favourable impression of the United States that permeated Quebec's popular culture was thus viewed as imperative to French Canadian *survivance*. Continentalists, for their part, condemned emigration without resorting to anti-American diatribes.

By the turn of the twentieth century, most French Canadian intellectuals had come to see the emigrant as a hapless victim of macroeconomic forces. Nevertheless, a few conservative thinkers continued the mid-nineteenth century tradition of blaming emigration on laziness and improvidence. Jean-Charles Harvey, whose family had lived for a time in Massachusetts, refuted these arguments in a 1920 pamphlet. Like many liberals, he saw economic problems as the root cause of emigration:

> Two million of our own live today in Massachusetts, New Hampshire, Vermont, Maine, Connecticut and Rhode Island. Two million! Almost half our population lost, irrevocably lost to us, with their admirable qualities of physical and moral endurance! What were they going to do there? Were they giving in to whims, to a taste for adventure? No. Too many powerful links attached them to their country of origin for them to exile themselves with a happy heart. If they left, it is because a defect in social organization drives them away; it is because, in order to live better, they have gone towards a prosperity that we do not have, just as people who are cold seek out a flame to warm them up.[33]

The crusade against emigration fit well into the wider conservative struggle against modernity. American life was presented as morally and physically corrosive to French-speaking Catholics. French Canadian migrants, it was argued, were exposed to the twin dangers of assimilation and apostasy. They often lived in poverty and were invariably subjected to harsh industrial labour and urban squalor. The emigrant, moreover, was also a dangerous and unwitting agent of Americanization. 'Even in the least affected parishes,' wrote abbé Georges-Marie Bilodeau in a 1926 monograph on emigration, 'there are cars parked pompously in front of the doors, with their American licence plates. They are most often sons, brothers, sons-in-law who are coming with all their wealth, but also their arrogance, to teach luxury, to show the way to the United States, to scandalize the humble inhabitants of our hamlets.'[34] Emigration also eroded Quebec's place in Confederation. In L'Action française, Father Alexandre Dugré (1887–1958), whose brother Adélard, also a Jesuit, had in 1925 published a novel, La campagne canadienne, to denounce emigration, went so far as to argue that the exodus had prevented a French Canadian reconquista: 'It is not the two million who still struggle as best they can in the United States that make up our national loss; no, more than this it is the millions of descendants of people long assimilated, the millions of possible families, families due to us, the vigorous generations, that would have been born for us and would have made Canada into a Catholic New France.'[35]

To put an end to emigration, nationalist intellectuals favoured solutions involving agriculture and rural development. The public and private sectors needed to promote colonization and access to rural credit – many *nationalistes* were active promoters of Alphonse Desjardins' *caisses populaires* – more vigorously. It was also argued that the development of decentralized, medium-size industry would help Quebec retain its surplus population – large-scale, centralized industrialization was regarded as an essentially counterproductive solution. Indeed, like emigration, the industrial metropolis was viewed as a threat to French Canadian *survivance*. Most continentalists did not share this perspective. Jean-Charles Harvey, for instance, believed that large-scale industrial development was the best way to put an end to the exodus. 'It was at the time when we had the least industry that rural desertion was most frequent: witness the millions of our own people who are today in the United States,' he wrote in 1920. 'The industrial awakening, if it did nothing more than stop on this side of the line the flow of emigrants, would render us a great service.'[36]

By the late nineteenth century, emigration was no longer viewed as an automatic cultural and moral death sentence. Emigrants could resist assimilation, conservatives and liberals argued, but they would have to struggle to retain their language and their faith. And those Franco-Americans who remained Catholic and French were not denied membership in the French Canadian nation, whose essence was viewed as fundamentally ethno-religious. Abbé Lionel Groulx, for instance, saw Franco-Americans as part of a wider *Amérique française*. 'If nationality rests on ties of blood, soul, and language, or – to talk like ethnologists and philosophers – on physiological, psychological, and moral identity, even though you have American citizenship, you are also French Canadian in nationality,' he told a group of Franco-Americans in 1922.[37]

For some intellectuals, the relative strength of the Franco-American diaspora appeared to confirm theories regarding French Canadian providentialism. French Canada possessed a divine mission, insisted Quebec's leading theologian, Msgr. Louis-Adolphe Pâquet (1859–1942), in his oft-quoted 1902 'Sermon sur la vocation de la race française en Amérique.' God had planted a French seed in the New World to convert North America to Roman Catholicism: 'Yes, making God known, publishing His name, spreading and defending everything that constitutes the precious heritage of Christian traditions, such is our vocation. We have seen the certain and unquestionable signs of it. What Europe's France was for the Old World, America's France must be for this New World.'[38] A number of turn-of-the-twentieth-century intellectuals, conservatives for the most part, argued that the Franco-American diaspora was part of this divine movement.

Providentialism loomed large in Father Édouard Hamon's analysis of emigration. Born in Brittany, Hamon entered the Society of Jesus in 1861. He immigrated to North America in 1868 and lectured briefly at Fordham College, New York's Jesuit university, before coming to teach at Montreal's Collège Sainte-Marie, where he would remain until 1879. Though nominally attached to the Montreal parish of l'Immaculée-Conception, Hamon would dedicate the next several years to preaching retreats throughout Canada and the United States. He was instrumental in the creation of the popular Ligue du Sacré-Cœur and served as the superior of the Jesuit Order's Quebec City residence from 1897 to 1900. Like most of Quebec's clergymen, Father Hamon was deeply concerned by the emigration of French Canadians to New England. A popular preacher, he had spent a great deal of time in New England's *petits Canadas* and was familiar with the emigrant's plight. In 1882, he published *Exil et patrie*, a play that condemned emigration and promoted the colonization of the Ottawa Valley. However, he is best remembered for *Les Canadiens-Français de la Nouvelle-Angleterre*, an 1891 essay that denounced emigration, but that nevertheless portrayed the emigrant as an instrument of God's will. 'This mass depopulation is certainly a calamity for Canada. It would have been much more preferable to keep these men in the country, where they would have started settler families attached to the soil,' Hamon wrote. Nevertheless,

I believe we must look higher to understand this strange migration. The speed with which it has occurred, the ease with which Canadians, transplanted to a foreign land, have immediately remade the Catholic mould of the parish that made them so strong in Canada; the energy that they have deployed in building churches, founding convents, gathering together and organizing themselves into flourishing congregations, sustained inside by everything that can nourish Christian piety, protected from pernicious outside influences by the strength of association and by a generally well-run press: all these elements of Catholic life organized in a quarter of a century, even in the heart of the citadel of old Puritanism, seem to indicate, as I have said already, a providential act as well as a mission, whose full significance will be revealed to us by the future alone.

For Father Hamon, there could be no doubt that 'the French Canadians are carrying out a providential mission; they are working for their part towards the peaceful conquest, in the name of religion, of the land of New England.' His providentialism was tinged with expansionism. Like Jules-Paul Tardivel, Hamon believed that both Canada and the United States would eventually disintegrate and that a French Canadian republic encompassing Quebec, New England, eastern Ontario, and northern New Brunswick would emerge from the ruins of the two federations. 'Looking at things exclusively from a religious and national point of view,' Hamon wrote in 1891, 'I think that before long, the two fractions of the Canadian people, the one that inhabits the land of its ancestors and the one that has already crossed the American border, will reunite and will thus be able to join hands and form but a single people.'[39]

In many ways, however, ultramontane predictions regarding the divine nature of emigration were hollow. Intellectuals like Father Hamon sought to make sense of a phenomenon which, by their own admission, was a disaster. And by the interwar years an increasing number of thinkers regarded the whole idea of a providential exodus as wishful thinking. Many continentalists, for their part, were inclined to dismiss providentialism. 'It is obvious that it is not to play the role of missionary in the United States that the farmer abandons his soil, that the worker leaves with him, separating himself from everything that he holds most dear in the world: his family, his friends, his country,' Jean-Baptiste Rouilliard wrote in 1893.[40] Migrants, he believed, were simply the unfortunate victims of economic circumstance and government neglect.

Emigration was not generally viewed as a life or death issue in English Canadian intellectual circles. At the turn of the twentieth century, tens of thousands of English-speaking Canadians were leaving the Dominion every year to settle permanently in the United States, but this loss was offset by immigration, particularly from Britain and the United States. Moreover, unlike in Quebec, where religious and moral considerations loomed large over the discussion of emigration, the moral fate of emigrants was of no particular concern to English Canadian observers, including those associated with the Tory tradition. Many imperialists showed a great deal of pride in the accomplishments of prominent Canadian emigrants. William Osler, for instance, was widely hailed for his rise to the top of the American medical profession. Imperialists were nonetheless concerned by the brain drain and its potential impact on Canadian development. As a university administrator, Robert Falconer was particularly troubled by the exodus of Canadian graduates to the United States. 'The rolls of Canadian colleges contain the names of nearly six hundred former students who hold academic appointments across the line,' he told an English audience in 1925. 'In addition to this there are possibly four thousand five hundred graduates of Canadian institutions, or about ten percent of the total number, who are making their living in the United States. This is not a high percentage relative to other walks of life, but in terms of quality the actual loss to Canada has been serious.' To help staunch the brain drain, Falconer suggested that the university sector be expanded, particularly at the post-graduate level. 'If we can divert some of this stream of college graduates to our own universities,' he wrote, 'we shall save many of them for the Dominion, and at the same time bring together from widely separated provinces those who will be leaders in the life of the nation.'[41]

On the whole, continentalist attitudes towards emigration did not significantly differ from those held by Canadian imperialists. Most continentalists registered some sense of loss when examining the exodus, which is to say that they were also concerned by emigration's qualitative cost to Canada. 'Apart from the French-Canadian laborers and the fishermen and mechanics from the Maritime provinces,' Hugh Keenleyside noted in 1929, 'Canada lost many of those who, by their exceptional qualifications for business or professional life, would have done much to speed the development of the Dominion.'[42] Keenleyside, who received his Ph.D. from Clark University in Worcester, Massachusetts, authored the first book-length study devoted to the history of Canadian-American relations. Published in 1929, *Canada and the United States: Some Aspects of the History of the Republic and the Dominion* was reissued in 1952, while Keenleyside was serving as the director general of the United Nations' Technical Assistance Administration.

A handful of continentalists, usually exiles themselves, regarded Canadian emigration as essentially positive. John Bartlet Brebner, who became an American citizen in 1943, saw the exodus as a factor contributing to the improvement of Canadian-American relations and, perhaps more importantly, to Canada's economic stability. In his *North Atlantic Triangle* (1945), he predicted that the significant reduction in

Canadian immigration that had been instituted by the U.S. Congress in 1930 might have serious long-term economic consequences for Canada:

> Canadians customarily speak of this situation as a 'national deficit' or a 'cruel loss,' yet these terms invite criticism. Indeed it can be argued that the Canadians who stayed at home may literally have gained because one-quarter of their stock went to live in the United States. The explanation is to be found in the maintenance and improvement of the North American standard of living. Largely because of their immense financial obligations for the systems of transportation which alone can bind the Dominion together, Canadians have normally enjoyed a slightly lower standard of living than Americans. Yet as long as the Republic lay open to them, the discrepancy could be kept small because those who found opportunity lacking at home could move to the United States ... Now that the Republic is no longer a safety valve for 'surplus' Canadian population, time may reveal some unexpected consequences of the novel ban on interchange of population which was laid down in 1930.[43]

In continentalist prose, American immigration to Canada – provided it was made up of Americans of European ancestry – was invariably presented in a positive light. The American immigrant was an asset to Canada. American immigrants, William Arthur Deacon argued in 1926, were easily integrated into Canada's body politic: 'Americans settled in Canada are seldom annexationists. Many of them are successful farmers in the West, and many have risen to prominence in business in the central provinces; but having become used to Canadian laws and customs, they are usually well satisfied with their adopted country and seldom express a desire for the merging of the two countries.'[44] Many imperialists would have agreed with this assessment. Indeed, in an unsigned 1910 editorial intended to refute 'the charge that Canadian writers in the *University Magazine* are animated by malice and misled by prejudice when they deal with matters concerning the people of the United States,' Andrew Macphail praised white, English-speaking American immigrants: 'They make our best citizens. We like them because they are simple people like ourselves, and they like us and our institutions so well that they quickly become Canadians, which is only a step backward to the race from which we both are sprung; and this without the least prejudice to our growing affection which pertains to England.'[45]

That said, some Tories did express concern regarding the large-scale influx of American immigrants. Robert Falconer noted in 1925 that most American immigrants 'have become excellent Canadians,' but he was nevertheless concerned that the presence of tens of thousands of American settlers in Alberta and Saskatchewan was fuelling Western populism, which was not well regarded in imperialist circles. 'As might have been expected, the American new-comer into the prairie provinces has not yet grasped fully the meaning of responsible government,' he warned. 'Being something of a radical he proposes more direct methods than he finds in the Dominion of Canada. Consequently on occasion, with his pioneering energy, he may suggest the Initiative, the Referendum and the Recall, though so far without much success.'[46]

In Quebec, American immigration did not generate a great deal of commentary. Nevertheless, like most foreign immigration, it was viewed with some suspicion in nationalist circles. In 1922, for instance, abbé Lionel Groulx warned the readers of L'Action française that the influx of American settlers was loosening the bonds of Confederation: 'An immigration policy that lacked foresight has allowed the American element, the very one that can most actively undermine Canadian unity, to park itself in the western part of the country.'[47] American immigrants were vectors of Americanization: they would invariably turn the Canadian West into a Yankee outpost.

America was regarded as a potentially transformative agency by Canadian intellectuals. Canadian-American trade, American investment, international labour unionism, and cross-border migration were believed to possess the power to fundamentally alter the Canadian experience. Like American mass culture, they were viewed as agents of sociocultural change, of Americanization. In Quebec's intellectual culture, cross-border migration loomed large, as did, to a lesser extent, American investment and international labour unionism. Continentalist and anti-American opinion appeared to converge in their assessment of emigration and American investment, though underlying divergences about the nature of American society precluded the emergence of a true consensus on these issues.

Major concerns surrounding the liberalization of Canadian-American trade scarcely arose in French Canadian intellectual commentary. Unlike the transborder movement of capital and labour, the flow of trade was not usually seen as potentially affecting French Canadian *survivance*. In English Canada, however, the issue of reciprocity spawned a great deal of passion. More often than not, it served as the flashpoint between continentalist and anti-American opinion; by contrast, American investment, international unionism, and cross-border migration did not generate much debate. Reciprocity, argued imperialists, would erode Canadian tradition and the imperial bond, and would eventually lead to annexation. Continentalists rejected this line of reasoning. They insisted that reciprocity would strengthen the Canadian nation. It would bring prosperity to Canadians and allow the Dominion of Canada to assume its modern, North American trajectory.

Conclusion

'The United States, though a young nation, shows all the signs of decadence,' wrote the secretary-general of the Ligue d'action française, Anatole Vanier, in 1922. An influential nationalist who practised law in Montreal, Vanier believed that 'irreligion, moral corruption, the destruction of the family through divorce, lynching, the internal divisions between whites and blacks and between capitalists and workers, the absolutism of the plutocracy, the awakening of the non-Anglo-Saxon races [and] the too great expanse of territory,' would ultimately destroy the American republic.[1] America's degeneracy and eventual collapse was not an uncommon theme in conservative commentary. At heart, like all pre–Second World War Canadian writing on the United States, it was about much more than specific American actions and policy, which have historically had little effect on underlying intellectual attitudes towards the United States. Predictions regarding America's disintegration were revelatory of the republic's deeper symbolic significance in Canadian thought and writing.

The present study has focused on this symbolic significance. Examining Canadian writing on America offers a fresh insight into the Canadian mind. It offers limited insight, however, into the American experience. America's regional, racial, and social diversity, for instance, was often poorly assessed in Canadian commentary. Yet Canadian intellectuals were well acquainted with American life. American ideas and culture permeated Canada's intellectual and cultural environment and many Canadian intellectuals worked or studied in the United States. Their tendency to homogenize the American experience, therefore, was not largely the result of ignorance. Rather, it was a sign in Canadian prose that the United States was more than simply a nation and neighbour. America was the embodiment of something more universal: modernity. America's standing as the quintessence of modernity rested on a number of factors. The nation, it was claimed, had rejected European continuity and wholeheartedly embraced, among other things, secularism and democracy. That these assertions often rested on weak reasoning was of little importance; they shaped the attitudes of generations of Canadian thinkers.

Modernity generates deep social and economic change which, in turn, corrodes traditional values, institutions, and social relations. These transformations engendered a conservative reaction which, in Canada, expressed itself through both imperialism and French Canadian nationalism. The intellectual reaction to modernity, however, was far from uniformly negative. On the contrary, many Canadian intellectuals embraced the mass age. Liberals and socialists alike rejected tradition as a guide to social welfare and were correspondingly enthused with the idea of progress, whether material, social, or cultural. During the inter-war years, these ideas came to dominate English Canadian intellectual discourse. In Quebec, radical discourse actually declined during the period under study, and from the late nineteenth century to the 1940s, the vital centre of French Canadian thought could be found on the right.

Canadian intellectuals devoted a great deal of energy to debating the merits of modernity. However, given that the Dominion of Canada shared a 5,000-mile border with a nation that was seen as the embodiment of the modern ethos, part of the wider discussion surrounding the mass age was masked by a debate regarding the merits of American society and the course of Canadian-American relations. Virtually every aspect of Canadian intellectual debate, including issues related to gender, identity, and the Dominion of Canada's relationship with Great Britain, could be discussed through the prism of the United States. American society offered an unsettling glimpse into the not-so-distant future. The United States, as viewed through conservative prose, was a dysfunctional society: the American Revolution had forever destabilized the nation's political and social order; crime was rampant and a racial or social conflict always seemed to be on the horizon; secularism and materialism were corroding the country's moral integrity and its culture; and massive industrialization was creating both a disaffected and unstable proletariat and a dangerous plutocracy of obscenely wealthy capitalists. To draw closer to such a society, Canadian conservatives argued, was dangerous. Canada, a fundamentally conservative nation, was permanently threatened by annexation and Americanization. Canada and the United States, to be sure, were presented as largely antithetical entities.

These ideas were expressed most fully in the writing of imperialists born before 1880 and by French Canadian nationalists born roughly between 1860 and 1900. These intellectuals were deeply affected by the whirlwind of change that swept across North America in the late nineteenth century. Subsequent generations of conservatives held less radical opinions of the United States and continental integration. Their overall assessment of American society, however, remained generally negative. Generations are important to the history of ideas. As intellectual variables, they are perhaps more significant to the present study than either region or religion. Nevertheless, neither region nor religion should be discounted in the intellectual history of Canadian-American relations. Certainly, anti-American sentiment was strongest among Roman Catholics and Anglicans. It was also more prevalent among the British-born and, to a lesser extent, among central Canadians.

Imperialism and French Canadian nationalism shared a wider conservative ethos. A shared respect for tradition, however, did not prevent imperialism and French Canadian nationalism from coming into conflict. On the contrary, the quarrel that opposed the two ideologies arose because they professed loyalty to two different traditions. That said, imperialist and *nationaliste* sentiment often converged on issues related to the United States. This, of course, did not mean that their outlooks were identical. They diverged in their level of intensity, in their focus, and in their evolution. *Nationaliste* anti-Americanism was at once more radical and less fixated than its imperialist counterpart. The most uncompromising critiques of the United States were usually the work of French Canadian nationalists. Yet French Canadian nationalists, though fervent in their anti-Americanism, were hardly obsessed with the United States. The bulk of the anti-American prose published in Canada before the Second World War, indeed, was the work of imperialist intellectuals. Anti-American differentialism was essential to the imperialist sense of nationhood. It was far less significant to the French Canadian identity.

Imperialist anti-Americanism reached its summit of intensity during the 1911 federal election, which was presented as a watershed moment in Canadian history. In Quebec, anti-American sentiment peaked during the Great Depression, which many nationalists blamed on the United States. Imperialist and nationalist attitudes towards the United States also diverged in their focus. Political institutions and the imperial bond were important to the imperialist sense of distinctiveness, and English Canadian writing on the United States tended to deal primarily with political and diplomatic issues. In Quebec, where political institutions were not generally viewed as vital elements of national distinctiveness, social and cultural affairs dominated writing on the United States. Economic affairs were of great interest in both English and French Canada, though reciprocity did not generate a passionate debate among Quebec's intellectuals.

Anti-American rhetoric served a variety of functions. In imperialist writing, its most evident purpose was to legitimize and grant a moral caution to economic protectionism. For instance, the torrent of anti-American prose that accompanied the federal elections of 1891 and 1911 ensured that many Canadians would view the National Policy not only as an instrument of economic development, but also, and perhaps most importantly, as a political, cultural, and moral prophylactic. In Quebec, anti-Americanism was a central feature of the campaign to discourage French Canadians from emigrating to the United States. Leading nationalists warned that emigrants would be exposed to moral decadence, violence, and debilitating industrial labour in the cities of the Northeast and the Midwest. To emigrate was to imperil one's body and soul.

Anti-American rhetoric also served more elusive purposes. It was a key element in the right-wing campaign to brand Canada a fundamentally conservative nation. Imperialists and French Canadian nationalists insisted on the conservative and anti-American nature of Canadian society, in part, to consolidate their power and influence. Canada's conservatives sought to monopolize the power to define what was and was not 'Canadian,' and externalized their political and intellectual adversaries by presenting them as foreign enemies.[2] Anti-Americanism also provided traditional elites with a means to legitimize their moral and cultural authority. The conservative assault on American culture, for instance, was essentially an attack on mass culture. By externalizing and disparaging mass culture, intellectuals like abbé Henri d'Arles sought to affirm both the pre-eminence of highbrow culture and their role as the arbiters of culture. Likewise, many clergymen sought to shore up their moral influence by externalizing secularism. To embrace a secular or materialistic world view, they argued, was not only to turn one's back on God, but also to turn one's back on Canada.

Nevertheless, the conservative rejection of America was seldom absolute. The anti-American ethos, indeed, possessed some degree of ambi-

guity. For instance, many French Canadian nationalists, though worried
by most aspects of Canadian-American convergence, held a relatively
ambivalent view of reciprocity. The protectionist impulse was present
in nationalist thought, but was generally expressed through calls for
cultural protectionism and censorship. In imperialist prose, reciprocity was presented as a major threat to Canada's nationhood. American
investment, on the other hand, scarcely raised an eyebrow. Moreover
though imperialists believed, as Carl Berger writes, 'that the republic
represented an undesirable social order,'[3] few appear to have lost sleep
over the fate that awaited the hundreds of thousands of Canadians emigrants who chose to settle in the industrial centres of the Northeast and
Midwest. More significantly, most anti-Americans harboured little or
no resentment towards *individual* Americans. Few of Canada's leading
anti-American intellectuals appear to have shunned the United States
in their private lives, and their critique of American society often drew
its inspiration from American sources. In the late nineteenth and early
twentieth centuries, antimodernism was itself ambivalent. In the writing of many British and American intellectuals, notes Jackson Lears, a
rejection of the mass age often coexisted with 'enthusiasm for material
progress.'[4]

A degree of ambiguity was present in most Canadian writing on the
United States. Perfectly coherent and unambiguous ideas only exist in
the abstract and, in practice, both anti-Americanism and continentalism
were imperfect sensibilities. For instance, in the work of a number of liberal and socialist intellectuals, continentalism coexisted with a vigorous
critique of American society. Nevertheless, throughout the period under study, an obvious dividing line existed between anti-Americanism
and continentalism. It was most apparent when intellectuals discussed
issues related to continental integration or Canadian-American distinctiveness. The issue of reciprocity, for example, tended to rapidly dif-
ferentiate anti-Americans and continentalists in English Canada. Even
during the Great Depression and the Second World War, when conservative intellectuals like R.G. Trotter or B.K. Sandwell were willing
to accept some degree of economic integration, their half-hearted approval of the measure stood in stark contrast to the enthusiastic support
for free trade that emanated from the Dominion's leading continentalists. Issues related to identity offered a similar dividing line. Imperialists and *nationalistes* alike balked at the continentalist contention that
Canada and the United States shared a wider ethos of rupture and renewal. They argued that the Canadian-American border was far more

than an administrative boundary; it marked a fundamental divide. On a deeper level, however, anti-Americans and continentalists differed in their appreciation of tradition. This dichotomy faithfully mirrored the dividing line between conservative and non-conservative thought. In the conservative hierarchy of values, tradition stood paramount. It offered a guide to social welfare and a haven from the turmoil of the mass age. America's apparent contempt for the very idea of tradition was undoubtedly enough, in the eyes of many imperialists and French Canadian nationalists, to justify condemnation. By contrast, liberals and socialists, who shared a common passion for change and progress, viewed America's apparent disregard for tradition as the foundation of its greatness. Even conservative liberals like Edmond de Nevers, who held tradition in some esteem, were inclined to look upon American indifference towards convention and custom with favour.

Continentalism was a dichotomous ideal. In the nineteenth century, it was an essentially liberal doctrine espoused more often than not by religious nonconformists. By the interwar years, however, its vital centre had shifted leftward. During that era, some of Canada's leading continentalists were active supporters of the Co-operative Commonwealth Federation. In English Canada, continentalism reached its summit of influence during the 1930s and 1940s. The generation of intellectuals that had come of age during the Great War was exceptionally receptive to continentalist ideas. In Quebec, intellectual continentalism had been steadily declining since the failed rebellions of 1837–38. By the interwar years, its exponents were largely confined to the margins of the province's intellectual culture. The vital centre of French Canadian continentalism remained solidly liberal during the period examined here. That said, it was not a homogeneous sensibility. Some of Quebec's leading continentalists were the intellectual successors of the radical Institut canadien, while others professed a more moderate form of liberalism.

In the late nineteenth century, some of continentalism's most radical exponents embraced annexationism. The idea of continental union was particularly appealing to intellectuals like Goldwin Smith and Louis-Honoré Fréchette, whose liberalism was essentially republican in nature. Annexationism's fortunes were tied to a wider pessimism regarding the future of Canada. During the late 1880s and early 1890s, economic depression and ethnic, religious, and sectional strife helped fuel annexationist sentiment. By 1900, however, economic prosperity had returned to Canada and annexationism had more or less disappeared from the nation's intellectual culture.

The intellectual unity of the continental ethos was based on two fundamental premises: first, that Canada was an American nation, and second, that it would benefit from some form of continental integration. On a deeper level, however, continentalists were united in their assessment of modernity. They tended to regard humanity as the central fact of the universe and held a profound faith in its perfectibility and in the illimitable progress of society. The United States, as they saw it, was the embodiment of these ideas. The United States was a liberal republic that embraced a certain conception of progress, equality, and secularism. Continental integration, for its part, was expected to further the progressive agenda by altering Canada's political, economic, cultural, and intellectual relationship with Europe. This, in turn, would weaken Canada's 'reactionary' impulses – anti-Americanism, imperialism, conservatism, and clericalism – and allow Canadians to fully embrace their Americanness.

Continentalists in both English and French Canada were inclined to view the Canadian-American relationship in terms of similarities and concord, rather than in terms of differences and conflict. They believed, moreover, that American wealth and power could contribute to Canadian development. Most continentalists, indeed, could be considered nationalists. They saw Britain, not the United States, as the main threat to Canada's sovereignty and hoped to draw Canada closer to the United States in order to affirm Canada's independence from Britain. There were, of course, differences between English and French Canadian continentalism. Their most significant difference lay in their assessment of their nation's Americanness. For the English Canadian continentalist, the similarities between Canada and the United States far outweighed the differences. In Quebec, on the other hand, continentalists did not argue that French Canadian and American society were essentially similar. Instead, intellectuals like Errol Bouchette insisted that a wider ethos of rupture with Europe united the various nations of the New World.

Continentalist rhetoric served similar purposes in both English and French Canada. On its most basic level it granted legitimacy to continental integration, in particular to the liberalization of Canadian-American trade. On a deeper level, however, continentalism sought to brand Canada a modern, North American nation. Reaction, argued intellectuals like Frank Underhill, was not a Canadian value. Indeed, continentalists were eager to defend their legitimacy as intellectual observers. They were fed up with conservative attempts to stifle domestic intellectual debate by portraying their principles as un-Canadian. Canada was an American nation and continentalism, in turn, was not a seditious doctrine.

Ideas matter to the study of Canadian-American relations. Indeed, though intellectual discourse is perhaps less significant than socioeconomic forces in its impact on historical development, it has nevertheless proved important to the evolution of the Canadian-American relationship. In certain instances, intellectual commentary helped strengthen prevailing attitudes towards a neighbour. For example, in the United States at the turn of the twentieth century, *Canada and the Canadian Question* was likely the most readily available book about Canada. Goldwin Smith's tome helped reinforce the persistent American belief that the Dominion of Canada was an unnatural entity whose ultimate destiny lay in annexation to the United States. This attitude undoubtedly had an impact on the course of Canadian-American relations until the interwar years, when most Americans eventually came to see Canada as a legitimate – and permanent – entity.

Intellectual commentary sometimes played a more direct role in shaping Canada's relationship with the United States. For instance, in 1911, the torrent of anti-American prose generated by Canada's imperialist intellectuals played a crucial role in turning English Canadian opinion against reciprocity. Most voters probably supported the trade agreement at the outset. However, after an intense barrage of propaganda generated by Canada's imperialist movement and distributed by the nation's leading manufacturing interests, scores of voters turned against an agreement that successive Canadian governments, both Liberal and Conservative, had hoped to secure since Confederation. Stephen Leacock, for his part, went on a speaking tour in Quebec and Ontario during the election campaign and played a key role in several local contests, including in Brome County, Quebec, where, writes Alan Bowker, 'he helped a political unknown defeat a cabinet minister.'[5]

In some cases, intellectuals were directly involved in Canadian-American diplomacy. Reverend James A. Macdonald, for instance, played a significant – and largely secret – role in negotiating the 1911 reciprocity agreement. During the early negotiations, he acted as an unofficial go-between for President William Howard Taft and Prime Minister Wilfrid Laurier. Other intellectuals, including O.D. Skelton and Hugh Keenleyside, rose to key positions within Canada's civil service. Skelton was appointed under-secretary of state for external affairs by Prime Minister Mackenzie King in 1925. He remained in place during the Conservative government of R.B. Bennett and died of a heart attack on his way to work in 1941. Skelton was the leading Canadian civil servant of his time and an architect of the modern Department of External Affairs.[6] Hugh Keenleyside entered the Department of External Affairs in 1928. He served as the Canadian secretary of the Permanent Joint Board of Defence during its first crucial years of existence and was appointed Canada's first ambassador to Mexico in 1944. Both Skelton and Keenleyside favoured continental integration.

From 1891 to 1945, the average Canadian's receptivity to intellectual discourse on the United States and Canadian-American relations varied a great deal. For instance, while anti-American diatribes may have convinced many voters to reject the 1911 reciprocity agreement, it is unlikely that the harsh criticism of the United States that was articulated at the turn of the twentieth century by many of the Dominion's imperialists was shared by the population at large. Likewise, though pro-American sentiment reached its high-water mark after the 1940 fall of France, many ordinary Canadians continued to view intellectual continentalism with some suspicion. Indeed, Frank Underhill's near dismissal from his teaching position in August 1940 clearly illustrates the pervasive ambivalence regarding *américanité* that characterized Canadian public opinion during the period under study.

In French Canada, where several historians have noted a significant *décalage élite-peuple* on matters related to the United States, this ambivalence was less pronounced. Popular perceptions of the United States, to be sure, were largely positive. Nevertheless, it would be a mistake to view the clerical and conservative campaign against emigration and American culture as an abject failure. Clerical censure did not prevent hundreds of thousands of French Canadians from emigrating to the United States, but it undoubtedly helped direct a large number of people towards various zones of agricultural colonization in Quebec, eastern Ontario, and the Prairies. A similar argument can be made regarding American popular culture. Indeed, though widely viewed as ineffective, the nationalist campaign against Americanization did have an impact on cultural consumption in Quebec. At the very least, it encouraged various governments to enact legislation aimed at reducing the influence of American culture. For instance, under intense clerical pressure, the government of Quebec passed a law in 1928 to prohibit children under the age of sixteen from attending movies.

In the Western world, the image of the United States as a modern, progressive nation gradually dissipated after 1945. The Cold War fundamentally altered America's symbolic significance. This, in turn, trig-gered a shift in Canadian attitudes towards the United States. In the 1960s and 1970s, conservative anti-Americanism withered away and left-of-centre continentalism became something of a contradiction in terms. 'During the last decade,' wrote James Laxer in 1970, 'left-wing thinkers in Canada increasingly have recognized that the goals of Ca-nadian independence and socialism are interdependent. Continental integration has become so pervasive that those who value an independ-ent Canada and those who reject the values of corporate capitalism are beginning to share a common agenda.' American imperialism, Laxer insisted, threatened 'the very existence of the Canadian nation' and was 'the chief enemy of the world social revolution which we believe es-sential to the creation of a more just and humane international order.'[7]

Conservatism and British tradition played little or no role in the new Canadian nationalism that fully emerged in the 1960s and 1970s. Nationalists sought to define Canada as a fundamentally progressive, tolerant, and peaceful country. The United States, by contrast, was presented as a nation whose ethos was embodied in the multinational corporation, the Vietnam War, MacCarthyism, and segregation. 'The United States,' claimed Robin Mathews in 1969, 'is a republican, rac-ist, imperialistic, two-party, chauvinistic, culturally aggressive commu-nity.'[8] Mathews, who launched a crusade against the Americanization of Canadian universities, was a key figure in the new anti-Americanism that emerged in the 1960s.

Nevertheless, though the intellectual underpinnings of both conti-nentalism and anti-Americanism fundamentally changed in the 1960s, many of their basic arguments remained the same. Calls for economic and cultural protectionism did not disappear with the imperial fed-eration movement. Neither did exacerbated Canadian-American dif-ferentialism or the tendency to externalize continentalist adversaries by presenting them as un-Canadian. These staples of Canadian anti-Americanism have lived on in the writing of left-wing luminaries like James Laxer and Maude Barlow. As had been the case with the impe-rialist movement, anti-Americanism was important to the new nation-alism's sense of distinctiveness and purpose. Continental integration was, of course, presented as a menace to the Canadian nation. In the late twentieth century, however, it was viewed as a threat to the social programs and left-of-centre values that were now believed to define the Canadian experience. The new anti-Americanism reached a fever pitch during the 1988 free trade debate. 'Think about your children being drafted for military duty in Central America,' wrote one commentator in the *Canadian Forum*. 'Think about not having medicare, and having our streets filled with the poor, the crazy and the elderly. If we become Americans we will be a hinterland. We will be poor, living out of shopping carts spiritually and perhaps literally.'[9]

Left-wing anti-Americanism was not without antecedents. During the interwar years, some elements within Canada's labour movement articulated a form of nationalism that combined progressivism and anti-Americanism. Later, in the 1960s and 1970s, George Grant's *Lament for a Nation* was a source of inspiration to many young nationalists. Grant's conservatism was discarded, but his critique of America and his belief that Canada and the United States were antithetical entities were enthusiastically adopted by intellectuals involved in the new left. *Lament for a Nation* was 'the most important book I ever read in my life,' James Laxer confided to a journalist in the 1980s. 'Here was this crazy old philosopher of religion at McMaster and he woke up half our generation. He was saying Canada is dead, and by saying it he was creating the country.'[10] Donald Creighton's anti-American reading of Canadian history also inspired the new left, though to a lesser extent. His dour conservatism and his lack of respect for minority rights made his work less appealing to socialists.

During Quebec's Quiet Revolution, anti-Americanism remained present in nationalist commentary, though to lesser extent than in English-speaking Canada. Nationalism's *virage à gauche* was not accompanied by a fundamental shift in the themes of anti-Americanism. In some senses, anti-American rhetoric in Quebec had scarcely changed since the nineteenth century. Indeed, conservative nationalists would no doubt have agreed with journalist and writer André Major when he stated in 1968 that the Americans 'confuse material power and civilization.' Major was a founding editor of *Parti Pris*, a left-wing review which played an important role in the evolution of Quebec's intellectual culture. Yet his criticism of the United States in many ways mirrored that of *L'Action française*: 'Instinctively I distrust the Americans because, though I also live on this continent, I am not bound up in any way with the civilization evolving here. The values of this New World seem to me so old already and so poisoned that I would rather seek refreshment among my old people and in the Old World, where at least the mind has always mastered barbarism, except in moments of grave crisis.'[11]

Likewise, continentalism's shift to the right was not accompanied by a corresponding change in its basic premises. Leading continentalists continued to downplay Canadian-American divergences and insist that American power could contribute to the development of the Canadian nation. Goldwin Smith's contention that the continent's natural divisions ran along a north-south axis and that each of Canada's regions was the prolongation of a contiguous American region found its contemporary expression in the borderlands concept. 'The premise of the Borderlands Project is that North America runs more naturally north and south than east and west as specified by national boundaries, and that modern communication and efficient transportation help to blur distinctions between regional neighbors,' wrote Lauren McKinsey and Victor Konrad in the preface to the 1989 booklet that launched the influential, though short-lived, Borderlands Monograph Series. 'While people living near the border pay allegiance to their respective sovereign authorities in Washington, D.C. and Ottawa, they sometimes have more in common with neighbors across the border than with their fellow citizens.' McKinsey and Konrad also articulated one of the core tenets of interwar continentalism: that the Canadian-American relationship, though exceptional, could serve as a model of international relations. 'Unlike many border antagonists around the globe,' they insisted, 'Canadians and Americans are able to marshal resources for constructive engagement. These two countries have shown that it is possible to achieve joint objectives without subordinating social or cultural diversity, and many see this successful and unique bilateral relationship as a model for the management of rising global interdependence.'[12]

Many of the values and symbols associated with the United States have evolved over time. What has remained constant, however, is the symbolic importance accorded to America by the intellectuals of the world. In Canada, this phenomenon has been even more pronounced. For Canadians, America is not only a powerful nation whose way of life possesses universal pretensions, it is also a neighbour whose geographic and cultural proximity is one of the central facts of the Canadian experience. The Canadian-American relationship is existential for Canadians: it is bound up with issues related to Canadian identity and distinctiveness and to Canada's place in the world. For this reason the debate surrounding Canada's Americanness has proven to be both an enduring and an essential feature of our nation's intellectual culture.

Appendix: Corpus

The present study rests primarily on the analysis of the texts listed below. Wholly or in part, each text selected for inclusion in this corpus explores an aspect of American life or of the relationship between Canada and the United States. To better illustrate the evolution of Canadian writing on the United States, the corpus has been arranged in chronological order.

1891

Bonpart, Adrien de. 'Le P.É. Hamon et l'émigration canadienne.' *La Revue canadienne* XXVI: 513–25.

Bourinot, John George. 'Canada and the United States: An Historical Retrospect.' *Papers of the American Historical Association* V (July): 273–333.

Clarke, S.R. *A New Light on Annexation: A Political Brochure.* Toronto: J. Murray. 22 p.

Duncan, Sara Jeannette. *An American Girl in London.* Toronto: Williamson. x+321 p.

Grant, George Monro. *Canada and the Canadian Question:* A Review. Toronto: C.B. Robinson. 37 p.

Hamon, Édouard. *Les Canadiens-Français de la Nouvelle-Angleterre.* Quebec: N.S. Hardy. xv+483 p.

Lefroy, A.H.F. *The British Versus the American System of National Government.* Toronto: Williamson. 42 p.

McEvoy, John M. 'Review of Goldwin Smith's *Canada and the Canadian Question.*' *Annals of the American Academy of Political and Social Science* II (Nov.): 381–6.

Smith, Goldwin. *Canada and the Canadian Question.* New York: Macmillan. x+325 p.

- *Loyalty, Aristocracy and Jingoism: Three Lectures Delivered before the Young Men's Liberal Club, Toronto.* Toronto: Hunter, Rose. 96 p.
Wiman, Erastus. 'Can We Coerce Canada?' *North American Review* CLII (Jan.): 91–102.
- *Impossibility of Canadian Annexation.* [New York: E. Wiman.] 10 p.
- 'The Struggle in Canada.' *North American Review* CLII (Mar.): 339–48.
- *Union between the United States and Canada: Political or Commercial? Which Is Desirable and Which Is Presently Possible?* New York: [n.p.] 42 p.

1892

Parkin, George R. *Imperial Federation: The Problem of National Unity.* London: Macmillan. xii+314 p.

1893

Bourinot, John George. 'Canadian Studies in Comparative Politics: Parliamentary Compared with Congressional Government.' *Proceedings and Transactions of the Royal Society of Canada* 1st Series, XI, Section II: 77–94.
Fréchette, Louis-Honoré. 'The United States for French Canadians.' *Forum* XVI (Nov.): 336–45.
Fronsac, Viscount de [X Frederic Gregory Forsyth]. 'Origin of the Social Crisis in the United States: A Monarchist's View.' *Canadian Magazine* I (Oct.): 660–4.
Hopkins, J. Castell. 'Canadian Hostility to Annexation.' *Forum* XVI (Nov.): 325–35.
Rouilliard, Jean-Baptiste. *Annexion: conférence: l'union continentale.* Montreal: [n.p.] 48 p.
St-Pierre, Télesphore. *Les Canadiens et les États-Unis: ce qu'on perd à émigrer.* Montreal: La Gazette. 16 p.
Smith, Goldwin. *The United States: An Outline of Political History, 1492–1871.* New York: Macmillan. x+312 p.
Wiman, Erastus. *Chances of Success: Episodes and Observations in the Life of a Busy Man.* Toronto: F.R. James. vi+359 p.
- 'A Whirlwind of Disaster: Its Lessons.' *Canadian Magazine* I (Sept.): 517–22.

1894

Bernier, T.A. 'Les écoles publiques aux États-Unis.' *La Revue canadienne* XXX (Apr.): 193–209.

Brown, Vere C. 'The Crisis in the United States.' *Journal of the Canadian Bankers' Association* I (June): 237–64.

Cooper, John A. 'Canadian Democracy and Socialism.' *Canadian Magazine* III (Aug.): 332–36.

– 'The Canadian Premier and the United States President.' *Canadian Magazine* II (Mar.): 415–21.

Cotes, Mrs Everard [X Sara Jeannette Duncan]. *A Daughter of Today: A Novel.* New York: D. Appleton. 392 p.

Douglas, James. *Canadian Independence, Annexation and British Imperial Federation.* New York: G.P. Putnam. vi+114 p.

Rogers, R. Vashon. 'How to Get Divorced.' *Queen's Quarterly* I (Jan.): 193–206.

Royal, Joseph. *Le Canada, république ou colonie.* Montreal: Eusèbe Sénécal & fils. 105 p.

– 'Le socialisme aux États-Unis et en Canada.' *Mémoires et comptes rendus de la Société royale du Canada* 1st Series, XII, Section I: 49–61.

Smith, Goldwin. 'Preface to Revised Edition.' In his *Essays on Questions of the Day: Political and Social,* revised edition, v–xv. New York: Macmillan.

1895

Bourinot, John George. 'Why Canadians Do not Favor Annexation.' *Forum* XIX (May): 276–88.

Daoust, Charles R. 'Chez nos voisins.' *La Revue nationale* I (Mar.): 146–60.

Denison, George T. 'Canada and her Relations to the Empire.' *Westminster Review* CXLIV (Sept.): 248–65.

Parkin, George R. *The Great Dominion: Studies of Canada.* London: Macmillan. viii+251 p.

Smith, Goldwin. 'The Colonial Conference.' *Contemporary Review* LXVII (Jan.): 105–16.

1896

Clute, Arthur R. 'Recent Labor Troubles in America.' *University of Toronto Quarterly* II (Mar.): 165–80.

DeCelles, Alfred Duclos. *Les États-Unis. Origine, institutions, développement.* Ottawa: A.D. DeCelles. xv+437 p.

Grant, George Monro. 'Canada and the Empire.' *National Review* XXVII (July): 673–85.

– 'Canada and the Empire: A Rejoinder to Dr Goldwin Smith.' *Canadian Magazine* VIII (Nov.): 73–8.

Meek, Edward. 'Representative Government and Federalism.' *Canadian Magazine* VI (Apr.): 561–8.

Nevers, Edmond de [X Edmond Boisvert]. *L'avenir du peuple canadien-français*. Paris: Henri Jouve. xlvii+441 p.

Rouleau, Charles-Edmond. *L'émigration. Ses principales causes*. Quebec: Léger Brousseau. 149 p.

Ryerson, George Sterling. *The After-Math of a Revolution*. Toronto: W. Briggs. 16 p.

Smith, Goldwin. 'A Reply.' *Canadian Magazine* VII (Oct.): 540–4.

1897

Farrer, Edward. 'New England Influences in French Canada.' *Forum* XXIII (May): 308–19.

1898

Badreux, Jean [X Henri Roullaud]. *La guerre, l'Espagne et les États-Unis*. Montreal: Leprohon. 32 p.

Bourinot, John George. 'Canada's Relations with the United States and her Influence on Imperial Councils.' *Forum* XXV (May): 329–40.

Buies, Arthur. 'Le rôle des Canadiens français en Amérique.' *L'Enseignement primaire* XIX (Jan.): 377–9.

Chapman, William. *À propos de la Guerre hispano-américaine*. Quebec: Léger Brousseau. x+14 p.

Harrison, Susie Frances. *The Forest of Bourg-Marie*. Toronto: G.N. Morang. 306 p.

Roberts, Charles G.D. *New York Nocturnes and Other Poems*. Boston: Lamson Wolffe. 84 p.

Walker, B.E. 'The Canadian and American Banking Systems.' In *Canada: An Encyclopaedia of the Country*, vol. I, J. Castell Hopkins, ed., 495–504. Toronto: Linscott.

1899

Lefroy, A.H.F. 'Canadian Forms of Freedom.' *Annual Transactions of the United Empire Loyalists' Association of Ontario* (1899): 104–14.

1900

Clapin, Sylva. *Histoire des États-Unis depuis les premiers établissements jusqu'à nos jours*. Montreal: Beauchemin. vi+218 p.

Nevers, Edmond de [X Edmond Boisvert]. *L'âme américaine*, 2 vols. Paris: Jouve et Boyer.

Tardivel, Jules-Paul. *La situation religieuse aux États-Unis. Illusions et réalités.* Montreal: Cadieux et Derome. viii+302 p.

Willison, J.S. *The American Spirit.* Toronto: G.N. Morang. 7 p.

1901

Barr, Robert. *The Victors: A Romance of Yesterday Morning & This Afternoon.* New York: F.A. Stokes. ix+567 p.

Burwash, Nathanael. 'The Moral Character of the U.E. Loyalists.' *Annual Transactions of the United Empire Loyalists' Association of Ontario* (1901–2): 58–65.

Laflamme, J.L.K. 'Les Canadiens aux États-Unis.' *La Revue canadienne* XXXIX–XL (June–Dec.): 485–93, 72–9, 153–9, 232–9, 311–19, 385–98, 471–8.

Lloyd, Wallace [X James Algie]. *Bergen Worth.* Toronto: Langdon and Hall. viii–276 p.

1902

[Beaudet, Henri.] *Esquisse des collèges américains.* [Lewiston, Maine: Haswell Press.] [18 p.]

Arnold, Matthew. *Études sur les États-Unis par Matthew Arnold*, translated, prefaced, and annotated by Edmond de Nevers [X Edmond Boisvert]. Quebec: Dussault et Proulx. xii+221 p.

Clapin, Sylva. *A New Dictionary of Americanisms.* New York: Louis Weiss. xvi+581 p.

Colquhoun, A.H.U. 'The Reciprocity of To-day.' *Canadian Magazine* XVIII (Jan.): 226–8.

Cotes, Mrs Everard [X Sara Jeannette Duncan]. *Those Delightful Americans.* New York: D. Appleton. 352 p.

Dooner, W.A. 'The Negro Problem in the United States.' *University of Ottawa Review* IV (May): 471–6.

Hopkins, J. Castell. 'Relations with Foreign Countries.' *Canadian Annual Review of Public Affairs* (1902): 173–88.

Huot, Antonio. 'Mœurs américaines. Blancs et noirs.' *La Nouvelle-France* I (Aug.): 368–80.

Pâquet, Louis-Adolphe. 'Sermon sur la vocation de la race française en Amérique' (1902). In his *Discours et allocutions*, 181–202. Quebec: Imp. franciscaine missionaire, 1915.

Smith, Goldwin. *Commonwealth or Empire? A Bystander's View of the Question*. New York: Macmillan. 82 p.

1903

Bouchette, Errol. *Robert Lozé. Nouvelle*. Montreal: A.P. Pigeon. 170 p.

Hopkins, J. Castell. 'Relations with the United States.' *Canadian Annual Review of Public Affairs* (1903): 346–400.

Milner, William S. 'Roman, Greek, English and American Conceptions of Liberty.' *Canadian Magazine* XXI (Oct.): 508–18.

Stringer, Arthur. *The Silver Poppy: A Novel*. New York: D. Appleton. vi+291 p.

Willson, Beckles. *The New America: A Study of the Imperial Republic*. London: Chapman and Hall. vii+268 p.

1904

Cappon, James. 'The Great American Democracy.' *Queen's Quarterly* XI (Jan.): 296–311.

Denison, George T. 'The United Empire Loyalists and their Influence upon the History of This Continent.' *Proceedings and Transactions of the Royal Society of Canada*, 2nd Series, X, Appendix A: xxv–xxxix.

Holmested, George S. 'The Alaskan Boundary.' *Canadian Law Review* III (Feb.): 59–69.

Nevers, Edmond de [X Edmond Boisvert]. 'L'évolution des peuples anciens et modernes.' *La Revue canadienne* XLVII (Aug., Sept., and Nov.): 167–80, 279–90, 538–60.

Osler, William. 'Anglo-Canadian and American Relations.' *Addresses Delivered before the Canadian Club of Toronto* (1904–5): 62–7.

Smith, Goldwin. 'Can Canada Make Her Own Treaties?' *Canadian Magazine* XXII (Feb.): 331–5.

1905

Bouchette, Errol. 'Le Canada parmi les peuples américains.' *La Revue canadienne* XLVIII (Jan.): 11–19.

Burpee, Lawrence J. 'Canada and the Joint High Commission.' *North American Review* CLXXXI (Oct.): 555–67.

Stewart, J.F.M. 'The Development of our National Sentiment and Spirit of Independence.' *University of Toronto Monthly* V (Mar.): 143–7.

Wickett, S. Morley. 'Canadians in the United States.' *University of Toronto Monthly* V (Feb.): 117–25.

1906

Farrer, Edward. 'Canada and the United States.' *Comtemporary Review* 90 (Oct.): 550–63.

Lefroy, A.H.F. 'A Century of Constitutional Development upon the North American Continent.' *Canada Law Journal* XLII (July): 449–91.

O'Higgins, Harvey J. *Don-A-Dreams: A Story of Love and Youth.* New York: Century. 412 p.

Rogers, R. Vashon. 'Difficulties in Marrying in the United States.' *Canadian Law Review* V (Mar.): 145–52.

Shortt, Adam. 'The Relations of Canada and the United States.' *The Westminster* IX (July): 54–8.

Willison, J.S. *Anglo-Saxon Amity.* [Toronto: n.p.] 15 p.

1907

Cappon, James. 'Current Events: The Growth of Federal Control in the United States.' *Queen's Quarterly* XIV (Apr.): 335–7.

Colquhoun, A.H.U. 'A Home of Lost Causes.' *University Magazine* VI (Feb.): 101–6.

Huot, Antonio. 'La question sociale aux États-Unis en 1907.' *La Revue canadienne* LII (Apr.): 419–27.

Leacock, Stephen. 'Greater Canada: An Appeal.' *University Magazine* VI (Apr.): 132–41.

– 'The Psychology of American Humour.' *University Magazine* VI (Feb.): 55–75.

Logan, Annie MacFarlane. 'The American Novel.' *University Magazine* VI (Apr.): 154–67.

Skelton, O.D. 'Current Events: Reform Tendencies in the United States.' *Queen's Quarterly* XV (July): 75–8.

1908

Arles, Henri d' [X Henri Beaudé, né Beaudet]. *Le collège sur la colline.* Paris: F. R. de Ruderval. 95 p.

Cappon, James. 'Current Events: Democracy and Panics.' *Queen's Quarterly* XV (Jan.): 237–48.

Chapman, William. 'Aux Canadiens des États-Unis.' *La Revue franco-américaine* I (1908): 241–3.

Ewart, John S. 'The Alaska Boundary.' In his *The Kingdom of Canada, Imperial Federation, the Colonial Conference, the Alaska Boundary and Other Essays,* 299–347. Toronto: Morang.

Falconer, Robert A. 'The Unification of Canada.' *University Magazine* VII (Feb.): 3–9.

Huot, Antonio. 'Aux États-Unis: La dernière crise.' *La Revue canadienne,* New Series, I (May): 410–16.

– 'Aux États-Unis: Les échos d'un centenaire.' *La Revue canadienne,* New Series, II (July): 169–74.

– 'Aux États-Unis: Les universités.' *La Revue canadienne,* New Series, II (Dec.): 550–7.

Johnston, Arthur. *Myths and Facts of the American Revolution: A Commentary on United States History as It Is Written.* Toronto: W. Briggs. 302 p.

Laflamme, J.L.K. 'La religion et les assimilateurs dans la Nouvelle-Angleterre.' *La Revue franco-américaine* I (May): 81–8.

MacPhail, Andrew. 'Protection and Politics.' *University Magazine* VII (Apr.): 238–55.

Smith, Goldwin. 'Party Government.' *North American Review* CLXXXVII (Nov.): 641–9.

Parkin, George R. 'The Relations of Canada and the United States.' *Empire Club Speeches* (1907–8): 157–68.

Walker, B.E. 'Abnormal Features of American Banking.' *Journal of the Canadian Bankers' Association* XVI (Oct.): 58–80.

Willison, J.S. *The United States and Canada.* New York: American Branch of the Association for International Conciliation. 13 p.

1909

Asselin, Olivar. *Le problème municipal. La leçon que Montréal doit tirer de l'expérience des États-Unis.* Montreal: O. Asselin. 16 p.

Denison, George T. *The Struggle for Imperial Unity. Recollections and Experiences.* London: Macmillan. x+422 p.

Héroux, Omer. 'En terre franco-américaine.' *La Revue franco-américaine* III (Sept.): 336–42.

Knowles, Robert E. *The Attic Guest: A Novel.* New York: F.H. Revell. viii+338 p.

Laflamme, J.L.K., et al. 'French Catholics in the United States.' In *The Catholic Encyclopedia,* vol. VI, ed. Charles G. Hebermann et al., 271–7. New York: Encyclopedia Press.

- 'La question des langues et l'épiscopat dans la Nouvelle-Angleterre.' *La Revue franco-américaine* II (Mar.): 324–33.

Leacock, Stephen. 'Canada and the Monroe Doctrine.' *University Magazine* VIII (Oct.): 351–74.

- 'Literature and Education in America.' *University Magazine* VIII (Feb.): 3–17.

LeBouthillier, Jean-Georges. 'Chronique américaine.' *La Revue franco-américaine* III (June): 101–11.

Maclaren, J.J. 'Our International Boundary.' *Queen's Quarterly* XVII (July): 23–7.

MacPhail, Andrew. 'New Lamps for Old.' *University Magazine* VIII (Feb.): 18–35.

Perrier, Philippe. 'L'école catholique d'été aux États-Unis.' *La Revue canadienne*, New Series, IV (Sept.): 210–19.

Skelton, O.D. 'Current Events: Government by Commission; The Poverty of Issues; Preference or Reciprocity.' *Queen's Quarterly* XVI (Jan.): 290–8.

Wrong, George M. 'The Attitude of Canada.' *The Nineteenth Century* LXVI (Oct.): 704–15.

1910

Arles, Henri d' [X Henri Beaudé, né Beaudet]. 'Le journalisme américain.' In his *Essais et conférences*, 9–31. Quebec: [n.p.], 1909. [This collection of essays was not published until Apr. 1910.]

Eckhardt, H.M.P. 'Americanizing Influences.' *Journal of the Canadian Bankers' Association* XVII (July): 285–93.

Falconer, Robert A. 'The Individuality of the Canadian People.' *University Monthly* X (June): 437–48.

Huot, Antonio. 'Aux États-Unis. L'enseignement de l'État et l'éducation.' *La Revue canadienne*, New Series, V (Apr.): 314–28.

Lemay, Henri. 'L'avenir de la race canadienne-française.' *La Revue canadienne*, New Series, V (Apr.): 289–313.

[MacPhail, Andrew.] 'Canadian Writers and American Politics.' *University Magazine* IX (Feb.): 3–17.

- *Essays in Fallacy*. London: Longmans. vi+359 p.

Riddell, William Renwick. 'The Canadian and American Constitutions: A Comparison.' *Canadian Magazine* XXXV (June): 108–14.

- 'Some Remarks on the Constitutions of Canada and the United States.' *Empire Club Speeches* (1909–10): 188–99.

Robinson, C.W. *Canada and Canadian Defence: The Defensive Policy of the Domin-*

ion in Relation to the Character of Her Frontier, the Events of the War of 1812 and her Position Today. Toronto: Musson. x-186 p.

Skelton, O.D. 'Current Events: Insurgency in the United States; The Canadian Movement.' *Queen's Quarterly* XVIII (Oct.): 168–73.

Wrong, George M. 'Canadian Nationalism and the Imperial Tie.' *University Monthly* X (Feb.): 173–83.

1911

Bélisle, Alexandre. *Histoire de la presse franco-américaine.* Worcester, Mass.: L'Opinion publique. [xvi] +432 p.

Bourassa, Henri. *The Reciprocity Agreement and Its Consequences as Viewed from the Nationalist Standpoint.* Montreal: Le Devoir. iv+43 p.

Cappon, James. 'Current Events: A Glance at the Surface: Hearst Journalism; President Taft's Message.' *Queen's Quarterly* XVIII (Jan.): 251–7.

Hammond, M.O. 'The Tragedy of Reciprocity.' *Canadian Magazine* XXXVIII (Nov.): 84–91.

Hawkes, Arthur. *An Appeal to the British-Born: To Promote the Sense of Canadian Nationality, as an Increasing Power within the British Empire, and to Preserve Unimpaired the Canadian and British Channels of Commerce on which the Prosperity of the Dominion Has Been Founded.* Toronto: Canadian National League. 8 p.

Hopkins, J. Castell. 'Reciprocity with the United States.' *Canadian Annual Review of Public Affairs* (1911): 17–141.

Leacock, Stephen. 'A Hero in Homespun: or, The Life Struggle of Hezekiah Hayloft.' In his *Nonsense Novels,* 95–111. New York: J. Lane.

MacPhail, Andrew. 'Certain Varieties of the Apples of Sodom.' *University Magazine* X (Feb.): 30–46.

– 'The Cleaning of the Slate.' *University Magazine* X (Apr.): 183–91.

– 'Why the Liberals Failed.' *University Magazine* X (Dec.): 566–80.

Sandwell, B.K. 'The Annexation of Our Stage.' *Canadian Magazine* XXXVIII (Nov.): 22–6.

Sibley, E.L. 'That Market of Ninety Millions.' *Industrial Canada* XI (June): 1166–8.

Skelton, O.D. 'Canada's Rejection of Reciprocity.' *Journal of Political Economy* XIX (Nov.): 726–31.

– 'Current Events: Reciprocity; The Advantage of Party Criticism; The Economic Balance; The Annexation Bogey.' *Queen's Quarterly* XVIII (Apr.): 329–33.

Wickett, S. Morley. 'Great Britain and the Canadian Preference.' *Industrial Canada* XII (Sept.): 162–7.

1912

Bourassa, Henri. *The Spectre of Annexation and the Real Danger of National Disintegration*. Montreal: Le Devoir. 42 p.

Cappon, James. 'Current Events: Government and Trusts in the United States.' *Queen's Quarterly* XIX (Jan.): 290–300.

Leacock, Stephen. *Sunshine Sketches of a Little Town*. New York: J. Lane. xii+264 p.

Macdonald, James A. 'Some International Fundamentals.' *Addresses Delivered before the Canadian Club of Montreal* (1912–13): 54–61.

Magnan, D.-M.-A. *Histoire de la race française aux États-Unis*. Paris: C. Amat. xvi+356 p.

Munro, William Bennett. *The Government of American Cities*. New York: Macmillan. viii+401 p.

Riddell, William Renwick. 'International Trade Relations and Reciprocity between Canada and the United States: A Historical Sketch.' *Queen's Quarterly* XIX (Apr.): 330–9.

Skelton, O.D. 'Current Events: Choosing a President.' *Queen's Quarterly* XX (July): 113–16.

– 'Current Events: The Presidential Campaign.' *Queen's Quarterly* XX (Oct.): 237–40.

1913

Allin, Cephas D. 'The Game of Politics.' *University Magazine* XII (Apr.): 215–31.

Chartier, Émile. 'En territoire franco-américain.' *La Nouvelle-France* XII (Nov.): 507–15.

Ewart, John S. 'The Canning Policy Sometimes Called the Monroe Doctrine.' *The Kingdom Papers* 16: 167–89.

[Grant, William Lawson.] 'Canada and Anglo-American Relations.' *The Round Table* IV (Dec.): 106–22.

Munro, William Bennett. 'Should Canadian Cities Adopt Commission Government?' *Queen's Quarterly* XX (Jan.): 262–74.

Skelton, O.D. 'The Referendum.' *University Magazine* XII (Apr.): 197–214.

Sutherland, John C. 'Teaching of History in the United States.' *University Magazine* XII (Feb.): 159–64.

1914

Leacock, Stephen. 'The American Attitude.' *University Magazine* XIII (Dec.): 595–7.

– *Arcadian Adventures with the Idle Rich*. New York: J. Lane. 310 p.

O'Keefe, J.C. 'American Immigration into the Canadian North West.' *University of Ottawa Review* XVI (Apr.): 277–9.

Saint-Pierre, Arthur. *La Fédération américaine du travail*. Montreal: l'École sociale populaire. 31 p.

Skelton, O.D. 'Canada and the American Tariff.' *University Magazine* XIII (Feb.): 45–54.

Sutherland, John C. 'American Historians.' *University Magazine* XIII (Feb.): 105–11.

Willson, Beckles. 'Must We Be Americans?' *University Magazine* XIII (Feb.): 59–67.

1915

Anonymous. 'Canada: Canada and the United States.' *The Round Table* V (Sept.): 840–4.

Macdonald, James A. *Democracy and the Nations: A Canadian View*. Toronto: S.B. Gundy. x+244 p.

Skelton, O.D. 'Current Events: The Position of the United States.' *Queen's Quarterly* XXIII (July): 105–10.

1916

Cappon, James. 'Current Events: President Wilson's Diplomacy; Dark Forces.' *Queen's Quarterly* XXIV (Oct.): 371–87.

Charbonneau, Jean. *Des influences françaises au Canada*, vol. I. Montreal: Beauchemin. xix+226 p.

Jordan, William George. 'Current Events: American.' *Queen's Quarterly* XXIII (Apr.): 477–88.

Skelton, O.D. 'Canadian Capital Requirements.' *Annals of the American Academy of Political and Social Science* LXVIII (Nov.): 216–25.

– 'Current Events: United States.' *Queen's Quarterly* XXIV (July): 142–51.

Vaughan, Walter. 'Woman Suffrage Today.' *University Magazine* XV (Dec.): 575–87.

1917

Bourassa, Henri. *L'intervention américaine, ses motifs, son objet, ses conséquences*. Montreal: Le Devoir. 51 p.

Cappon, James. 'Current Events: The Conflict over the Classics in the United

States; Princeton University; The Classical Conference; Senator Lodge's Address.' *Queen's Quarterly* XXV (July): 91–112.

Hopkins, J. Castell. 'The United States and the War.' *Canadian Annual Review of Public Affairs* (1917): 213–81.

King, Basil. *The High Heart*. New York: Harper. 419 p.

Macdonald, James A. *The North American Idea*. New York: F.H. Revell. 240 p.

Riddell, Willam Renwick. *The Constitution of Canada in Its History and Practical Working*. New Haven: Yale University Press. xi-170 p.

1918

Colquhoun, A.H.U. 'Canada and the United States.' *Canadian Magazine* L (Jan.): 204–7.

Falconer, Robert A. '1776 and 1914, a Contrast in British Colonial Action.' *Proceedings and Transactions of the Royal Society of Canada*, 3rd series, XII, section II: 241–50.

Montpetit, Édouard. 'Six jours à Berkeley.' *Revue trimestrielle canadienne* IV (May): 1–20.

Morin, Léo-Pol. 'La mare aux grenouilles: La musique et les Américains.' *Le Nigog* I (May): 204–5.

1919

Arles, Henri d' [X Henri Beaudé, né Beaudet]. 'Le français dans le Connecticut.' *La Revue nationale* I (Jan.): 6–18.

– 'Le français dans le New Hampshire.' *La Revue nationale* I (Mar.): 98–116.

Bourassa, Henri. *Syndicats nationaux ou internationaux?* Montreal: Le Devoir. 46 p.

Courchesne, Georges. *Nos légitimes aspirations*. Montreal: Ligue de ralliement français en Amérique. 24 p.

King, Basil. *The City of Comrades*. New York: Grosset and Dunlap. 405 p.

Leacock, Stephen. 'The Warning of Prohibition in America.' *National Review* LXXIII (July): 680–7.

[MacPhail, Andrew.] 'Article Nineteen.' *University Magazine* XVIII (Oct.): 311–26.

Munro, William Bennett. *The Government of the United States: National, State and Local*. New York: Macmillan. x+660 p.

Phelps, Arthur L., et al. 'The Deluge of American Magazines in Canada.' *Canadian Bookman* I (Apr.): 10–13.

1920

Baker, Ray Palmer. *A History of English-Canadian Literature to the Confederation: Its Relation to the Literature of Great Britain and the United States.* Cambridge: Harvard University Press. ix+200 p.

Charpentier, Alfred. *Dans les serres de l'aigle. Historique de l'entreprise du trade-unionisme américain sur le mouvement ouvrier au Canada.* Montreal: Bibliothèque de l'Action française. 32 p.

– *De l'internationalisme au nationalisme.* Montreal: l'École sociale populaire. 40 p.

Désy, Jean. 'La Société des nations et l'opposition américaine.' *Revue trimestrielle canadienne* VI (Dec.): 357–68.

Gérin-Lajoie, Marie. 'Entre nous: L'orientation sociale catholique aux États-Unis.' *La Bonne parole* VIII (Apr.): 3–4.

Harvey, Jean-Charles. *La chasse aux millions: l'avenir industriel du Canada-français [sic].* Quebec: Crédit industriel. 40 p.

Lecompte, Édouard. *La YMCA aux États-Unis, au Canada: L'antidote.* Montreal: L'Oeuvre des tracts. 16 p.

McArthur, Peter. *The Affable Stranger.* New York: Houghton Mifflin. xvi+216 p.

MacMechan, Archibald. 'Canada as a Vassal State.' *Canadian Historical Review* I (Dec.): 347–53.

[Patton, H.S.] 'A Canadian at Harvard.' *Canadian Forum* I (Dec.): 75–6.

1921

Audet, Francis J., and A.H.U. Colquhoun. 'Correspondence: Canada as a Vassal State.' *Canadian Historical Review* II (Mar.): 69–73.

Durand, Louis-D. 'Par delà nos frontières.' *L'Action française* V (Apr.): 220–6.

Laut, Agnes C. *Canada at the Cross Roads.* Toronto: Macmillan. 279 p.

Mavor, James. 'The Art of the United States.' *Canadian Forum* I (Feb.): 144–5.

Munro, William Bennett. 'Problems of City Government.' *Dalhousie Review* I (July): 139–50.

Patton, H.S. 'Reciprocity with Canada: The Canadian Viewpoint.' *Quarterly Journal of Economics* 35 (Aug.): 574–96.

Wrong, George M. *The United States and Canada: A Political Study.* New York: Abingdon Press. 191 p.

1922

Action française, L' [X Lionel Groulx]. 'Notre avenir politique.' *L'Action française* VII (Jan.): 4–25.

Gascon, Wilfrid. 'Vers l'indépendance du Canada.' *L'Action française* VIII (Aug.): 100–16.

Groulx, Lionel. *L'amitié française d'Amérique*. Montreal: Bibliothèque de l'Action française. 32 p.

Harvey, Jean-Charles. *Marcel Faure*. Montmagny, Que.: Imp. de Montmagny. 214 p.

[Sandwell, B.K.] 'America' and 'American.' *Canadian Bookman* IV (Sept.): 229–30.

Turc [X Victor Barbeau]. 'La politique: La méthode américaine.' *Les Cahiers de Turc* V (Feb.): 29–34.

Vanier, Anatole. 'Notre avenir politique: L'État français et les États-Unis.' *L'Action française* VII (June): 322–38.

Villeneuve, J.-M.-R. 'Notre avenir politique: Et nos frères de la dispersion?' *L'Action française* VIII (July): 4–27.

Willison, J.S. *From Month to Month: A Survey of American Conditions and Problems*. Toronto: [n.p.] 11 p.

1923

Alexander, Henry. 'The American Language.' *Queen's Quarterly* XXX (Apr.): 353–62.

Burpee, Lawrence J. 'An International Experiment.' *Dalhousie Review* III (July): 163–79.

Dale, E.A. 'The Drama in North Dakota and Elsewhere.' *Canadian Forum* III (Aug.): 341–2.

Jackson, G.E. 'Emigration of Canadians to the United States.' *Annals of the American Academy of Political and Social Science* CVII (May): 25–34.

Minville, Esdras. 'Les Américains et nous.' *L'Action française* X (Aug.): 97–105.

Raîche, Joseph. 'Une randonée aux États-Unis.' *Le Canada français* XI (Oct.): 116–40.

Willison, J.S. *Partners in Peace; the Dominion, the Empire and the Republic*. Toronto: Warwick and Rutter. 94 p.

1924

Bernard, Harry. 'L'ennemi dans la place: Théâtre et cinéma.' *L'Action française* XII (Aug.): 69–80.

Brown, George W. 'Elections: British and American.' *Canadian Forum* IV (Feb.): 138–9.

Davis, Allan Ross. 'Canada, the United States, and Great Britain.' *United Empire*, New Series, XV (Dec.): 667–72.

Durand, Louis-D. 'L'ennemi dans la place: La perte du capital humain.' *L'Action française* XI (Mar., Apr.): 130–9, 194–212.

Leacock, Stephen. 'Little Glimpses of the Future in America.' In his *The Garden of Folly*, 223–33. Toronto: S.B. Gundy.

Minville, Esdras. 'L'ennemi dans la place: Le capital étranger.' *L'Action française* XI (June): 323–49.

Ollivier, Maurice. 'Méthodes législatives et formes de gouvernement. Parallèle entre l'Angleterre, les États-Unis et le Canada.' *Revue trimestrielle canadienne* X (Dec.): 384–90.

Stevenson, J.A. 'The Political Situation in the United States.' *Canadian Forum* IV (May): 236–8.

– 'The Presidential Campaign in the United States.' *Canadian Forum* V (Nov.): 43–5.

Stevenson, Lionel. 'Manifesto for a National Literature.' *Canadian Bookman* (Feb.): 35–6, 46.

Trotter, Reginald G. 'Some American Influences upon the Canadian Federation Movement.' *Canadian Historical Review* V (Sept.): 213–27.

1925

Anonymous. 'Canadian Prosperity and the United States.' *The Round Table* XV (June): 569–72.

Dugré, Adélard. *La campagne canadienne. Croquis et leçons.* Montreal: Le Messager. 235 p.

Dumont, Armand. 'Les cours d'été à l'Université d'Harvard.' *Le Canada français* XIII (Nov.): 190–6.

Falconer, Robert A. *The United States as a Neighbour from a Canadian Point of View.* Cambridge: Cambridge University Press. viii+259 p.

Maclellan, W.E. 'Topics of the Day: The Tennessee Trial.' *Dalhousie Review* V (Oct.): 395–400.

Parizeau, Gérard. 'Relations commerciales entre le Canada et les États-Unis.' *L'Actualité économique* I (July–Aug.): 16–17.

Wrong, George M. 'The Evolution of the Foreign Relations of Canada.' *Canadian Historical Review* VI (Mar.): 4–14.

1926

Alexander, Henry. 'Is There an American Language?' *Queen's Quarterly* XXXIV (Oct.): 191–202.

Bilodeau, Georges-Marie. *Pour rester au pays. Étude sur l'émigration des Canadiens français aux États-Unis. Causes. Remèdes.* Quebec: L'Action sociale. 168 p.

Deacon, William Arthur. 'The Bogey of Annexation.' In his *Poteen: A Pot-Pourri of Canadian Essays*, 1–25. Ottawa: Graphic Publications.

Falconer, Robert A. 'The United States as Canada's Friend.' *Current History* XXIV (May): 181–8.

Jackson, G.E. 'American Prosperity.' *Canadian Forum* VI (Feb.): 162–5.

MacKay, Douglas. 'The Americanization of Canada.' *Century* CXII (June): 190–4.

Minville, Esdras. 'L'industrie américaine de l'automobile.' *L'Actualité économique* I (Feb.): 10–12.

Van der Hoek, J. Marjorie. 'The Penetration of American Capital in Canada.' *Canadian Forum* VI (Aug.): 333–5.

1927

Ayre, Robert. 'The American Empire.' *Canadian Forum* VIII (Jan.): 105–6.

Ewart, John S. 'Canada, the Empire and the United States.' *Foreign Affairs* VI (Oct.): 116–27.

Gratton, Valmore. 'Le capital étranger au Canada.' *L'Actualité économique* II (Feb.): 11–13.

Grove, Frederick Philip [X Felix Paul Greve]. *A Search for America.* Ottawa: Graphic Publications. 448 p.

Keenleyside, Hugh L. 'The American Economic Penetration of Canada.' *Canadian Historical Review* VIII (Mar.): 31–40.

Ladouceur, Lucien. 'Les États-Unis à vol d'oiseau.' *L'Actualité économique* III (Oct.): 128–32.

Lyon, Alexander. 'National Unions or American Trade Trusts.' *Canadian Unionist* 1 (June): 13.

Trotter, Reginald G. 'Canadian History in the Universities of the United States.' *Canadian Historical Review* VIII (Sept.): 190–207.

1928

Bastien, Hermas. 'Sur les États-Unis.' *L'Action canadienne-française* XX (Aug.): 111–17.

Brisay, Richard de. 'The American Election.' *Canadian Forum* IX (Nov.): 39–40.

Dafoe, John W. 'The Problems of Canada.' In Cecil J.B. Hurst et al. *Great Britain and the Dominions*, 131–260. Chicago: University of Chicago Press.

Dugré, Alexandre. 'Comment orienter l'émigration.' *L'Action canadienne-française* XX (Aug.): 73–90.

Grignon, Claude-Henri. *Le secret de Lindbergh*. Montreal: Éd. de la Porte d'or. iv+211 p.

Groulx, Lionel. *Nos responsabilités intellectuelles*. Montreal: Association catholique de la jeunesse canadienne-française. 40 p.

Leman, Beaudry. 'Les Canadiens français et le milieu américain.' *Revue trimestrielle canadienne* XIV (Sept.): 263–75.

Minville, Esdras. 'M. Hoover et nous.' *L'Actualité économique* IV (Nov.): 105–7.

Underhill, Frank H. 'Canadian and American History – and Historians.' *Canadian Forum* VIII (June): 685–8.

1929

Bastien, Hermas. 'William James.' In his *Itinéraires philosophiques*, 53–102. Montreal: A. Lévesque.

Brisay, Richard de. 'Our Neighbours to the South.' *Canadian Forum* IX (Jan.): 111–13.

Bush, Douglas. 'Pride and Prejudice.' *Canadian Mercury* I (June): 136–7.

Keenleyside, Hugh L. *Canada and the United States: Some Aspects of the History of the Republic and the Dominion*. New York: Knopf. xxi+396+xlii p.

King, Tom. 'The Testing of Herbert Hoover.' *Queen's Quarterly* XXXVI (Summer): 406–19.

Lower, A.R.M. 'New France in New England.' *New England Quarterly* II (June): 278–95.

– 'Some Neglected Aspects of Canadian History.' Canadian Historical Association *Annual Report*, 65–71.

McInnis, Edgar W. 'This Insubstantial Pageant: Reflections on the American Political Scene.' *Canadian Forum* IX–X (June, Aug., Sept., and Nov.): 305–6, 378–9, 413–15, 45–6.

Munro, William Bennett. *American Influences on Canadian Government*. Toronto: Macmillan. xi+153 p.

Trotter, Reginald G. 'Canadian Interest in the History of the United States.' *Queen's Quarterly* XXXVI (Winter): 92–107.

Underhill, Frank H. 'O Canada.' *Canadian Forum* X (Oct.): 10–12.

– 'O Canada.' *Canadian Forum* X (Dec.): 79–80.

Willson, Beckles. *America's Ambassadors to England (1785–1929): A Narrative of Anglo-American Diplomatic Relations*. New York: Stokes. xiv+497 p.

Wilson, J. 'The Need of a National Outlook.' *Canadian Unionist* III (Nov.): 73–4.

1930

Bilodeau, Georges-Marie. 'L'américanisme.' *La Voix nationale* III (Apr.): 6–7.

Burford, W.T. 'Labour Is National.' *Canadian Forum* X (Apr.): 236–8.

Corbett, P.E. 'Anti-Americanism.' *Dalhousie Review* X (Oct.): 295–300.

Dafoe, John W. 'Canada and the United States.' *Journal of the Royal Institute of International Affairs* IX (Nov.): 721–8.

Falconer, Robert A. 'American Influence on the Higher Education of Canada.' *Proceedings and Transactions of the Royal Society of Canada*, 3rd Series, XXIV, Section II: 23–38.

Martin, J.B. 'Neighborliness or Absurdity.' *Canadian Republic Magazine* I (May): 6–7.

– 'Who Owns Our Theatres?' *Canadian Independence Magazine* I (July): 14–17.

Massey, Vincent. *Good Neighbourhood and Other Addresses in the United States.* Toronto: Macmillan. xiii+362 p.

Stevenson, J.A. 'Canadian Sentiment toward the United States.' *Current History* XXXIII (Oct.): 60–4.

Underhill, Frank H. 'O Canada.' *Canadian Forum* X (Jan.): 115–16.

1931

Alexander, Henry. 'What Is Good English?' *Queen's Quarterly* XXXVIII (Spring): 350–8.

Brebner, John Bartlet. 'Canadian and North American History.' Canadian Historical Association *Annual Report*, 37–48.

– 'Oxford, Toronto, Columbia.' *Columbia University Quarterly* XXIII (Sept.): 224–40.

Choquette, Robert. *Metropolitain Museum.* [Montreal]: [Herald Press.] 29 p.

Corbett, P.E. 'The New Canadianism.' *Contemporary Review* CXL (Oct.): 479–84.

Creighton, D.G. 'Ten Years of the Noble Experiment.' *Canadian Forum* XI (July): 371–2.

Denison, Merrill. 'Thoughts on Radio.' In *Open House*, ed. William Arthur Deacon and Wilfred Reeves, 107–20. Ottawa: Graphic Publications.

Desrosiers, Léo-Paul. *Nord-Sud. Roman canadien.* Montreal: Le Devoir. 199 p.

Greenaway, C. Roy. 'Big Shots.' In *Open House*, ed. William Arthur Deacon and Wilfred Reeves, 219–45. Ottawa: Graphic Publications.

Héroux, Omer, ed. *En Louisiane.* Montreal: Imp. populaire. 126 p.

King, Tom. 'Half-Way Through the Hoover Administration.' *Queen's Quarterly* XXXVIII (Winter): 76–88.

Lamarche, M.-A. 'Le scandale de New York.' *Revue dominicaine* XXXVII (June): 321–5.

McCulloch, John H. 'Monstrosities of the Movies.' In *Open House*, ed. William Arthur Deacon and Wilfred Reeves, 41–52. Ottawa: Graphic Publications.

Montreal Branch of the Canadian Institute for International Affairs. 'Canadi-
an-American Relations.' *International Affairs* X (July): 493–503.
Underhill, Frank H. 'O Canada.' *Canadian Forum* XI (Feb.): 168–70.
– 'American Political Thought.' *Canadian Forum* XI (July): 383–4.
Vézina, François. 'Le capital étranger au Canada.' *L'Actualité économique* VI
(Feb.): 407–12.

1932

Bastien, Hermas. 'La philosophie américaine.' In his *La défense de l'intelligence,*
169–74. Montreal: A. Lévesque.
McKay, Colin. 'The USA on the Brink.' *Canadian Unionist* 6 (June): 3.
R [X Norman Robertson]. 'Neighbors, A Canadian View.' *Foreign Affairs* X
(Apr.): 417–30.
Stevenson, J.A. 'The Presidential Election in the United States.' *Queen's Quar-
terly* XXXIX (Aug.): 529–44.
Trotter, Reginald G. 'George Washington and the English-Speaking Heritage.'
Queen's Quarterly XXXIX (May): 297–306.

1933

Anonymous. 'Canadian-American Relations.' *The Round Table* XXIII (Mar.):
410–19.
Bastien, Hermas. 'La critique américaine.' In his *Témoignages. Études et profils
littéraires,* 33–51. Montreal: A. Lévesque.
Corbett, P.E. 'A Foreign Policy for Canada.' In *The Liberal Way: A Record of
Opinion on Canadian Problems as Expressed and Discussed at the First Liberal
Summer Conference, Port Hope, Sept., 1933,* ed. Liberal party of Canada, 129–
43. Toronto: J.M. Dent.
Deacon, William Arthur. *My Vision of Canada.* Toronto: Ontario Publications.
309 p.
Hall, Frank. 'Canada and the United States Are One People.' *Canadian Con-
gress Journal* XII (Feb.): 12.
MacDermot, T.W.L. 'The Significance for Canada of the American New Deal.'
In *The Liberal Way: A Record of Opinion on Canadian Problems as Expressed and
Discussed at the First Liberal Summer Conference, Port Hope, Sept., 1933,* ed.
Liberal party of Canada, 185–96. Toronto: J.M. Dent.
McKay, Colin. 'Roosevelt's Plan – So Far.' *Canadian Unionist* VII (Aug.):
39–40.
Minville, Esdras. 'La crise bancaire aux États-Unis.' *L'Actualité économique* VIII
(Mar.): 536–42.

Perry, Anne Anderson. 'New Deal for American Women.' *Canadian Comment* 2 (July): 12–13.

Roy, Lionel. 'Roosevelt travaille.' *Le Canada français* XXI (Dec.): 310–26.

Trotter, Reginald G. 'The Canadian Back-Fence in Anglo-American Relations.' *Queen's Quarterly* XL (Aug.): 383–97.

1934

Brebner, John Bartlet. 'The Interplay of Canada and the United States.' *Columbia University Quarterly* XXVI (Dec.): 331–8.

Brown, E.K. 'The National Idea in American Criticism.' *Dalhousie Review* XIV (July): 133–47.

Goldenberg, H. Carl. 'Economic Recovery in Great Britain and the United States.' *Empire Club of Canada Addresses* (1934–5): 374–89.

Guimont, Paul-Henri. 'La crise agraire aux États-Unis.' *L'Actualité économique* X (Oct.): 306–26.

MacKenzie, Norman. 'Canadian-American Relations.' *Canadian Bar Review* XII (Oct.): 479–90.

Shotwell, James T. *The Heritage of Freedom: The United States and Canada in the Community of Nations*. New York: Scribners. ix+136 p.

Surveyer, Arthur. 'Le plan Roosevelt.' *Revue trimestrielle canadienne* XX (Mar.): 12–25.

Willson, Beckles. *Friendly Relations: A Narrative of Britain's Ministers and Ambassadors to the United States (1791–1930)*. London: Lovat, Dickson and Thompson. 350 p.

1935

Benoit, Josaphat. *L'âme franco-américaine*. Montreal: A. Lévesque. 245 p.

Connor, Ralph [X Charles W. Gordon]. *The Rebel Loyalist*. Toronto: McClelland and Stewart. 328 p.

Dafoe, John W. *Canada: An American Nation*. New York: Columbia University Press. 134 p.

Ells, Margaret. 'Loyalist Attitudes.' *Dalhousie Review* XV (Oct.): 320–34.

Gregory, Claudius. *Solomon Levi*. Toronto: G.J. MacLeod. 400 p.

Groulx, Lionel. 'Notre avenir en Amérique.' In his *Orientations*, 275–310. Montreal: Éditions du Zodiaque.

Guimont, Paul-Henri. 'Coup d'œil sur l'Amérique contemporaine.' *L'Actualité économique* XI (Apr.): 28–56.

Le Bel, Paul. 'Panorama de la crise économique mondiale.' *Le Canada français* XXII (Feb.–Apr.): 497–524, 601–19, 705–32.

Liane [X Camille Lessard]. *Canuck.* Lewiston, Me: Le Messager, 1936. 131 p. [First appeared in serialised form in *Le Messager* of Lewiston, Me, in late 1935.]

Lower, A.R.M. 'Foreign Policy and Canadian Nationalism.' *Dalhousie Review* XV (Apr.): 29–36.

Shotwell, James T. 'Canadian-American Relations.' *Queen's Quarterly* XLII (Autumn): 391–402.

Simpson, J.H. 'Our Friends the Americans.' *Journal of the Canadian Bankers' Association* XLII (July): 530–6.

Stevenson, J.A. 'The NRA to Date.' *Queen's Quarterly* XLII (Autumn): 403–14.

Trotter, Reginald G. 'The Basis of Canadian-American Relations.' *Addresses Delivered before the Canadian Club of Toronto* (1935–6): 99–107.

Underhill, Frank H. 'Review of J.W. Dafoe's *Canada, An American Nation.*' *Canadian Forum* XV (July): 301.

Wrong, George M. *Canada and the American Revolution: The Disruption of the First British Empire.* New York: Macmillan. xii+497 p.

1936

Bastien, Hermas. 'L'américanisation par la philosophie.' *Revue dominicaine* XLII (Apr.): 197–214.

Bruchési, Jean. 'Notre américanisation par le magazine.' *Revue dominicaine* XLII (July–Aug.): 5–21.

Corey, Albert B., Walter W. McLaren, and Reginald G. Trotter, eds. Conference on Canadian-American Affairs held at the St Lawrence University, Canton, New York, 17–22 June 1935, *Proceedings.* Boston: Ginn. xi+301 p.

Desbiens, Lucien. 'L'infiltration américaine par la radio.' *Revue dominicaine* XLII (Mar.): 134–49.

Forest, M.-Ceslas. 'Notre américanisation par les sports.' *Revue dominicaine* XLII (June): 348–63.

Goldenberg, H. Carl. '"Americanization" of Canada.' *Fortnightly Review* CXLV (June): 688–95.

Janin, Alban. 'Notre américanisation par le cinéma.' *Revue dominicaine* XLII (Feb.): 69–88.

Jasmin, Damien. 'L'américanisation et nos pratiques financières.' *Revue dominicaine* XLII (Nov.): 187–201.

Lamarche, M.-A. 'Notre américanisation.' *Revue dominicaine* XLII (Jan.): 1–5.

– 'Notre américanisation: Aperçus complémentaires et mot de la fin.' *Revue dominicaine* XLII (Dec.): 249–60.

Lawson, William. 'Father Coughlin.' *New Frontier* I (July): 24–6.

Leacock, Stephen. 'Canada Won't Go Yankee.' *American Mercury* XXXVIII (Sept.): 37–40.

Llloyd, Cecil Francis. 'American Literature Then and Now.' *Canadian Bookman* XVIII (June): 7–9.

McKay, Colin. 'United States Labour Begins to Learn from Britain.' *Canadian Unionist* X (July): 36–7.

Marshall, Herbert, Frank A. Southard, Jr, and Kenneth W. Taylor. *Canadian-American Industry: A Study in International Investment*. New Haven, Conn.: Yale University Press. xiii+360 p.

Pelletier, Georges. 'Notre américanisation par le journal.' *Revue dominicaine* XLII (May): 273–82.

Pineault-Léveillé, Ernestine. 'Notre américanisation par la femme.' *Revue dominicaine* XLII (Oct.): 127–49.

Ryan, J. Arthur. 'Two Essays in American Critical Realism.' *Revue de l'Université d'Ottawa* VI (July, Oct.): 102*–8*, 262*–96*.

Simpson, J.H. 'Social Security in the United States.' *Journal of the Canadian Bankers' Association* XLIII (Jan.): 187–97.

Trotter, Reginald G. 'America's "New Neutrality."' *Queen's Quarterly* XLIII (Spring): 68–73.

Voyer, Raymond-M. 'L'américanisme et notre vie religieuse.' *Revue dominicaine* XLII (Jan.): 6–25.

1937

Alexander, Henry. 'American English.' *Queen's Quarterly* XLIV (Summer): 169–75.

Bruchési, Jean. 'Les États-Unis et les rébellions de 1837–1838 dans le Bas-Canada.' *Revue trimestrielle canadienne* XXIII (Mar.): 1–20.

Corbett, P.E. *The Settlement of Canadian-American Disputes: A Critical Study of Methods and Results*. New Haven, Conn.: Yale University Press. viii+134 p.

Corey, Albert B., Walter W. McLaren, and Reginald G. Trotter, eds. Conference on Canadian-American Affairs held at Queen's University, Kingston, Ontario, 14–18 June 1937, *Proceedings*. Boston: Ginn. xii+274 p.

Creighton, D.G. *The Commercial Empire of the St Lawrence, 1760–1850*. Toronto: Ryerson Press. vii+441 p.

Gosselin, Paul-Émile. 'Nos frères des États-Unis.' *Le Canada français* XXIV (Aug.): 750–9.

Innis, H.A., ed. *The Dairy Industry in Canada*. Toronto: Ryerson Press. xxvii+299 p.

– *Labor in Canadian-American Relations: The History of Labor Interaction.* Toronto: Ryerson Press. xxxviii+212 p.

Lanctot, Gustave. 'Influences américaines dans le Québec.' *Mémoires et comptes rendus de la Société royale du Canada,* 3rd Series, XXXI, Section I: 119–25.

Laurendeau, André. 'Commentaires: Menaces de l'américanisme.' *L'Action nationale* X (Dec.): 312–23.

Lower, A.R.M. 'Canada and the Americas.' *Dalhousie Review* XVII (Apr.): 17–21.

Martin, Chester. 'The United States and Canadian Nationality.' *Canadian Historical Review* XVIII (Mar.): 1–11.

Potter, Lloyd. 'The International Labour Illusion.' *Labour Review* I (Sept.): 243–4, 250.

Sandwell, B.K. 'Public Affairs: Canada and Anglo-American Entente.' *Queen's Quarterly* XLIV (Summer): 247–55.

1938

Angus, H.F., ed. *Canada and Her Great Neighbor: Sociological Surveys of Opinions and Attitudes in Canada Concerning the United States.* Toronto: Ryerson Press. xxxvi+451 p.

Bilodeau, Charles. 'Le recul économique aux États-Unis.' *Le Canada français* XXV (Apr.): 849–56.

Burpee, Lawrence J. 'Canada's Debt to the Carnegie Corporation.' *Queen's Quarterly* XLV (Summer): 232–7.

Corbett, P.E. 'American Foreign Policy.' *University of Toronto Quarterly* VII (Jan.): 209–27.

Gelber, Lionel M. *The Rise of Anglo-American Friendship: A Study in World Politics, 1898–1906.* London: Oxford University Press. 292 p.

Glazebrook, G.P. de T. *A History of Transportation in Canada.* Toronto: Ryerson Press. xxv+475 p.

Laing, Lionel H., and Norman MacKenzie, eds. *Canada and the Law of Nations: A Selection of Cases in International Law, Affecting Canada or Canadians, Decided by Canadian Courts, by Certain of the Higher Courts in the United States and Great Britain and by International Tribunals.* Toronto: Ryerson Press. xxvii+ 567 p.

Lower, A.R.M., and W.A. Carrothers. *The North American Assault on the Canadian Forest: A History of the Lumber Trade between Canada and the United States.* Toronto: Ryerson Press. xxvii+377 p.

MacKay, R.A., and E.B. Rogers. *Canada Looks Abroad.* London: Oxford University Press. xx+402 p.

Ringuet [X Philippe Panneton]. *30 arpents. Roman.* Paris: Flammarion. 292 p.

Scott, F.R. *Canada Today: A Study of Her National Interests and National Policy.* London: Oxford University Press. xii+163 p.

Trotter, Reginald G. 'Which Way Canada?' *Queen's Quarterly* XLV (Autumn): 289–98.

1939

Alexander, William Hardy. 'Counting America In.' *Canadian Forum* XIX (Aug.): 142–3.

Brebner, John Bartlet. 'Canada's Choice in Foreign Affairs.' *Quarterly Journal of Inter-American Relations* I (Jan.): 50–7.

– 'The Survival of Canada.' In *Essays in Canadian History Presented to George MacKinnon Wrong*, ed. R. Flentley, 253–77. Toronto: Macmillan.

Corbett, P.E. 'Canada and Pan Americanism.' *Quarterly Journal of Inter-American Relations* I (Oct.): 30–4.

Denison, Merrill. *An American Father Talks to His Son: A Radio Play.* New York: Columbia Broadcasting System. 7 p.

– *Haven of the Spirit: Play in One Act.* New York: Dramatists Play Service. 34 p.

Gelber, Lionel M. 'Review of H.F. Angus' *Canada and her Great Neighbor.' Canadian Journal of Economics and Political Science* V (Feb.): 125–8.

Humphrey, John P. 'Canadian-American Friendship.' *University of Toronto Quarterly* VIII (Jan.): 242–6.

Leacock, Stephen. *All Right, Mr Roosevelt: Canada and the United States.* Toronto: Oxford University Press. 40 p.

Lower, A.R.M. 'The United States through Canadian Eyes.' *Quarterly Journal of Inter-American Relations* I (July): 104–11.

McInnis, Edgar W. 'Two North American Federations: A Comparison.' In *Essays in Canadian History Presented to George MacKinnon Wrong*, ed. R. Flentley, 94–118. Toronto: Macmillan.

Macdonald, W.L. 'Towards a Canadian Foreign Policy.' *Canadian Forum* XIX (Aug.): 145–7.

Morrow, Rising Lake, ed. Conference on Educational Problems in Canadian-American Relations held at the University of Maine, Orono, Maine, 21–3 June 1938, *Proceedings.* Orono, Me: University of Maine Press. viii+248 p.

Saint-Pierre, Albert. 'Le mirage de l'or aux États-Unis.' *Revue dominicaine* XLV (Sept.): 87–96.

Sandwell, B.K. *Canada and United States Neutrality.* Toronto: Oxford University Press. 34 p.

– 'Democracy.' *Queen's Quarterly* XLVI (Spring): 95–103.

1940

Angers, François-Albert. 'L'américanisation du Saint-Laurent.' *L'Actualité économique* XV (Feb.): 359–64.

Brebner, John Bartlet. 'Ogdensburg: A Turn in Canadian-American Relations.' *Inter-American Quarterly* II (Oct.): 18–28.

Burpee, Lawrence J. *Good Neighbours*. Toronto: Ryerson Press. 30 p.

Burt, A.L. *The United States, Great Britain, and British North America from the Revolution to the Establishment of Peace after the War of 1812*. New Haven: Yale University Press. vii+448 p.

Corey, Albert B., Walter W. McLaren, and Reginald G. Trotter, eds. Conference on Canadian-American Affairs held at the St Lawrence University, Canton, New York, 19–22 June 1939, *Proceedings*. Boston: Ginn. viii+250 p.

Gordon, J. King. 'Neutral Corner.' *Canadian Forum* XIX (Jan.): 316–17.

Guimont, Paul-Henri. *La canalisation du Saint-Laurent*. Montreal: École sociale populaire. 31 p.

Hansen, Marcus Lee. *The Mingling of the Canadian and American Peoples*, vol. I: *Historical*, completed and prepared for publication by John Bartlet Brebner. New Haven: Yale University Press. xviii+274 p.

Innis, H.A. *The Cod Fisheries: The History of an International Economy*. New Haven, Conn.: Yale University Press. xviii+520 p.

Lower, A.R.M. 'Canada and Foreign Policy.' *Queen's Quarterly* XLVII (Winter): 418–27.

– 'The Maritimes as a Strategic Point in North America.' *Public Affairs* IV (Nov.): 57–60.

MacCormac, John. *Canada: America's Problem*. New York: Viking Press. 287 p.

– 'What Will America Do about Canada?' *Current History* LI (June): 35–6, 60.

McInnis, Edgar W. 'Canada's American Problem.' *University of Toronto Quarterly* X (Oct.): 101–5.

– 'Washington Looks Ahead.' *Canadian Forum* XIX (Feb.): 347–8.

Richer, Léopold. *Le Canada et le bloc anglo-saxon*. Montreal: Le Devoir. 155 p.

Scott, F.R. 'Mr Roosevelt Keeps Going.' *Canadian Forum* XX (Dec.): 267–8.

Stacey, C.P. *The Military Problems of Canada: A Survey of Defence Policies and Strategic Conditions, Past and Present*. Toronto: Ryerson Press. vii+184 p.

Simpson, J.H. 'America's Wonder City.' *Canadian Banker* XLVII (Apr.): 338–43.

Trotter, Reginald G. 'More on Canada and Pan Americanism: A Reply to Professor Corbett.' *Inter-American Quarterly* II (Jan.): 5–10.

– *North America and the War*. Toronto: Oxford University Press. 40 p.

Underhill, Frank H. 'Canada's Problem.' *Canadian Forum* XX (Aug.): 134–5.

– 'North American Front.' *Canadian Forum* XX (Sept.): 166–7.

1941

Action nationale, L' [X André Laurendeau]. 'There'll Always Be an England, mais y aura-t-il un Canada?' *L'Action nationale* XVII (June): 439–42.

Angers, François-Albert. 'Québec, 57e étoile sur le drapeau de l'Oncle Sam.' *L'Action nationale* XVII (June): 481–99.

Anonymous. 'The Canadian-American Defence Agreement and Its Significance.' *The Round Table* XXXI (Mar.): 347–57.

Bernard, Harry. 'L'Américain du peuple nous ignore, et après?' *L'Action nationale* XVIII (Sept.): 19–34.

Brebner, John Bartlet. 'Soyons nous-mêmes?' *Le Canada français* XXIX (Dec.): 252–60.

– 'The U.S.A.: Canada's Problem.' *Survey Graphic* XXX (Apr.): 221–5.

Corbett, P.E. 'Canada in the Western Hemisphere.' *Foreign Affairs* XIX (July): 778–89.

Corey, Albert B., and Reginald G. Trotter, eds. Conference on Canadian-American Affairs held at Queen's University, Kingston, Ontario, 23–6 June 1941, *Proceedings*. Boston: Ginn. xiii+287 p.

Cousineau, Jacques. 'Ne nous induisez pas en tentation...' *L'Action nationale* XVII (June): 508–21.

Dafoe, John W., ed. *Canada Fights: An American Democracy at War*. New York: Farrar and Rinehart. vi+280 p.

Denison, Merrill. *The United States vs. Susan B. Anthony: Play in One Act*. New York: Dramatists Play Service. 29 p.

Desautels, Adrien. 'Regards sur la vie américaine.' *Le Canada français* XXVIII (Mar.): 701–13.

Faludi, E.G. 'America and Modern Art.' *Canadian Forum* XXI (June): 74–7.

Ferguson, George V. 'Canada the Interpreter.' *University of Toronto Quarterly* XI (Oct.): 40–5.

Gordon, J. King. 'The United States and the War.' *Canadian Forum* XXI (Oct.): 203–5.

Groulx, Lionel. 'L'annexionnisme au Canada français.' *L'Action nationale* XVII (June): 443–54.

Hamel, Philippe. 'La canalisation du Saint-Laurent.' *L'Action nationale* XVII (June): 546–79.

Humphrey, John P. 'Pan-America in the World Order.' *Canadian Forum* XXI (Oct.): 199–202.

– 'The Twenty-Second Chair: Is It for Canada?' *Inter-American Quarterly* III (Oct.): 5–13.

Kerr, W.B. *The Maritime Provinces of British North America and the American Revolution.* Sackville: Busy East Press. 172 p.

Lanctot, Gustave, ed. *Les Canadiens français et leurs voisins du sud.* Montreal: Éditions Bernard Valiquette. ix+322 p.

– 'Le Québec et la Révolution américaine.' *Mémoires et comptes rendus de la Société royale du Canada,* 3rd Series, XXXV, Section I: 91–111.

Landon, Fred. *Western Ontario and the American Frontier.* Toronto: Ryerson Press. xvi+305 p.

Laurendeau, André. 'Conclusion.' *L'Action nationale* XVII (June): 534–7.

– 'Connaissance des États-Unis.' *L'Enseignement secondaire* XXI (Dec.): 203–8.

– 'Vers l'accomplissement de notre destin américain.' *L'Action nationale* XVIII (Oct.): 151–4.

Lemieux, Edmond [X André Laurendeau]. 'De l'optimisme juridique au pessimisme politique.' *L'Action nationale* XVII (June): 473–80.

Maheux, Arthur. 'Entre voisins.' *Le Canada français* XXIX (Sept.): 7–12.

Montpetit, Édouard. *Reflets d'Amérique.* Montreal: B. Valiquette. 255 p.

Nicolet, Jean [X Roger Duhamel]. 'Si nous étions américains.' *L'Action nationale* XVII (June): 500–7.

Normandin, Rodrigue. '*Reflets d'Amérique.* Réflexions en marge d'un livre récent.' *Revue de l'Université d'Ottawa* XI (Oct.): 472–6.

Pemberton, J.S.B., ed. *Ogdensburg, Hyde Park – and After: Joint Economic Defence.* Toronto: Canadian Institute of International Affairs. 23 p.

Perrault, Jacques. 'Un aspect favorable de l'annexionnisme.' *L'Action nationale* XVII (June): 455–72.

Phelps, Arthur L. *These United States: A Series of Broadcasts.* Toronto: CBC Publications Branch. 60 p.

Richer, Léopold. *Vers l'accomplissement de notre destin américain.* [Quebec]: Éd. Cap Diamant. 38 p.

Sandwell, B.K. 'Canada and the U.S.A.' *Public Affairs* V (Winter): 113–18.

– 'The Neutrality Act.'*Queen's Quarterly* XLVIII (Winter): 414–19.

Scott, F.R. *Canada and the United States.* Boston: World Peace Foundation. 80 p.

– 'Canada and Hemispheric Solidarity.' In *Inter-American Solidarity,* ed. Walter H.C. Laves, 139–73. Chicago: University of Chicago Press.

– 'Currents of American Opinion.' *Canadian Forum* XXI (July): 104–5.

Trotter, Reginald G., and R.A. MacKay. 'Pan Americanism Is not Enough: Two Opinions.' *Public Affairs* V (Winter): 118–23.

1942

Angus, H.F., ed. *British Columbia and the United States: The North Pacific Slope from Fur Trade to Aviation.* Toronto: Ryerson Press. xv+408 p.

Bernard, Harry. 'Nationalisme du roman américain.' *Revue de l'Université d'Ottawa* XII (Jan.): 123–38.

– 'Filiation de Mark Twain.' *Revue de l'Université d'Ottawa* XII (July): 327–41.

– 'Les noirs des États-Unis et le roman régionaliste.' *Revue de l'Université d'Ottawa* XII (Oct.): 408–27.

Brosseau, Vincent. *Ottawa regarde vers Washington.* [n.p.] xii+285 p.

Brown, George W. 'Have the Americas a Common History?: A Canadian View. *Canadian Historical Review* XXIII (June): 132–9.

Burt, A.L. 'The American Key.' *Revue de l'Université d'Ottawa* XII (Apr.): 153–66.

Creighton, D.G. 'The Course of Canadian Democracy.' *University of Toronto Quarterly* XI (Apr.): 255–68.

Eby, Frederick. 'Current Educational Theory in America.' *Queen's Quarterly* XLIX (Spring): 20–30.

Frye, Northrop. 'Reflections at a Movie.' *Canadian Forum* XXII (Oct.): 212–13.

Humphrey, John P. *The Inter-American System: A Canadian View.* Toronto: Macmillan. xi+329 p.

MacCormac, John. *America and World Mastery: The Future of the United States, Canada, and the British Empire.* New York: Duell, Sloan and Pierce. 338 p.

McInnis, Edgar W. *The Unguarded Frontier: A History of American-Canadian Relations.* New York: Doubleday. 384 p.

Sauriol, Paul. *Notre continent est-il anglo-saxon?* Montreal: Le Devoir. 8 p.

Trotter, Reginald G. 'Canada and Pan-Americanism.' *Queen's Quarterly* XLIX (Autumn): 252–60.

Underhill, Frank H. 'Anglo-American Dream.' *Canadian Forum* XXII (Apr.): 10–12.

Watt, C.D. 'A Chance for Continental Integration.' *Canadian Forum* XXI (Mar.): 376–7.

1943

Brebner, John Bartlet. 'Relations of Canada and the United States: Persistent Problems.' *Canadian Historical Review* XXIV (June): 117–26.

Coates, R.H., and M.C. MacLean. *The American-Born in Canada: A Statistical Interpretation.* Toronto: Ryerson Press. xviii+176 p.

Dafoe, John W. 'The Unguarded Frontier.' *University of Toronto Quarterly* XII (Jan.): 221–5.

Duhamel, Roger. 'L'avenir du livre américain au Canada français.' *Relations* III (Nov.): 299–300.

Hertel, François. [X Rodolphe Dubé]. 'Le Canada français en Amérique.' *La Nouvelle Relève* II (Sept.): 537–42.

Léry, Louis Chaussegros de. 'Écoles publiques étatsuniennes.' *Relations* III
    (Dec.): 319–21.
McInnes, Graham. 'U.S. on the Move.' *Canadian Forum* XXII (Feb.): 331–2.
Maurault, Olivier. *Aux Louisianais*. Montreal: Éditions des Dix. 160 p.
Rand, William. 'America's "Solid South."' *Dalhousie Review* XXIII (July):
    166–76.
Trotter, Reginald G. 'Relations of Canada and the United States: Reciprocity of
    Attitudes.' *Canadian Historical Review* XXIV (June): 126–34.

1944

Bernard, Harry. 'La culture intellectuelle aux États-Unis.' *Relations* IV (Feb.):
    46–7.
Brown, George W. 'Canada in the Making.' Canadian Historical Association
    Annual Report, 5–15.
– *The United States, Past and Present*. Ottawa: Canadian Legion Educational
    Services. 23 p.
Clark, S.D. 'The Social Development of Canada and the American Continental
    System.' *Culture* V (June): 132–3.
Landon, Fred. 'Our Neighbours and Ourselves.' *Quarterly Review of Commerce*
    XI (Winter): 53–7.
Ledit, Joseph-H. 'Le problème des races aux États-Unis.' *Relations* IV (Oct.):
    255–8.
McInnis, Edgar W. 'The United States and World Settlement.' *Canadian Histori-
    cal Review* XXV (June): 151–65.
Sauriol, Jacques. 'L'Amérique serait-elle 'fasciste'?' *L'Action nationale* XXIV
    (Aug.–Sept.): 20–8.
Scott, F.R. *Cooperation for What? United States and British Commonwealth*. New
    York: American Council, Institute of Pacific Relations. 64 p.
Underhill, Frank H. 'Trends in American Foreign Policy.' *University of Toronto
    Quarterly* XIII (Apr.): 286–97.
Watson, J.W., and W.R. Mead. 'Canada in the American Balance.' *Culture* V
    (Sept.): 385–402.

1945

Brebner, John Bartlet. *North Atlantic Triangle: The Interplay of Canada, the United
    States and Great Britain*. New Haven, Conn.: Yale University Press. xxii+
    385 p.
Comité permanent de la survivance française en Amérique [X Antoine Ber-

nard, ed.] *La vocation de la race française en Amérique du Nord*. Quebec: Comité permanent de la survivance française en Amérique. 199 p.

Creighton, D.G. 'Canada in the English-Speaking World.' *Canadian Historical Review* XXVI (June): 119–27.

Girard, René. 'Villes catholiques des États-Unis.' *Relations* V (Apr.): 102–3.

– 'La grande centrale catholique des États-Unis.' *Relations* V (July): 187–90.

Grant, George. *The Empire, Yes or No?* Toronto: Ryerson Press. 34 p.

Montpetit, Édouard. 'Quantité et qualité.' *La Nouvelle Relève* IV (Dec.): 479–98.

Trotter, Reginald G. 'Canada and World Organization.' *Canadian Historical Review* XXVI (June): 128–47.

– 'Future Canadian-American Relations.' *Queen's Quarterly* LII (Summer): 215–29.

Notes

Introduction

1 Douglas Bush, 'Pride and Prejudice,' *Canadian Mercury* I (1929): 136.
2 Anti-American rhetoric in Canada is discussed in William M. Baker, 'The Anti-American Ingredient in Canadian History,' *Dalhousie Review* 53 (1973): 57–77; idem, 'A Case Study of Anti-Americanism in English-Speaking Canada: The Election Campaign of 1911,' *Canadian Historical Review* 51 (1970): 426–49; Carl Berger, *The Sense of Power: Studies in the Ideas of Canadian Imperialism, 1867–1914* (Toronto, 1970); Charles F. Doran and James P. Sewell, 'Anti-Americanism in Canada?' *Annals of the American Academy of Political and Social Science* 497 (1988): 105–19; J.L. Granatstein, *Yankee Go Home? Canadians and Anti-Americanism* (Toronto, 1996); John C. Kendall, 'A Canadian Construction of Reality: Northern Images of the United States,' *American Review of Canadian Studies* 4 (1974): 20–36; George Rawlyk, '"A Question of Self or no Self": Some Reflexions on the English-Canadian Identity within the Context of Canadian-U.S. Relations,' *Humanities Association Review* 30 (1979): 281–301; Reginald C. Stuart, 'Anti-Americanism in Canadian History,' *American Review of Canadian Studies* 27 (1997): 293–310; S.F. Wise and Robert Craig Brown, *Canada Views the United States: Nineteenth-Century Political Attitudes* (Toronto, 1967); and Patricia K. Wood, 'Defining "Canadian": Anti-Americanism and Identity in Sir John A. Macdonald's Nationalism,' *Journal of Canadian Studies* 36 (2001): 49–69.
3 In a recent monograph on the Anglo-Saxon ideal, Edward P. Kohn criticises North American historians for not 'looking beyond traditional American Anglophobia and Canadian anti-Americanism' and 'treating these trends of thought as unquestionable constants of their respective national histories.' Both of these negative faiths, he believes, were undermined

during the brief period of Anglo-Saxon fervour fuelled by the Anglo-American rapprochement that occurred between 1895 and 1903. Kohn, *This Kindred People: Canadian-American Relations and the Anglo-Saxon Idea, 1895–1903* (Montreal and Kingston, 2004), 5.

4 Berger, *Sense of Power*, 175.

5 Granatstein, *Yankee Go Home*, x, 286. The instrumental nature of anti-American rhetoric has also been examined by Patricia K. Wood. In an article on the 1891 federal election, she argues that 'while the campaign revolved around anti-Americanism, its language, images and symbols were referential to specific discourses of ethnicity, gender and class. These discourses privileged British-Canadian, middle-class males, who used this election to further entrench their positions of social, cultural, and political power.' Indeed, Wood insists that anti-American rhetoric contained powerful cues related to gender, class, ethnicity, and race. It was used by the Conservatives to claim ownership over the power to define what was and was not 'Canadian.' Wood, 'Defining "Canadian,"' 49.

6 Continentalism is discussed in Ian Grant, 'Erastus Wiman: A Continentalist Replies to Canadian Imperialism,' *Canadian Historical Review* 53 (1972): 1–20; Graham Carr, '"All We North Americans": Literary Culture and the Continentalist Ideal, 1919–1939,' *American Review of Canadian Studies* 17 (1987): 145–57; and Allan Smith, 'Doing the Continental: Conceptualizations of the Canadian-American Relationship in the Long Twentieth Century,' *Canadian-American Public Policy* 44 (2000): 2–70.

7 Reginald Stuart, 'Continentalism Revisited: Recent Narratives on the History of Canadian-American Relations,' *Diplomatic History* 18 (1994): 406.

8 Smith, 'Doing the Continental,' 5.

9 French Canadian attitudes towards the United States are discussed in Gérard Bouchard, *Genèse des nations et cultures du Nouveau Monde. Essai d'histoire comparée* (Montreal, 2000); idem and Yvan Lamonde, eds. *Québécois et Américains: la culture québécoise aux XIXe et XXe siècles* (Montreal, 1995); Jacques Cotnam, 'Americans Viewed Through the Eyes of French-Canadians,' *Journal of Popular Culture* 10 (1977): 784–96; idem, 'La prise de conscience d'une identité nord-américaine au Canada français, 1930–1939,' in *Les grands voisins*, ed. G. Kurgan (Brussels, 1984), 53–79; Richard Jones, 'French Canada and the American Peril in the Twentieth Century,' *American Review of Canadian Studies* 14 (1984): 333–50; idem, 'Le spectre de l'américanisation,' in *Les rapports culturels entre le Québec et les États-Unis*, ed. C. Savary (Quebec, 1984), 145–69; Yvan Lamonde, *Ni avec eux ni sans eux: le Québec et les États-Unis* (Montreal, 1996); and Guildo Rousseau, *L'image des États-Unis dans la littérature québécoise, 1775–1930* (Sherbrooke, 1981).

10 Gérard Bouchard, 'Le Québec comme collectivité neuve. Le refus de l'américanité dans le discours de la survivance,' in Bouchard and Lamonde, *Québécois et Américains*, 16.

11 The *américanité* paradigm is not without its critics. Chief among them is Joseph Yvon Thériault. In a recent monograph, Thériault argues that the concept impedes the understanding of Quebec's historical singularity. Moreover, he contends that Quebec's conservative and clerical elite did not reject the province's essential continentalism and were not completely out of step with its populace. These elites merely refused to accept that the American model – rupture – was endemic to the New World. Thériault, *Critique de l'américanité. Mémoire et démocratie au Québec* (Montreal, 2002), passim.

12 The term 'English Canadian' has been used in this study to describe a fairly heterogeneous group of English-speaking individuals drawn from different regions, ethnicities, and religious denominations. I am aware of the difficulties this usage poses. However, the constraints of comparative research make it necessary.

13 As Fernande Roy has observed, nationalism is typically 'a polymorphous value that embraces various ideologies. Nationalism is present to such a degree that it has concealed everything else; it makes the history of Quebec ideologies more complex and explains unexpected alliances.' Roy, *Histoire des idéologies au Québec aux XIXe et XXe siècles* (Montreal, 1993), 11. The same could be said for English Canadian forms of nationalism, which have complicated the study of discourse and have led many writers to neglect the left-right cleavage in Canadian history. More often than not, nationalism is merely the vehicle for a wider ideology. Imperialism, for instance, was the primary means of expression for turn-of-the-twentieth-century English Canadian conservatism. Accordingly, Andrew Macphail and Stephen Leacock were imperialists because they were conservatives, not the other way around.

14 A handful of American scholars have viewed the international phenomenon of anti-Americanism as a rejection of modernity. For instance, in a recent article, James W. Ceaser suggests that the interest of anti-American thinkers 'was not always with a real country or people, but more often with general ideas of modernity, for which 'America' became the name or symbol.' Ceaser, 'A Genealogy of Anti-Americanism,' *Public Interest* 152 (2003), 5. Paul Hollander, who sees anti-American sentiment as the product of nationalism and 'the rejection of (or ambivalence toward) modernization and anti-capitalism,' goes a step further than Ceaser in his assessment of the phenomenon: 'It has become increasingly clear,' he writes,

'that to the extent that "Americanization" is a form of modernization, the process can inspire understandable apprehension and anguish among those who seek to preserve a more stable and traditional way of life in various parts of the world.' Hollander, *Anti-Americanism: Critiques at Home and Abroad, 1965–1990* (New York: Oxford University Press, 1992), xi, 7.

15 Alexis Nouss, *La modernité* (Paris, 1995), 15, 19.

16 Massolin, *Canadian Intellectuals, the Tory Tradition, and the Challenge of Modernity*, 8.

17 James Cappon, 'Current Events: Government and Trusts in the United States,' *Queen's Quarterly* 19 (1912): 290.

18 Theodore Zeldin, 'Foreword,' in *The Rise and Fall of French Anti-Americanism*, x. In this sense, foreign writing on America has generally contained more than simply a discourse on otherness. For instance, as Michel Winock has noted regarding French reactions to America, 'the *other*, the American – even if we hate him – we don't talk about him like we used to talk about the "Britisher" or the "Jerry" because he isn't radically different from us: he is a part of ourselves, a bad side that needs repressing. The old hereditary enemy, it was easy to be unable to stand him, because his ethnic difference jumped out at you. The exteriority of the threat stirred up unmitigated hatred. But America, made up of fragments of the whole world, opens up a planetary civilisation; we fear it because it is inside us, because it is one of the high-probability potentialities of our own future.' Winock, '"U.S. go home": l'antiaméricanisme français,' *L'Histoire* 50 (1982): 7.

19 Wood, 'Defining "Canadian,"' 49–50.

20 Carl Berger in Goldwin Smith, *Canada and the Canadian Question* (Toronto, 1971), xvi.

21 Elisabeth Wallace, *Goldwin Smith, Victorian Liberal* (Toronto, 1957), 275.

22 J.A. Hobson quoted in Alan Bowker, 'Introduction,' in Stephen Leacock, *The Social Criticism of Stephen Leacock* (Toronto, 1973), xii.

23 Stuart, 'Continentalism Revisited,' 411.

24 Stephen Brooks, *America through Foreign Eyes: Classical Interpretations of American Political Life* (Don Mills, 2002), 152.

25 This method corresponds to what French historian Pierre Ronsanvallon calls 'the conceptual history of politics.' Broadly defined, its goal is to examine 'the way in which a period, a country, or social groups seek to construct responses to what they perceive, more or less vaguely, as a problem.' Ronsanvallon, 'Pour une histoire conceptuelle du politique,' *Revue de synthèse* 4 (1986): 100.

26 Historian Pascal Ory's definition of the 'intellectual' has been applied in this study. Ory argues that 'the intellectual is a man of culture in the posi-

tion of a man of politics, a producer and consumer of ideology.' He has 'not so much a post as a mission; he is following a vocation.' Ory, 'Qu'est-ce qu'un intellectuel?' in his *Dernières questions aux intellectuels et quatre essais pour y répondre* (Paris, 1990), 14, 24; Ory and Jean-François Sirinelli, *Les intellectuels en France, de l'Affaire Dreyfus à nos jours* (Paris, 1986), 10.

27 S.E.D. Shortt, *The Search for an Ideal: Six Canadian Intellectuals and their Convictions in an Age of Transition, 1890–1930* (Toronto, 1976), 6. Some work by erudite labour leaders and businessmen, in particular Alfred Charpentier (1888–1982), Erastus Wiman (1834–1904), B.E. Walker (1848–1924), and Beaudry Leman (1878–1951), who might not fit the standard definition of the 'intellectual' has been included in an effort to diversify and strengthen the study's corpus. Career politicians were systematically excluded from this study, but the work of a few independent or sometime politicians, most notably Henri Bourassa (1868–1953) and Vincent Massey (1887–1967), has been analysed.

28 Jean-François Sirinelli, 'Effets d'âge et phénomènes de génération dans le milieu intellectuel français,' *Cahiers de l'IHTP* 6 (1987): 7, 11 (original emphasis).

29 Robert A. Skotheim, *American Intellectual Histories and Historians* (Princeton, 1966), 259.

1 Canadian-American Relations: An Intellectual History

1 S.F. Wise quoted in Carl Berger, *The Sense of Power: Studies in the Ideas of Canadian Imperialism, 1867–1914* (Toronto, 1970), 154.

2 George Grant quoted in Robin Winks, *The Relevance of Canadian History: U.S. and Imperial Perspectives* (Toronto, 1979), 84.

3 Allan Smith, 'The Continental Dimension in the Evolution of the English-Canadian Mind,' in his *Canada: An American Nation? Essays on Continentalism, Identity, and the Canadian Frame of Mind* (Montreal and Kingston, 1994), 42.

4 'N'est-il pas singulier de voir les Canadiens instruits, au courant des faits et gestes des Grecs et des Egyptiens, des causes de la grandeur et de la décadence des Romains, des annales de l'Europe, ou très peu ou nullement renseignés sur les Etats-Unis? C'est là, convenons-en, une anomalie qui ne devrait pas exister, car aucun pays au monde n'influe autant que la Confédération américaine, sur nos intérêts et sur notre situation économique.' A.D. Decelles, *Les États-Unis. Origine, institutions, développement* (Ottawa, 1896), vi.

5 A.R.M. Lower, *My First Seventy-Five Years* (Toronto, 1967), 149.

6 André Laurendeau, 'Connaissance des États-Unis,' *L'Enseignement secondaire* XXI (1941): 208.

7 Claude Galarneau, 'Edmond Boisvert,' in *Dictionary of Canadian Biography*, vol. XIII.

8 'Un des plus intéressants qu'on ait publiés depuis longtemps sur l'Amérique.' Ferdinand Brunetière quoted in Claude Galarneau, *Edmond de Nevers, essayiste* (Quebec, 1960), 32.

9 Louis Balthazar, 'Les relations canado-américaines: nationalisme et continentalisme,' *Études internationales* 14 (1983): 33.

10 Norman Knowles, *Inventing the Loyalists: The Ontario Loyalist Tradition and the Creation of Usable Pasts* (Toronto, 1997), 113.

11 A.R.M. Lower, 'The United States through Canadian Eyes,' *Quarterly Journal of Inter-American Relations* I (1939): 104.

12 Ramsay Cook, 'Many Are Called, But None Is Chosen,' in his *The Maple Leaf Forever: Essays on Nationalism and Politics in Canada*, 2nd ed. (Toronto, 1977), 186.

13 Carl Berger, for instance, notes that 'one of the curious features of Canadian views of the United States was that, while geographical proximity afforded countless opportunities to examine the nature of American society, Canadians have never produced significant interpretations of American life that could rank with the travelogues of Charles Dickens or Mrs Trollope, let alone the monumental study of Alexis de Tocqueville.' Berger, *Sense of Power*, 153.

14 Ibid.

15 Pascal Ory, 'From Baudelaire to Duhamel: An Unlikely Antipathy,' in *The Rise and Fall of French Anti-Americanism: A Century of French Perception*, ed. D. Lacorne et al. (New York, 1990), 42.

16 Charles F. Doran and James P. Sewell, 'Anti-Americanism in Canada?' *Annals of the American Academy of Political and Social Science* 497 (1988): 119.

17 Goldwin Smith, *Loyalty, Aristocracy and Jingoism: Three Lectures Delivered before the Young Men's Liberal Club, Toronto* (Toronto, 1891), 21. Most anti-Americans did not consider themselves to be antagonistic to the United States. For example, in 1910, the editor of the conservative *University Magazine*, Andrew Macphail, insisted that 'it is not a sign of prejudice but a desire for self-preservation to fly the yellow flag over a plague spot.' Macphail, 'Canadian Writers and American Politics,' *University Magazine* IX (1910): 5.

18 Gérard Bouchard, 'Le Québec comme collectivité neuve. Le refus de l'américanité dans le discours de la survivance,' in Bouchard and Lamonde, eds., *Québécois et Américains: la culture québécoise aux XIXe et XXe siècles* (Montreal, 1995), 23–4.

19 David Strauss, *Menace in the West: The Rise of French Anti-Americanism in Modern Times* (Westport, 1978), 67.

20 Not every imperialist was anti-American. A handful of unconventional thinkers, including journalist John S. Willison (1856–1927), had come to the imperialist movement from the Liberal party and professed a non–anti-American form of imperialism. Others, like physician William Osler (1849–1919), had spent so much time in the United States that their imperialism had become largely purged of anti-American impulses. 'Too often I have heard and seen expressed in the newspapers a carping spirit towards the Americans,' Osler told the Canadian Club of Toronto in 1904. 'You should bear in mind that your fellow countrymen are living over there and are treated in a way which certainly should make you who live at home remember that whatever feelings you may entertain towards the United States as a nation, it ill becomes you to speak in any way at all derogatory of its people among whom we live as brothers and could not be treated any better if we lived at home.' Osler, 'Anglo-Canadian and American Relations,' *Addresses Delivered Before the Canadian Club of Toronto* (1904–5): 64.

21 A less prominent form of French Canadian conservatism, loyalism, was also present in pre-1945 discourse. It combined key elements of both the imperialist and *nationaliste* traditions into a unique conservative synthesis. During the period under study, loyalism's principal exponents were Thomas Chapais (1858–1946), Gustave Lanctot (1883–1975), and Arthur Maheux (1884–1967).

22 Sylvie Lacombe, *La rencontre de deux peuples élus. Comparaison des ambitions nationale et impériale au Canada entre 1896 et 1920* (Quebec, 2002), passim.

23 Philip Massolin, *Canadian Intellectuals, the Tory Tradition, and the Challenge of Modernity* (Toronto, 2001), 5; Russell Kirk, *The Conservative Mind from Burke to Eliot*, 7th rev. Ed. (Chicago, 1986), 8–9.

24 Nevertheless, as Pierre Trépanier notes, 'ultramontanism, like moderate conservatism, referred back to a tradition not only of the French counter-revolution, but above all to a truly French Canadian synthesis, partially integrating British traditionalism with its particular feature of parliamentarianism. French Canadian ultracism would never perfectly match its French counterpart.' Trépanier, 'Notes pour une histoire des droites intellectuelles canadiennes-françaises à travers leurs principaux représentants (1770–1970),' *Cahiers des Dix* 48 (1993): 122.

25 Yvan Lamonde, 'Les "intellectuels" francophones au Québec au XIXe siècle: questions préalables,' *Revue d'histoire de l'Amérique française* 48 (1994): 164–7.

26 Jackson Lears, *No Place of Grace: Antimodernism and the Transformation of American Culture, 1880–1920* (New York, 1981), passim.

27 Guy Sorman, 'United States: Model or Bête Noire?' in Lacorne et al., eds., *The Rise and Fall of French Anti-Americanism*, 213.

28 George Grant, *Lament for a Nation: The Defeat of Canadian Nationalism*, new ed. (Toronto, 1970 [1965]), 54.

29 A.Z. Rubinstein and D.E. Smith, 'Anti-Americanism: Anatomy of a Phenomenon,' in their *Anti-Americanism in the Third World: Implications for U.S. Foreign Policy* (New York, 1985), 17.

30 The notion that industrialization was accompanied by a 'status revolution' was first advanced by Richard Hofstadter in *The Age of Reform*. He contended that most turn-of-the-twentieth-century American reformers 'were Progressives not because of economic deprivations but primarily because they were victims of an upheaval in status that took place in the United States during the closing decades of the nineteenth and early years of the twentieth century. Progressivism, in short, was to a very considerable extent led by men who suffered from the events of their time not through a shrinkage in their means but through the changed pattern in the distribution of deference and power.' Hofstadter, *The Age of Reform from Bryan to FDR* (New York, 1955), 135.

31 Ibid., 135, 136

32 Lears, *No Place of Grace*, 5.

33 Alan Bowken, 'Introduction,' in Stephen Leacock, *The Social Criticism of Stephen Leacock* (Toronto, 1973), xv.

34 Doran and Sewell, 'Anti-Americanism in Canada?' 110; J.L. Granatstein, *Yankee Go Home? Canadians and Anti-Americanism* (Toronto, 1996), x.

35 Murray Barkley, 'The Loyalist Tradition in New Brunswick: The Growth and Evolution of an Historical Myth, 1825–1914,' *Acadiensis* 4 (1975): 44.

36 'L'influence anglaise peut nous paraître redoutable, mais elle s'exerce à distance et, considérée comme civilisation, nous est moins hostile [que] la civilisation américaine.' André Laurendeau, 'Commentaires: Menaces de l'américanisme,' *L'Action nationale* X (1937): 312.

37 'Ce résidu de civilisation anglo-saxonne jeté dans une immense éprouvette a donc produit une civilisation à part, éblouissante par certains côtés. Mais *le déchet est immense et nous cueillons le déchet*.' M.-A. Lamarche, 'Notre américanisation: Aperçus complémentaires et mot de la fin,' *Revue dominicaine* XLII (1936): 253 (original emphasis).

38 'Si donc Edmond de Nevers a usé dix ans de sa vie à scruter des documents, s'il a tourné son regard original et perspicace vers nos voisins du sud, c'est qu'à son avis *les destinées des États-Unis sont d'une importance suprême pour nous, Canadiens-Français* [sic]. On ne saurait exiger un effort aussi soutenu de la part de tous les esprits cultivés, à plus forte raison de tous

les futurs bacheliers. Mais l'avenir étatsunien devant peser d'un tel poids sur notre avenir national, n'est-il pas légitime de s'attendre à ce qu'on ait fourni aux collégiens des notions simples, justes et vraies sur le passé et le présent de la grande République? ... Questionnons autour de nous, et dans l'ensemble, nous découvrirons les mêmes pauvretés, le même néant. Certains amis, dont la sympathie avait été éveillée de ce côté, se sont donné une demi-culture personnelle. Leur spécialité en a forcé d'autres à chercher plus avant. Plusieurs ont voyagé outre quarante-cinquième, noué des relations d'affaires, etc. Mais tous tombent d'accord: le collège les avait mis en garde contre l'américanisme, c'est-à-dire contre une très réelle maladie de l'âme et de l'esprit, c'est-à-dire encore contre un péril national, moral et religieux, mais leur avait révélé fort peu de chose sur le fait américain.' André Laurendeau, 'Connaissance des États-Unis,' *L'Enseignement secondaire* XXI (1941): 205 (original emphasis).

39 Allan Smith, 'Doing the Continental: Conceptualizations of the Canadian-American Relationship in the Long Twentieth Century,' *Canadian-American Public Policy* 44 (2000): 5.

40 Kirk, *Conservative Mind*, 9–10.

41 Knowles, *Inventing the Loyalists*, 168.

42 Gerald L. Caplan and James Laxer, 'Perspectives on Un-American Traditions in Canada,' in *Close the 49th Parallel etc.: The Americanization of Canada*, ed. Ian Lumsden (Toronto, 1970), 310.

43 John P. Humphrey, *The Inter-American System: A Canadian View* (Toronto, 1942), 253.

44 Smith, 'Doing the Continental,' 4.

45 In the introduction to *In Search of Canadian Liberalism*, Frank Underhill described how his war service helped shape his perception of Britain: 'I did my military service in France as a subaltern officer in an English infantry battalion. I discovered that this Edwardian-Georgian generation of Englishmen made the best regimental officers in the world and the worst staff officers. The stupidity of G.H.Q. and the terrible sacrifice of so many of the best men among my contemporaries sickened me for good of a society, national or international, run by the British governing classes.' Underhill, 'Introduction,' in his *In Search of Canadian Liberalism* (Toronto, 1960), x.]

46 Carl Berger, *The Writing of Canadian History: Aspects of English-Canadian Historical Writing Since 1900*, 2nd ed. (Toronto, 1986), 145.

47 Graham Carr, '"All We North Americans": Literary Culture and the Continentalist Ideal, 1919–1939,' *American Review of Canadian Studies* 17 (1987): 153.

48 Berger, *Writing of Canadian History*, 137.

49 Underhill quoted in Robert Bothwell et al., *Canada since 1945: Power, Politics, and Provincialism* (Toronto, 1981), 57.

50 Alexandre Bélisle, *Histoire de la presse franco-américaine* (Worcester, 1911) 54, 289.

51 Gérard Bouchard, *Genèse des nations et cultures du Nouveau Monde. Essai d'histoire comparée* (Montreal, 2000), 143–4.

52 André Laurendeau, 'Commentaires: Menaces de l'américanisme,' *L'Action nationale* X (1937): 316.

53 J.H. Thompson and S.J. Randall, *Canada and the United States: Ambivalent Allies*, 3rd ed. (Montreal and Kingston, 2002), 17.

54 Arthur Johnston, *Myths and Facts of the American Revolution: A Commentary on United States History as It Is Written* (Toronto, 1908), iii; Knowles, *Inventing the Loyalists*, 110.

55 [Macphail], 'Canadian Writers and American Politics,' 3.

56 Canadian anti-Americanism and American critical introspection could indeed, at times, nurture one another. For instance, Canadian detractors of America's Indian policy frequently echoed the work of American critics such as Helen Hunt Jackson, whose 1884 *Century of Dishonor*, in turn, praised the Dominion for its treatment of Native People. Thompson and Randall, *Canada and the United States*, 50.

57 Frederick Jackson Turner also exerted a great deal of influence on continentalist thought, most notably on sociologist S.D. Clark (1910–2003) and historians Frank Underhill and Arthur Lower. Their work explored the significance of the frontier in Canadian history.

58 'Ce grand polémiste catholique, une des plus belles figures de l'Église des États-Unis, et tout à fait comparable à Louis Veuillot.' Jules-Paul Tardivel, *La situation religieuse aux États-Unis. Illusions et réalités* (Montreal, 1900), 167.

59 George R. Parkin, *Imperial Federation: The Problem of National Unity* (London, 1892), passim; Sara Jeannette Duncan, *Those Delightful Americans* (New York, 1902), 236.

60 James T. Shotwell, *The Autobiography of James T. Shotwell* (New York, 1961), 35.

61 Michel Winock, '"U.S. Go Home": l'antiaméricanisme français,' *L'Histoire* 50 (1982): 8.

62 'André Siegfried essaye d'être objectif mais, malgré lui, ses jugements, ses appréciations laissent trop voir qu'il est protestant. Son credo l'empêche d'avoir de la question une vue totale.' Hermas Bastien, 'Sur les États-Unis,' *L'Action canadienne-française* XX (1928): 115.

63 'Notre avenir! Tous les stigmates de cette civilisation dévorante, nous

pourrons, avant vingt ans, les découvrir sur les membres de l'Europe.' Georges Duhamel, *Scènes de la vie future* (Paris, 1930), 220.

64 'Le cycle présent de l'évolution humaine aboutit peu à peu à une "dépersonnalisation" de l'individu, devenu machine lui-même.' Lucien Romier, *Qui sera le maître, Europe ou Amérique?* (Paris, 1927), 238.

65 Pierre Trépanier, 'Le maurrassisme au Canada français,' *Cahiers des Dix* 53 (1999): 167.

2 American Politics and Philosophy

1 Douglas Bush, 'Pride and Prejudice,' *Canadian Mercury* I (1929): 136.

2 Brandon Conron, 'Essays, 1920–1960,' in *Literary History of Canada: Canadian Literature in English*, vol. 2, ed. C.F. Klinck (Toronto, 1976), 119.

3 A.R.M. Lower, 'The United States through Canadian Eyes,' *Quarterly Journal of Inter-American Relations* I (1939): 110.

4 Beckles Willson, *The New America: A Study of the Imperial Republic* (London, 1903), 248.

5 'Le matériel accapare la portion la plus considérable de l'énergie américaine,' warned the Université de Montréal's professor of American literature, Hermas Bastien, in 1936. America, he continued, was a 'civilisation d'essence économique' that embodied 'le libéralisme à l'état pur, oublieux des personnes et des distinctions ethniques.' Hermas Bastien, 'L'américanisation par la philosophie,' *Revue dominicaine* XLII (1936): 201.

6 'Bref, il semble que ce peuple vise plus bas que Dieu, ce qui, pour une civilisation chrétienne, est le commencement de tout désordre.' Lionel Groulx, *Nos responsabilités intellectuelles* (Montreal, 1928), 28.

7 'Sa qualité saillante est l'énergie, et on l'accuse de trop d'âpreté dans sa poursuite de la richesse matérielle. Mais il est aussi faux de dire que l'Américain adore uniquement le dollar que de prétendre que les Anglais sont une nation de boutiquiers.' The republic, Bouchette continued, 'ne manque pas de vie intellectuelle,' and had produced, among other things, 'une littérature plus brillante et plus variée que la nôtre.' Errol Bouchette, 'Le Canada parmi les peuples américains,' *La Revue canadienne* XLVIII (1905): 14-15.

8 ' – Ah! Les Américains! Parlons-en, dit le vieux Brégent, rouge de colère. Un tas d'abrutis! Une nation de païens où le mariage est un jeu et le divorce un sport. Les Américains! Des chercheurs de plaisir et d'excitations sensuelles, qui ne trouvent pas d'autre but à la vie que fabriquer des bretelles et jeter leur gourme! Et pas intelligents, pas artistes, bourrés de littérature de foot-ball et ahuris de jazz band. Ah! Ah!

' – Calmez-vous, je vous prie. Je connais leurs défauts. Peuple très jeune, il est trop fort pour son âge. Il a l'exubérance de l'adolescent qui, trop tôt, a pris conscience de sa puissance: il dépense sa surabondance de vie. Mais restons dans le sujet: la prospérité matérielle, dis-je, donne le confort au foyer et à l'État, la fierté aux citoyens qui s'éprennent d'une terre où l'on vit mieux et plus qu'ailleurs. Avec la richesse, la science, les lettres et les arts deviennent nécessairement l'apanage du grand nombre; les grandes institutions se multiplient, bref, on achète la civilisation.' Jean-Charles Harvey, *Marcel Faure* (Montmagny, 1922), 138–9.

9   Willson, *New America*, 244.

10   Robert Falconer, *The United States as a Neighbour from a Canadian Point of View* (Cambridge, 1925), 174.

11   George Grant, *The Empire, Yes or No?* (Toronto, 1945), 30–1.

12   'Le plus grand problème moral dont la solution s'impose, aujourd'hui, au peuple américain est celui-ci: où mettre les bornes entre la liberté et la licence?' Antonio Huot, 'Aux États-Unis: Les universités,' *La Revue canadienne*, New Series, II (1908): 554.

13   'En Angleterre on a quelques notions de liberté. Aux États-Unis on parle beaucoup de liberté. La langue anglaise a même deux mots pour exprimer la chose: *liberty* et *freedom*; deux beaux mots, certes, qui arrondissent admirablement une phrase et qui font toujours éclater des applaudissements pourvu qu'on les prononce avec un peu d'emphase. Mais la *Land of freedom* n'a réellement pas la moindre idée de ce que c'est que la vraie liberté … La liberté qui existe aux États-Unis, est la liberté libérale ou maçonnique. Et cette liberté là – une fausse liberté – est très nuisible à l'Église, en ce sens qu'elle lui enlève de nombreux enfants et affaibli l'esprit de foi chez beaucoup de ceux qu'elle ne lui arrache pas entièrement.' Jules-Paul Tardivel, *La situation religieuse aux États-Unis* (Montreal, 1900), 38, 195–6.

14   J.A. Macdonald, *The North American Idea* (New York, 1917), 73–4.

15   J.W. Dafoe, ed., *Canada Fights: An American Democracy at War* (New York, 1941), 205.

16   'L'individualisme américain … s'appelle, en bon français, esprit d'insubordination.' 'En effet,' he continued, 'l'individualisme américain a horreur de la discipline, de tout ce qui peut gêner ses mouvements. Il veut bien croire aux dogmes, mais ne cherchez pas à lui imposer une règle de conduite.' And though Tardivel understood that individualism 'est une qualité … lorsqu'il ne dépasse pas les bornes de la modération,' he could not condone a form of individualism which he believed destabilized society. Tardivel, *La situation religieuse aux États-Unis*, 19, 28.

17   Grant, *The Empire*, 32.

18 'Fondée par l'individualisme, arrivée à la plus haute prospérité en s'appuyant sur ses propres forces, la république devra répugner à la loi de la collectivité qui serait la mainmise sur l'énergie de chacun au profit de tous.' DeCelles, *Les États-Unis*, 402.

19 Colin McKay, 'Roosevelt's Plan – So Far,' *Canadian Unionist* VII (1933): 39.

20 James Cappon, 'The Great American Democracy,' *Queen's Quarterly* XI (1904): 298.

21 Willson, *New America*, 13, 35.

22 'L'utopie égalitaire … est dans tous les discours du tribun; zéro dans la société. C'est le plus stupide contresens qui soit jamais sorti de la bouche d'un homme. Mieux que cela: elle est contre nature.' Antonio Huot, 'La question sociale aux États-Unis en 1907,' *La Revue canadienne* LII (1907): 421.

23 'Les hommes sont crées égaux dans ce sens que tous sont composés d'une âme et d'un corps, que tous sont mortels, que tous ont la même fin surnaturelle à laquelle ils ne peuvent parvenir que par la même aide d'En-Haut, la pratique des mêmes vertus, l'éloignement des mêmes péchés. Mais ce n'est pas dans ce sens métaphysique que les Révolutionnaires, tant Américains que Français, entendent l'égalité. Ils parlent de l'égalité sociale et politique. Or cette égalité n'a jamais existé, n'existera jamais, ne peut pas exister. Il n'y a peut-être pas deux hommes "créés égaux" dans ce sens; il n'y a pas deux hommes qui possèdent exactement les mêmes qualités intellectuelles, les mêmes aptitudes, les mêmes dons physiques. Tous ne sont pas appelés aux mêmes rôles dans la société. Le fils est-il "créé égal" à son père? L'imbécile, le *minus habens*, est-il l'égal, socialement, et politiquement parlant, de l'homme d'étude et de génie?' Tardivel, *La situation religieuse aux États-Unis*, 128.

24 S.J. Duncan, *A Daughter of Today: A Novel* (New York, 1894), 113.

25 F.P. Grove, *A Search for America* (Ottawa, 1927), 30.

26 Edmond de Nevers, who saw deference as 'un reste des époques de servitude,' praised democratic egalitarianism in *L'âme américaine* (1900). De Nevers had been repelled by 'la servilité des garçons de café, ouvriers, manœuvres' that he had encountered while travelling in Europe. By contrast, he marvelled at American society, where 'chaque homme traite son semblable comme un *homme*.' Indeed, in spite of America's insidious love of titles, 'l'égalité règne aux États-Unis, aussi complète que cela peut être compatible avec les lois de la nature qui en feront toujours une chose paradoxale. Le mouvement de la richesse, la constitution de grandes fortunes ne lui ont pas été fatals, comme on aurait pu le croire.' E. de Nevers, *L'âme américaine*, vol. II (Paris, 1900), 237–9, 241 (original emphasis).

27 Andrew Macphail, 'New Lamps for Old,' *University Magazine* VIII (1909): 31; 'Canadian Writers and American Politics,' *University Magazine* IX (1910): 6–7.

28 G.T. Denison, 'The United Empire Loyalists and Their Influence upon the History of this Continent,' *Proceedings and Transactions of the Royal Society of Canada*, 2nd Series, X (1904): xxvii; 'Canada and Her Relations to the Empire,' *Westminster Review* CXLIV (1895): 249.

29 W.B. Munro, *The Government of the United States: National, State and Local* (New York, 1919), 1.

30 'C'étaient des hommes absolument modérés que Washington, Hamilton et les principaux constituants de Philadelphie. On aurait tort de voir en eux des révolutionnaires; ils ne l'avaient été qu'un instant, et à leur corps défendant. Profondément imbus des traditions anglaises, ils restèrent, sous la république, prisonniers de leur passé et de leurs traditions.' DeCelles, *Les États-Unis. Origine, institutions, développement* , 408.

31 'L'esprit de la Révolution américaine ne diffère guère, quoi qu'on en ait dit, de l'esprit de la Révolution française.' Tardivel, *La situation religieuse aux États-Unis*, 127.

32 'Plusieurs chefs de la Révolution américaine inclinaient vers le déisme.' Louis Chaussegros de Léry, 'Écoles publiques étatsuniennes,' *Relations* III (1943): 320.

33 Falconer, *United States as a Neighbour*, 106.

34 J.W. Dafoe, 'Canada and the United States,' *Journal of the Royal Institute of International Affairs* IX (1930): 723.

35 John MacCormac, *America and World Mastery: The Future of the United States, Canada, and the British Empire* (New York, 1942), 5.

36 R.P. Baker, *A History of English-Canadian Literature to the Confederation: Its Relation to the Literature of Great Britain and the United States* (Cambridge, 1920), viii, 69.

37 S.R. Clarke, *A New Light on Annexation: A Political Brochure* (Toronto, 1891), 19.

38 J.B. Brebner, 'The Interplay of Canada and the United States,' *Columbia University Quarterly* XXVI (1934): 335.

39 O.D. Skelton, 'Current Events: Choosing a President,' *Queen's Quarterly* XX (1912): 113–14.

40 In many ways, Wrong and Falconer's interwar judgement of American politics and government was not significantly different from that of liberal continentalists like J.W. Dafoe or W.B. Munro. Their moderate anti-Americanism did emerge, however, when they discussed issues pertaining to trade and identity.

41 Andrew Macphail, 'Certain Varieties of the Apples of Sodom,' *University Magazine* X (1911): 33.

42 'Les diverses formes de gouvernement que les peuples se donnent, pourvu qu'elles ne sortent pas du cadre légitime, n'intéressent pas l'Église.' Tardivel, *La situation religieuse aux États-Unis*, 12.

43 A.H.F. Lefroy, *The British Versus the American System of National Government* (Toronto, 1891), 9.

44 R.C.B. Risk, 'Augustus Henry Frazer Lefroy,' in *Dictionary of Canadian Biography*, vol. 14.

45 'Le système républicain … possède une supériorité indéniable, indiscutable, car il ne pourrait, comme l'hérédité, donner des chefs ou des pontifs ignorants, vulgaires, criminels mêmes.' J.-B. Rouilliard, *Annexion: conférence: l'union continentale* (Montreal, 1893), 13.

46 Goldwin Smith, *Canada and the Canadian Question* (New York, 1891), 252.

47 J.T. Shotwell, *The Heritage of Freedom: The United States and Canada in the Community of Nations* (New York, 1934), 126–7.

48 Macphail, 'New Lamps for Old,' 35.

49 In the late nineteenth century some European Catholics looked to America's less confrontational secularism as a possible alternative to the radical separation of church and state that had occurred in the French and Italian republics. Moreover, they saw the progress of the American Church as a sign that Catholicism could adapt to modernity. The Vatican, however, had little patience for theological modernism during this era. As a result, 'Americanism' – the so-called phantom heresy – was promptly condemned by Pope Leo XIII in 1899. The papal condemnation of 'Americanism' is discussed in Condé B. Pallen, 'Testem Benevolentiæ,' *Catholic Encyclopedia*.

50 'Depuis que Jésus-Christ est venu sur la terre, il n'y a que deux esprits qui animent les individus et les gouvernements: l'esprit chrétien et l'esprit antichrétien. L'esprit gouvernemental des États-Unis n'étant manifestement pas l'esprit chrétien doit être, de toute nécessité, l'esprit antichrétien. Si cet esprit antichrétien y paraît moins violent qu'ailleurs, c'est uniquement parce qu'il y trouve moins de résistance. Le fleuve, large et profond, coule silencieux vers la mer, tandis que la petite rivière, dont le cours est obstrué par des digues et des rochers, fait grand bruit. Cependant la puissance du fleuve l'emporte de beaucoup sur celle de la rivière … Le vrai Dieu du peuple américain et du gouvernement américain, c'est l'humanité, c'est l'homme' Tardivel, *La situation religieuse aux États-Unis*, 125–6, 135.

51 Henri Bourassa, *The Spectre of Annexation and the Real Danger of National Disintegration* (Montreal, 1912), 17.

52 'La population hétérogène des États-Unis, la multiplicité des croyances

que l'on y trouve, l'absence même de toute foi religieuse chez un grand nombre, ont rendu [le laïcisme] nécessaire. Dans de telles circonstances, c'est incontestablement le moindre mal.' Tardivel, *La situation religieuse aux États-Unis*, 88.

53 Indeed, though antidemocratic sentiment was present in pre-1945 conservative thought, the rejection of parliamentarism was virtually non-existent in both English and French Canada. As historian Pierre Trépanier has pointed out, 'except among the fascists and in spite of the denunciations of the ravages of partisanship, doctrinal anti-parliamentarianism would scarcely register with Quebec intellectuals.' Trépanier, 'Notes pour une histoire des droites intellectuelles canadiennes-françaises à travers leurs principaux représentants (1770–1970),' *Cahiers des Dix* 48 (1993): 162.

54 'La Déclaration d'Indépendance contient un principe essentiellement faux et subversif. '*Deriving their just powers from the consent of the governed.*' Les auteurs de la République Américaine [*sic*] attribuèrent donc formellement une origine humaine au pouvoir civil. L'Église, parlant par la bouche de Léon XIII, dans l'encyclique *Diuturnum*, déclare "qu'il faut chercher en Dieu la source du pouvoir dans l'État. "' Tardivel, *La situation religieuse aux États-Unis*, 129 (original emphasis).

55 Henri Bourassa, *L'intervention américaine, ses motifs, son objet, ses conséquences* (Montreal, 1917), 18.

56 Andrew Macphail, 'Protection and Politics,' *University Magazine* VII (1908): 250.

57 'Notre République est vraiment la chose du peuple; elle pratique le suffrage universel, qui est, pour de grands esprits, "le règne de l'incompétence. "' Henri d'Arles, 'Le français dans le Connecticut,' *La Revue nationale* I (1919): 15.

58 Viscount de Fronsac [X Frederic Gregory Forsyth], 'Origin of the Social Crisis in the United States: A Monarchist's View,' *Canadian Magazine* I (1893): 663–4.

59 Smith, *Canada and the Canadian Question*, 173.

60 Macdonald, *North American Idea*, 54.

61 J.C. Hopkins, 'Canadian Hostility to Annexation,' *Forum* XVI (1893): 332.

62 Edgar W. McInnis, 'This Insubstantial Pageant: Reflections on the American Political Scene,' *Canadian Forum* IX (1929): 305–6.

63 A.H.F. Lefroy, 'Canadian Forms of Freedom,' *Annual Transactions of the United Empire Loyalists' Association of Ontario* (1899): 106.

64 Munro, *Government of the United States*, 51.

65 Clarke, *New Light on Annexation*, 19.

66 Bagehot in Macphail, 'Certain Varieties of the Apples of Sodom,' 30.

67 John G. Bourinot, 'Canadian Studies in Comparative Politics: Parliamentary Compared with Congressional Government,' *Proceedings and Transactions of the Royal Society of Canada*, 1st Series, XI (1893): 81.

68 Munro, *Government of the United States*, 58.

69 Donald G. Creighton, 'The Course of Canadian Democracy,' *University of Toronto Quarterly* XI (1942): 263–4.

70 W.B. Munro, *American Influences on Canadian Government* (Toronto, 1929), 20.

71 'Les états américains reçoivent et exercent les pouvoirs que la Constitution ne réserve pas au gouvernement fédéral; quand, au Canada, c'est le gouvernement central qui est revêtu des pouvoirs que la Constitution n'accorde pas aux provinces. Autrement dit, l'état américain possède, en matière de législation, un champ plus étendu, une autorité plus large.' Édouard Montpetit, *Reflets d'Amérique* (Montreal, 1941), 34.

72 Macphail, 'New Lamps for Old,' 21.

73 W.S. Milner, 'Roman, Greek, English and American Conceptions of Liberty,' *Canadian Magazine* XXI (1903): 516.

74 Stephen Leacock, *Arcadian Adventures with the Idle Rich* (New York, 1914), 307–8.

75 Munro, *American Influences on Canadian Government*, 91.

76 Munro, *Government of the United States*, 97.

77 F.H. Underhill, 'O Canada,' *Canadian Forum* X (1929): 11.

78 Cappon, 'The Great American Democracy,' 297.

79 'Le système fédéral ne constitue-t-il pas une force formidable au profit de l'ordre? En effet, sur la vaste étendue de la république se dressent quarante-cinq gouvernements particuliers, comme autant de citadelles en état d'imposer respect aux ennemis de la société.' DeCelles, *Les États-Unis*, 405.

80 McInnis, 'This Insubstantial Pageant,' 305–6.

81 F.H. Underhill, 'O Canada,' *Canadian Forum* X (1930): 116.

82 Dafoe, ed., *Canada Fights*, 35.

83 'Une rupture dans la hiérarchie des personnes et une confusion dans leurs rapports avec le politique et le culturel. En ces dernières années, tels symptômes se sont accusés chez nous et nous nous croyons autorisés à les dénoncer comme une influence américaine en morale politique.' Bastien, 'L'américanisation par la philosophie,' 211–12.

3 Religion and Culture in the United States

1 'Regardons vers New York lorsqu'il s'agit de finances et vers Chicago lorsqu'il s'agit de cochons. Mais lorsqu'il y va de littérature, d'art, de

science, de culture, rappelons-nous que les Dieux n'ont pas encore traversé l'Atlantique.' Victor Barbeau, 'La politique: La méthode américaine,' *Les Cahiers de Turc* V (1922): 34.

2 'Le jazz que nous servent le plus fréquemment les postes radiophoniques américains n'a pas été purifié par l'art de compositeurs remarquables, il n'est pas manié non plus par des musiciens mais par des faiseurs de bruit quelconques. Ce qu'on nous sert est donc le jazz *original*, c'est-à-dire, selon Paul Whiteman – l'un des rénovateurs de musique syncopée – un bruit épileptique dans lequel s'immisce une musique informe et bête.' Lucien Desbiens, 'L'infiltration américaine par la radio,' *Revue dominicaine* XLII (1936): 140 (original emphasis).

3 J.H. McCulloch, 'Monstrosities of the Movies,' In *Open House*, ed. William Arthur Deacon and Wilfred Reeves (Ottawa, 1931), 47.

4 'Pour le peuple, le cinéma, c'est en quelque sorte le rêve éveillé. Concrète, presque palpable, c'est la belle illusion que chacun, sans peut-être y croire beaucoup, conserve dans un recoin de l'âme. Le spectacle détachera l'être de la réalité vivante et de ses tristesses, pour le transporter dans un monde factice d'où il ne descendra qu'avec peine. Pour beaucoup, cette transposition dans l'irréel aura pour effet de rendre plus durs la vie et le renoncement qu'elle comporte.' Harry Bernard, 'L'ennemi dans la place: Théâtre et cinéma,' *L'Action française* XII (1924): 75.

5 'S'il se rencontre encore, aux États-Unis, plusieurs magazines dont le ton et la forme littéraire rappellent les premières publications du genre,' he wrote in 1936, 'la grande majorité des magazines américains est devenue synonyme d'une des formes les plus détestable et dangereuses de la réclame en faveur des manifestations les moins intéressantes des mœurs de nos voisins.' These included 'l'apologie du crime, du divorce, de l'amour libre,' and 'la glorification des étoiles de cinéma et des as du base-ball.' Jean Bruchési, 'Notre américanisation par le magazine,' *Revue dominicaine* XLII (1936): 6, 9.

6 Stephen Leacock, 'Literature and Education in America,' *University Magazine* VIII (1909): 3, 13, 16–17; 'The Psychology of American Humour,' *University Magazine* VI (1907): 57–8.

7 'Quels sont ceux que les jeunes Américains connaissent, admirent et envient? Les littérateurs, les savants, les artistes? Nullement. Ce sont les étoiles de l'écran, pour leur beauté; les étoiles du sport, pour leur force ou leur adresse ... Certains d'entre eux sont de véritables gloires nationales. Ils jouissent d'une célébrité qu'aucun homme public, qu'aucun savant, qu'aucun artiste n'oserait ambitionner. Leurs traits que les journaux ne se lassent pas de reproduire sont souvent plus familiers aux jeunes américains que ceux du Président des États-Unis. Lors du Congrès eucharistique

de Chicago, un journal reproduisit une photo où l'on voyait Babe Ruth donnant la main au Cardinal Légat. Il n'est pas douteux que pour un grand nombre d'Américains, tout l'honneur était pour le Légat du Saint-Siège.' Ceslas Forest, 'Notre américanisation par les sports,' *Revue dominicaine* XLII (1936): 350–1.

8 Northrop Frye, 'Reflections at a Movie,' *Canadian Forum* XXII (1942): 212.

9 Merrill Denison, 'Thoughts on Radio,' In *Open House*, 115.

10 Graham Carr, '"All We North Americans": Literary Culture and the Continentalist Ideal, 1919–1939,' *American Review of Canadian Studies* XVII (1987): 149.

11 'Le grand obstacle qui s'oppose à l'avènement de l'état de liberté absolue auquel doivent aspirer tous les patriotes sincères, c'est le vasselage intellectuel dans lequel l'Amérique se trouve encore vis-à-vis de l'Europe et surtout de l'Angleterre.' Edmond de Nevers, *L'âme américaine*, vol. II (Paris, 1900), 387.

12 E.G. Faludi, 'America and Modern Art,' *Canadian Forum* XXI (1941): 75–6.

13 'Sur le terrain du journalisme la supériorité des Américains sur leurs concurrents s'affirme sans conteste. Sous la poussée de leur génie entreprenant, la feuille éphémère a pris un développement en rapport avec la soif de savoir qui dévore leur société enfiévrée … Le journal devait, certes, atteindre ce prodigieux développement dans un pays où l'instruction s'est infiltrée partout.' A.D. DeCelles, *Les États-Unis. Origine, institutions, développement* (Ottawa, 1896), 376.

14 Goldwin Smith, *Canada and the Canadian Question* (New York, 1891), 50.

15 Sylva Clapin, *A New Dictionary of Americanisms* (New York, 1902), vi.

16 The American, he wrote, 'n'est pas toujours un athée, mais le côté surnaturel de la religion ne le préoccupe pas. D'ailleurs il est issu du protestantisme dont le principe fondamental repose sur la foi seule, sans les œuvres. Le libre examen, autre principe protestant le pousse à se faire une religion à lui, et c'est ainsi que le naturalisme toujours croissant, selon l'attrait de la nature viciée, en fait pratiquement un païen.' Georges-Marie Bilodeau, 'L'américanisme,' *La Voix nationale* III (1930): 6.

17 'Ce peuple de 120 millions d'hommes' was ravaged by 'tous les microbes de son néo-paganisme.' 'N'est-il pas en train de s'acheminer vers une civilisation athée,' he asked, 'n'admettant d'autres lois que la dure loi des surhommes économiques, d'autres fins que la jouissance sensuelle ou l'élevage des meilleures races de l'animal humain?' Lionel Groulx, *Nos responsabilités intellectuelles* (Montreal, 1928), 25–6. Groulx borrowed the expression 'néo-paganisme' from Lucien Romier's *Qui sera le maître, Europe ou Amérique?* (Paris, 1927).

18 Stephen Leacock, *Arcadian Adventures with the Idle Rich* (New York, 1914), 154, 239.

19 Robert Falconer, *The United States as a Neighbour from a Canadian Point of View* (Cambridge, 1925), 184–5.

20 'La secte la plus nombreuse et la plus agissante, celle des calvinistes,' was 'écartelée par deux tendances adverses, celle des modernistes en train de vider la vie religieuse de tout dogme et de tout rite, et celle des fondamentalistes qui, tout autant qu'une religion, figure une réaction nationaliste anglo-saxonne contre les races et les croyances étrangères.' Groulx, *Nos responsabilités intellectuelles*, 29.

21 'L'Église d'Amérique est libre,' wrote Jules-Paul Tardivel in 1900, 'tant qu'elle ne sort pas de chez elle, de ses conciles, de ses temples, de ses écoles. Mais quelque désir qu'elle ait de se faire petite, de s'effacer, de se confondre avec la foule des sectes, il lui faut, nécessairement, prendre contact avec les pouvoirs publics. Et alors commence la véritable persécution.' Indeed, he continued, 'l'esprit public et les pouvoirs publics sont hostiles à l'Église et aux catholiques.' Roman Catholics, Tardivel noted, were effectively barred from such highly symbolic offices as the presidency: 'Aucun parti politique ne songerait à proposer un catholique au poste de premier magistrat de la République. Si, par impossible, un des partis faisait une telle proposition, il serait littéralement balayé aux élections comme une vile poussière. On ne peut pas se figurer un *catholique* ou un *nègre* président des États-Unis. C'est une impossibilité morale.' Tardivel, *La situation religieuse aux États-Unis. Illusions et réalités* (Montreal, 1900), 90–1, 111. Tardivel also believed that American society bred unorthodox Catholicism. Indeed, his ultramontane essay on American Catholicism read like a veritable catalogue of apparently heretical transgressions perpetrated by some members of the American clergy. For Tardivel, 'Americanism' was hardly a phantom heresy; it was a very real movement led by a number of American bishops who sought to adapt Catholicism to the modern world. This was, of course, completely unacceptable to the editor of *La Vérité*, who was a fervent opponent of religious modernism.

22 'Divorce, enseignement neutre et socialisme, voilà bien les trois plaies sociales qui menacent de ruiner complètement, de nos jours, les forces vitales de la république américaine,' warned abbé Antonio Huot in 1908. Mercifully, however, 'l'Église catholique se dresse, dans toute la majesté de son immuable doctrine, pour barrer la route à ces trois ennemis de l'ordre social.' Huot, 'Aux États-Unis: Les échos d'un centenaire.' *La Revue canadienne*, New Series, II (1908): 172–3.

23 'Une autre force milite chez nos voisins en faveur de l'ordre; c'est le sen-

timent religieux qui pénètre encore toutes les classes de la société et qui
s'affirme dans les circonstances un peu importantes de la vie nationale.'
DeCelles, *Les États-Unis*, 402–3.

24 'Aux États-Unis, quoi qu'en disent les optimistes, les religions sont en
décadence; dans tous les cultes se sont accumulées des ruines, un vent de
scepticisme et d'indifférence souffle sur les consciences.' de Nevers, *L'âme
américaine*, II, 143.

25 Fred Landon, *Western Ontario and the American Frontier* (Toronto, 1941),
75.

26 'Il y a peut-être une chose que l'Europe a réellement empruntée à l'Amérique: le principe radicalement faux et souverainement funeste qui fait de
l'éducation de l'enfance une fonction de l'État, une œuvre politique; doctrine qui, entre les mains de la franc-maçonnerie, nous a conduits à l'école
sans Dieu.' Tardivel, *La situation religieuse aux États-Unis*, 153.

27 'En *biologie* prévaut uniquement le système de l'évolution sans Dieu,
où disparaît toute idée de création. Tout phénomène vital, y compris la
pensée, a pour cause une mutation chimique dans l'organisme. Le droit
à l'avortement et au suicide en découle naturellement.' M.A. Lamarche,
'Notre américanisation: Aperçus complémentaires et mot de la fin,' *Revue
dominicaine* XLII (1936): 254–5 (original emphasis).

28 'Il ne nous paraît pas que la constitution mentale de la femme soit propre
à des matières surtout faites pour l'esprit positif, froid et raisonneur de
l'homme et s'adapte à un programme de cours classique … D'ailleurs,
quoiqu'en pensent les féministes, ce n'est pas du tout comprendre le rôle
social de la femme, tel que voulu par Dieu, sa mission, sa vocation dans le
monde, que de la préparer, par ces sortes d'études, à sortir de sa sphère naturelle d'influence et d'action, et, non pas à aider l'homme, plus tard, mais
à le supplanter, non pas à en être la compagne accomplie, mais le compagnon, l'égal absolu dans l'exercice de ces professions libérales, autrefois
regardées comme son inaliénable domaine. Pareille œuvre nous semble
être une déformation du plan divin.' [Henri d'Arles], *Esquisse des collèges
américains* [Lewiston, 1902], [9–10].

29 Falconer, *United States as a Neighbour*, 236–7.

30 Andrew Macphail, 'The Fallacy in Education,' in his *Essays in Fallacy* (London, 1910), 116.

31 Leacock, 'Literature and Education in America,' 8–9.

32 'Dans ces pays, l'éducation est à la portée de tous et l'entreprise de
s'instruire n'offre pas des difficultés insurmontables. Tous ont libre accès
à la source des connaissances, mais tous n'y puisent pas.' Errol Bouchette,
Robert Lozé (Montreal, 1903), 49.

33 J.B. Brebner, 'Oxford, Toronto, Columbia,' *Columbia University Quarterly* XXIII (1931): 238–9.
34 'Nulle part au monde plus qu'aux États-Unis voit-on l'adolescent mieux préparé à la lutte pour l'existence, envisager l'avenir avec plus de confiance,' he wrote. 'Le jeune Américain sort de l'école parfaitement équipé pour accomplir sa mission. Son savoir est la résultante d'une instruction toute positive, excluant comme bagage inutile les connaissances d'agrément que l'on regarde comme indispensables en Europe. Il les acquerra plus tard, après fortune faite. En somme, éducation très démocratique, très précise, menant droit à un but déterminé: l'aisance ou la richesse.' DeCelles, *Les États-Unis*, 369–70.
35 W.B. Munro, *American Influences on Canadian Government* (Toronto, 1929), 114.
36 John MacCormac, *Canada: America's Problem* (New York, 1940), 149.

4 Race and Gender in the United States

1 Racial violence, especially lynching, was particularly offensive to the conservative sense of justice and order. For instance, in an apocalyptic footnote to *La situation religieuse aux États-Unis*, Jules-Paul Tardivel predicted that the widespread practice of lynching would sow the seeds of a horrible racial war that would devastate America. Tardivel, *La situation religieuse aux États-Unis. Illusions et réalités* (Montreal, 1900), 202–3, n1. The issue of lynching even crept into Canadian literature. In his best-selling work of fiction, *The Attic Guest* (1909), Robert Knowles (1868–1946) told the story of a courageous Scottish minister, Gordon Laird, who breaks the colour barrier in the American South. In a poignant scene, Laird tries to save a Black man from being lynched and almost loses his life in the process. The reader is left with a strong sense of British moral superiority. Knowles was ordained in the Presbyterian Church in 1891, and served as the pastor of Knox Church, in Galt, Ontario, for most of his career. A proponent of church union, he eventually joined the United Church.
2 Huot condemned 'l'infranchissable *color line*, comme on dit en ce pays, qui empêche les blancs et les noirs de voyager en chemin de fer, dans le même wagon, et de dîner au restaurant à la même table, dans les anciens États esclavagistes.' Yet, in the same breath, he noted that 'la race noire est une race inférieure, et il serait absolument chimérique de croire qu'il soit possible au nègre, placé dans les mêmes conditions que le blanc, d'atteindre le niveau intellectuel de celui-ci.' Antonio Huot, 'Mœurs américaines. Blancs et noirs,' *La Nouvelle-France* I (1902): 370, 376.

3 Beckles Willson, *The New America: A Study of the Imperial Republic* (London, 1903), 186–7.

4 'Primitifs pour un bon nombre, illettrés ou peu instruits, persécutés par des blancs indignes ou dégénérés, ils acquièrent en certaines régions ce que l'Américain appelle un *inferiority complex*. Ils se montrent alors timides et fuyants, obséquieux, serviles [et] leurs mœurs atteignent souvent un niveau assez bas.' Harry Bernard, 'Les noirs des États-Unis et le roman régionaliste,' *Revue de l'Université d'Ottawa* XII (1942): 409.

5 Goldwin Smith, *The United States: An Outline of Political History, 1492–1871* (New York, 1893), 43; *Commonwealth or Empire? A Bystander's View of the Question* (New York, 1902), 43.

6 W.A. Deacon, *My Vision of Canada* (Toronto, 1933), 118–22.

7 Ibid., 121.

8 G.R. Parkin, *Imperial Federation: The Problem of National Unity* (London, 1892), 136.

9 'Malgré la distance qui sépare le blanc du Peau-Rouge, le français en fait son ami, le compagnon de ses courses, et cette confraternité le conduit jusqu'au mariage avec la femme indigène … Tant de condescendance gagne le cœur de l'aborigène et le prestige du nom français sert de sauf-conduit au coureur des bois … tandis que le puritain, odieux aux enfants de la forêt, n'ose pas se risquer isolé en dehors de sa demeure.' A.D. DeCelles, *Les États-Unis. Origine, institutions, développement* (Ottawa, 1896), 391.

10 J.B. Brebner, 'Canadian and North American History,' Canadian Historical Association *Annual Report* (1931): 44.

11 'L'on a coutume de considérer comme un élément de faiblesse, dans un État politique, la pluralité des races ou des origines. Cependant, l'histoire démontrerait peut-être que les États et les empires les mieux musclés et par conséquent doués de longévité, furent précisément les États et les empires de structure composite, comme si l'équilibre de génies divers leur avait donné plus de souplesse dans la conduite de leur destin, les avait mieux protégés contre les emportements irréfléchis, les aventures catastrophiques. Les plus cultivés des Américains savent fort bien que les exigences de la vie internationale interdisent à tout grand peuple de se passer, à l'heure actuelle, de l'un ou l'autre des grandes cultures humaines, et en particulier de la culture française.' Lionel Groulx, 'Six semaines après,' in *En Louisiane*, ed. Omer Héroux (Montreal, 1931), 98–9.

12 'L'unification linguistique que vous prônez chez vous serait-elle avantageuse à aucun point de vue? Ce serait amoindrir les races diverses qui pullulent ici, par conséquent amoindrir le capital national, si je puis ainsi parler, attaquer les réserves foncières sur lesquelles reposent nos plus

grandes destinées.' Henri d'Arles, 'Le français dans le Connecticut,' *La Revue nationale* I (1919): 17.

13 Willson, *New America*, 170.

14 Nathanael Burwash, 'The Moral Character of the U.E. Loyalists,' *Annual Transactions of the United Empire Loyalists' Association of Ontario* (1901–2): 63.

15 J.A. Macdonald, 'Some International Fundamentals,' *Addresses Delivered before the Canadian Club of Montreal* (1912–13): 58.

16 Goldwin Smith, *Loyalty, Aristocracy and Jingoism: Three Lectures Delivered before the Young Men's Liberal Club, Toronto* (Toronto, 1891), 87.

17 W.B. Munro, *The Government of American Cities* (New York, 1912), 35; *The Government of the United States: National, State and Local* (New York, 1919), 576.

18 Parkin, *Imperial Federation*, 135.

19 Smith, *The United States: An Outline of Political History*, 216.

20 John MacCormac, *America and World Mastery: The Future of the United States, Canada, and the British Empire* (New York, 1942), 276.

21 'Depuis sa venue aux États-Unis,' Laflamme wrote in 1908, 'l'élément irlandais … a surtout été un élément d'opposition … il est aujourd'hui l'âme du parti démocratique qui a donné naissance aux quatre ou cinq partis radicaux qui existent dans la république.' The Irish were, he believed, a violent and disruptive group: 'L'abondance de liberté qu'ils trouvent en arrivant en Amérique les porte à tyranniser ceux qui les entourent et n'ont pas l'avantage d'être les plus nombreux.' Irish-American bishops 'veulent empêcher les catholiques de différente provenance de former en Amérique des groupes compacts nationaux: allemands, italiens, polonais, tchèques, hongrois, franco-canadiens. Les évêques, à l'exemple de Mgr Ireland, cherchent à les américaniser, si bien que l'Église est devenue un instrument d'américanisation.' J.L.K. Laflamme, 'La religion et les assimilateurs dans la Nouvelle-Angleterre.' *La Revue franco-américaine* I (1908): 86–7; 'Les Canadiens aux États-Unis,' *La Revue canadienne* XXXIX (1901): 486; 'La question des langues et l'épiscopat dans la Nouvelle-Angleterre,' *La Revue franco-américaine* II (1909): 329.

22 James Algie, *Bergen Worth* (Toronto, 1901), 5–6.

23 'Les pellicules qu'on nous montre sont, à de rares exceptions près, de provenance américaine, ou, pour mieux dire, judéo-américaine.' 'Les Juifs, outre le but de déchristianisation qu'on leur prête, ont pour principal objet de réaliser de l'argent et de mettre la main sur les finances du monde. En s'emparant du cinéma, ils ne songent pas tant à faire de l'art qu'à s'accaparer la richesse. Pour arriver à leurs fins, rien ne sera négligeable ni trop bas; ils exploiteront les passions sous toutes les formes, flatteront les

instincts. Ils n'ont aucun souci de la morale ni de l'ordre, et le merveilleux moyen d'éducation qu'est le cinéma deviendra entre leurs mains, à cause de leur soif d'or et de leur rage de domination, un outil de dépravation, une école de corruption et de révolution. S'ils y voient une raison d'attirer les foules, et d'emplir la caisse, ils propageront les idées anti-sociales, se feront les champions du divorce ou de l'amour libre, à l'occasion des pratiques malthusiennes. Naturellement ennemis de l'ordre, ils accorderont un appui bienveillant au socialisme le plus destructeur. Pour eux, il n'y a d'important que ce qui fait recette.' Harry Bernard, 'L'ennemi dans la place: Théâtre et cinéma,' *L'Action française* XII (1924): 70, 71–2.

24 Desmond Pacey, 'Fiction, 1920–1940,' in *Literary History of Canada: Canadian Literature in English*, vol. 2, ed. C.F. Klinck (Toronto, 1976), 197.

25 S.J. Duncan, *An American Girl in London* (Toronto, 1891), 1.

26 Munro, *Government of the United States*, 82.

27 A.A. Perry, 'New Deal for American Women,' *Canadian Comment* 2 (1933): 12–13.

28 Andrew Macphail, 'The American Woman,' in his *Essays in Fallacy* (London, 1910), 7.

29 'Devant ces hommes si simplement maîtres chez eux, qui avaient une idée si nette et si ferme de ce que doit être la famille, le docteur américain se sentait humilié de l'anarchie qui régnait à son foyer. Vraiment sa femme y prenait trop de place. Qu'elle eût une voix prépondérante quand il s'agissait des choses de son ressort, passe. Qu'elle s'occupât seule de meubler la maison, de choisir ou de renvoyer les servantes, qu'elle allât même jusqu'à déterminer l'emploi des soirées libres, le but et l'itinéraire de leurs voyages, passe encore; mais qu'elle se chargeât d'orienter la carrière de son mari, de choisir sa clientèle et de lui indiquer son gagne-pain, c'était trop fort. En cela c'est lui, François, qui devait être juge suprême et maître souverain. Il était temps que Fanny l'apprît et l'acceptât. Il y a des cas majeurs où la femme doit obéir et se taire, si elle ne peut pas approuver et se réjouir.' Adélard Dugré, *La campagne canadienne. Croquis et leçons* (Montreal, 1925), 202.

30 'L'Américaine humiliée, ravalée par le divorce, la pratique anti-conceptionelle et le "birth control, " n'a pas d'enfants. Elle élève des toutous et leur lègue en mourant, fortune, palais et cimetière.' Ernestine Pineault-Léveillé, 'Notre américanisation par la femme,' *Revue dominicaine* XLII (1936): 145.

31 'Le malthusianisme, pour ne pas dire l'onanisme, ce qui en pratique est la même chose, est la plaie des mariages, non seulement entre protestants et incroyants, mais aussi entre chrétiens.' Georges-Marie Bilodeau, *Pour rester*

au pays. Étude sur l'émigration des Canadiens français aux États-Unis. Causes. Remèdes (Quebec, 1926), 46.

32 'Ce qui frappe d'admiration, c'est le progrès matériel de notre voisin. Ce qui épouvante, c'est le néo-paganisme de la grande masse des Américains. Idée religieuse, doctrine spiritualiste, solidité de la famille, ces bases des nations chrétiennes sont en Amérique sapées par le divorce stérilisateur, le pragmatisme utilitaire, le panthéisme mystique.' Hermas Bastien, 'La critique américaine,' in his *Témoignages. Études et profils littéraires* (Montreal, 1933), 35.

33 J.C. Hopkins, 'Canadian Hostility to Annexation,' *Forum* XVI (1893): 330.

34 Smith, *Loyalty, Aristocracy, Jingoism*, 87–8.

35 Godwin Smith, *Canada and the Canadian Question* (New York, 1891), 167.

36 S.J. Duncan, *Those Delightful Americans* (New York, 1902), 237.

5 The Perils of Prosperity and the Search for Order

1 'Dans la formation de son économie, elle avait fondé sur la formule nouvelle et vulgaire de la standardisation industrielle d'extravagantes et insatiables ambitions. Elle avait méprisé le génie créateur et conservateur de la vieille Europe. L'originalité dans la conception lui était inconnue. Elle s'était gratifiée d'une superstructure industrielle excessive à laquelle correspondait une population trop peu nombreuse.' Paul-Henri Guimont, 'Coup d'œil sur l'Amérique contemporaine,' *L'Actualité économique* XI (1935): 55.

2 Andrew Macphail, 'The American Woman,' in his *Essays in Fallacy* (London, 1910), 11, 12–13, 14.

3 James Algie, *Bergen Worth* (Toronto, 1901), 1.

4 G.S. Ryerson, *The After-Math of a Revolution* (Toronto, 1896), 11.

5 'Nulle part, les conflits entre patrons et ouvriers n'ont été plus âpres, plus dangereux qu'aux États-Unis; nulle part les grèves n'ont revêtu un caractère plus menaçant pour l'ordre public qu'à Pittsburg [*sic*], Baltimore et Chicago. C'étaient, dans leur cadre restreint, comme les combats d'avant-poste d'une guerre sociale. Plusieurs causes ont provoqué la lutte anti-capitaliste; l'influence de l'Europe dévorée par le socialisme, influence exercée par la propagande de nombreux déclassés que l'immigration traîne avec elle et qui, par leurs discours révolutionnaires, attisent la discorde et enveniment le conflit; la concentration rapide, en quelques mains, d'énormes fortunes plus ou moins avouables et, partant, de nature à exaspérer le travailleur honnête.' A.D. DeCelles, *Les États-Unis. Origine, institutions, développement* (Ottawa, 1896), 399.

6 'Faut-il nous adapter au milieu américain? Il me semble que nous devons répondre: Oui, dans le domaine économique. Que l'on regrette, voire même que l'on déplore la tendance de plus en plus marquée vers la standardisation et vers la disparition de la petite industrie spécialisée et du travail individuel, à la fois créateur et novateur, je le comprends, mais serait-il permis de suggérer que cette forme de l'activité industrielle n'est pas la mieux adaptée à notre condition et à nos besoins. D'ailleurs, à cet égard, l'Europe s'américanise rapidement et ne vit pas seulement de ses petites industries. Elle en a, comme l'Amérique, de très grandes, et, toutes proportions gardées, elle adopte les méthodes qui assurent le meilleur rendement. Chacun est enclin, suivant ses sympathies, à généraliser la louange ou le blâme. Tout n'est pas condamnable dans la standardisation, qui a donné des résultats vraiment extraordinaires ... Je ne puis concevoir que notre culture latine et notre humanisme soient sérieusement menacés du fait que nous aurons à notre disposition moins de formes de bouteilles, moins d'espèces de roues d'automobile et moins de genres de pneus.' Beaudry Leman, 'Les Canadiens français et le milieu américain,' *Revue trimestrielle canadienne* XIV (1928): 269.

7 'Des étourdissantes cités, des quais souillés, des gratte-ciel provoquants, des usines tentaculaires et des vaudevilles burlesques.' Hermas Bastien, 'William James,' in his *Itinéraires philosophiques* (Montreal, 1929), 53

8 Erastus Wiman, *Chances of Success: Episodes and Observations in the Life of a Busy Man* (New York, 1893), 172, 256.

9 Renée Legris, 'Metropolitan Museum,' in *Dictionnaire des œuvres littéraires du Québec*, vol. II.

10 W.B. Munro, *The Government of American Cities* (New York, 1912), 50.

11 'La femme du monde n'est plus la femme d'un rang social élevé, d'une éducation soignée, d'une culture plus poussée. L'intérêt et l'argent ont tout nivelé avec quelques degrés dans l'égalité suivant la capacité de réception et d'adaptation des uns et des autres. On n'est plus bien souvent qu'une femme riche, ou simplement un membre anonyme, falot, sans influence dans la société.' Ernestine Pineault-Léveillé, 'Notre américanisation par la femme,' *Revue dominicaine* XLII (1936): 146.

12 Stephen Leacock, 'Literature and Education in America,' *University Magazine* VIII (1909): 16.

13 'Les compagnies de voies ferrées, les puissants syndicats accapareurs et monopoleurs, les *trusts* de toute sorte, les *combines* – institutions qui n'existaient pas aux premiers jours de la République, – exercent aujourd'hui une influence aussi grande que néfaste sur la législation, sur la direction des affaires publiques, sur les destinées nationales.' Jules-Paul Tardivel,

La situation religieuse aux États-Unis. Illusions et réalités (Montreal, 1900), 12.

14 O.D. Skelton, 'Current Events: Choosing a President,' *Queen's Quarterly* XX (1912): 114.

15 'Je crois les États-Unis destinés à résoudre les grands problèmes sociaux; car c'est là que la lutte entre le capital et le travail arrivera tout d'abord, à son point culminant,' de Nevers wrote in 1904. 'L'ouvrier n'est pas, dans la république voisine, l'homme asservi, pressuré aigri des grands centres européens; c'est un homme libre, ayant conscience de sa dignité et habitué aux formes constitutionnelles. Quand le régime capitaliste aura donné tout ce qu'il peut donner, il s'entendra avec l'élément ouvrier. Et je pressens que la réforme que l'on inaugurera alors, sera une œuvre géniale que le reste du monde imitera.' Edmond de Nevers, 'L'évolution des peuples anciens et modernes,' *La Revue canadienne* XLVII (1904): 559–60.

16 F.R. Scott, *Canada and the United States* (Boston, 1941), 12–13.

17 Andrew Macphail, 'New Lamps for Old,' *University Magazine* VIII (1909): 26.

18 Robert Falconer, *The United States as a Neighbour from a Canadian Point of View* (Cambridge, 1925), 177.

19 G.T. Denison, 'The United Empire Loyalists and Their Influence upon the History of this Continent,' *Proceedings and Transactions of the Royal Society of Canada*, 2nd Series, X (1904): xxxi–xxxii.

20 'Les déportements de toute une catégorie de la société américaine, les criminels et les *gangsters* immanquablement victorieux sur la police, les divorces répétés d'acteurs et d'étoiles du cinéma, d'industriels ou de financiers en vedette, d'as du théâtre ou du sport professionnel: tout cela, avec des histoires de *love's nests*, d'exploits de *gunmen*, figure au premier plan de ce type de presse.' Georges Pelletier, 'Notre américanisation par le journal,' *Revue dominicaine* XLII (1936): 276.

21 'Celle-là est bien la plus dangereuse des innovations de la démocratie, exposant la justice aux pires soupçons,' he wrote in 1896. Without a doubt, 'l'indépendance de la magistrature, qui est la première sauvegarde de son honnêteté, a reçu un coup fatal le jour où elle est devenue une fonction élective. Il est difficile de comprendre comment les Américains, qui n'osent jamais faire fonds sur la probité humaine, ont pu consentir à accepter un principe qui en est le plus sûr destructeur?' DeCelles, *Les États-Unis*, 240.

22 W.A. Deacon, *My Vision of Canada* (Toronto, 1933), 115–16.

23 S.D. Clark, 'The Social Development of Canada and the American Continental System,' *Culture* V (1944): 134–5.

24 Roy Greenaway, 'Big Shots,' in *Open House*, ed. W.A. Deacon and Wilfred Reeves (Toronto, 1931), 220, 235–6.

25 Generally speaking, America's 'noble experiment' was not popular among interwar Canadian intellectuals. Many continentalists blamed prohibition for rising crime rates on both sides of the border and argued that the unpopular eighteenth amendment had bred a general disrespect for law and order among Americans. Similar arguments were made on the right.

6 Canadian Identity and America

1 Anti-British sentiment in nineteenth-century America was founded on a rejection of hereditary privilege, deference, and militarism. It affirmed the nation's faith in democratic republicanism.

2 Patricia K. Wood, 'Defining "Canadian": Anti-Americanism and Identity in Sir John A. Macdonald's Nationalism,' *Journal of Canadian Studies* 36 (2001): 50.

3 G.T. Denison, 'Canada and her Relations to the Empire,' *Westminster Review* CXLIV (1895): 248.

4 Norman Knowles, *Inventing the Loyalists: The Ontario Loyalist Tradition and the Creation of Usable Pasts* (Toronto, 1997), 162.

5 R.G. Trotter, 'The Canadian Back-Fence in Anglo-American Relations,' *Queen's Quarterly* XL (1933): 391–2.

6 Wood, 'Defining "Canadian"' 49.

7 Anonymous, 'Canadian Prosperity and the United States,' *The Round Table* XV (1925): 572.

8 R.G. Trotter, 'The Canadian Back-Fence in Anglo-American Relations,' *Queen's Quarterly* XL (1933): 395.

9 Robert Falconer, *The United States as a Neighbour from a Canadian Point of View* (Cambridge, 1925), 7–8.

10 French Canadian society was 'simple, patriarcale, essentiellement catholique et conservatrice,' while American society was 'éblouissante et tapageuse, protestante et matérialiste.' 'Il existe actuellement, dans l'Amérique du Nord, deux civilisations fort différentes: l'une est représentée par cent millions d'Anglo-Saxons, l'autre par trois ou quatre millions de Canadiens d'origine française. Ce qui distingue ces deux groupes inégaux, ce n'est pas seulement la langue qu'ils parlent et la foi religieuse de la grande majorité de ceux qui les composent, c'est aussi la diversité dans les manières d'agir, la divergence de vues dans la façon d'envisager la vie, ses jouissances et ses devoirs. On a hérité, au Canada français, du tempérament et des traditions de la France catholique du dix-septième siècle; on a hérité,

chez les Américains anglo-saxons, du libre examen et de l'esprit utilitaire des Anglais du règne d'Élisabeth … Cette opposition dans le caractère des deux groupes ethniques se trahit constamment dans la pratique de la vie: l'exercice du culte divin, les coutumes familiales, l'éducation, la littérature, le commerce et la réclame, les procédés électoraux, les fêtes populaires, tout traduit à l'observateur le moins attentif les profondes différences qui distinguent le Canadien resté français de l'Américain-type.' Adélard Dugré, *La campagne canadienne. Croquis et leçons* (Montreal, 1925), 5–6, 234.

11 'Le caractère français est juste aux antipodes du caractère anglo-saxon-américain. Autant l'un est gai, expansif, sans souci, compatissant avec les misères des autres, prêt aux sacrifices les plus généreux, autant l'autre est froid, concentré, calculateur et égoïste.' Édouard Hamon, *Les Canadiens-Français de la Nouvelle-Angleterre* (Quebec, 1891), 120.

12 'L'aigle américain n'a pas aujourd'hui notre sympathie, encore moins notre amour. Notre amour! Nous le donnons à l'Espagne … Les Espagnols sont, pour ainsi dire, nos frères, ils sentent, comme nous, couler dans leurs veines le sang inaltérable de la race latine, leur langue ressemble à la nôtre comme le paros ressemble au carrare, et leur foi catholique est l'étoile qui guide la barque portant nos destinées religieuses et nationales.' William Chapman, *À propos de la Guerre hispano-américaine* (Quebec, 1898), ii, v.

13 French Canadians, wrote abbé Lionel Groulx, 'comptent … parmi les plus vieux Américains.' Indeed, he continued, 'nul n'est plus enraciné que nous en cette Amérique, ne s'est plus identifié avec ce continent.' Lionel Groulx, 'Notre avenir en Amérique,' in his *Orientations* (Montreal, 1935), 278.

14 'Le Québécois moyen, également libéré des inhibitions européennes, s'apparente à l'Américain moyen par son démocratisme politique, son égalitarisme social, son incuriosité intellectuelle, sa bienveillance inlassable et ses goûts aventureux.' Gustave Lanctot, 'Influences américaines dans le Québec,' *Mémoires et comptes rendus de la Société royale du Canada*, 3rd Series, XXXI (1937): 123.

15 J.W. Dafoe, 'Canada and the United States,' *Journal of the Royal Institute of International Affairs* IX (1930): 723.

16 F.R. Scott, *Canada Today: A Study of Her National Interests and National Policy* (London, 1938), 104.

17 P.E. Corbett, 'The New Canadianism,' *Contemporary Review* CXL (1931): 483.

18 S.D. Clark, 'The Importance of Anti-Americanism in Canadian National Feeling,' in *Canada and Her Great Neighbor*, 243.

19 A.R.M. Lower, 'The United States through Canadian Eyes,' *Quarterly Journal of Inter-American Relations* I (1939): 105.

20 Goldwin Smith, *Canada and the Canadian Question* (New York, 1891), 5.
21 J.B. Brebner, 'Canadian and North American History,' Canadian Historical Association *Annual Report* (1931): 43.
22 P.E. Corbett, 'Anti-Americanism,' *Dalhousie Review* X (1930): 300.
23 Ibid., passim.
24 J.W. Dafoe, *Canada: An American Nation* (New York, 1935), 92–3.
25 'C'est un grand et noble peuple que celui des États-Unis, un peuple éminemment civilisateur et où la question sociale a déjà sur plusieurs points trouvé des solutions. Nous devons admirer ses vertus et rechercher son amitié. Mais jamais nous ne pourrons nous fondre en lui parce que nous sommes différents, que notre âme n'est pas son âme, et que la Providence nous réserve évidemment une mission autre et non moins noble que la sienne.' Errol Bouchette, 'Le Canada parmi les peuples américains,' *La Revue canadienne* XLVIII (1905): 15.
26 'Il n'est pas exact de dire qu'on retrouve l'Espagne au Mexique, une Angleterre rajeunie aux États-Unis, une France nouvelle sur les bords du Saint-Laurent,' Bouchette wrote in the *Revue canadienne*. 'Que ces peuples parlent l'espagnol, l'anglais, le français, qu'ils conservent beaucoup de choses de la mère patrie, cela ne les empêche pas d'être des peuples différents.' Ibid., 16.
27 Smith, *Canada and the Canadian Question*, 1–2. Continentalists often suggested that physical maps better reflected the realities of North American geography than political maps. Smith's magnum opus contained a fold-out physical map of the Dominion, and every volume in the series on Canadian-American relations sponsored by the Carnegie Endowment for International Peace contained a physical map of North America on its end-papers.
28 Ibid., 160.
29 John W. Dafoe, 'The Problems of Canada,' in Cecil J. B. Hurst et al., *Great Britain and the Dominions* (Chicago, 1929), 137.
30 The borderlands concept is outlined in Lauren McKinsey and Victor Konrad, *Borderlands Reflections: The United States and Canada* (Orono, 1989).
31 Falconer, *United States as a Neighbour*, 1–3.
32 G.M. Grant, *Canada and the Canadian Question: A Review* (Toronto, 1891), 9, 31; 'Canada and the Empire,' *National Review* XXVII (1896): 682.
33 J.C. Hopkins, 'Canadian Hostility to Annexation,' *Forum* XVI (1893): 327, 335.
34 H.A. Innis, 'Introduction to the Canadian Economic Studies,' in his *The Dairy Industry in Canada* (Toronto and New Haven, 1937), vi.
35 Henri Bourassa, *The Reciprocity Agreement and Its Consequences as Viewed from the Nationalist Standpoint* (Montreal, 1911), 28.

36 Goldwin Smith, 'Can Canada Make Her Own Treaties?' *Canadian Magazine* XXII (1904): 334.

37 Lionel Groulx, *Mes mémoires*, vol. 2, *1920–1928* (Montreal, 1971), 303.

38 'Entre l'Est et l'Ouest, il y a la *distance ennemie*. En vain a-t-on espéré effacer cet éloignement qui donne à notre pays l'étendue d'un empire, par la construction d'interminables et coûteux chemins de fer. Le pays y aurait trouvé la banqueroute, à moins que les provinces qui n'ont point à s'en servir ne paient pour celles qui en ont l'usage; ce qui n'est guère une répartition propre à cimenter l'unité. Du reste, les divisions naturelles, en un territoire qui est, comme on l'a dit, une *absurdité géographique*, partagent nettement les intérêts, imposant le libre-échange là-bas, réclamant la protection tarifaire ici. Je sais bien que la *géographie humaine* ne prend pas fatalement ses mesures sur les fleuves ni sur les montagnes, et que les frontières politiques qui demeurent sont plutôt celles de l'esprit national que les tracés de l'arpentage. Mais c'est par une solidarité étroite d'intérêts et d'esprit commun que les fossés géographiques peuvent être comblés. Dans l'espèce, c'est ce qui fait précisément le plus défaut.' Rodrigue Villeneuve, 'Notre avenir politique: Et nos frères de la dispersion?' *L'Action française* VIII (1922): 12–13 (original emphasis).

39 'Un climat froid, une nature calme, des conditions économiques difficiles, une foi religieuse robuste ont développé chez les Canadiens français l'endurance dans les travaux pénibles et la facilité de contentement; un climat tempéré, une nature généreuse, l'abondance des richesses, ont développé chez les Américains le goût de vivre et l'attachement aux biens terrestres, tandis que le mysticisme des pionniers puritains faisait place chez eux à une indifférence religieuse de plus en plus accentuée.' Dugré, *La Campagne canadienne*, 5–6.

40 William Osler, 'Anglo-Canadian and American Relations,' *Addresses Delivered before the Canadian Club of Toronto* (1904–5): 65.

41 G.R. Parkin, 'The Relations of Canada and the United States,' *Empire Club Speeches* (1907–8): 160. Parkin argued, moreover, that Canada's climate was not merely repelling undesirable immigrants, it was also keeping indigence in check: 'Nature takes [indigents] firmly in her hand and says, If you do not have foresight and prudence, and get fuel and food and a roof over your head, you are going to die in that climate … That is one of the immense advantages which we have over the people to the south of us. In the future that means everything for us. It means that we are going to have a people more carefully selected, more fit for the struggle of life, breeding a better race than those who take people from all kinds and conditions and permit a submerged tenth.' Ibid., 160–1.

42 Andrew Macphail, 'Canadian Writers and American Politics,' *University Magazine* IX (1910): 7.
43 J.A. Macdonald, *Democracy and the Nations: A Canadian View* (Toronto, 1915), 80–81.

7 Twin Perils: Annexation and Americanization

1 Goldwin Smith, *Canada and the Canadian Question* (New York, 1891), 267.
2 Smith, *Loyalty, Aristocracy and Jingoism: Three Lectures Delivered before the Young Men's Liberal Club, Toronto* (Toronto, 1891), 95–6.
3 Smith, *Canada and the Canadian Question*, 275.
4 Ibid., 277.
5 S.R. Clarke, *A New Light on Annexation:A Political Brochure* (Toronto, 1891), 11, 22.
6 'L'union continentale, par l'annexion aux États-Unis, assurerait un tarif uniforme, un tarif protecteur élevé, contre les pays transatlantiques, et libre échangiste avec les peuples des Amériques.' J.-B. Rouilliard, *Annexion: conférence: l'union continentale* (Montreal, 1893), 26.
7 L.-H. Fréchette, 'The United States for French Canadians,' *Forum* XVI (1893): 345.
8 Ibid.
9 'Nous savons, enfin, qu'un jour viendra où la frontière qui sépare le Canada des États-Unis aura disparu, où l'Amérique du nord [*sic*] ne formera plus qu'une vaste république et nous avons l'ambition de constituer dans l'Est, un foyer de civilisation française qui fournira son apport au progrès intellectuel, à la moralité et à la variété de l'Union.' E. de Nevers, *L'âme américaine*, vol. II (Paris, 1900), 368.
10 In some ways, de Nevers' annexationism resembled the ultramontane expansionism of Father Édouard Hamon and Jules-Paul Tardivel. Hamon and Tardivel believed that both Canada and the United States would eventually disintegrate and that a French Canadian republic encompassing Quebec, New England, eastern Ontario, and northern New Brunswick would emerge from the ashes of the two federations.
11 'Quand l'heure aura sonné de la séparation définitive entre l'ancien monde et le nouveau, la destinée s'accomplira pacifique et solennelle, et rien ne troublera la tranquillité de l'univers.' E. de Nevers, *L'avenir du peuple canadien-français* (Paris, 1896), 394.
12 J.G. Bourinot, 'Why Canadians Do not Favor Annexation,' *Forum* XIX (1895): 277.
13 G.M. Grant, 'Canada and the Empire,' *National Review* XXVII (1896): 676.

14 G.R. Parkin, *The Great Dominion: Studies of Canada* (London, 1895), 185.

15 J. Castell Hopkins, 'Canadian Hostility to Annexation,' *Forum* XVI (Nov.): 328–9.

16 G.M. Grant, *Canada and the Canadian Question: A Review* (Toronto, 1891), 21.

17 Ibid., 29–30.

18 Erastus Wiman, *Union between the United States and Canada: Political or Commercial? Which Is Desirable and which Is Presently Possible?* (New York, 1891), 29.

19 O.D. Skelton, 'Current Events: The Annexation Bogey,' *Queen's Quarterly* XVIII (1911): 332.

20 P.E. Corbett, 'Canada in the Western Hemisphere,' *Foreign Affairs* XIX (1941): 786.

21 Henri Bourassa, *The Spectre of Annexation and the Real Danger of National Disintegration* (Montreal, 1912), 3, 16, 18.

22 'Au premier rang des signataires du document, figurent un bon nombre des dirigeants anglais du monde financier et politique de Montréal. Tous les groupes, conservateurs, réformistes, rouges, s'y trouvent représentés, avec cette particularité savoureuse, toutefois, que l'élément tory tient la prépondérance.' Lionel Groulx, 'L'annexionnisme au Canada français,' *L'Action nationale* XVII (1941): 447.

23 'Les annexions peuvent changer l'allégeance politique et quelques formes administratives; elles ne peuvent atteindre directement l'être de la nation.' Lionel Groulx, *Nos responsabilités intellectuelles* (Montreal, 1928), 13.

24 'L'annexion … tendrait à troubler pour longtemps le métabolisme religieux de l'individu canadien-français. Une partie de la bourgeoisie, retenue dans l'Église par les cadres sociaux plutôt que par adhésion personnelle, se détacherait plus ou moins lentement … L'accent rural et la solide continuité de notre vie chrétienne se verront encore atténués par l'attirance accrue vers les villes et par la prépondérance alarmante que prendront les coutumes urbaines de piété.' Jacques Cousineau, 'Ne nous induisez pas en tentation…' *L'Action nationale* XVII (1941): 516–17.

25 'Québec deviendrait donc, dans la grande République, un État d'agriculteurs, de bûcherons, de mineurs et de centrales électriques, avec sans doute un minimum d'industrialisation fixée sur place dans les cas où le facteur matières premières l'emporte sur tous les autres pour la localisation. Dans ces conditions, Québec pourrait rester français, mais sans espoir de retenir son accroissement de population.' F.-A. Angers, 'Québec, 57e étoile sur le drapeau de l'Oncle Sam,' *L'Action nationale* XVII (1941): 495.

26 'Ce sont eux, en tout cas, que les Américains y emploient. Le pays en est

infesté d'une rive à l'autre. Vassal économique des États-Unis, le Canada est en passe de devenir également son vassal spirituel. Canadiens-anglais et Canadiens-français ne pensent, ne vivent, ne jugent que par leurs voisins. Dans tous les étages de la société leur influence pénètre et se développe. On ne va au cinéma que pour voir glorifier leurs prouesses, admirer leur ingéniosité, applaudir leur drapeau. On ne lit leurs journaux, leurs revues que pour apprendre les derniers de leurs exploits, les plus beaux de leurs accomplissements politiques ou sportifs. Ils nous écrasent de leur vie nationale. Nous ne semblons exister que pour nous féliciter de les avoir comme voisins et nous appliquer à leur ressembler le plus possible.' [Victor Barbeau], 'La politique: La méthode américaine,' *Les Cahiers de Turc* V (1922): 31, 34.

27 'La femme est l'un des grands facteurs responsables de l'américanisme au Canada. L'américanisme a désaxé la femme. En lui proposant toutes les libertés, en la sortant du foyer dont elle est la reine et maîtresse naturelle, en obnubilant sa conscience et troublant sa foi, il brisa du même coup la famille, aggrava le problème économique et disqualifia la société.' Ernestine Pineault-Léveillé, 'Notre américanisation par la femme,' *Revue dominicaine* XLII (1936): 132.

28 'Il faut noter que cette infiltration s'exerce surtout dans les grandes villes, mais pénètre infiniment moins et par remous seulement dans les campagnes, de sorte qu'elle n'atteint réellement qu'une moitié de la population.' Gustave Lanctot, 'Le Québec et les États-Unis, 1867–1937,' in his *Les Canadiens français et leurs voisins du sud* (Montreal, 1941), 306–7.

29 'Si nous voulons combattre, autant que la chose est possible, la littérature de rebut qui nous vient des États-Unis, ayons, pour la masse, au moins un magazine bien fait, vivant, présenté avec goût, où la variété des sujets soit égale à l'excellence de la forme littéraire, où la première place soit donnée aux choses et gens de chez nous.' Jean Bruchési, 'Notre américanisation par le magazine,' *Revue dominicaine* XLII (1936): 20.

30 'Une campagne d'éducation anti-américanisante, à la fois scolaire et populaire … s'impose d'urgence.' 'Il est contradictoire et vain de prétendre éveiller chez les jeunes comme chez les anciens le sentiment national (je parle d'un sentiment raisonné, éprouvé au contact de la doctrine catholique), sans les prévenir et prémunir du même coup contre ce qu'on nomme l'annexion morale américaine.' M.A. Lamarche, 'Notre américanisation: Aperçus complémentaires et mot de la fin,' *Revue dominicaine* XLII (1936): 258.

31 'Parce qu'il reste fidèle à sa tradition,' Gustave Lanctot told the Royal Society of Canada in 1937, 'le Québec remplit devant l'américanisme, comme

en 1775, en 1849 et en 1887, le rôle de barrière, barrière qui force le pays à s'arrêter et à réfléchir avant de sauter dans l'inconnu de l'assimilation américaine. Il accomplit ainsi une œuvre nationale, tout en poursuivant son but particulier qui est le maintien intégral de la langue, de la religion et des institutions reçues des ancêtres.' Gustave Lanctot, 'Influences américaines dans le Québec,' *Mémoires et comptes rendus de la Société royale du Canada*, 3rd Series, XXXI (1937): 125.

32 'Si l'on ne se résout pas à une attitude nationale qui soit le reflet d'une culture anglo-française, le rayonnement de la civilisation américaine, toute proche et munie de moyens puissants de pénétration, se propagera.' Édouard Montpetit, *Reflets d'Amérique* (Montreal, 1941), 78.

33 'En pays canadien, des provinces entières sont déjà toutes américanisées, non seulement par la langue commune, mais par les idées, les sentiments et les goûts; par les intérêts, les affaires, les amusements; par les sectes, l'école, le théâtre, les magazines et les journaux quotidiens; par une égale licence dans la vie morale, indifférentisme religieux, divorce, malthusianisme, féminisme, démocratie libertaire, égalitarisme social.' Rodrigue Villeneuve, 'Notre avenir politique: Et nos frères de la dispersion?' *L'Action française* VIII (1922): 11.

34 Stephen Leacock, 'Canada Won't Go Yankee,' *American Mercury* XXXVIII (1936): 37.

35 Archibald MacMechan, 'Canada as a Vassal State,' *Canadian Historical Review* I (1920): 347, 349–50.

36 Douglas Bush, 'Pride and Prejudice,' *Canadian Mercury* I (1929): 136.

37 H.C. Goldenberg, '"Americanization" of Canada,' *Fortnightly Review* CXLV (1936): 688.

38 Lionel Gelber, 'Review of H.F. Angus' *Canada and Her Great Neighbor*,' *Canadian Journal of Economics and Political Science* V (1939): 125–6.

39 J.B. Brebner, 'Canadian and North American History,' Canadian Historical Association *Annual Report* (1931): 41.

40 F.H. Underhill, 'O Canada,' *Canadian Forum* X (1929): 11–12.

8 Canadian-American Relations and American Foreign Policy

1 G.T. Denison, *The Struggle for Imperial Unity. Recollections and Experiences* (London, 1909), 369.

2 G.R. Parkin, *The Great Dominion: Studies of Canada* (London, 1895), 234.

3 Beckles Willson, *America's Ambassadors to England (1785–1929): A Narrative of Anglo-American Diplomatic Relations* (New York, 1929), ix.

4 J.G. Bourinot, 'Canada's Relations with the United States and Her Influence on Imperial Councils,' *Forum* XXV (1898): 340.

5 J.C. Hopkins, 'Canadian Hostility to Annexation,' *Forum* XVI (1893): 326.

6 Arthur Johnston, *Myths and Facts of the American Revolution: A Commentary on United States History as It Is Written* (Toronto, 1908), 7.

7 Bourinot, 'Canada's Relations with the United States,' 336.

8 Stephen Leacock, 'Greater Canada: An Appeal,' *University Magazine* VI (1907): 139–40.

9 [W.L. Grant], 'Canada and Anglo-American Relations,' *The Round Table* IV (1913): 108–9, 121-122.

10 Robert Falconer, *The United States as a Neighbour from a Canadian Point of View* (Cambridge, 1925), 244.

11 B.K. Sandwell, 'Canada and the U.S.A,' *Public Affairs* V (1941): 118.

12 R.G. Trotter, 'Which Way Canada?' *Queen's Quarterly* XLV (1938): 295.

13 B.K. Sandwell, *Canada and United States Neutrality* (Toronto, 1939), 32.

14 R.G. Trotter, 'Defense and External Obligations: Discussion,' in Conference on Canadian-American Affairs held at the St Lawrence University, Canton, New York, 19–22 June, 1939, *Proceedings*, ed. A.B. Corey, W.W. McLaren, and R.G. Trotter (Boston, 1940), 206; 'Canada and Pan-Americanism,' *Queen's Quarterly* XLIX (1942): 256–7.

15 George Grant, *The Empire, Yes or No?* (Toronto, 1945), 18.

16 Edgar W. McInnis, *The Unguarded Frontier: A History of American-Canadian Relations* (New York, 1942), 3.

17 F.H. Underhill, 'O Canada,' *Canadian Forum* X (1929): 10.

18 A.R.M. Lower, 'The United States through Canadian Eyes,' *Quarterly Journal of Inter-American Relations* I (1939): 105.

19 J.A. Macdonald, *The North American Idea* (New York, 1917), 188–9.

20 J.T. Shotwell, 'Foreword,' in Charles C. Tansill, *Canadian-American Relations, 1875–1911* (New Haven and Toronto, 1943), viii.

21 P.E. Corbett, *The Settlement of Canadian-American Disputes: A Critical Study of Methods and Results* (New Haven and Toronto, 1937), 128–9.

22 Graham Carr, '"All We North Americans": Literary Culture and the Continentalist Ideal, 1919–1939,' *American Review of Canadian Studies* XVII (1987): 149.

23 W.A. Deacon, *My Vision of Canada* (Toronto, 1933), 100, 104–5.

24 J.S. Ewart, 'The Canning Policy Sometimes Called the Monroe Doctrine,' *The Kingdom Papers* 16 (1913): 188.

25 F.R. Scott, 'Canada and Hemispheric Solidarity,' in *Inter-American Solidarity*, ed. Walter H.C. Laves (Chicago, 1941), 148.

26 J.P. Humphrey, 'Pan-America in the World Order,' *Canadian Forum* XXI
     (1941): 201–2.
27 'Loin de bouder une politique de rapprochement canado-américain, loin
     de nous arrêter aux dangers qu'une politique d'indépendance représente,
     nous devons l'appuyer et l'encourager de toutes nos forces, afin qu'elle
     puisse donner des fruits à la fin du conflit actuel. Pour toutes les nations,
     la nation canadienne comprise, l'indépendance est un bien désirable en
     soi. Non pas une indépendance qui méprise les droits des autres nations et
     qui conduit aux pires catastrophes: la République voisine nous empêche-
     rait bien de tenter la folle aventure. Mais une indépendance réelle, qui
     s'appuierait sur une collaboration étroite et amicale avec les États-Unis.
     Une indépendance, enfin, qui nous délivrerait des liens factices actuels,
     pour accepter ceux que la géographie nous a façonnés, qui correspond-
     ent, par conséquent, à des nécessités … Il importe de nous habituer à
     l'idée que le Canada, tout en reconnaissant les obligations que sa situation
     géographique et économique lui impose, peut vivre libre et prospère, en
     collaboration avec les Etats-Unis.' Léopold Richer, *Vers l'accomplissement de
     notre destin américain* (Quebec, 1941), 3–4, 37.
28 'Grâce au zèle, à l'intelligence et à la générosité déployés sans relâche par
     les hommes d'État et les diplomates britanniques pour servir les intérêts
     américains, le Canada est devenu une incohérence géographique, une
     enfilade de pays sans contact immédiat, séparés par d'immenses barrières
     naturelles et attirés, chacun séparément, par l'énorme et croissante force
     d'attraction qui émane de la république américaine, leur unique voisine …
     Un Canada indépendant serait plus à l'abri des cupidités américaines que
     le Canada, dépendance britannique.' Henri Bourassa, *Syndicats nationaux
     ou internationaux?* (Montreal, 1919), 28; *L'intervention américaine, ses motifs,
     son objet, ses conséquences* (Montreal, 1917), 51.
29 F.A. Angers, 'Institutional and Economic Bases of the Entente between
     British Countries and the United States: Discussion,' in Conference on
     Canadian-American Affairs held at Queen's University, Kingston, Ontario,
     23–6 June 1941, *Proceedings*, ed. A.B. Corey and R.G. Trotter (Boston, 1941),
     163–4.
30 'Il devient clair à tous qu'un nouveau classement des régions de la terre
     se prépare et qu'une rupture d'équilibre s'accomplit au détriment de
     l'Europe … Seule, il faut bien le dire, notre effroyable insouciance d'État
     en tutelle, a pu nous permettre d'observer, sans émoi, le vaste mouvement
     panaméricaniste qui s'est développé dans les deux Amériques depuis
     1914 … J'ai toujours cru qu'il fallait chercher de ce côté-là un contrepoids
     à l'influence omnipotente de Washington.' Lionel Groulx, 'Notre avenir

politique,' *L'Action française* VII (1922): 5; Mes mémoires, vol. 2, *1920–1928* (Montreal, 1971), 335.

31 J.C. Harvey, 'Defense and External Obligations: Discussion,' in Conference on Canadian-American Affairs ... 19–22 June 1939, *Proceedings*, 210.

32 Beckles Willson, *The New America: A Study of the Imperial Republic* (London, 1903), vii, 28, 34–5, 189. Nevertheless, Willson saw U.S. reluctance to create a large standing army as a serious obstacle to imperial greatness. Like many Canadian imperialists, he believed that the United States lacked a truly martial spirit. 'For a bellicose and jingoistic folk, ready at all times to take and give offence, the Americans are still surprisingly unmilitary,' he noted in 1903. 'Perhaps I should say that there is an absence of a scientific military spirit in the country. They do not take the profession of arms seriously; and our recent experience in South Africa has rather disposed them to believe that a regular army has very little advantage, if any, over the untrained volunteer.' This absence of martialism, Willson and others insisted, was tied to the more general lack of order in the United States. Martialism, it was argued, required manly, conservative virtues which America did not possess in spades. For instance, Willson maintained that Americans lacked the discipline to produce good soldiers. 'Subordination is never easy to the average American, in whatever capacity,' he wrote. The American everyman could scarcely be turned into a true soldier 'because he lacks the leading essential, discipline; because he has never been made to learn that hard lesson, implicit obedience.' Ibid., 126.

33 Ibid., 89, 90n1, 91–2.

34 Stephen Leacock, 'Canada and the Monroe Doctrine,' *University Magazine* VIII (1909): 3701. During the interwar years, most imperialists would cease to regard the Monroe Doctrine as a direct threat to Canadian security. Nevertheless, few Tories were willing to acknowledge that the Monroe Doctrine, and U.S. might in general, were the mainstays of Canadian security. 'In the past some Canadians as well as Americans have been in the habit of saying that Canada's main source of security was the American policy embodied in the Monroe Doctrine,' wrote R.G. Trotter in 1940. 'Actually the strength of Canada's position has always mainly consisted ... in the prestige and power afforded her by the British connection.' Trotter, *North America and the War* (Toronto, 1940), 35–6.

35 Ewart, 'Canning Policy,' 171, 185.

36 Goldwin Smith, *Commonwealth or Empire? A Bystander's View of the Question* (New York, 1902), 2.

37 Ibid., 26, 34, 74.

38 'La Constitution, la Déclaration de l'Indépendance, les enseignements de

Washington, de Jefferson et de Monroe.' Edmond de Nevers, *L'âme américaine*, vol. I (Paris, 1900), 311.

39 'Un esprit guerrier pouvant pousser aux pires aventures ... Le militarisme, qu'on croyait impossible aux États-Unis, commence à s'implanter chez nos voisins ... L'armée régulière a aujourd'hui atteint un chiffre considérable, et des armements formidables se poursuivent dans tous les chantiers de la marine. Bien plus, l'annexion de Porto-Rico et des îles Philippines a fait naître, surtout chez les républicains, toute une politique d'agrandissement qu'on a résumée d'un mot: l'impérialisme.' Sylva Clapin, *Histoire des États-Unis depuis les premiers établissements jusqu'à nos jours* (Montreal, 1900), 210–12.

40 'Cette guerre est ignominieuse,' he asserted in 1898, 'et ce qui nous la fait trouver plus criminelle encore, c'est la déclaration hypocrite des Américains qui prétendent ne vouloir répandre le sang que pour servir l'humanité. Nous connaissons l'amour des enfants de l'oncle Sam pour l'humanité; nous savons comment ils ont traité et comment ils traitent encore la race noire sous le drapeau semé d'étoiles; nous avons encore devant les yeux l'exemple abominable qu'ils ont donné au monde civilisé en souffrant dans l'Utah la polygamie, en laissant Brigham Young abaisser des milliers de chrétiens policés au niveau de véritables bêtes humaines perdues dans les ténèbres de l'ignorance et de la perversité.' William Chapman, *À propos de la Guerre hispano-américaine* (Quebec, 1898), ii–iii. Chapman would tone down the anti-American rhetoric in a subsequent edition of this poem. Jean Ménard, 'À propos de la Guerre hispano-américaine, poème de William Chapman,' in *Dictionnaire des œuvres littéraires du Québec*, vol. 2.

41 'Il devra endosser la politique wilsonienne et collaborer d'une manière plus étroite et moins sentimentale sur le plan international, ce qu'il n'a encore guère recherché et ce que l'esprit américain ne semble guère disposé à admettre. Le salut économique de la nation américaine ne doit pas être laissé à la merci d'un peuple en désarroi, d'un peuple encore borné par la hantise de ses propres frontières. La participation aux affaires mondiales est un attribut de la virilité d'un people.' P.H. Guimont, 'Coup d'œil sur l'Amérique contemporaine,' *L'Actualité économique* XI (1935): 39.

42 'Leur participation à la vie internationale n'est ni plus brillante, ni plus onéreuse que celle des autres nations. Leur politique est avant tout nationale.' Lionel Roy, 'Roosevelt travaille,' *Le Canada français* XXI (1933): 311.

43 J.T. Shotwell, *The Heritage of Freedom: The United States and Canada in the Community of Nations* (New York, 1934), 88.

44 J.W. Dafoe, 'Final Luncheon,' in Conference on Canadian-American Affairs ... 17–22 June 1935, 285.

45 Peter McArthur, *The Affable Stranger* (New York, 1920), 58–9.
46 H.F. Angus, 'General Analysis of Opinions and Attitudes in Canada,' in his *Canada and Her Great Neighbor: Sociological Surveys of Opinions and Attitudes in Canada Concerning the United States* (Toronto, 1938), 21.
47 O.D. Skelton, 'Current Events: The Position of the United States,' *Queen's Quarterly* XXIII (1915): 107.
48 F.R. Scott, 'Currents of American Opinion,' *Canadian Forum* XXI (1941): 104.
49 F.H. Underhill, 'Review of J.W. Dafoe's *Canada, An American Nation,*' *Canadian Forum* XV (1935): 301.
50 'I am not an isolationist,' insisted F.R. Scott in mid-1939. 'I do not believe that Canada can live by herself. I think she should join the Pan-American Union immediately. But I would insist that Canadians themselves must determine when and where we intervene in any part of the world. Our choice should always be determined by the real interests of Canada. I do not happen to see those interests demanding our intervention in the expected European war. This, however, is far from a policy of isolation.' Scott, 'Defense and External Obligations: Discussion,' in Conference on Canadian-American Affairs ... 19–22 June 1939, 215.
51 R.G. Trotter, 'Some American Influences upon the Canadian Federation Movement,' *Canadian Historical Review* V (1924): 226–7.

9 Canadian-American Trade, Unionism, and Migration

1 Andrew Macphail stands out as one of the few imperialists of his generation to support reciprocity. He did not believe that reciprocity threatened the British connection and he heaped scorn on his fellow citizens for their 1911 rejection of the measure: 'These terrified Canadians distrusted not the Americans but themselves, and they disclosed to the world that they had no faith in their own citizenship ... In no other country in the world but China could the like be seen, a nationality declaring that its existence depended upon the limitation of trade with a neighbour.' Macphail, 'Why the Liberals Failed,' *University Magazine* X (1911): 572, 575.
2 G.R. Parkin, *The Great Dominion: Studies of Canada* (London, 1895), 186–7.
3 Arthur Hawkes, *An Appeal to the British-Born: To Promote the Sense of Canadian Nationality, as an Increasing Power within the British Empire, and to Preserve Unimpaired the Canadian and British Channels of Commerce on which the Prosperity of the Dominion Has Been Founded* (Toronto, 1911), 1, 7.
4 H.C. Goldenberg, '"Americanization" of Canada,' *Fortnightly Review* CXLV (1936): 690.
5 Goldwin Smith, *Canada and the Canadian Question* (New York, 1891), 291–2.

6 O.D. Skelton, 'Current Events: The Canadian Movement,' *Queen's Quarterly* XVIII (1910): 173.
7 J.W. Dafoe, 'Tariffs: Discussion,' in Conference on Canadian-American Affairs held at the St Lawrence University, Canton, New York, 17–22 June 1935, *Proceedings*, ed. A.B. Corey, W.W. McLaren, and R.G. Trotter (Boston, 1936), 52.
8 P.E. Corbett, 'A Foreign Policy for Canada,' in *The Liberal Way: A Record of Opinion on Canadian Problems as Expressed and Discussed at the First Liberal Summer Conference, Port Hope, September, 1933*, ed. Liberal party of Canada (Toronto, 1933), 134.
9 Erastus Wiman, 'The Struggle in Canada,' *North American Review* CLII (1891): 348.
10 Ian Grant, 'Erastus Wiman: A Continentalist Replies to Canadian Imperialism,' *Canadian Historical Review* LIII (1972): 4.
11 Henri Bourassa, *The Reciprocity Agreement and Its Consequences as Viewed from the Nationalist Standpoint* (Montreal, 1911), 12, 23, 40.
12 Minville's economic nationalism is examined in Dominique Foisy-Geoffroy, *Esdras Minville. Nationalisme économique et catholicisme social au Québec durant l'entre-deux-guerres* (Sillery, 2004).
13 'L'industrialisation du Canada s'est effectuée sans méthode, et, eu égard au chiffre de notre population, trop rapidement. Des troubles d'ordre social et politique en sont la conséquence … Chaque arrivage de capital étranger dans notre province signifie le recul du jour où notre nationalité pourra enfin secouer le joug économique qui lui pèse aujourd'hui si lourdement.' Esdras Minville, 'L'ennemi dans la place: Le capital étranger,' *L'Action française* XI (1924): 330–1, 338–9.
14 La plus grande république démocratique du monde n'est pas sans prétentions impérialistes,' Minville wrote in 1924, 'elle obéit aux tendances de notre époque et imite l'exemple des grandes puissances européennes … Le dollar est leur arme, et le peuple qui monopolise à l'heure actuelle 48% des réserves d'or du monde, entend bien s'en servir pour propager ses idées et étendre son influence.' Ibid., 333.
15 'L'industrialisation de la province de Québec se poursuivra inévitablement, soit par des Canadiens-français, soit par des étrangers,' Harvey wrote in 1920. 'Il se peut qu'elle comporte parfois des inconvénients; mais dans ce cas nous appliquerons le proverbe: 'Entre deux maux, il faut choisir le moindre.' Or, mieux vaut que nos richesses deviennent la propriété des nôtres que la chose de nos voisins.' J.C. Harvey, *La chasse aux millions: l'avenir industriel du Canada-français* (Quebec, 1920), 5–6, 12.
16 'Convaincus, par auto-suggestion, que notre idéalisme atavique devait

nous tenir au-dessus des biens de ce monde, induits par notre éducation même à mépriser les nations commerciales, nous avons vécu en marge des réalités de la matière, laissant nos voisins, concrets et pratiques, entrer dans notre maison et s'y installer en maîtres ... Par milliers, nos ouvriers font métier de serfs sous une férule étrangère. Un jour viendra, s'il n'est pas venu, où notre prolétariat, conscient de son servage, n'obéissant qu'à des hommes qui ne parlent pas sa langue et ne connaissant rien de ses traditions, croira appartenir à une race inférieure. De cet apparente infériorité naîtra le mépris des siens, et de ce mépris, l'apostasie nationale.' J.C. Harvey, *Marcel Faure* (Montmagny, 1922), 16; *La chasse aux millions*, 15–16.

17 'L'asservissement économique entraîne généralement et à brève échéance la domination politique; si nous tardons davantage à nous qualifier pleinement pour répondre à notre vocation de Français d'Amérique, nous cesserons d'être de bons Canadiens et nous nous préparerons à devenir des Américains quelconques ... La menace la plus sérieuse n'est pas celle qui pénètre sous forme de capital-argent mais celle qui est représentée par le capital moral et intellectuel d'hommes mieux préparés que nous à tirer parti de richesses naturelles que la Providence avait mises à notre disposition et que nous aurons laissées glisser entre nos mains inhabiles ou paresseuses en nous contentant de recevoir en échange un plat de lentilles.' Beaudry Leman, 'Les Canadiens français et le milieu américain,' *Revue trimestrielle canadienne* XIV (1928): 273, 275.

18 Robert Falconer, *The United States as a Neighbour from a Canadian Point of View* (Cambridge, 1925), 164.

19 Herbert Marshall, F.A. Southard, and K.W. Taylor, *Canadian-American Industry: A Study in International Investment* (New Haven and Toronto, 1936), 1.

20 Ibid., 290–1.

21 Ibid., 175, 294.

22 Ibid., 291.

23 It is nevertheless worth noting that one of the earliest intellectual validations of American investment in English Canada was published in the *Canadian Forum*. See J. Marjorie Van der Hoek, 'The Penetration of American Capital in Canada,' *Canadian Forum* VI (1926): 333–5.

24 F.H. Underhill, 'O Canada,' *Canadian Forum* X (1929): 80.

25 'Le syndicalisme international et neutre est pernicieux en soi et dans tous les pays, parce qu'il ne tient aucun compte, dans la recherche des avantages qu'il propose à ses adhérents, de Dieu, de la famille et de la patrie, ces trois assises fondamentales de l'ordre social chrétien.' However, he coninued, 'le péril est incomparablement plus grand ici que partout ail-

leurs, à cause de l'unique voisinage des États-Unis. Le syndicalisme international veut dire, au Canada, le complet assujettissement des travailleurs
canadiens aux caprices et à la domination du travail américain syndiqué.
C'est l'une des manifestations les plus complètes et les plus prenantes de
la conquête morale et économique du Canada par les Etats-Unis.' Henri
Bourassa, *Syndicats nationaux ou internationaux?* (Montreal, 1919), 3.
26 'La neutralité a fait du syndicalisme américain un champ propice à la
contagion des erreurs (révolutionnaires, socialistes); il n'aspire sans cesse
qu'à des réformes de plus en plus égalitaires; il se fait de la sorte, plus ou
moins à son insu, le précurseur du socialisme.' Alfred Charpentier, *De
l'internationalisme au nationalisme* (Montreal, 1920), 13.
27 'Le syndicat ouvrier n'a pas seulement une fonction économique ... il a
aussi une fonction sociale et, par conséquent, morale à remplir.' Catholic
unionism, therefore, 'était nécessaire pour vulgariser et diffuser les princi-
pes supérieurs de la morale sociale catholique, sans laquelle il n'y a point
de solution véritable possible aux problèmes économiques.' Ibid., 11, 14.
28 W.T. Burford, 'Labour Is National,' *Canadian Forum* X (1930): 236–8.
29 Ernest Ingles, 'Labour Organization,' in Conference on Canadian-American Affairs held at Queen's University, Kingston, Ontario, 14–18 June 1937,
Proceedings, ed. A.B. Corey, W.W. McLaren, and R.G. Trotter (Boston, 1937),
177.
30 F.R. Scott, *Canada Today: A Study of Her National Interests and National Policy*
(London, 1938), 67.
31 Yolande Lavoie, *L'émigration des Québécois aux États-Unis de 1840 à 1930*
(Quebec, 1979), 45; L.E. Truesdell, *The Canadian-Born in the United States:
An Analysis of the Statistics of the Canadian Element in the Population of the
United States, 1850 to 1930* (New Haven and Toronto, 1943), 9–10, 26–7, 47.
32 Statistics Canada, *Statistiques historiques du Canada*, 2nd ed. (Ottawa, 1983),
A297–A326; R.H. Coats and M.C. MacLean, *The American-Born in Canada: A
Statistical Interpretation* (Toronto and New Haven, 1943), 3, 56.
33 'Deux millions des nôtres peuplent aujourd'hui le Massachusetts, le New-
Hampshire, le Vermont, le Maine, le Connecticut et le Rhode-Island. Deux
millions! Presque la moitié de notre population perdue, irrévocablement
perdue pour nous avec ses admirables qualités d'endurance physique
et morale! Qu'allaient-ils faire là-bas? Céderaient-ils à un caprice, à un
goût d'aventures? Non. Trop de liens puissants les rattachaient au pays
d'origine pour qu'ils s'exilassent de cœur-joie. S'ils sont partis, c'est qu'un
vice d'organisation sociale les chassait de chez nous; c'est que, pour mieux
vivre, ils sont allés vers une prospérité que nous n'avions pas, comme des
êtres qui ont froid cherchent la flamme qui les réchauffera.' Harvey, *La
chasse aux millions*, 13–14.

34 'Même dans les paroisses les moins affectées, il faut voir les automobiles qui campent pompeusement devant les portes, avec numéro de licence américaine. Ce sont le plus souvent des fils, des frères, des gendres qui viennent avec toute leur richesse, mais aussi avec arrogance, enseigner le luxe, montrer le chemin des États-Unis, scandaliser les humbles habitants de nos hameaux.' G.M. Bilodeau, *Pour rester au pays. Étude sur l'émigration des Canadiens français aux États-Unis. Causes. Remèdes* (Quebec, 1926) 9.

35 'Ce ne sont pas les deux millions qui surnagent encore vaille que vaille aux États-Unis qui constituent notre coulage national; non, ce sont encore les millions de descendants des assimilés de longue date, ces millions de familles possibles, de familles dues, ces générations vigoureuses, qui seraient nées pour nous et qui auraient fait du Canada une Nouvelle-France catholique.' Alexandre Dugré, 'Comment orienter l'émigration,' *L'Action canadienne-française* XX (1928): 77.

36 'C'est à l'époque où nous avions le moins d'industries que la désertion du sol a été la plus fréquente: témoins les millions des nôtres qui sont aujourd'hui aux Etats-Unis. Le réveil industriel, n'eut-il pour résultat que d'arrêter en deçà des lignes le flot des émigrants, nous aurait rendu déjà un fier service.' Harvey, *La chasse aux millions*, 16–17.

37 'Si la nationalité repose sur la parenté du sang, de l'âme et de la langue, ou – pour parler comme les ethnologues et les philosophes – sur l'identité physiologique, psychologique et morale, vous ne pouvez faire que, tout en étant de nationalité américaine, vous ne soyez aussi de nationalité canadienne-française.' Lionel Groulx, *L'amitié française d'Amérique* (Montreal, 1922), 14.

38 'Oui, faire connaître Dieu, publier son nom, propager et défendre tout ce qui constitue le précieux patrimoine des traditions chrétiennes, telle est bien notre vocation. Nous en avons vu les marques certaines, indiscutables. Ce que la France d'Europe a été pour l'ancien monde, la France d'Amérique doit l'être pour ce monde nouveau.' L.A. Pâquet, 'Sermon sur la vocation de la race française en Amérique,' in his *Discours et allocutions* (Quebec, 1915), 193.

39 'Cette dépopulation en masse est sans doute une calamité pour le Canada. Il eût été bien préférable de garder ces hommes au pays, où ils auraient fondé des familles de colons attachés au sol ... Il faut, je crois, regarder plus haut pour comprendre cette migration étrange. La rapidité avec laquelle elle s'est accomplie, la facilité avec laquelle les Canadiens, transplantés sur une terre étrangère, ont immédiatement reformé le moule catholique de la paroisse qui les fit si forts au Canada; l'énergie qu'ils ont déployée pour bâtir des églises, élever des couvents, se grouper ensemble et s'organiser en congrégations florissantes, soutenus au dedans par tout

ce qui peut alimenter la piété chrétienne, défendues contre les influences pernicieuses du dehors par la force de l'association et d'une presse généralement bien dirigée: tous ces éléments de vie catholique organisés en un quart de siècle, au sein même de la citadelle du vieux puritanisme, semblent indiquer, comme je l'ai déjà dit, une action aussi bien qu'une mission providentielle dont l'avenir seul nous révélera toute l'importance ... les Canadiens-Français [sic] accomplissent une mission providentielle; ils concourent pour leur part à la conquête pacifique, au nom de la religion, du sol de la Nouvelle-Angleterre ... Me plaçant exclusivement au point de vue religieux et national, je pense qu'avant longtemps, les deux fractions du peuple Canadien, celle qui habite la terre des ancêtres et celle qui a déjà franchi la frontière américaine se rejoindront et pourront alors se donner la main pour ne plus former qu'un seul peuple.' Édouard Hamon, *Les Canadiens-Français de la Nouvelle-Angleterre* (Quebec, 1891), 5, 11, 145, 155.

40 'Il est évident que ce n'est pas pour jouer le rôle de missionnaire aux États-Unis que le cultivateur abandonne sa terre, que l'ouvrier, s'éloigne avec lui, en se séparant de ce qu'il a de plus cher au monde, sa famille, ses amis, sa patrie.' J.B. Rouilliard, *Annexion: conférence: l'union continentale* (Montreal, 1893), 9.

41 Falconer, *United States as a Neigbour*, 206; 'The Unification of Canada,' *University Magazine* VII (1908): 8–9.

42 Hugh Keenleyside, *Canada and the United States: Some Aspects of the History of the Republic and the Dominion* (New York, 1929), 345.

43 J.B. Brebner, *North Atlantic Triangle*, 302.

44 W.A. Deacon, 'The Bogey of Annexation,' in his *Poteen: A Pot-Pourri of Canadian Essays* (Ottawa, 1926), 20.

45 [Andrew Macphail], 'Canadian Writers and American Politics,' *University Magazine* IX (1910): 3.

46 Falconer, *United States as a Neigbour*, 33–4, 180.

47 'Une politique d'immigration imprévoyante a laissé se parquer dans la partie occidentale du pays, l'élément américain, celui-là même qui pouvait miner le plus activement l'unité canadienne.' [Lionel Groulx], 'Notre avenir politique,' *L'Action française* VII (1922): 11.

Conclusion

1 'Les États-Unis quoique jeunes ont tous les signes de la décadence,' wrote the secretary-general of the Ligue d'action française, Anatole Vanier, in 1922. An influential nationalist who practised law in Montreal, Vanier believed that 'l'irréligion, la·corruption des mœurs, la ruine des familles par

le divorce, le lynch, les divisions intestines entre blancs et noirs, entre capitalistes et ouvriers, l'absolutisme de la ploutocratie, le réveil des races non-anglo-saxonnes [et] la trop grande étendue de territoire,' would ultimately destroy the American Republic. Anatole Vanier, 'Notre avenir politique: L'État français et les États-Unis,' *L'Action française* VII (1922): 334.

2 Patricia K. Wood, 'Defining "Canadian": Anti-Americanism and Identity in Sir John A. Macdonald's Nationalism,' *Journal of Canadian Studies* 36 (2001): 50.

3 Carl Berger, *The Sense of Power: Studies in the Ideas of Canadian Imperialism, 1867–1914* (Toronto, 1970), 153.

4 Jackson Lears, *No Place of Grace: Antimodernism and the Transformation of American Culture, 1880–1920* (New York, 1981), xiii.

5 Alan Bowker, Introduction, in Stephen Leacock, *The Social Criticism of Stephen Leacock* (Toronto, 1973), xv.

6 Norman Hillmer, 'Skelton, Oscar Douglas,' *Canadian Encyclopedia*, 2nd ed.

7 James Laxer, 'The Americanization of the Canadian Student Movement,' in *Close the 49th Parallel etc.: The Americanization of Canada*, ed. Ian Lumsden (Toronto, 1970), 276; Gerald L. Caplan and James Laxer, 'Perspectives on Un-American Traditions in Canada,' in ibid., 306.

8 Robin Mathews quoted in J.L. Granatstein, *Yankee Go Home? Canadians and Anti-Americanism* (Toronto, 1996), 206–7.

9 Brian Fawcett quoted in ibid., 259.

10 James Laxer quoted in Charles Taylor, *Radical Tories: The Conservative Tradition in Canada* (Toronto, 1982), 148.

11 André Major, 'The Decline of America,' in *The New Romans: Candid Canadian Opinions of the U.S.*, ed. Al Purdy (New York, 1968), 141.

12 Lauren McKinsey and Victor Konrad, *Borderlands Reflections: The United States and Canada* (Orono, Maine, 1989), iii, 1.

Bibliography

Serials Examined

Over one hundred Canadian serials were examined for this study. Although a number of articles in this study's corpus were drawn from British and American publications, only five foreign reviews were systematically scrutinized for relevant material: the *North American Review*, the *Quarterly Journal of Inter-American Relations*, the *Inter-American Quarterly*, the *Annals of the American Academy of Political and Social Science*, and the *Round Table*. These journals actively sought the contribution of Canadian authors and devoted sufficient space to Canadian affairs to justify a detailed examination. The dates following a journal's title indicate the period examined and are preceded by its place of publication. In many instances, these dates correspond to the time when the journal appeared and when publication ceased.

Acadiensis (St John, NB, 1901–8)
L'Action canadienne-française (Montreal, 1928)
L'Action française (Montreal, 1917–27)
L'Action nationale (Montreal, 1933–45)
L'Action universitaire (Montreal, 1934–45)
L'Actualité économique (Montreal, 1925–45)
Addresses Delivered before the Canadian Club of Montreal (Montreal, 1912–19)
Addresses Delivered before the Canadian Club of Toronto (Toronto, 1903–39)
Addresses Read before the Canadian Club of Ottawa (Ottawa, 1903–18)
Amérique française (Montreal, 1941–45)
Annals of the American Academy of Political and Social Science (Philadelphia, 1891–1945)
Annual Transactions of the United Empire Loyalists' Association of Canada (Toronto, 1914–45)

Annual Transactions of the United Empire Loyalists' Association of Ontario
   (Toronto, 1898–1913)
The Anvil (Vancouver, 1931)
Behind the Headlines (Toronto, 1940–5)
La Bonne parole (Montreal, 1913–45)
The British Columbia Argonaut (Victoria, BC, 1931)
British Columbia Historical Quarterly (Victoria, BC, 1937–45)
The British Pacific (Cumberland, BC, 1902)
Les Cahiers de Turc (Montreal, 1921–2, 1926–7)
Canada First (Toronto, 1905–7)
Le Canada-Français (Quebec, 1891)
Le Canada français (Quebec, 1918–45)
Canada Law Journal (Toronto, 1891–1922)
Canadian Annual Review of Public Affairs (Toronto, 1902–38)
Canadian Banker (Toronto, 1936–45)
Canadian Bar Review (Ottawa, 1923–45)
Canadian Bookman (Toronto, 1919–39)
Canadian Comment (Toronto, 1932–8)
Canadian Congress Journal (Ottawa, 1924–44)
Canadian Defence (Welland, Ont., 1912–17)
Canadian Defence Quarterly (Ottawa, 1923–39)
Canadian Field (Welland, Ont., 1909–11)
Canadian Forum (Toronto, 1920–45)
Canadian Historical Association *Annual Report* (Ottawa, 1922–45)
Canadian Historical Review (Toronto, 1920–45)
Canadian Independence Magazine (Montreal, 1930)
Canadian Journal of Economics and Political Science (Toronto, 1935–45)
Canadian Journal of Religious Thought (Toronto, 1924–32)
Canadian Law Review (Toronto, 1901–7)
Canadian Magazine (Toronto, 1893–1937)
Canadian Mercury (Montreal, 1928–9)
Canadian Methodist Review (Toronto, 1894–5)
Canadian Republic Magazine (Montreal, 1929–30)
Canadian Unionist (Hull, Que., 1927–45)
Les Carnets viatoriens (Joliette, Que., 1939–45)
Culture (Quebec, 1940–5)
Dalhousie Review (Halifax, 1921–45)
Dominion Magazine (Toronto, 1908)
Dominion Review (Montreal, 1896–9)
L'École sociale populaire (Montreal, 1911–45)

Empire Club of Canada Addresses (Toronto, 1912–45)
Empire Club Speeches (Toronto, 1903–11)
L'Enseignement secondaire au Canada (Quebec, 1915–45)
First Statement (Montreal, 1942–5)
The Great West Magazine (Winnipeg, 1891–8)
Les Idées (Montreal, 1935–9)
Industrial Canada (Toronto, 1900–45)
Inter-American Quarterly (Washington, DC, 1940–1)
Journal of the Canadian Bankers' Association (Toronto, 1893–1936)
Labour Review (Hull, Que., 1936–40)
Knox College Monthly and Presbyterian Magazine (Toronto, 1891–6)
Laval théologique et philosophique (Quebec, 1945)
McGill Fortnightly Review (Montreal, 1925–7)
The McGilliad (Montreal, 1930–1)
McGill University Magazine (Montreal, 1901–6)
Masses (Toronto, 1932–4)
Methodist Magazine (Toronto, 1891–4)
Methodist Magazine and Review (Toronto, 1896–1906)
The Moccasin Prints (Montreal, 1912–13)
Morang's Annual Register of Canadian Affairs (Toronto, 1901)
National Monthly of Canada (Toronto, 1902–5)
New Brunswick Magazine (St John, NB, 1898–1905)
New Frontier (Toronto, 1936–7)
Le Nigog (Montreal, 1918)
North American Notes and Queries (Quebec, 1900–1)
North American Review (New York, 1891–1939)
La Nouvelle-France (Quebec, 1902–18)
La Nouvelle Relève (Montreal, 1941–5)
L'Œuvre des tracts (Montreal, 1919–45)
Oxford Pamphlets on World Affairs: Canadian Series (Toronto, 1939–40)
Les Pamphlets de Valdombre (Sainte-Adèle, Que., 1936–43)
Preview (Montreal, 1942–5)
Prince Edward Island Magazine (Charlottetown, PEI, 1899–1905)
Proceedings and Transactions of the Royal Society of Canada (Ottawa, 1891–1945)
Public Affairs (Halifax, 1937–45)
Quarterly Journal of Inter-American Relations (Cambridge, Mass., 1939)
Queen's Quarterly (Kingston, Ont., 1893–1945)
The Rebel (Toronto, 1917–20)
Regards (Quebec, 1940–2)
Relations (Montreal, 1941–5)

La Relève (Montreal, 1934–41)

Report on the Work of the Canadian Institute of International Affairs (Toronto, 1933–45)

Review of Historical Publications Relating to Canada (Toronto, 1896–1918)

La Revue acadienne (Montreal, 1917–18)

Revue du barreau (Montreal, 1941–5)

La Revue canadienne (Montreal, 1891–1922)

Revue dominicaine (Saint–Hyacinthe, Que., 1915–45)

Revue du droit (Quebec, 1922–39)

Revue économique canadienne (Montreal, 1911–14)

La Revue franco-américaine (Montreal, 1908–13)

La Revue libre (Montreal, 1915–16)

La Revue nationale (Montreal, 1895–6)

La Revue nationale (Montreal, 1919–32)

Revue trimestrielle canadienne (Montreal, 1915–45)

Revue de l'Université d'Ottawa (Ottawa, 1931–45)

Le Rosaire (Saint-Hyacinthe, Que., 1902–14)

The Round Table (London, 1910–45)

Selected Papers from the Transactions of the Canadian Military Institute (Toronto, 1891–1945)

Semaines sociales du Canada (Montreal, 1920–45)

Le Semeur (Montreal, 1904–35)

Trades and Labor Congress Journal (Ottawa, 1944–5)

University Magazine (Montreal, 1907–20)

University Monthly (Toronto, 1907–18)

University of Ottawa Review (Ottawa, 1898–1915)

University of Toronto Monthly (Toronto, 1900–7)

University of Toronto Quarterly (Toronto, 1895–6)

University of Toronto Quarterly (Toronto, 1931–45)

The Westminster (Toronto, 1896–1916)

Willison's Monthly (Toronto, 1925–9)

Secondary Sources

Works of Reference

Amtmann, Bernard. *Contributions to a Dictionary of Canadian Pseudonyms and Anonymous Works Related to Canada*. Montreal: Amtmann, 1973.

Bullock, Alan, and Oliver Stallybrass, eds. *The Harper Dictionary of Modern Thought*. New York: Harper and Row, 1977.

Cook, Ramsay, ed. *Dictionary of Canadian Biography*, vols. XII–XIV. Toronto: University of Toronto Press, 1990–1998.

Dion-Lévesque, Rosaire. *Silhouettes franco-américaines*. Manchester, NH: Association canado-américaine, 1957.

Hamel, Réginald, John Hare, and Paul Wyczynski. *Dictionnaire des auteurs de langue française en Amérique du Nord*. Montreal: Fides, 1989.

Hamelin, Jean, and André Beaulieu. *Les journaux du Québec de 1764 à 1964*. Quebec: Presses de l'Université Laval, 1965.

Hart, James D. *The Oxford Companion to American Literature*, 4th ed. New York: Oxford University Press, 1965.

Johnson, Thomas H., and Harvey Wish. *The Oxford Companion to American History*. New York: Oxford University Press, 1966.

Lemire, Maurice, ed. *Dictionnaire des œuvres littéraires du Québec*, vols. I–III, 2nd ed. Montreal: Fides, 1987–1995.

Marsh, James H., ed. *The Canadian Encyclopedia*, 4 vols., 2nd ed. Edmonton: Hurtig, 1988.

Morgan, Henry James, ed. *The Canadian Men and Women of the Time: A Hand-Book of Canadian Biography*, 1st ed. Toronto: Briggs, 1898.

– *The Canadian Men and Women of the Time: A Hand-Book of Canadian Biography of Living Characters*, 2nd ed. Toronto: Briggs, 1912.

Myers, Jan. *The Fitzhenry and Whiteside Book of Canadian Facts and Dates*, revised and updated by Larry Hoffman and Fraser Sutherland. Richmond Hill: Fitzhenry and Whiteside, 1991.

Story, Norah. *The Oxford Companion to Canadian History and Literature*. Toronto: Oxford University Press, 1967.

Toye, William, ed. *The Oxford Companion to Canadian Literature*. Toronto: Oxford University Press, 1983.

– *Supplement to the Oxford Companion to Canadian History and Literature*. Toronto: Oxford University Press, 1973.

Vinet, Bernard. *Pseudonymes québécois*. Quebec: Éditions Garneau, 1974.

Wallace, W. Stewart. *The Macmillan Dictionary of Canadian Biography*, 3rd ed. Toronto: Macmillan, 1963.

Wiener, Philip P., ed. *Dictionary of the History of Ideas*, 5 vols. New York: Scribners, 1968.

Books

Allen, Donald Roy. *French Views of America in the 1930s*. New York: Garland, 1979.

Bélanger, Damien-Claude, Sophie Coupal, and Michel Ducharme, eds. *Les idées en mouvement: perspectives en histoire intellectuelle et culturelle du Canada.* Quebec: Presses de l'Université Laval, 2004.

Berger, Carl. *The Sense of Power: Studies in the Ideas of Canadian Imperialism, 1867–1914.* Toronto: University of Toronto Press, 1970.

– *The Writing of Canadian History: Aspects of English-Canadian Historical Writing Since 1900,* 2nd ed. Toronto: University of Toronto Press, 1988.

Bergeron, Gérard. *Quand Tocqueville et Siegfried nous observaient...* Sillery, Que.: Presses de l'Université du Québec, 1990.

Bothwell, Robert, Ian Drummond, and John English. *Canada since 1945: Power, Politics, and Provincialism.* Toronto: University of Toronto Press, 1981.

Bouchard, Gérard. *Genèse des nations et cultures du Nouveau Monde. Essai d'histoire comparée.* Montreal: Boréal, 2000.

Bouchard, Gérard, and Yvan Lamonde, eds. *Québécois et Américains: la culture québécoise aux XIXe et XXe siècles.* Montreal: Fides, 1995.

Bothwell, Robert, Ian Drummond, and John English. *Canada, 1900–1945.* Toronto: University of Toronto Press, 1987.

Brooks, Stephen. *America through Foreign Eyes: Classical Interpretations of American Political Life.* Don Mills: Oxford University Press, 2002.

Brown, Robert Craig, and Ramsay Cook. *Canada, 1896–1921: A Nation Transformed.* Toronto: McClelland and Stewart, 1974.

Bryce, James. *The American Commonwealth,* 2 vols., 2nd ed. Chicago: C.H. Sergel, 1891.

Charle, Christophe. *Naissance des 'intellectuels,' 1880–1900.* Paris: Éd. de Minuit, 1990.

Chassay, Jean-François. *L'ambiguité américaine..Le roman québécois face aux États-Unis.* Montreal: XYZ, 1995.

Cook, Ramsay. *The Politics of John W. Dafoe and the* Free Press. Toronto: University of Toronto Press, 1963.

– *The Maple Leaf Forever: Essays on Nationalism and Politics in Canada,* 2nd ed. Toronto: Macmillan, 1977.

– *The Regenerators: Social Criticism in Late Victorian English Canada.* Toronto: University of Toronto Press, 1985.

Courville, Serge. *Immigration, colonisation et propagande: du rêve américain au rêve colonial.* Sainte-Foy, Que.: Éditions MultiMondes, 2002.

Djwa, Sandra. *F.R. Scott, une vie.* Montreal: Boréal, 2001.

Duhamel, Georges. *Scènes de la vie future.* Paris: Mercure de France, 1930.

Edmunds, June, and Bryan S. Turner. *Generations, Culture, and Society.* Buckingham: Open University Press, 2002.

Francis, R. Douglas. *Frank H. Underhill, Intellectual Provocateur.* Toronto: University of Toronto Press, 1986.

Gagnon, Serge. *Quebec and Its Historians*, 2 vols. Montreal: Harvest House, 1982–1985.

Galarneau, Claude. *Edmond de Nevers, essayiste*. Quebec: Presses de l'Université Laval, 1960.

Granatstein, J.L. *How Britain's Weakness Forced Canada into the Arms of the United States*. Toronto: University of Toronto Press, 1989.

– *Yankee Go Home? Canadians and Anti-Americanism*. Toronto: Harper Collins, 1996.

Grant, George. *Lament for a Nation: The Defeat of Canadian Nationalism*, new ed. Toronto: McClelland and Stewart, 1970 [1965].

Greenlee, James G. *Sir Robert Falconer: A Biography*. Toronto: University of Toronto Press, 1988.

Hofstadter, Richard. *The Age of Reform from Bryan to F.D.R.* New York: Vintage Books, 1955.

Hollander, Paul. *Anti-Americanism: Critiques at Home and Abroad, 1965–1990*. New York: Oxford University Press, 1992.

Innis, Hugh, ed. *Americanization*. Toronto: McGraw-Hill and Ryerson, 1972.

Kirk, Russell. *The Conservative Mind from Burke to Eliot*, 7th rev. ed. Chicago: Regnery Books, 1986.

Klinck, Carl F., ed. *Literary History of Canada: Canadian Literature in English*, 3 vols., 2nd ed. Toronto: University of Toronto Press, 1976.

Knowles, Norman. *Inventing the Loyalists: The Ontario Loyalist Tradition and the Creation of Usable Pasts*. Toronto: University of Toronto Press, 1997.

Kohn, Edward P. *This Kindred People: Canadian-American Relations and the Anglo-Saxon Idea, 1895–1903*. Montreal and Kingston: McGill-Queen's University Press, 2004.

LaCapra, Dominick. *Rethinking Intellectual History: Texts, Contexts, Language*. Ithaca, NY: Cornell University Press, 1983.

Lacombe, Sylvie. *La rencontre de deux peuples élus. Comparaison des ambitions nationale et impériale au Canada entre 1896 et 1920*. Quebec: Presses de l'Université Laval, 2002.

Lacorne, Denis, Jacques Rupnik, and Marie-France Toinet, eds. *The Rise and Fall of French Anti-Americanism: A Century of French Perception*. New York: St Martin's Press, 1990.

Lamonde, Yvan. *Ni avec eux ni sans eux: le Québec et les États-Unis*. Montreal: Nuit Blanche, 1996.

– *Allégeances et dépendances. Histoire d'une ambivalence identitaire*. Quebec: Nota bene, 2001.

– *Histoire sociale des idées au Québec, 1896–1929*. Montreal: Fides, 2004.

Leacock, Stephen. *The Social Criticism of Stephen Leacock*, edited and introduced by Alan Bowker. Toronto: University of Toronto Press, 1973.

Lears, T.J. Jackson. *No Place of Grace: Antimodernism and the Transformation of American Culture, 1880–1920*. New York: Pantheon Books, 1981.

Levine, Lawrence. *Highbrow/Lowbrow: The Emergence of Cultural Hierarchy in America*. Cambridge, Mass.: Harvard University Press, 1988.

Lower, A.R.M. *Canada: Nation and Neighbour*. Toronto: Ryerson Press, 1952.

– *My First Seventy-Five Years*. Toronto: Macmillan, 1967.

Lumsden, Ian, ed. *Close the 49th Parallel etc.: The Americanization of Canada*. Toronto: University of Toronto Press, 1970.

McKillop, A.B. *A Disciplined Intelligence: Critical Inquiry and Canadian Thought in the Victorian Era*. Montreal: McGill-Queen's, 1979.

McKinsey, Lauren, and Victor Konrad. *Borderlands Reflections: The United States and Canada*. Oronro, Me: Borderlands Project, 1989.

Mahant, Edelgard E., and Graeme S. Mount. *An Introduction to Canadian-American Relations*, 2nd ed. Scarborough: Nelson Canada, 1989.

Massolin, Philip. *Canadian Intellectuals, the Tory Tradition, and the Challenge of Modernity, 1939–1970*. Toronto: University of Toronto Press, 2001.

Masters, D.C. *Reciprocity, 1846–1911*. Ottawa: Canadian Historical Association, 1965.

Moffett, Samuel E. *The Americanization of Canada*, reprinted with an introduction by Allan Smith. Toronto: University of Toronto Press, 1972.

Morton, W.L. *The Canadian Identity*. Toronto: University of Toronto Press, 1964.

Nouss, Alexis. *La modernité*. Paris: Presses universitaires de France, 1995.

Novick, Peter. *That Noble Dream: The 'Objectivity Question' and the American Historical Profession*. Cambridge: Cambridge University Press, 1988.

Ory, Pascal, and Jean-François Sirinelli. *Les intellectuels en France, de l'Affaire Dreyfus à nos jours*. Paris: Armand Colin, 1986.

Phillips, Kevin. *The Cousins' Wars: Religion, Politics, and the Triumph of Anglo-America*. New York: Basic Books, 1999.

Revel, Jean-François. *L'obsession anti–américaine: son fonctionnement, ses causes, ses inconséquences*. Paris: Plon, 2002.

Roby, Yves. *Les Québécois et les investissements américains (1918–1929)*. Quebec: Presses de l'Université Laval, 1976.

– *Les Franco-Américains de la Nouvelle-Angleterre. Rêves et réalités*. Sillery, Que.: Septentrion, 2000.

Romier, Lucien. *Qui sera le maître, Europe ou Amérique?* Paris: Hachette, 1927.

Romney, Paul. *Getting It Wrong: How Canadians Forgot their Past and Imperilled Confederation*. Toronto: University of Toronto Press, 1999.

Rousseau, Guildo. *L'image des États-Unis dans la littérature québécoise (1775–1930)*. Sherbrooke, Que.: Naaman, 1981.

Roy, Fernande. *Histoire des idéologies au Québec aux XIXe et XXe siècles*. Montreal: Boréal, 1993.

Roy, Mario. *Pour en finir avec l'antiaméricanisme*. Montreal: Boréal, 1993.

Roz, Firmin. *L'évolution des idées et des mœurs américaines*. Paris: Flammarion, 1931.

Rudin, Ronald. *Faire de l'histoire au Québec*. Sillery, Que.: Septentrion, 1998.

Ryan, Pascale. *Penser la nation. La Ligue d'action nationale, 1917–1960*. Montreal: Leméac, 2006.

Savard, Pierre. *Jules-Paul Tardivel, la France et les États-Unis, 1851–1905*. Quebec: Presses de l'Université Laval, 1967.

Shortt, Samuel Edward D. *The Search for an Ideal: Six Canadian Intellectuals and Their Convictions in an Age of Transition, 1890–1930*. Toronto: University of Toronto Press, 1976.

Shotwell, James T. *The Autobiography of James T. Shotwell*. New York: Bobbs-Merrill, 1961.

Siegfried, André. *Le Canada: les deux races: problèmes politiques contemporains*. Paris: Armand Colin, 1906.

– *Les États-Unis d'aujourd'hui*. Paris: A. Colin, 1927.

Skotheim, Robert Allen. *American Intellectual Histories and Historians*. Princeton: Princeton University Press, 1966.

Smith, Allan. *Canada: An American Nation? Essays on Continentalism, Identity and the Canadian Frame of Mind*. Montreal and Kingston: McGill-Queen's University Press, 1994.

Smith, Goldwin. *Canada and the Canadian Question*, reprinted with an introduction by Carl Berger. Toronto: University of Toronto Press, 1971.

Strauss, David. *Menace in the West: The Rise of French Anti-Americanism in Modern Times*. Westport: Greenwood Press, 1978.

Taylor, Charles. *Radical Tories: The Conservative Tradition in Canada*. Toronto: Anansi, 1982.

Thériault, Joseph Yvon. *Critique de l'américanité. Mémoire et démocratie au Québec*. Montreal: Québec Amérique, 2002.

Thompson, John Herd, and Stephen J. Randall. *Canada and the United States: Ambivalent Allies*, 3rd ed. Montreal and Kingston: McGill-Queen's University Press, 2002.

Tocqueville, Alexis. *De la démocratie en Amérique*, 2 vols., preface and bibliography by François Furet. Paris: Flammarion, 1981.

Trofimenkoff, Susan Mann. *Action française: French Canadian Nationalism in the Twenties*. Toronto: University of Toronto Press, 1975.

Underhill, Frank H. *In Search of Canadian Liberalism*. Toronto: Macmillan, 1960.
– *The Image of Confederation*. Toronto: CBC Publications, 1964.
Wallace, Elisabeth. *Goldwin Smith, Victorian Liberal*. Toronto: University of Toronto Press, 1957.
Warner, Donald F. *The Idea of Continental Union: Agitation for the Annexation of Canada to the United States, 1849–1893*. [n.p.]: University of Kentucky Press, 1960.
Warren, Jean-Philippe. *Edmond de Nevers: portrait d'un intellectuel, 1862–1906*. Montreal: Boréal, 2005.
Wiebe, Robert H. *The Search for Order, 1877–1920*. New York: Hill and Wang, 1967.
Winks, Robin W. *The Relevance of Canadian History: U.S. and Imperial Perspectives*. Toronto: Macmillan, 1979.
Wise, S.F., and Robert Craig Brown. *Canada Views the United States: Nineteenth-Century Political Attitudes*. Toronto: Macmillan, 1967.

Articles

Aggarwalla, Rohit T. '"Non-Resident Me": John Bartlet Brebner and the Canadian Historical Profession.' *Journal of the Canadian Historical Association* 10 (1999): 237–77.
Baker, William M. 'A Case Study of Anti-Americanism in English-Speaking Canada: The Election Campaign of 1911.' *Canadian Historical Review* 51 (1970): 426–49.
– 'The Anti-American Ingredient in Canadian History.' *Dalhousie Review* 53 (1973): 57–77.
Balthazar, Louis. 'Les relations canado-américaines: nationalisme et continentalisme.' *Études internationales* 14 (1983): 23–37.
Barkley, Murray. 'The Loyalist Tradition in New Brunswick: The Growth and Evolution of an Historical Myth, 1825–1914.' *Acadiensis* 4 (1975): 3–45.
Bélanger, Damien-Claude. 'Lionel Groulx and Franco-America.' *American Review of Canadian Studies* 33 (2003): 373–89.
Berger, Carl. 'Internationalism, Continentalism and the Writing of History: Comments on the Carnegie Series on the Relations of Canada and the United States.' In *The Influence of the United States on Canadian Development: Eleven Case Studies*, ed. R.A. Preston, 32–54. Durham: Duke University Press, 1972.
Bourinot, John G. 'Canada and the United States: A Study in Comparative Politics.' *Annals of the American Academy of Political and Social Science* 1 (1890): 1–25.

Brown, Robert Craig. 'Goldwin Smith and Anti-Imperialism.' *Canadian Histori-cal Review* 43 (1962): 93–105.

– 'The Commercial Unionists in Canada and the United States.' Canadian Historical Association *Annual Report* (1963): 116–24.

Campbell, Sandra. 'From Romantic History to Communications Theory: Lorne Pierce as Publisher of C.W. Jeffreys and Harold Innis.' *Journal of Canadian Studies* 30 (1995): 91–116.

Carr, Graham. '"All We North Americans": Literary Culture and the Conti-nentalist Ideal, 1919–1939.' *American Review of Canadian Studies* 17 (1987): 145–57.

Ceaser, James W. 'A Genealogy of Anti-Americanism.' *The Public Interest* 152 (2003): 3–18.

Cotnam, Jacques. 'Americans Viewed through the Eyes of French-Canadians.' *Journal of Popular Culture* 10 (1977): 784–96.

– 'La prise de conscience d'une identité nord-américaine au Canada français, 1930–1939.' In *Les grands voisins*, ed. G. Kurgan, 63–79. Brussels: Éditions de l'Université de Bruxelles, 1984.

Creighton, D.G. 'The Ogdensburg Agreement and F.H. Underhill.' In *The West and the Nation: Essays in Honour of W.L. Morton*, ed. C. Berger and R. Cook, 300–20. Toronto: McClelland and Stewart, 1976.

Cumming, Carman. 'The Toronto *Daily Mail*, Edward Farrer, and the Question of Canadian-American Union.' *Journal of Canadian Studies* 24 (1989): 121–39.

Distad, N. Merrill, and Linda Merrill. 'Canada.' In *Periodicals of Queen Vic-toria's Empire: An Exploration*, ed. J. Don Vann and R.T. Vanarsdel, 60–174. Toronto: University of Toronto Press, 1996.

Doran, Charles F., and James P. Sewell. 'Anti-Americanism in Canada?' *Annals of the American Academy of Political and Social Science* 497 (1988): 105–19.

Duncan, Sara Jeannette. 'American Influence on Canadian Thought' [1887]. In *The Search for English-Canadian Literature: An Anthology of Critical Articles from the Nineteenth and Early Twentieth Centuries*, ed. Carl Ballstadt, 36–41. Toronto: University of Toronto Press, 1975.

Gaudreau, Guy, and Micheline Tremblay. 'Harry Bernard (1898–1979): érudit et homme de lettres.' *Mens* 2 (2001): 35–65.

Gilbert, A.D. 'On the Road to New York: The Protective Impulse and the English-Canadian Cultural Identity, 1896–1914.' *Dalhousie Review* 58 (1978): 405–17.

Gilpin, Robert. 'American Direct Investment and Canada's Two National-isms.' In *The Influence of the United States on Canadian Development: Eleven Case Studies*, ed. R.A. Preston, 124–43. Durham: Duke University Press, 1972.

Grant, Ian. 'Erastus Wiman: A Continentalist Replies to Canadian Imperialism.' *Canadian Historical Review* 53 (1972): 1–20.

Johnston, Richard, and Michael B. Percy. 'Reciprocity, Imperial Sentiment, and Party Politics in the 1911 Election.' *Canadian Journal of Political Science* 13 (1980): 711–29.

Jones, Richard A. 'French Canada and the American Peril in the Twentieth Century.' *American Review of Canadian Studies* 14 (1984): 333–50.

– 'Le spectre de l'américanisation.' In *Les rapports culturels entre le Québec et les États-Unis*, ed. C. Savary, 145–69. Quebec: Institut québécois de recherche sur la culture, 1984.

Kendall, John C. 'A Canadian Construction of Reality: Northern Images of the United States.' *American Review of Canadian Studies* 4 (1974): 20–36.

Kresl, Peter. 'Before the Deluge: Canadians on Foreign Ownership, 1920–1955.' *American Review of Canadian Studies* 6 (1976): 86–126.

Lacombe, Sylvie. 'La comparaison pour quoi faire? À la recherche des "totalités sociales" dans le contexte canadien.' In *La nation dans tous ses États: le Québec en comparaison*, ed. G. Bouchard and Y. Lamonde, 205–20. Montreal: Harmattan, 1997.

Lamonde, Yvan. 'La modernité au Québec: pour une histoire des brèches (1895–1950).' In *L'avènement de la modernité culturelle au Québec*, ed. Y. Lamonde and E. Trépanier, 299–311. Quebec: Institut québécois de recherche sur la culture, 1986.

– 'Les "intellectuels" francophones au Québec au XIXe siècle: questions préalables.' *Revue d'histoire de l'Amérique française* 48 (1994): 153–85.

– 'Le regard sur les États-Unis: le révélateur d'un clivage social dans la culture nationale québécoise.' *Journal of Canadian Studies* 30 (1995): 69–74.

– '"Être de son temps": pourquoi, comment?' In *Constructions de la modernité au Québec*, ed. G. Michaud and É. Nardout-Lafarge, 23–36. Montreal: Lanctôt éditeur, 2004.

– 'Américanité et américanisation. Essai de mise au point.' *Globe* 7 (2004): 21–9.

LeBlanc, Robert G. 'The Francophone Conquest of New England: Geopolitical Conceptions and Imperial Ambition of French-Canadian Nationalists in the Nineteenth Century.' *American Review of Canadian Studies* 15 (1985): 288–310.

Lennox, John. 'Canadian-American Literary Relations in the 1920s: A Canadian Perspective.' In *Les grands voisins*, ed. G. Kurgan, 43–61. Brussels: Éditions de l'Université de Bruxelles, 1984.

Mackey, William F. 'Les grands voisins des Anglo-Canadiens: une histoire de triple identité nationale.' In *Les grands voisins*, ed. G. Kurgan, 109–18. Brussels: Éditions de l'Université de Bruxelles, 1984.

McAndrew William J. 'Weighing a Wild-Cat on the Kitchen Scales: Canadians Evaluate the New Deal.' *American Review of Canadian Studies* 4 (1974): 23–45.

Ory, Pascal. 'Qu'est-ce qu'un intellectuel?' In his *Dernières questions aux intellectuels et quatre essais pour y répondre*, 11–50. Paris: Olivier Orban, 1990.

Page, Donald M. 'Canada as the Exponent of North American Idealism.' *American Review of Canadian Studies* 3 (1973): 30–46.

Rawlyk, George A. '"A Question of Self or no Self": Some Reflexions on the English-Canadian Identity within the Context of Canadian-U.S. Relations.' *Humanities Association Review* 30 (1979): 281–301.

Roby, Yves. 'Un Québec émigré aux États-Unis: bilan historiographique.' In *Les rapports culturels entre le Québec et les États-Unis*, ed. C. Savary, 103–29. Quebec: Institut québécois de recherche sur la culture, 1984.

Ross, Malcom. 'Goldwin Smith.' In *Our Living Tradition, Seven Canadians*, ed. Claude T. Bissell, 29–47. Toronto: University of Toronto Press, 1957.

Rubinstein, Alvin Z., and Donald E. Smith. 'Anti-Americanism: Anatomy of a Phenomenon.' In their *Anti-Americanism in the Third World: Implications for U.S. Foreign Policy*, 1–30. New York: Praeger, 1985.

Ryan, Pascale. 'Des intellectuels en Europe et en Amérique. Un état de la question.' *Mens* 4 (2003): 9–37.

Sénécal, André. 'La thèse messianique et les Franco-Américains.' *Revue d'histoire de l'Amérique française* 34 (1981): 557–67.

Sénécal, Gilles. 'Les idéologies territoriales au Canada français: entre le continentalisme et l'idée du Québec.' *Journal of Canadian Studies* 27 (1992): 49–62.

Sirinelli, Jean-François. 'Effets d'âge et pénomènes de génération dans le milieu intellectuel français.' *Cahiers de l'IHTP* 6 (1987): 5–18.

Smith, Allan. 'Doing the Continental: Conceptualizations of the Canadian-American Relationship in the Long Twentieth Century.' *Canadian-American Public Policy* 44 (2000): 2–70.

Stuart, Reginald C. 'Continentalism Revisited: Recent Narratives on the History of Canadian-American Relations.' *Diplomatic History* 18 (1994): 405–14.

– 'Anti-Americanism in Canadian History.' *American Review of Canadian Studies* 27 (1997): 293–310.

Tausky, Thomas E. 'In search of a Canadian Liberal: The Case of Sara Jeannette Duncan.' *Ontario History* 83 (1991): 85–108.

Trépanier, Pierre. 'Notes pour une histoire des droites intellectuelles canadiennes-françaises à travers leurs principaux représentants (1770–1970).' *Cahiers des Dix* 48 (1993): 119–64.

– 'Le maurrassisme au Canada français,' *Cahiers des Dix* 53 (1999): 167–233.

Winks, Robin W. 'The American Exile.' In *Ireland and America, 1776–1976: The*

American Identity and the Irish Connection, ed. D.N. Doyle and O.D. Edwards, 43–56. Westport: Greenwood Press, 1980.

Winock, Michel. '"U.S. Go Home": l'antiaméricanisme français.' *L'Histoire* 50 (1982): 7–20.

Wood, Patricia K. 'Defining "Canadian": Anti-Americanism and Identity in Sir John A. Macdonald's Nationalism.' *Journal of Canadian Studies* 36 (2001): 49–69.

Wright, Donald A. 'W.D. Lighthall and David Ross McCord: Antimodernism and English-Canadian Imperialism, 1880s–1918.' *Journal of Canadian Studies* 32 (1997): 134–53.

Unpublished Theses and Dissertations

Bélanger, Damien-Claude. 'Pride and Prejudice: Canadian Intellectuals Confront the United States, 1891–1945.' Ph.D. dissertation, McGill University, 2005.

Bragdon, Chandler. 'Canadian Attitudes to the Foreign Policy of the United States, 1935–1939.' Ph.D. dissertation, University of Rochester, 1961.

Ronyk, Gwenneth H. 'The United States in the Twenties as Seen by the Western Canadian Press.' M.A. thesis, University of Regina, 1979.

Weaver, John C. 'Imperilled Dreams: Canadian Opposition to the American Empire, 1918–1930.' Ph.D. dissertation, Duke University, 1973.

Index

African Americans, 96–9, 122, 142
American English, 82, 84
American Federation of Labor, 196, 197
Americanism (heresy), 265n49, 270n21
américanité (concept), 4, 253n11
American Revolution, 59–61, 116, 122–3, 163, 181
American sources and inspiration for Canadian writing on the United States, 42–4
Angers, François-Albert, 153–4, 172–3
Anglo-American relations, 162, 165, 168
Anglo-Saxon unity, 60–1, 146, 150, 162, 172–3, 251n3
Angus, Henry F., 180
annexationism, 33, 40–1, 144, 146, 211
anti-Americanism, Canadian, 7–8, 9, 21–2, 210–11; ambiguities within, 22, 209–10; basic premises of, 22; and Canadian identity, 126; and conservatism, 22–3; criticism of, 128–9, 133–4, 187; and education, 89; and ethnicity, 128; evolution in English Canada, 26–8, 214–16;

evolution in French Canada, 29–31, 216; as the expression of antimodernism, 23, 24–5; instrumental aspects of, 127, 209; justifications of, 133, 256n17; and nationalism, 22–3, 215; and public opinion, 5, 42, 214; regional intensity of, 23–4, 28; and religion, 85; role of American sources and inspiration in, 42–3, 44, 260n56; role of British sources and inspiration in 45; role of French sources and inspiration in, 29, 45–7, 56; scholarly interpretations of, 4, 5, 251n2, 252n5, 252n9; and socialism, 216
anti-Americanism, worldwide, 253n14, 254n18
anti-British sentiment in the United States, 126, 279n1
anti-Irish sentiment, 26, 103–5
antimodernism, 24, 25, 210
antiparliamentarism, 266n53
anti-Semitism, 22, 105–6
Arles, Henri d', 16, 66–7, 91, 93, 101, 209
Arnold, Matthew, 19, 44
Asselin, Olivar, 17, 29, 30

free trade. *See* liberalization of Canadian-American trade
French sources and inspiration for Canadian writing on the United States, 45–7
Fronsac, Viscount de, 67

Gelber, Lionel, 159
generations in the study of intellectual history, 12, 16, 208
geography and the dynamics of Canadian-American relations, 135–40, 281n27
George III, 59
German-Americans, 103
Gibbons, James, 44
Goldenberg, H. Carl, 158–9, 185–6
Good Neighbor Policy, 171
Gordon, King, 11
Gordon, Walter, 192
Granatstein, J.L., 4
Grant, George Monro, 20, 26, 53, 137, 149, 150
Grant, George Parkin, 4, 14, 20, 24, 28, 53, 55, 151, 167
Grant, Ian, 188
Grant, William Lawson, 53, 164
Great Britain's role in Canadian-American relations, 161–2, 163–4, 170, 172
Great Depression, 17–18, 30, 114–15
Greenaway, Roy, 124–5
Gregory, Claudius, 106
Groulx, Lionel, 8, 30, 86, 110; on American immigration to Canada, 204; on American materialism, 50; on annexation, 152, 153; on Franco-America, 199; on French Canada's Americanness, 130; and Goldwin Smith, 139; on immigration to the United States, 100; influence of Lucien Romier on, 47, 50, 269n17; influence of Jacques Maritain on, 50; on pan-Americanism, 173; on religion in the United States, 86, 87
Grove, Frederick Philip, 57, 103
Guimont, Paul-Henri, 114–15, 178–9

Hamilton, Alexander, 42, 72
Hamon, Édouard, 17, 130, 200–1, 283n10
Harvey, Jean-Charles, 16, 33, 41, 51–2, 85, 134, 173–4, 190–1, 198
Hawkes, Arthur, 184–5
Hobson, J.A., 10
Hofstadter, Richard, 25, 258n30
Hollywood, 79–80, 106
Hopkins, John Castell, 16, 68, 111, 137–8, 149, 163
Hosmer, James, 42
Humphrey, John P., 34, 35, 133, 171
Huot, Antonio, 17, 53–4, 56, 87–8, 96–7
Hyde Park Agreement, 18, 39, 165, 170

immigration of Americans to Canada, 203–4
immigration to the United States, 100–3, 122
imperial federation, 29, 147, 149, 150, 164
imperialism, American, 174–8
imperialism, Canadian, 7, 8–9, 25–28, 58, 128, 137, 162, 208, 253n13; and anti-Americanism, 22–3; condemned by Bourassa, 152; existence of a non–anti-American current within, 257n20